About the Author

He was introduced to birds at the tender age of five, when taken to his local park in Birmingham to feed the ducks. His first real involvement was egg collecting, but he quickly became more interested in watching and studying birds. Over the next eighty years, he has studied birds in most European countries, plus Egypt. He has written many features for various publications; jointly presented a countryside radio programme for BBC Radio Birmingham; was a tutor for both Birmingham and Keele universities teaching bird study, and has taken parties of birders on study tours in the UK and Europe. The author, now in his eighty-nineth year, is still learning and enjoying his study of birds.

Searching:
Volume II

Brian C. George

Searching
Volume II

Olympia Publishers
London

www.olympiapublishers.com
OLYMPIA PAPERBACK EDITION

Copyright © Brian C. George 2023

The right of Brian C. George to be identified as author of
this work has been asserted in accordance with sections 77 and 78 of the
Copyright, Designs and Patents Act 1988.

All Rights Reserved

No reproduction, copy or transmission of this publication
may be made without written permission.
No paragraph of this publication may be reproduced,
copied or transmitted save with the written permission of the publisher, or in
accordance with the provisions
of the Copyright Act 1956 (as amended).

Any person who commits any unauthorised act in relation to
this publication may be liable to criminal
prosecution and civil claims for damage.

A CIP catalogue record for this title is
available from the British Library.

ISBN: 978-1-80074-668-8

This is a work of creative nonfiction. The events are portrayed to the best of the author's memory. While all the stories in this book are true, some names and identifying details have been changed to protect the privacy of the people involved.

First Published in 2023

Olympia Publishers
Tallis House
2 Tallis Street
London
EC4Y 0AB

Printed in Great Britain

Acknowledgements

I dedicate this book to my late wife, Dorothy, whose love and friendship made it all possible.

INTRODUCTION

When I first commenced to write this book, I did not think it would be necessary to have an introduction to Volume II, but I did not visualise the circumstances under which I would be completing it. One thing I now realise is that it is a good thing we do not know what the future holds.

I will be brief. Dorothy passed away on 26th July, although expected, it still came hard, and life can obviously never be the same again. We are always being told that time heals, I am about to find out the truth in that. The only thing I do believe at present, is that it is necessary to fill the mind with positive thoughts, and allow the memories to remain. The mind, I understand, is a selective machine, and if allowed to run, filters out the good from the bad, the happy from the sad. I hope who ever said that is correct, and was quoting from experience.

My future now is down to the birds. I still have much to learn and lots to see and enjoy. The fact that much of it will now be solitary cannot be changed, but I frequently tell people you are never alone with the birds, that is now about to be put to the test.

I am at least fortunate in having many friends to share my life with, the Rosliston Bird Study Group will be a regular part of my life, and my daughter, Sarah, shares my interest, so the future is not all grey.

It is now seventy years since I saw my first kingfisher which really started this whole business, my aim is to see what the next ten years produces. If I can complete an eighty years love with the birds, that will not have been a bad life, especially as Dorothy shared over fifty of those years.

Read on and see how we fare.

CHAPTER I
THE LATER YEARS

After over fifty years of knowing and living with Dorothy, I now faced a totally different future than I ever imagined. I was fortunate in having my daughter, Sarah, still at home, and I had many friends and colleagues in the bird world, so lonely I was unlikely to be. Direction is what was required and my interest in birds was to provide this for me. One of the final things Dorothy ever said to me was, 'Life is for living'. and when you love someone, as I know Dorothy did me, then those words were seriously said.

Sorrow is a most difficult thing to express, it is a most personal feeling, but I recently came across a poem which I thought summed it all up most beautifully. It was written by an American poet, Mary Frye, who is probably only known because of this one work. I will repeat it here.

Do Not Stand at My Grave and Weep.

Do not stand at my grave and weep,
I am not there, I do not sleep,
I am a thousand winds that blow,
I am the diamond glints of snow,
I am the sunlight on ripened grain,
I am the gentle autumn rain,
When you awakened in the morning hush,
I am the swift uplifting rush
Of quiet birds, in circled flight,
I am the soft stars that shine at night,
Do not stand at my grave and cry,
I am not there, I did not die.

I could not have improved on those words to express my feelings at that time.

Now, back to birding. In the midst of all the recent emotion, I said that birding had gone on the back burner, it certainly had. My total number of birds seen in the UK during 2007 was one hundred and ninety-eight, my lowest total since 1986, when I last failed to reach the two hundred mark.

For a few weeks now Sarah had been getting on at me about having a break and going on holiday somewhere, obviously our two cruises had been cancelled. I finally succumbed to her 'bullying', and come early September I was off to Anglesey for five days. That year had been the first for many that I had not visited Bempton Cliffs, and I hoped that on Anglesey I may catch up on a few of the birds previously missed and see some birds on passage.

It was going to be a little unusual for me. I had never been away, apart from on business, on my own previously, so it was going to be a newish experience doing so for the first time. But it is something I am going to have to get used to.

The journey to Anglesey produced several red kites, ravens and buzzards, so that was a very good start, and I arrived in almost perfect conditions from a birding point of view. A fairly strong wind was coming in from the west which should keep passing birds close to land, and this was forecast to stay much the same for at least a further three days.

My first evening at the hotel, which incidentally, was very comfortable, passed by fairly pleasantly. A very good meal, accompanied by a pleasant half bottle of wine, and an interesting conversation or two at the bar later, made a welcome start to my holiday. It is amazing how simple things can help raise your confidence, I felt better than I had done for quite some time. I now really looked forward to the few days ahead.

As events turned out the birding was very good. A few razorbills and guillemots were still on the cliffs at South Stack, fulmars were gliding around, the odd kittiwake was evident and gannets were out at sea. Cormorants were very active along with the occasional shag, and five choughs were visible on one occasion, the largest number I have ever seen together. The coffee at South Stack tasted very good after that, and to cap it all, two peregrine falcons appeared on the scene, it looked like a female and a juvenile. A most enjoyable and productive day it had proved.

I spent most of my time on the coast. At that time of the year it was going to be the most productive. I managed to catch up with a small number of Sandwich terns, little terns and Arctic terns, all new species for the year, and near to Cemlyn Bay I picked up two black guillemots, the birds of the holiday.

On the final full day of the holiday, the wind had strengthened considerably, so I visited Carmel Head to do some sea watching. I managed to find a sheltered spot where I did not feel the full force of the wind, and set up my tripod and 'scope. I was very pleased I had brought those with me. Way out on the sea was a large flock of common scoter where, after much searching, I spotted two velvet scoters, well worth the hard work. Further out the odd Manx shearwater could be found, and odd was the operative word, but one is enough to get it on your list.

A flock of very small birds appeared close in, several hundred of them and I was delighted to see they were petrels, the question now, was which? Looking down on them as I was, I could only see their upper surfaces, but they looked all black with a very bold white rump and a squared-off tail. I was happy. They were storm petrels, the first I had seen for many years, and I mean many—twenty plus. They were flying in an almost straight line, just above the surface of the sea. I was sure if I had been at sea level, I would have seen their feet actually dangling into the water. From my elevated position they looked almost like a black bat, as they flew with fast fluttering wingbeats interspersed by short glides, those were worth the trip to Anglesey alone. You do not get petrels inland, and apart from where they breed, you do not see them so close to land. Most of their lives are spent at sea.

During my stay I saw sixty-seven species, the bulk of which were my first sightings of the year, with only one disappointment—no puffins. The birding had been first class, the accommodation equally so, but above all it had done me a power of good. I had now started to live again, and I knew that was what Dorothy would have wanted. My love affair with birds was back on track.

Later in the month it was time to take the Rosliston Birders on a day's trip, so we chose a visit to Old Moor Nature Reserve in the Dearne Valley, Yorkshire. Reports of bearded tits and bitterns had been creeping out from there, a good enough reason for a visit it was decided. We had a good turnout, five cars, eighteen birders, took the trip, a round journey of about 200 miles.

Being an RSPB reserve, the facilities are good and it has a very pleasant restaurant, so some of us decided not to bother with food, we would make a day of it.

The journey up was straightforward. A38, M1 with the final few miles or so just off the M1, south of Barnsley. After a quick coffee in the restaurant, we ventured forth. We had been informed that the bearded tits were proving rather elusive, but if we were lucky the bittern had been seen flying about occasionally. The information regarding the bearded tits was correct, not a peep, the bittern, however, had not read the script, and weren't we glad?

We entered the family hide to have a birder put his finger to his lips and point out of the hide, we could not believe our luck. Standing still, in open water, was the bittern, I had never experienced such a sighting ever. Not twenty yards away, in full view, stood one of our rarest breeding birds. We watched this bird for several muinutes, hardly daring to breathe before it leapt in the air, and with very slow and deep wingbeats, it was off. It landed in the reed bed, not to be seen again. What a greeting we had experienced.

Our next stop was the Wader Scrape Hide, very aptly named as things turned out. The water levels are obviously controlled, and good areas of open mud were visible, and these had attracted a goodly selection of waders. Black-tailed godwits, common sandpipers, well one to be strictly accurate, curlews, dunlins, a green sandpiper and a flock of golden plovers. Ducks included teals, shovelers, shelducks, pochards, wigeons, tufted ducks and mallards plus mute swans, Canada geese, grey-lag geese and barnacle geese. Add to these coots, moorhens, a solitary water rail, great crested grebes and little grebes, you will see we had more than enough to get on with. Due to my little birding so far that year, I was chalking up 'year ticks' without any effort, it was almost like the start of a new year.

Time for lunch, which was most enjoyable. This saved me having to worry about a meal when I got home, things had changed somewhat, and it was not fair for Sarah to have to wait for my homecoming.

After lunch we all met up in the Wath Ings Hide, and there we encountered the completely unexpected. In a tree at the back of the scrape, was a large bird of prey. At first glance I presumed it to be a buzzard, but on focusing up my 'scope I found it not to be, but what had I got? It was a bird I had never seen before, even in picture form; I knew it not to be a British or European species, but what? We got our field guides out obviously, but this only confirmed my original thought, it was in none of those. I commenced to make a few notes when one of the wardens walked in the hide. 'What do you think of our hawk then?' he asked. He quickly explained what we had, it was an escaped Harris hawk, a North American species which is a common bird amongst falconers, easily trained apparently. I did raise the question regarding not so easy to keep!

The hawk had been at Old Moor for over a week by then, it was catching food easily enough, so there was no reason why it could not survive. Whether the local birds were impressed with it being there is another matter.

Back to birds we had a chance of recognising. To the waders previously mentioned we added lapwings, spotted redshanks, snipes, a little stint and a jack snipe. Making it a very good selection. On the day we totalled fifty-nine species, well worth the trip up north, and we may never see another Harris hawk!

Anglesey and Old Moor had quickly got me back into the swing of things, and birds and friends had made it so.

Sarah and I had also got back into birding again. We were having a couple of hours out birding together on a Saturday morning, when we could, and that was proving to be most enjoyable, and at times productive. On one such morning we picked up both a little stint and a wood sandpiper at Blithfield Reservoir, and the osprey was still hanging around. Not bad being only seven miles or so from home!

A few more local visits were made, and then I decided on another week's break. This time I returned to Norfolk, The Pheasant called once more, and I booked myself in for a week this time. Being there on my own would certainly be different from all my previous stays, which had been either with Dorothy or a group.

I arrived at The Pheasant early and I was able to get in a couple of hours birding prior to my unpacking, and took a walk down to The Quag. A large flock of linnets welcomed my arrival, and on the water, I was delighted to see a red-necked grebe. Approaching the shore, a male hen harrier flew past and on the sea were three red-throated divers, quite a greeting, but Norfolk is like that. As I was about to turn back a small skein of about twenty Brent geese flew close in to the shore, they looked like they were heading for Cley.

Talking to a few of the birders over a drink that evening; I was informed of many of the high-quality birds that were to be seen. If managed those I was in for an exceptional week, only time would tell. I decided that Titchwell would be my first destination.

Things commenced well. Approaching Titchwell I saw a group of birders staring intently along the hedgerow, I managed to pull in. They were studying a pair of hawfinches, not a common bird in Norfolk I was informed. Birding is a small world in many respects, I mentioned Cromford to them, and much to my surprise, they all knew about it and had visited it on occasion, just to see the hawfinches and dippers.

Titchwell was fairly quiet on the birders front, birds on the other hand were very good. Both godwits were to be seen, three avocets were still about, little egrets were plentiful as were Brent geese, the latter well into the hundreds, and amongst the Canada geese was a lesser Canada goose (cackling goose as it is now called). Moving on down to the shore I was pleased to see several spotted redshanks in one of the lagoons. Out at sea were many gulls, nothing of note amongst them and on the sea were two drake smews and a great northern diver. Enough there to keep the keenest of birders happy. In total I saw fifty-one species that day.

Back in the hotel that evening, talking to other birders, at Cley apparently, they had seen a Wilson's phalarope, now that is a bit special. It is a rare North American vagrant and I have only ever seen one previously. The following day had now become a 'twitch' day.

Cley was certainly busy, the phalarope had seen to that. The one consolation regarding that was the fact you did not need to search for the phalarope, you just looked for the crowd! They did not take long to find. A group of twenty or so birders were standing out in the open, gazing across a meadow at a nearby stretch of water.

Among the few ducks on the water, a small wader was feeding in the shallow water, and unlike our two phalaropes which spin in the water, this bird was just walking and swimming when the water got deeper. It was a uniform grey in colour and looked a larger bird than our species. A great start to my day. I had not even entered the reserve at this stage. One of the birders I knew slightly, and he jokingly said to me, "If I had known where the bird was, I need not have paid my entrance fee." He was right, we were on a public footpath!

Wader numbers were very good, many of the commoner species were seen, ducks were also very evident, especially teals and wigeons. Working my way through this, I was very pleased to find a drake scaup, this bird had not been mentioned by any birders I spoke with. They are probably more common in Norfolk than they are at home, and are not worthy of comment!

I was pleased to see hen harrier again, this time a female, and on the sea were two long-tailed ducks. Cley had been well worth the visit, and I did not begrudge them the entrance fee!

Nothing special was reported at the hotel that evening, so the following day I decided to take a trip down memory lane. Some years ago, when on holiday in Norfolk with Dorothy, we had visited Sandringham and then gone on to an area we birders know, as The Triangle, near to Wolferton, then famous for golden pheasants.

Were they still to be seen was the question, time will tell.

Driving near to Holkham I had a pleasant surprise. Standing in the middle of a field, full of sheep, stood a great white egret. It was worth pulling over and enjoying for a few minutes. I had not seen many of those in the UK. Whilst there, a flock of a couple of hundred or so golden plovers flew across, so it had been a good place to stop.

Whilst passing through Holkham I stopped for a coffee, and picked up something for lunch, not that I needed a lot, the hotel knew how to look after you.

Walking back to my car I heard geese calling and a skein of pink-footed geese flew across. That had turned out to be a good coffee break.

I called in at Hunstanton for a few minutes, the tide was almost fully in, gulls were plentiful, including a few common gulls. The odd fulmar was still flying round the cliffs and a good-sized flock of curlews were on the golf course.

I finally reach The Triangle. As this is not on any map by name, I will give you the map reference. Sheet No 132, TF282672. I have my light lunch and then proceeded to walk round The Triangle, a walk of a little over a mile. It is all wooded, the golden pheasant being a woodland species unlike our native pheasants. At this time of the year our woods are relatively quiet, so any large bird moving through should be heard. Golden pheasants originally were brought over from central China where they are a mountain bird. Having been either released or escaped, they have set up home in one or two areas of the UK, East Anglia being one of them.

I heard a noise from the wood, but it was a bird in flight, and when it called, I did not need to see it, the bird was a jay, no mistaking him vocally.

I was almost back to the main road, the A149, when a loud scuffling noise came from the wood. That was no bird in flight, it sounded as though something was scratching at the ground. I slowly made my way in the direction of the sound, stopping on the edge of the wood, and waited. I was very lucky, I did not have to wait for long. Out of the wood came a magnificent male golden pheasant, a glamour bird if there ever was one. They are a larger bird than our native pheasant, with a much longer tail. I stood stock still, not even lifting my binoculars, not that I needed to, he was so close. It did not even look in my direction, it obviously had other things on its mind and just walked on down the lane for a short distance, before returning to the wood. Although I waited for several minutes it did not reappear, although I heard it on a couple of occasions.

That concluded my day, a magnificent bird which brought back happy memories of seeing the bird with Dorothy, she also had been impressed with the bird.

Now what would the 'morrow hold?

Nothing unusual had been seen by other birders so I decided to visit Holkham Hall Park and then go on down to Holkham Bay for a bit of sea watching. The deer showed well as I drove up to park near the hall, intending to walk round the lake.

Initially I made my way to the monument, here in the past I had seen both little and tawny owls, it would be interesting to see if they were still in residence. After a good half an hour of searching I did at least find a little owl, but no tawny.

The lake had a good selection of birds, and in particular one, a black-necked grebe, was worthy of note, it being an adult bird. Among the ducks, which were plentiful, were a pair of mandarins, those two birds were very active and frequently took to the air, they were free fliers, no question there. Egyptian geese were also well accounted for, and if what local birders claim is correct, it was here that many captive Egyptian geese escaped to set up the local wild population. Be that true of not, most of the geese seen that day were fully fledged. On now down to the sea.

It was my lucky day. The parking attendant was not on duty so parking at Holkham Gap was for free! I did not make the sea. I met up with a group of birders who had just come out of the Holkham Meals and they told me they had just seen a yellow-browed warbler down near Meals House, and that it should not be difficult to find as there were several birders still down there.

On the walk down I had a good mixed flock of titmice, a small party of siskins and heard, but did not see, crossbills. The birders were correct, a dozen or so people could be seen near to Meals House, so I quickly joined them.

The warbler was making frequent excursions out into a nearby bush, so it was just a question of patience, and my first view of the bird did not take long. It flicked onto the bush, sat out on the top for a second or two, before vanishing deep into the bush, then flying out and going into some nearby conifer trees. During the next hour or so it repeated this pattern on several occasion, providing decent views.

Yellow-browed warblers are an annual vagrant from the Siberian taiga, and are a distinctive little bird, with a long yellowish supercilium (hence the name), and two yellow wingbars. Both features showed up well on this bird. Although I have seen the odd yellow-browed warbler in the past, this bird certainly gave me the best views I have ever had. I am very pleased I met those birders on arrival, had I not I may have gone towards the sea without knowing about the bird. Luck plays a big part in this game.

That evening I had something to tell the other birders about, no need to wonder where many of them would be off to. I decided to visit Salthouse where I could do my sea watching, the car park being right on the coast.

A couple of cars were parked up at Salthouse, neither had bird stickers on the windscreens so they were probably not birders, so I had the birding all to myself. In puddles on the car park were three turnstones and a ringed plover, whilst over Gramborough Hill a buzzard was soaring. I presumed it was just a common buzzard, it vanished before I could get my binoculars focused on it. Walking towards the hill, a small flock of pipits drew my attention, but before I could sort them all out, they were up and away, a merlin chose that moment to fly through.

On the slopes of the hill two small birds caught my attention, one of them had a black head, but this was no reed bunting. It also had a white stripe over the eye which connected with a white collar, bingo, I had a pair of Lapland buntings, a male and a female. I had not expected them, although Norfolk does well with those birds most years. Once again we are talking about a bird which is a winter visitor to the UK, as you can tell by the name of the bird, it breeds much further north, although the odd pair have nested in Scotland.

Time to concentrate on the sea. Way out gannets were flying south and among the many gulls were good numbers of common gulls. The odd auk could be picked out, mostly guillemots, plus a small group of great northern divers. There were six birds in this group, I had never seen that many together previously. Due to the height of the tide, there was little shoreline exposed but the odd dunlin, knot and sanderling could be seen.

Returning to my car for a snack, I then moved along the shore towards the area which borders the Cley Marshes. Along the edge of the New Cut, a canal cut through the marshes, a white egret was standing out on the bank, which I at first took to be a little egret. As I got nearer, the bird proceeded to walk off, and I was delighted to see it was a cattle egret, it still showed some of the buff on its back. Unlike its cousin the little egret, they are still a rare bird with just the odd report of their breeding in southern England. Seeing the buff on this bird took me back to my time in Egypt.

They were a common bird out there, but at that time they were known as buff-backed herons. Their current name is apt enough, they frequently associate with cattle and will even perch on the cattles backs to catch large insects. Who knows, in the future they may even become as well spread as the little egret.

For my final day, I decided to visit Cley once again, it was local to where I was staying, and as events tuned out it was a good choice. I initially drove down to Cley Eye to spend a few minutes looking over the sea, where I again saw red-throated and great northern divers and enjoyed several skeins of Brent geese flying into Cley.

Whilst studying the divers, a smaller bird popped up on the surface, a Slavonian grebe, that gave me my fifth grebe of the week, I have already mentioned black-necked and red-necked grebes, but I had also seen little and great crested grebes.

Now for Cley reserve. Entrance fee paid, no Wilson's phalarope, it had departed. Approaching one of the hides I stopped to look at a scrape in a lagoon, several small waders were feeding along it, dunlins, knots and two green sandpipers, when a small dark looking wader dashed in. I could not believe my luck, it was a purple sandpiper, had I not have stopped I would not have seen it. I enjoyed the bird for a few minutes before it moved off.

From the hides the usual selection of waterfowl could be seen, shoveler and shelduck numbers were very high, as were teals and wigeons as I have previously commented on. A young birder in the hide called my attention to a duck he was looking at, he did not know what it was. I was very pleased he had drawn my attention to it, it was a drake blue-winged teal, a rare vagrant from North America.

The bird was not illustrated in his field guide, luckily it was in mine, so I could show him the pictures of the bird. I had a feeling he would shortly be buying himself a new field guide.

That was my final top bird of the week, a week in which I saw one hundred and nine species, that was going to improve my year's totals.

The remainder of the year was just a question of mopping up a few species, and this was all done locally. Blithfield Reservoir, Belvide and Whitemoor Haye all contributed and I ended up on two hundred and six. A very good number in view of the circumstances. A year of mixed emotions, but friends rallied round, my daughter Sarah was wonderful support, and the birds, as usual, were magnificent. As I frequently say to people, birds will certainly frustrate you at times, but I have yet to have an argument with one!

What would 2009 bring?

CHAPTER II

Initially a few pleasant trips out birding locally, mostly on a Monday with the Rosliston Birders, and we did very well. Come the end of January I had notched up one hundred and five species, which considering I had hardly been out of the county, was very good.

The following two months saw things slow down appreciably. I was beginning to have trouble walking, my left knee was giving me a lot of pain. Another hospital visit, and a further knee replacement was called for. The waiting list was now very lengthy for this type of operation, so I chose to go private, and I was able to get into hospital very quickly, within ten days as it so happened.

Things went well I am pleased to say. After a short time I was able to be taken birding, walking was a recommended remedy, and by the spring I was able to drive again, so back to serious birding.

After last year's experiences, locations such as the Staffordshire Moorlands, Bempton Cliffs, Little Paxton and Weeting Heath were firmly pencilled in. I did not intend to miss out on some of my favourite summer birds such as ring ouzels, puffins, nightingales, turtle doves, woodlarks and stone curlews, which I had done the previous year.

The Moors came up trumps. Red grouse were seen as I crossed Axe Edge Moor, well up into double figures, the ring ouzel was equally accommodating, as were a pair of wheatears. As I returned over Axe Edge raven put on an aerial display, no complaints there.

Bempton Cliffs was its usual self. A bright day with a light wind coming in off the sea, perfect birding conditions. The resident birds were all now well into breeding, and the noise from the cliffs was quite incredible. I frequently refer to Bempton as a bird city, and today it was living up to it.

Due to the wind direction, birds out at sea were in close and I was pleased to note a few more shags than normal and terns were passing through, Sandwich terns and Artctic terns especially so. A few eiders were also on the sea, and it was noticeable all were drakes, the ducks were no doubt sitting eggs. I was also delighted to see two Manx shearwaters drift past on their journey northwards. Bempton had turned up trumps once again.

My trip to Little Paxton started off rather damp, but conditions improved as the morning progressed. The rain did not seem to dampen the nightingales' enthusiasm, one was heard just a minute or two's walk from my parked car. A turtle dove was also very accommodating, it was purring away from nearby overhead wires.

I can never remember seeing my two target birds so quickly, I had heard and seen them in the matter of a few minutes.

As I walked round the reserve, I heard several nightingales, approaching double figures, they had obviously had a good year here at Little Paxton. Warblers were also in good voice, blackcaps especially so, several males were letting forth.

The sound of summer was also to be heard, three or four cuckoos were in attendance, this is at least one call you do not have to be an expert to recognise.

I called in to the Kingfisher Hide on my return. I did not see the kingfisher, but I was able to enjoy two hobbies which were causing concern to the many hirundines present. A very satisfactory conclusion to my day out.

Weeting Heath brought the month to its conclusion, and here again luck favoured me. Before I even entered the reserve, I had my first stone curlew in the bag.

I stopped to view the field opposite the reserve as I had caught sight of a bird standing out in the open, and it was a stone curlew. This is birding made easy. As I went to drive off, I noticed a movement at the edge of the field, two roe deer had walked into view. Unfortunately, they did not hang around and quickly returned to cover. Not a bad welcoming that!

There were not many birders on the reserve, which was surprising as it is usually very busy here, being a small reserve. They had probably all seen the bird opposite and driven on. Walking on down to the first hide a small bird flew out of a tree, caught a flying insect, and returned to the tree—a spotted flycatcher was at work I spent a few minutes enjoying seeing this bird go about its business, and as I walked on I noticed a nest box in the tree—the bird was no doubt feeding a sitting female.

The stone curlews did not disappoint, I had several views of different birds. A grey partridge was also in one of the meadows, just a male bird, his partner was no doubt sitting eggs by now. A turtle dove was also heard purring away, but due to the density of the trees in the area, I could not locate him. I spent a few more minutes watching the spotted flycatcher prior to departing.

As I drove off, I had another look at the meadow opposite, the stone curlew was still in the open, if he had not been in a different position, you would have thought it was stuffed! Another great day concluded, and the month also as it so happened.

I had now reached one hundred and seventy-eight. Things were definitely on the up, and I was now fully back into the swing of things. Dorothy had got it right, that was for sure. 'Life was definitely for the living there of'.

June commenced with an evening on the Chase. Last year I did not go nightjar hunting and the Rosliston Birders were very interested in seeing them again, so the first Friday of the month saw us on the Chase, and twelve of us turned out for the event.

It was a warm evening, and small insects were very active unfortunately, attacking any piece of exposed skin. Oh, to be in England now that summer is here!

The hobbies were very active down in the Sherbrook Valley, where we saw one bird catch a large moth. As well as taking small birds they do feed on large insects such as dragonflies and moths, and are frequently seen feeding late evenings on the latter.

We also had brief views of a long-eared owl in flight. They have bred on the Chase in recent years, so it looks as though they are doing so again. There were also at least four cuckoos calling, one of which gave us a close fly-past, much to the pleasure of two of my colleagues who had never seen cuckoos previously. They commented on the fact that due to the bird's tail length it almost looked like a small bird of prey. Which is how I frequently describe the bird, myself.

Darkness was now falling, time to take our position for the

nightjars. We were not the only birders out seeking the birds, a dozen or so were already *in situ*, most of them known to me.

We heard a bird churing away in the distance, which after a few minutes was responded to by a bird close by. The bird stopped calling and we heard a clapping sound. The nightjar flew almost overhead, providing very good views, and it came that close the white spots on its primaries were clearly seen, the bird being a male, the female lacks these. The flight is almost owl-like I always feel, silent, ghost-like, apart from the occasional claps of the wings. We spent a further half an hour listening to and occasionally seeing the bird, before moving off home. Another superb evening, thanks to the birds.

The rest of the month was spent on chasing down the remaining summer migrants, and most off our visits were to the Chase. We did well. The pick of the warblers locally put on a good show, well two of them did, the wood warbler is a bird which appears to be declining rapidly. It does not seem all that long ago that several pairs bred regularly on the Chase, now I know of only two locations where you are likely to see and hear the bird. Fortunately for us, two pairs were again in residence.

A few pairs of redstarts were found, these being near Seven Springs and Penkridge Bank, and the pick of the remaining birds were probably stonechats, tree pipits and woodlarks from near the cadet huts.

As the month progressed and my walking was back to normal, I decided on a piece of nostalgia.

Locally there was a walk which Dorothy and I had done frequently. It was a circular walk of about three miles or so which took us down a local lane, Meadow Lane as it is known, and brought us back along the River Swarbourn into the village. A very pleasant walk, level ground and with little or no traffic, very peaceful in fact. I was lucky in having chosen a most pleasant day, not too hot for walking.

Meadow Lane has few properties along it, and the few it has are principally at the end of the lane, and I would not be walking that far. The land here is mainly grazing and it was a flood plain habitat prior to the planting of the Heart of England Forest, two rivers running through, the Swarbourn and the River Trent. I must confess, much as I like trees, I did not agree with this. The land originally supported breeding birds such as curlew, common snipe, lapwing and skylark, as the trees have grown these birds have vanished being replaced by woodland species. We have plenty of woodlands, we have all too few wetland sites.

Back to my walk. The lane has an old hedge running for most of the length, and the usual birds were in good voice. Chiffchaff were calling, willow warblers and blackcaps were singing, with a song thrush joining in. I often think these birds are so typically English, sorry to my Welsh and Scottish friends. Passing the forested area, garden warbler could be heard and a family party of magpies were adding their calls to things, although in their case it was hardly musical.

Continuing on down the lane the expected birds were seen and heard, blackbirds, robins, dunnocks and chaffinches, with titmice being active on the alder trees. Reaching the bend in the lane I moved into open country, the forest having finished, and here it is the land of sheep and cattle. I was very pleased to see at least one pair of lapwings in attendance, a few years ago they would have been in double figures, and probably more interesting, a grey partridge popped its head up, and seeing me promptly flew off into the distance. A brief encounter, but grey partridge, are not a common bird.

Walking down the lane I had a very pleasant surprise. Walking along in front of me were a covey of red-legged partridge, seven of them, two adults and five juveniles, the latter were not very large, I would think only a few weeks old. I stop, not wanting to frighten them, and watch them slowly make their way under a gate and into a neighbouring field. It has been a long time since I saw both of our partridges almost together.

I reach the Swarbourn and turn in off the lane to walk back along the river. I am almost instantly greeted by two mallards which fly off upstream with much noise, disturbing a grey heron as they do so. A moorhen is on the river, accompanied by two very small chicks, looking more like balls of fluff, than a bird. Delightful little things, let us hope the grey heron does not see them.

Further along the river a flash of yellow is seen, a male yellow wagtail is flitting along the bank, obviously collecting food. I sat down to watch. He was not aware of my presence, fortunately, so for several minutes I watch him going about his business. He has a beak full of insects, or so it appears, and then he flies off and vanished into the river bank. A family of yellow wagtails are due their dinner.

More moorhens, this time with four larger chicks, and the odd pheasant is seen among the sheep grazing nearby, with two further grey herons in the river. Not for long, seeing me they are off, croaking away, sounding almost as though they were angry at my approach, which they may well have been.

I now had to leave the river as the footpath concludes just outside the village, but my walk was not over. A kestrel was hovering, very energetically over the field, in which several rooks and jackdaws were busily feeding. I was more than happy with that. Nothing extra special, but a most pleasant walk with many interesting and colourful birds seen, plus many a happy memory, and that was more important.

That concluded the month for me, half the year completed, and I had now reached a total of one hundred and ninety-two.

The year then proceeded at a slow rate from then on. July only adding three species to my 'year list'. After a good start, things had almost stopped.

Then July 26th arrived. Twelve months since Dorothy died. I visited Sutton Coldfield Crematorium, where Dorothy was cremated, to spend a little time with her. I took some of her favourite flowers, yellow carnations, and spread those on the ground where her ashes had been scattered. I sat on a bench in deep thought, with, I must confess, a tear or two running down my cheek, when a robin landed on the arm of the bench. It just sat there, staring at me with its large black eyes, and the tears stopped. It was almost as though Dorothy had returned and was telling me to be happy and just enjoy treasured memories. I will remember that robin forever. Call it sentimentality if you like, but the crying stopped that day..

August was to be another slow month, and to compensate I organised another week's birding in Norfolk, to be taken next month. Short notice, but we birders do things by impulse! What would Norfolk do—it did its best, read on.

The weather started off very pleasantly, and whilst driving across to Norfolk we saw a group of birders staring intently into a field: we obviously stopped, and were pleased we had. They were studying three quail, we quickly joined in, some start to our week.

We then drove on, straight to The Pheasant for a quick lunch and an hour or two down The Quag. Here we were delighted to see a Slavonian grebe on the water and a hen harrier was quartering the ground nearby. Along with the quail seen earlier, those three birds gave us a good start to our holiday, things were looking good.

Over a pleasant after dinner drink, we decided that we would visit Titchwell the next day; it would be good if we could get avocet, bearded tit, bittern and marsh harrier on our list for the week.

It was a bit misty when we arrived but we had been assured it would quickly disperse, and it did. The avocets, bearded tits and marsh harriers behaved themselves perfectly, but the bittern did not cooperate. As compensation we did see barnacle geese, bean geese, Brent geese, a cattle egret, a hawfinch, which was a complete surprise, especially as it was almost on the car park. Golden plovers were in very good numbers, some still showing much of their summer plumage. A long-eared owl gave us a brief fly-past, but we happily accepted that! Curlews, ruffs and spotted redshanks were showing well, with good numbers of dunlins and knots. A few 'year ticks' were being notched up there.

After lunch we made our way down to the shore to do some sea watching, and that also proved to be productive. All three divers were to be seen, red-throated, great northern and black-throated, a flock of several hundred common scoter, but hard as we searched, we could find nothing else tucked away amongst them. Wigeon and teals were also on the water and sanderlings were scampering along the tideline. The odd Arctic and little terns were still evident, along with fieldfares and redwings which had commenced their arrival from northern Europe. Not a bad day at all.

Day two, Cley was our destination.

No mist to worry about on that occasion, it was just a dull grey day, but no rain had been forecast. Birdwatcher numbers were low, which was not a good sign but we were there, so we just got on with it, and we were pleased we had.

Almost the first bird we saw was a bittern, if we had nothing else, that would be worth the visit on its own. Needless to say, it was not. Three spoonbills were strutting their stuff on the lagoon right in front of the hide, swishing their spoon-shaped bill from side to side, if ever a bird was aptly named, this is the one. A good number of grey plovers were also to be seen, as with the golden plovers the previous day, some of those were also still in their summer finery. When seen in all their glory I frequently think they are mis-named, they should be called the silver plover, nothing grey about this!

On the shore were sanderlings, bar-tailed godwits, black-tailed godwits, common gulls and common sandpipers. Out at sea a few common terns were still passing through and black-necked grebe and great crested grebe were riding the waves. A real gaggle of grey-lag geese were on the shore, what had attracted them there it was hard to say. Could be they were real migrants which had just arrived and were resting up after their efforts.

Back on the reserve proper we met up with a group of excited birders. In a bush near to a hide, they had seen a firecrest, it was associating with a small flock of six goldcrests. No need to ask where we shot off to. We quickly located the hide and a small group of birders were already there, one pointed, and bingo, there was our firecrest. It could not have been easier. Firecrests are a rather special bird, they are not a mega rarity, but they are a bird you do not see all that often, and today's sighting was a 'lifer' for some of my colleagues. It cannot get much better than that I think you will agree!

Driving from Cley we stopped to look over a field in which were a flock of geese, grey geese, but they did not look like grey-lags. We were right, it was a flock of pink-footed geese, over one hundred of them, and they made a superb picture to finish of our day. Norfolk was providing the goods once again.

That evening we were in discussion with a couple of birders who were also staying at The Pheasant. That afternoon they had spent a few hours at Salthouse and had seen snow buntings, Lapland buntings, a twite, turnstones and ringed plovers.

Out at sea they had seen the odd skua and shearwater. Although right next door to Cley, sea watching from Salthouse does look more easterly, whereas from Cley you are looking more northerly, which probably accounted for the fact that we had seen none of those species from Cley. We now knew what day three was bringing.

The weather was still hanging on, dry and clear, a good day for sea watching in fact. Driving onto the car park at Salthouse we had to stop. The locals had been out feeding the birds and the turnstones were busily feeding on the seed and bathing in the puddles which were right in the middle of the road. If there is one thing I have learned about Salthouse and its turnstones, is the fact the birds will not be rushed, you pass when they allow you to. Eventually they allowed us through. A few photographs were taken of the turnstones, and the ringed plovers too. We must not forget them.

Whilst enjoying these birds I heard a familiar voice. An old friend of mine was also in Norfolk birding, and he was able to tell us where he had just seen three Lapland buntings and the twite. I am sorry turnstones and ringed plovers, you are just history now!

These two interesting birds were on the slopes of Gramborough Hill, just at the end of the car park. Back home we would just call this a mound, in Norfolk, not well known for hills, anything over twenty or so metres, is a hill!

The first birds we found were wheatears, a dozen or so of those and amongst them was a bird looking suspiciously like a Greenland wheatear, but we just could not get a clear enough view to be certain. They all flew off in any case, so that was another 'nearly bird'.

Rounding the path, we spotted the Lapland buntings (I will have to tell my friend he cannot count, we had seven), three of which were attractive males. We were able to enjoy those for a few minutes, as they were not too concerned about us. It is something I have noticed with Arctic or near-Arctic birds, they are far more tolerant of man. I can only presume man is not frequently met up with where they breed, so they have no built-in fear. We probably walk differently to a polar bear!

Whenever I see Lapland buntings, I remember sharing them with Dorothy when in Norway—happy memories.

Back to Norfolk. We turned our attention back inland, and our timing could not have been better. Flashing across the ground, at zero feet, was a merlin. What speed he was doing I have no idea, but the small bird it was pursuing, probably a skylark, had no chance. The merlin struck, a few feathers flew, the merlin had its dinner. As I have said before, it is a cruel world, but it certainly is also a spectacular world. I may also have mentioned this fact before, if so bear with me.

Unlike man who kills for sport, so-called, the merlin only kills to survive, and that is the nature of things. Incidentally, the merlin looked like a juvenile. If so, it had learned the tricks of the trade very well. An obvious survivor.

Whilst all of this was going on, a small greyish looking bird, popped up on a nearby fence post, someone shouted, 'Linnet'. I swung round, linnet be blowed, we had our twite. With their decline in numbers, for many of my party, this was a 'lifer'.

Lunchtime had arrived. So we went back into Salthouse for a bit of lunch, and then returned for our sea watch. The tide had now turned and was racing in, hopefully bringing the birds in closer to land, well, that was the theory, had we got it right?

Initially it did not matter. Arriving back in the car park, once the turnstones allowed us, we were delighted to see two snow buntings feeding away on the seed, and both were superb males. What a wonderful greeting. The two bunting species had been very early migrants, I would not have expected to see them for a least another month. Is this a sign of the winter ahead, or as is more likely, an indication of the weather in the north.

Now settled down, tripods and 'scopes up, the hard work of the day followed.

Teals, wigeons and common scoters were on the sea, along with a red-throated diver and two black-necked grebes, but what interested us most was the number of birds passing through way out to sea, a definite movement was on.

Gannets, Sandwich terns and mixed flocks of Arctic and common terns were passing in quite large flocks, thirty to forty birds a time and occasional flocks of auks were to be seen, guillemots and razorbills, no puffins unfortunately were seen.

Further out at sea, shearwaters and skuas could be seen, but much too far distant to be absolutely certain which they were, we needed them in closer.

Fortunately, on the north Norfolk coast, the tide does come in quite quickly, and that day it was a high tide, so that would also help. After a relatively short period of time, the tide was almost fully in, and it had done the trick. The passing birds had followed the movement of the tide and were much closer in.

Arctic skuas were in small parties of a dozen or so birds a time. Great skuas were mainly single sightings and occasionally pairs. A solitary pomarine skua gave us a very close fly-past, needless to say, greatly appreciated by all. A 'Lifer' for many.

Manx shearwaters were gliding through, wings just clipping the waves, effortless flight, accompanied by the odd sooty shrearwater, and to add noise and effect to it all, a large flock of Brent geese flew, and they do nothing silently. Our sea watch had produced the goods.

How could we follow that? We decided to go north again, this time to visit Thornham and Holme-next-the-Sea, where, if time allowed, we could finish off at Hunstanton for a view off the cliffs. One benefit from this area is the fact it has one or two good cafes, and as we had now moved into October, they could prove to be most appreciated.

The day proved to be fine and we called in at Thornham first, deciding to walk along the Peddars Way towards Holme. The tide was out and the creeks at Thornham had a decent selection of waders. Nothing unusual, but the ringed plovers were most cooperative, providing very good views and we had both godwits, bar-tailed and black-tailed. A large mixed flock of linnets and goldfinches were on the dunes and a female hen harrier put on a very majestic aerial display for us, this almost drew a round of applause! Not to be outdone, a peregrine flashed through, this disturbed the waders somewhat and we picked up three green sandpipers we had not noted previously. Two spoonbills were feeding in one of the creeks, they only appeared briefly, before retreating from view and out on the salt marsh three little egrets were busily foraging away. A reasonable enough spread, now for Peddars Way.

For those of you unfamiliar with Norfolk, Peddars Way is the name for the Norfolk Coast Path, and here, near to Holme you have The Wash to your west and Brancaster Bay to your north, so you are about as far north in Norfolk as you can go.

It is wild countryside in many respects, and if you deviate from the signed pathways, you could easily find yourselves in trouble, as I have mentioned previously, the tide comes in fast along this coast. I never travel in Norfolk without a tide table. Our walk to Holme was a little quiet, birds were not over responsive. A few waders, mainly redshanks, did fly overhead and further flocks of linnets were seen, but arriving at Holme things did pick up.

In the conifer plantation titmice were actively feeding, coal tits especially so, and we were told to look closely at the crossbills as two parrot crossbills had been reported, plus siskins and lesser redpolls. It was concentration time, but fortunately, all the birds mentioned were usually vocal when feeding, so it was a case of both eyes and ears.

The titmice were no problem, they are noisy at the best of times, and it was not too long before the 'kip, kip, kip' of crossbills was heard. We tracked those down quite easily, but they were feeding right at the top of the conifers, not providing good viewing opportunities.

Eventually, our patience was rewarded. Parrot crossbills will frequently hold onto a cone with one claw, whilst hanging clinging to a twig with the other, this they were doing. 'Lifer' time for some of my colleagues. Crossbills are fascinating birds, the males being brightly coloured, and thanks to the shape of their bills, they are aptly named.

The siskins and lesser redpolls were not so cooperative, but after much searching, we did spot one or two, so our walk to Holme was fully repaid.

A café now called and we did have time for Hunstanton Cliffs.

Cliffs are quite a rarity in Norfolk, and in the summer months fulmars breed here, along with the odd kittiwake, or so we had been informed. What would we have that day?

The tide by now was retreating and the beach below the cliffs was becoming visible, gulls were plentiful, five species, lesser black-backed, herring, black-headed, common and the odd great black-backed gull, but no kittiwakes. The latter were probably way out at sea, they are the most marine of our gulls and only return to land to breed. Two fulmars were gliding along the cliff face, and way out at sea, gannets were passing. Meadow pipits were on the adjoining grassy areas and here a solitary gull caught our attention. One of my colleagues got it in his 'scope, and turned to me saying, "It has no black feathers on the wings, the tips are white." I swung round at this, had a quick look through his 'scope, it was jackpot time, he had found us a

Mediterranean gull. Hunstanton had been well worth the visit.

Day five was upon us, the week was beginning to race away with us, we now only had two days of birding left. We had heard of a great grey shrike being seen at Holt, so we decided to visit Holt Country Park to try to track that bird down. I had been fortunate enough to get a map reference of where the bird had last been seen, so we just hoped the bird would stay *in situ*! Should we be lucky enough to see the shrike we could then have the rest of the day looking for woodland species.

Events did not quite go to plan. The shrike had not been reported that morning and we spent nearly two hours before we were rewarded and located the bird.

Fortunately, shrikes are not shy, they do not hide away, and this bird, a male as it so happened, was no exception. It was a very active bird, constantly diving and chasing small birds, and eventually its efforts were rewarded, a blue tit met his 'maker'. Not very pleasant for the blue tit, but very spectacular for us, and as stated before, it is only nature going about its business, the blue tit being food.

The remainder of that day was spent in clocking up common woodland and heathland species, and we increased our Norfolk list by twenty-one species, the pick of the day, after the shrike, being stonechat and marsh tit. We were more than happy. Now, what to do for our last day.

The weather forecast made that decision for us, heavy rain was coming in from out at sea, so hides would be necessary. Titchwell became our chosen venue, and if the rain should pass, we could pop into Wells-next-the-Sea for the last hour.

The weather forecasters were not wrong, it was sheeting down when we drove off, one or two of my party even declined and decided to visit Norwich for the day.

Twelve of us ventured forth and an early coffee at Titchwell was certainly much appreciated. We quickly made our way down to the first hide where, fortunately, the rain was to the side of the hide so we did not have to contend with it being driven through the viewing slots.

The birds were much as seen on day one, geese numbers seemed to have increased, and a few white-fronted geese were amongst them. A couple of birders tucked away in the corner of the hide became excited so we went across to join them.

They had picked up a little stint, well worthy of their excitement, a 'lifer' for three of my companions. The rain suddenly did not seem to matter!

On the water amongst the ducks, I was fortunate to spot a drake garganey, this was unexpected. Garganey are a summer migrant which breed in the UK in very small numbers, and I must confess was not a bird I normally looked for in October, maybe I had better start! The bird was still in its full plumage and looked very smart, another 'lifer' for one or two of my colleagues.

We did not visit the shore due to the weather, we remained where we were for the rest of the morning. Birds were flying in and out so we had plenty to occupy our time. Several of the dunlin still showed their black bellies, and one curlew sandpiper was still in almost full summer plumage, he even stood out in the rain!

We made our way back to the café for a warm snack, and as the rain seemed to be increasing in volume, we decided to call it a day and returned to our hotel where we did our packing nice and early.

A damp end to our week, but no one was complaining. One hundred and eighteen species in the week, a few of which were cracking birds to see. Norfolk had done it once again. We will no doubt be back.

October, and I was back at Rutland Water, a couple of grebes had been reported, so a day chasing those was not to be missed. On my drive across I had two red kites for company. I had pulled in on a layby to make a phone call, and the two birds glided in, landing on a nearby tree. They stayed there for several minutes, and in that day's sunlight you could really appreciate why they were called red kites. A wonderful experience, and my phone call was somewhat delayed!

The grebes I was interested in were not on the reserve, they were in the North Arm, I believe that is the name, so I drove a short distance towards Upper Hambleton and parked up where I could overlook the North Arm. I had noticed a couple of cars parked down a side road, and I had chosen well. Three birders were walking back to one of the cars, and yes, both the Slavonian grebe and black-necked grebe could be seen a short distance down the road. Two other birders were down there, so I would know where to stop. I thanked them and walked on.

They were right. I quickly found the birders and did not have to do any work to find the grebes, they were only too pleased to point them out to me. This was birding made easy, and I was not complaining. It is always good when you find birds for yourself, but I see no harm in having them found for you.

These birders also told me about a scaup they had seen further down the Arm, towards Armley Wood, and one of them was able to show me exactly where on his map. I now knew where I was going next. First of all I enjoyed the grebes, I had not driven this distance just to have a glance. They were both now in their winter plumage, but were adult birds, so enjoy them I did.

I was pleased to have been showed where to see the scaup. A gate on the side of the road was close to the shore of the lake, and this was open so access was available. A dead tree was on the water's edge and the bird had been diving close by, hopefully he would remain so, the bird being a drake, this made identification a little easier.

The gateway was located, and I was able to park close by, the road having a wide verge. They were right about the gate being open, looking at it I doubted it could be closed, the condition it was in. I was not gate watching, I had other things on my mind.

The tree was quickly located, being the only one there, and fortunately, the scaup was still in close attendance. They are a bulky looking bird, principally a black, white and grey duck with a heavy rounded head, at a distance, they could be mistaken for a drake tufted duck except the tufted has a black back, the scaup a grey. They are very much a marine duck and we only see them during the winter months as they are a near Arctic breeding species, with the odd one appearing on inland waters. They are more frequently seen round the coast. Another bird thoroughly enjoyed, and totally unexpected. Rutland Water had hit the jackpot today, a most enjoyable trip out.

The remainder of the year saw us visiting familiar places with the Rosliston Bird Sudy Group. Croxall, Blithfield and Cannock Chase principally. We had a few interesting species, scaup again, red-breasted merganser, great grey shrike, crossbill and lesser redpoll being the pick of those. They helped me reach two hundred and nine species in the year, which in view of the start to the year, I did not consider that to be too bad. More importantly, I felt I was on the road to recovery thanks to the birds and my many friends.

One of my colleagues, Roy, had been up to Scotland for a week's birding, and he suggested we should try that for a holiday. Several others agreed and we booked ourselves in at The Grant Arms Hotel in Grantown-on-Spey for a week commencing 26th April. The hotel is well known as the wildlife hotel, and they really do cater for the naturalist. I would be visiting an area completely new to me, although having visited Scotland previously, not this part.

Prior to that, I had booked another week in Norfolk for the group and this was taking place in February, was it tempting fate with the weather once again? Time alone would tell.

The Rosliston Bird Study Group now had thirty-one members and we decided to no longer have indoor meetings, instead we would meet up for a morning's birding locally, with still the occasional full day.

CHAPTER III

Prior to Norfolk, all our meetings were local and we did very well numerically, all of us reached the hundred mark, before the end of January, with a few bits of quality among them. The pick of those being the great grey shrike, still to be seen on Cannock Chase, great northern diver, black-necked grebe, glaucous gull, yellow-legged gull, peregrine falcon and an early chiffchaff, probably an over- wintering bird. This bird could easily have been a Siberian race, but the view we had of it was not conclusive. The 18th February saw us on the way to Norfolk, and the weather forecast for the week ahead was not bad. Cold, with frost and a bit of mist, but no snow mentioned. We hoped they had it right.

As with previous holidays in Norfolk at this time of the year, we drove straight to the hotel so we could get an hour or so down The Quag. Once again this proved to be a good decision. As we walked down the hedgerow we had a group of goldcrests for company, and at The Quag, we saw the following: grey partridge, little egret, the male hen harrier once again (I am beginning to think this bird probably over-winters here), pintail, a drake ruddy duck—a delightful surprise, woodcock and a black swan.

I think you will agree, that was a good enough start to our week.

We visited the usual locations, which you must be well familiar with by now, and the pick of the one hundred and twenty birds we saw in the week were as follows. Avocet, barn owl, black-throated diver, Brent goose, both races, corn bunting, crane, curlew, Egyptian goose, marsh harrier, mealy redpoll, merlin, pink-footed goose, red kite (this bird was whilst in transit, not actually in Norfolk), red-necked grebe, red-throated diver, rock pipit, scaup, smew, snow bunting, snow goose, the inevitable turnstones at Salthouse, still being fed, and white-fronted goose.

A bit of quality there I think you will agree. I am sure you just cannot fail in Norfolk. Thanks to Norfolk, I had broken the one hundred and fifty mark before the end of February, it looked as though I was heading for a good year, especially as I had Scotland to look forward to.

The usual species moved through during the weeks prior to our visiting Scotland, plus a most memorable species, an Arctic warbler, seen at Blithfield Reservoir. That was a mega 'lifer' for eighteen of us who just happened to be visiting Blithfield, not being aware of the bird's presence. As we arrived, two birders I knew came running across to me. 'Get yourselves down to St Stephen's Hill Bay, in the shrubby area below the farm, there is an Arctic warbler,' they shouted. We needed no second bidding, we were on our way. Fortunately, as we were all members of the West Midland Bird Club, we had permits and keys, so we were able to drive in and park up without any problems.

The bird was hiding away in a tangle of bramble and shrub hawthorn, just putting in an appearance occasionally, so it was a real question of patience. This was eventually rewarded, and we all had good views of the little fellow.

The Arctic warbler is not dissimilar to the willow warbler, being a slightly larger and more stout looking bird. It also has a more distinct pale eyebrow and a prominent dark line through the eye. Those we eventually saw, plus the darker legs, so we were happy with our diagnosis, plus the fact early March was a bit early for returning willow warblers.

What a bird which normally winters in South East Asia and does not usually return to Scandinavia until early June, was doing in middle England in March is anyone's guess. Mind you, there were many happy birders who did not ponder the question for too long, they just celebrated the occasion. Some bird to get on your local bird list.

What did surprise me, and I did not find this out for a year or two, although my two birding colleagues reported the bird, it was not accepted by the bird club's rarity committee. Even up to the present day, the only record of an Arctic warbler in Staffordshire goes back to 1993. Some of us know better! I no longer report any unusual sighting, it is just a waste of time and effort. You have to be well known or have supportive evidence, photographs etc., and even those are not always enough. A photograph of a bird in a tree could be taken anywhere. I will say no more, I have had my arguments and I have long decided birding is for pleasure and knowledge—mine!

Scotland finally arrived. Len picked me up and we joined Roy, just taking the one car. I must confess I was looking forward to being driven round for a few days, normally I was the one doing the driving.

On our way up to Grantown-on-Spey we called in at Loch Alvie where osprey were breeding, they are not all at Loch Garten, just the 'famous' pair are there. We had superb views of the bird and of the nest, and goldeneyes were also on the loch.

The most perfect way to start a birding holiday north of the border. We all had 'hit lists' of the birds we would most want to see, mine, due to my years of experience, only had three species on it, capercaillie, crested tit and Scottish crossbill. I needed those to complete my list of all the regular breeding species in the UK. Rare breeding species which may have bred on the very odd occasion were not included in this, my list was just the birds which bred every year, not occasionally.

Day one saw us off after the capercaillie, and here we went to Loch Garten, where we would see the ospreys and possibly crested tits. Could be in for a good start.

We were off early that day, leaving at 6.00 a.m., as entrance to the reserve is regulated and at that time of the year it is a very popular venue. We were lucky, we managed to get into the hide with the first intake. The ospreys were in full view, the nest being quite close. The female was on the nest and the male roosting up nearby.

He apparently had just brought in a fish so the female was devouring this. The male already having eaten his part of the catch.

The RSPB organised things so that you only had a certain time in the hide before the next batch of visitors were allowed in. With the volume of visitors this was necessary, otherwise people, who were paying, would not have gained entry. The majority of watchers were only interested in the ospreys, many had probably never heard of the capercaillie. We were in the minority, and concentrated our efforts in looking for that species.

I was beginning to think our allocated time would run out, when a warden touched me on the shoulder, and pointed. There he was, a magnificent male, strutting across an open area of ground, providing us with the finest of views. They are our largest game bird, and as one of my colleagues commented, if he had not known better, he would have thought he was looking at a turkey. I doubt we saw the bird for more than thirty seconds, but it was a time of pure magic. My long wait was over!

The tail was half raised, as though it was preparing itself for a 'lek', where the males display themselves to attract a female. We, unfortunately, did not see this, but we were more than happy with the short time we had shared with the bird.

Our time was up, back to the hotel for a late breakfast. Mind you, saying late, we were back by 9.00 a.m., our bird in the bag and a full day ahead.

Whilst at Loch Garten we had been told about an area where black grouse were regularly seen, so after breakfast, we were back near to Loch Garten. We travelled down a minor road which crossed the moors, and we had been told to look for a screen on the side of the road. This had been erected so birders could study the black grouse at their 'lek'. We were too late in the day for watching a 'lek', but the grouse could be seen throughout the day in this area. Our informants were not wrong. Black grouse were active at regular intervals during the hour or so we were there, those certainly were a good compensation for the loss of our local black grouse on the Staffordshire Moorlands.

It was now time for a bite of lunch, so we drove into Aviemore to partake of refreshments, and then, we had been told of a small loch nearby which had black-necked grebes breeding on it. Our afternoon's activities were decided upon.

I had the necessary map reference, so we quickly located the loch, parked up, and walked down the farm track to the loch. The loch was only the size of a park pool, so locating the grebes was not going to be difficult. Unlike great crested grebes which build a floating nest attached to low twigs, which can rise or lower depending upon water levels, the black-necked tend to nest on land, and frequently in colonies.

Ours that day was certainly nesting on the land, but not in a colony, we had just the one pair, we were happy enough with that.

Black-necked grebe are a northern breeding species, only

occasionally do they breed south of the border, although a pair did breed in Staffordshire a few years ago. They are only slightly larger than the little grebe, but in their breeding plumage they are a very smart bird. Black neck and head with a golden blaze on their cheeks, and a distinctive 'retrousse' bill, they are unmistakable.

Although being only late April I was pleasantly surprised by the number of hirundines we saw, especially at this loch. No swifts, however, probably too early for their arrival. I had not seen any back home.

Warblers were another species which we had not met up with so far, still it was early days, we still had time to go to put that right.

We decided that we would visit the Cairngorms the next day, the weather looked bright and clear, not much point in 'mountaineering' in a mist!

We drove through the Glenmore Forest Park, seeing buzzards and hooded crows whilst in transit, and parked up at the ski centre where we took the funicular railway up to the Ptarmigan View Point, aptly named we hoped, as it was ptarmigans we were after. The day was most pleasant and many were walking up, we took the easy route. Large areas of snow were still visible, although the walkways were clear for the walkers. What it must be like up here in winter is anyone's guess.

A mug of coffee was enjoyed on our arrival, and we went outside to do some birding. At this height it was quite chilly, and snow was close in, so we stayed at the viewpoint. A movement on a nearby grassy area caught our attention, a group of small, pale looking birds, had dropped in. To say we were pleased they had, is putting it mildly, we were studying six snow buntings, three pairs and the three males looked magnificent. Apart from Norway and Iceland, those were the only ones I had ever seen in full summer plumage. I had seen them in Norfolk with a good amount of colour remaining, but not like those. They brought back a few memories, I do not mind admitting.

According to my map we were standing over 1200 metres above sea level, it had gone very cloudy and a decided chill had descended. Time for another coffee we thought. It was just a pity a certain Scottish beverage could not have been added to it!

We birders do not give in that easily. Suitably fortified, we ventured forth once again to stare into the cold air. After several minutes our persistence was rewarded as three ptarmigans flew in and landed in a rocky area close to where we stood. These were all males, and they still showed some white in their plumage, they had not completely moulted out of their winter colours. We enjoyed the birds for two or three minutes before they flew off, they did not return, but we were more than happy.

As we were about to go back inside, a golden eagle was heard and shortly afterwards the bird came gliding past, putting on a wonderful fly-past. It cannot get much better than that.

On our return journey down, we saw a further group of eight ptarmigans, three of which were females, so that gave us eleven birds on the day. We all felt that most satisfactory.

In the car park, a further pleasure awaited. Ring ouzels could be heard calling and we located two males looking very smart in their brilliant white waistcoats. A wonderful end to our day out. Not a great number of species seen, just birds of quality.

After dinner that evening, we were talking to two birders who had seen crested tits that morning. They had visited Loch Garten, not the RSPB reserve, the loch itself, and in a local café they had seen crested tits visiting a feeder in the café gardens.

We now knew where we would be that next day.

We quickly found the café, confirmed with the proprietor that crested tits did visit her garden, ordered coffees and sat outside to wait, full of expectancy. About one hour and two further coffees later, we gave up.

A very pleasant wooded area lies on the shores of the loch and a good path leads through the wood down to the shores of Loch Mallachie, and back round the shores of Loch Garten. We decided to do that walk, if crested tits were in the area, we may pick them up in the wood.

As soon as we entered the wooded area, we picked up the song of a willow warbler, and the call of a common whitethroat quickly followed. Crossbills could also be heard from a stand of Scot's pines. We spent some time on those, had very good views, but to us they all looked and sounded like the ones back home. So if there were Scottish crossbills amongst them, we did not find them.

On reaching the shores of Loch Mallachie we had a very pleasant and unexpected surprise. On the water were a pair of Slavonian grebes, displaying, well the male was. We spent a most enjoyable few minutes watching this spectacle. As with the black-necked, Slavs as we call them, are a northern breeding species so we rarely see them in breeding plumage. It was almost as though we were seeing them for the first time.

Turning back, we walked along the shore of Loch Garten and here we saw the osprey out hunting. After several attempts he caught a large fish and flew with this into a nearby tree. Here he killed his catch and proceeded to eat part of the fish.

Watching him, we realised he was only eating the head, and apparently, this is what they regularly do. Could this be that the head is the most difficult part of the fish to eat and the female and any young need the more easily digestible parts of the fish?

Whatever the reason, once the head was consumed, off he flew back to the nest at Loch Garten reserve. The provider had done his job once again.

We called in back at the café, the crested tits had not been back that morning, had a coffee, and then decided to go red grouse hunting. They were to be seen on the open moorland not far from where we had seen the black grouse a day or so back.

We stopped for a quick look for black grouse, only saw two, but we were rewarded by a passing goshawk, which may have accounted for the scarcity of the black grouse.

A mile or so further on we stopped, according to our information that was a good spot. We were delighted to hear the plaintive call of golden plover and quickly realised this was also the breeding location for this delightful bird. We saw several of those birds, and in the height of the breeding season they are most spectacular.

Believe me, they are not called golden plover without good reason.

Whilst enjoying the plovers, a loud 'go'bak, go'bak' rang out—red grouse. We quickly located them and saw five males, the females no doubt already sitting eggs. In that day's sunlight, they really did look red, another case of a bird being aptly named.

Along with the red grouse, meadow pipits were plentiful, and they were in full voice. They may not rival the skylark, but they put on a very good show. In the far distance, what looked like a hen harrier was quartering the moors, but it was too far away to be absolutely certain, another 'nearly' bird.

In a couple of days we had seen the four most special of the UK's game birds—capercaillie, black grouse, ptarmigan and finally the red grouse. There are few places where you could manage that, and relatively speaking, not that far away from each other, especially the capercaillie, black and red grouse. I doubt if they were ten miles apart.

Another good day's weather was forecast, so we decided a visit to the coast would be a good idea. We headed in the general direction of Forres, where we could explore the coastal area at our leisure. It was a pleasant journey up, seeing several hooded crows whilst in transit, and a golden eagle also gave us a few seconds of its time. We did thank it!

Many more birds are to be seen in coastal habitats, on moors and mountains they are a bit specialised and not always easy to find. At the coast they almost come to see you, well some of the gulls do, they are after food.

We saw some interesting waders in full summer plumage, we are not used to this. South of the border we tend to see those species when on passage and they are not normally decked up in their summer regalia. Special amongst those were purple sandpiper, sanderling and turnstones, all at their immaculate best. The turnstones were almost tame, they just about stopped short of actually coming right up to you.

As one of my friends put it, 'Do you think these are the birds we saw in Norfolk at Salthouse?' Who knows, he could have been right!

In one of the tributaries goosander and red-breasted mergansers were showing well, one female red-breasted merganser actually had five largish ducklings, the first I had ever seen outside collections. Eiders were well accounted for, although it was noticeable, we were only seeing drakes, the ducks being obviously otherwise engaged!

One bird which did surprise me was a small flock of pink-footed geese, eighteen of them. I would have expected those to be on their northern breeding grounds by now, not still in the UK, even though they were almost at our northern limits.

As we drove on, we stopped by the side of a smallish loch, I do not know the name, on my map it did not have one, not that that was important. What was, was the fact a black-throated diver, again in full summer plumage, was sailing, majestically, across the loch. Another bird we rarely see in full summer plumage, when we do see them, they are either in a juvenile state or in winter plumage. As with the Slav, almost a new bird!

Common gulls do live up to their name in Scotland. In several locations as we crossed the moors, colonies of the birds were seen, in some two to three hundred pairs were breeding. We usually only see this bird in small numbers, and mostly during the winter months. Here they were common, living up to their name!

As with the black-headed gull back home, many of which do not breed along the coast, they prefer freshwater, here the common gulls were doing the same near to freshwater lochs. I frequently tell people, there is no such thing as a sea gull, they are just gulls of various species, and many never, ever, see the sea.

Curlews were plentiful, with much of the moorland being damp, conditions were ideal, and at times the air was full of their exotic calls. A wonderful sound from a truly wonderful bird. They certainly made the hairs on the back of my neck rise, the most evocative sound to be heard in the countryside in my opinion. As I regularly say, if the sound of a curlew does not turn you on, I am sorry, you have no soul.

We had heard rumour of crested tits being seen at Grantown. A large wooded area lies adjacent to the town, through which runs the River Spey, so we decided to spend some hours there, and have a rest from driving.

After a leisurely breakfast we walked down to the woods to concentrate our efforts on the crested tits. We need not have bothered, we saw none. We did however see a good range of woodland species, including amongst those, cuckoo, dipper on the Spey, a golden eagle heard but not seen, great spotted woodpecker, grey wagtail also along the Spey, raven, siskin, sparrowhawk, treecreeper, a very early tree pipit, heard a wood warbler and saw a pair of yellow wagtails, those were also along the Spey. If we include the common species seen or heard, we chalked up thirty-six birds in that area alone.

Our final day arrived, we would have one last fling after crested tits and Scottish crossbills, and the Abernethy Forest was our chosen destination. Loch Garten lies in this forest area, but we would not be visiting there that day. We had been given a map reference where both the birds we were seeking, had been reported recently. There was no guarantee, needless to say, but when you have come this far, you have to try.

We parked up at the allotted spot, just a clearing on the side of a minor road crossing the forest, no name, no one lived there. One thing in its favour was it had a tight small area of Scot's pines, much favoured by the crossbills.

Titmice were very evident, not the species we were seeking, we were beginning to wonder if they existed! To concentrate the mind, however, crossbills could be heard.

A flock of twenty or so flew into the Scot's pines, and our work started. We watched those birds for over twenty minutes, and the more we watched the more we were convinced they were just the common crossbill we see at home. The 'experts' talk of slight differences in their calls and in the bill shape. We could not see or hear anything different with these birds.

I am slowly becoming convinced that the Scottish crossbill is just a myth, along with 'Nessie', put out to bring tourists into Scotland. A friend of mine, a most experienced birder and photographer, has photographed birds claimed to be Scottish crossbills, and when he has studied them, he could find no evidence of any difference with those found south of the border. I agree.

Our holiday had drawn to its conclusion. Ninety-two birds seen, not a great number when compared with Norfolk, but among them, a few birds you would only see in Scotland. Hooded crows, golden eagles (now we had lost the only pair breeding in England, the Lake District birds), ptarmigan, capercallie and birds in breeding plumage, which do not breed south of the border. I was sure we would be back, I still needed the Scottish crossbill, presuming I believe it does exist, and the crested tit, which certainly does!

Back now to normality. The usual summer trips were made, with the customary results. The nightingales at Little Paxton put on a great display, I had at least five separate males singing their little hearts out. Even the turtle dove behaved itself, sitting on an overhead wire, gently purring away.

The nightjar numbers on Cannock Chase seemed to be on the increase and the woodcock were much in evidence. A pair of hobby were also seen, these were no doubt breeding, which was very good news, unless you were a moth or dragonfly!

Early July, and I had a three-day break, this time I visited Anglesey, after choughs and black guillemots in particular. The weather was not good, unfortunately, it was a case of birding between the showers. That did not stop me from seeing some quality birds, the choughs and black guillemots obliged well. The choughs were again to be seen at South Stack, where according to a local birder, they are regularly seen by the RSPB centre/café. The black guillemots were seen at two locations, their usual spot in Holyhead and on the cliffs on the east side of Cemaes Bay near Lanbadrig. Here I must have seen at least six different birds, one sitting out on the cliffs providing a wonderful view.

I also saw a cattle egret which was a bit special to say the least. Little terns, two roseate terns and Sandwich terns showed well and a small passage of Manx shearwaters also occurred, which all helped me break the two hundred mark for the year. Just how well I could do I did not know, but I still had almost six months to go.

The 26th July saw me back at Sutton Coldfield Crematorium. I took some seed with me this time just in case the robin was still there. He was not, he had done his job last year, and that day it was just happy memories, and no tears.

September saw me back in Norfolk for a few days, four in fact, and I stayed at The Pheasant, needless to say. I saw ninety-six species over the four days, nine of which were 'year ticks'. One a real beauty.

At Salthouse, I arrived to see a group of very excited birders, one of whom shouted across to me, "It's here." What 'it' was I had no idea, but I quickly found out.

A male Shorelark was on show, I have only seen them on rare occasions before, and this fellow was a real poser, and it intended to be seen. Binoculars were not required for this bird, it hopped about just feet away, and on one occasion, it actually hopped through a group of birders. A few cameras were whirring away that was for sure. The bird of the week was almost talking to me. It cannot get better than that! I should not have said that, because it did. I had my only second ever Arctic warbler, this one at Titchwell, and it was a much more accommodating bird than the one I had seen at Blithfield the previous year.

The other seven birds which were 'year ticks' being Arctic skua, bittern, dotterel, great skua, Lapland bunting, sooty shearwater and spoonbill. Norfolk had again produced the goods.

By the end of my short stay, I had reached two hundred and twenty-three species for the year, whether it would continue or not, who knew?

Early in December I had a long weekend in Norfolk, Friday till Sunday. I had arranged to meet a friend there. This did not materialise, unfortunately, he had to go abroad on business, but the birds compensated, ninety-one in total. A few 'year ticks' were added to my year's total, including a 'lifer'. Much work had been done recently with splitting the hen harrier into different species, inventing a new bird if you like, and one of those is now called the northern harrier. Whilst at Cley, one such bird was reported, a male fortunately, and the 'twitchers' arrived in number. I found myself in the middle of a major 'twitch'.

Fortunately, I was in the hide just before the news broke, mobile mania was taking place. I just sat there and let it all boil over my head, at times birders can become a little aggressive, and we had one or two there. Luckily for the harrier, he was outside the hide, bedlam was inside!

One or two of Norfolk's top birders were there, and it was very interesting listening to them as they pointed out the small differences in the bird's behaviour and plumage compared with a hen harrier. Thanks to them I was happy enough to have the bird as a 'lifer', had I been there on my own I am sure it would have gone down as a male hen harrier. Whether I would recognise the bird, if I ever saw one again, is open to conjecture!

I ended 2010 on two hundred and thirty-eight species, I have only ever exceeded that twice. What had 2011 in store?

CHAPTER IV

It commenced with my doctor suggesting I applied for a blue badge, with my knees, hip and pacemaker, he thought it would be sensible to have this. Walking at times was now becoming a bit of a problem and opening the car door wide enough to get in and out of my car was also diffcult. I applied for and was granted a badge.

This also set me off on the thoughts of a book. Much of my birding was now being done from or near to my car, and for any walking I was using an elbow crutch. I was also limited in where I took my telescope as I could not manage to carry a tripod any more. I could only take my hide clamp.

Given decent conditions underfoot I could just about manage to walk a mile or so, very slowly, but my friends were only too happy to accommodate me, so birding continued.

Back to thoughts of a book. There had never been a bird book written specifically for the disabled, advising them on places to go and how best to deal with it. Many birders are mature folk, need aids for walking and knowledge of where to go. The idea was sown, and I started to work on my book which would be titled, *A Journal of a Year in the Life of a Blue Badge Birder*, and this was to be based on that year's birding. 2011 was going to be a special year in many respects.

I was fortunate in quickly finding a publisher who was interested in my idea, so my birding for the year ahead had changed somewhat. Apart from a holiday I had organised for a week in Norfolk during March, my birding locations would have to be accessible to disabled birders. Fortunately, I knew of many places which fitted that bill, and we saw many interesting birds. I will not go into the year here in detail, it is already available in my book which was published in 2012, so I will just provide a quick resume of the top birds seen, when and where.

The year commenced dramatically in a way. On January 1st, I had a waxwing in my own garden, some start to a new year. January 3rd, long-eared owl at Park Hall Country Park, and red grouse on Axe Edge Moor. January 9th, whooper swan and pink-footed goose at Croxall Lakes Nature Reserve. Chasewater gave me smew and Iceland gull on 15th January. The end of the month provided hawfinch and dipper at Cromford and I closed on ninety-four species.

On 6th February, there was a great northern diver and yellow-legged gull at Carsington Water. The 11th provided a merlin at Whitemoor Haye, a Mediterranean gull at Blithfield on the 13th, and a Caspian gull at Carsington Water on 21st. One hundred and nine for the year.

What would March do? It started off well on the 8th, a great white egret at Blithfield Reservoir, and then we had Norfolk. During the week we saw one hundred and five species, the pick being avocet, Brent goose, shorelark, spoonbill, marsh harrier, Cetti's warbler, peregrine falcon, Ross's goose, and a red kite. By the end of the month, I had seen one hundred and forty-five species.

April commenced with swallows on the 1st, these were in my own village, Yoxall. The 3rd provided a wood duck at Wolseley Bridge Nature Reserve, and the gate opened up with the arrival of the usual summer migrants, two of which were rather special.

A ring ouzel at Croxall Lakes Nature Reserve on 24th April, and a pied flycatcher at Rosliston Forestry Centre on the 27th. The month closed on one hundred and seventy-one.

During May, I made the annual trips to Bempton Cliffs and Little Paxton, with the usual results. During the month I also had black tern at Blithfield on 3rd, quail at Whitemoor Haye on 12th, black-throated diver at Shustoke Reservoir on 14th, Temminck's stint at Croxall Lakes on 19th, Staunton Harold Reservoir gave me an osprey and goshawk on 27th, and we finished the month off with a little stint at Croxall Lakes on 29th. One hundred and ninety-two for the year so far.

Things were going to slow down now that was for sure. June 5th, wood sandpiper at Blithfield and honey buzzard at Hoar Cross, an escapee—Harris hawk at Lichfield on 14th. This bird attacked a man, and a hen harrier at Alrewas Arboretum on 19th. One hundred and ninety-eight for the year.

July came in with a garganey at Blithfield on 3rd, Slavonian grebe and American wigeon at Pitsford Reservoir on 10th, and the month finshed off with marsh sandpiper and bearded tit at Blacktoft. Two hundred and three for the year.

All August gave us was a snow goose at Rocester on 20th, number two hundred and four.

In September things woke up a bit. On the 22nd a curlew sandpiper visited Blithfield, a black-necked grebe at King's Mill Reservoir on 23rd, a scaup at Blithfield on 27^{th,} a rough-legged buzzard also at Blithfield on 29th, and the month closed with a visit to Frampton Marsh and Feiston Shore, two RSPB reserves in Lincolnshire where I saw pectoral sandpiper, long-billed dowitcher and red-throated pipit, some quality that. Two hundred and eleven for the year.

It was now a question of chasing the special birds and October saw me doing so. On 16th I was at Daventry Country Park for a grey phalarope, the 21st a water rail at Old Moor, at Rutland Water I saw a white-rumped sandpiper on the 23^{rd,} a hybrid pochard/tufted duck at Whitemoor Haye on 26th, a great grey shrike on Cannock Chase 28th, a jack snipe at Croxall on 30th and finished off the month with a squacco heron at Attenborough. Two hundred and eighteen.

November, and I was back in Norfolk for a few days, and whilst there I added cattle egret, Dartford warbler, black redstart, red-throated diver, velvet scoter, little auk, pomerine skua, bittern, melodious warbler, yellow-browed warbler, desert wheatear, Lapland bunting and crane. Norfolk did me proud that was for sure. Two hundred and thirty-one.

I finished off the year with a bean goose (Tundra race) at Whitemoor Haye on December 21st and my final bird of the year was seen on 26th, a glaucous gull at Albert Village Lake. I closed on two hundred and thirty-three species.

The great thing about those birds was the fact that nearly two hundred of them were seen either from my car or within a very short distance of my car. With careful planning and the right optical equipment, they are there to be seen. A car makes a wonderful hide, but just one thing to keep in mind, always have your windows down prior to parking, the lowering of windows can be quite noisy on some cars.

CHAPTER V

2012 saw us with two group holidays organised. First Norfolk called once again, March 11th would see us back at The Pheasant and in May we would return to Scotland, the lure of crested tits and Scottish crossbills was all demanding!

I also decided that 2012 would, hopefully, be a bit special. I do not make New Year resolutions, they are rarely kept, but I did resolve to try to make this a most special year on the bird watching front. At the back of my mind, I had always had two birding ambitions, the first was to see two hundred and fifty different birds in the UK in a single year, and the second to pass the four hundred mark on UK sightings. The latter is fully in the lap of the Gods, but the first is possible, it just requires time, effort and a bit of luck. I shall be seventy-nine this year and I do not know for how much longer I will be driving, nor have the energy. I am already struggling, so this could well be my final chance. I have Norfolk and Scotland which will help, the rest is down to effort, planning and luck. The year sees me in 'twitch' mode, how will I fare is the question.

For the first time in a number of years, I managed to break the fifty mark on January 1st—just. I saw fifty-one. Amongst those were a few good quality birds to start the year. Glaucous gull (it took me almost a full year to see one the previous year, now I had it on day one!), yellow-legged gull, little egret, golden plover and Egyptian goose. Not bad for so close to home. Mind you I had used every hour of daylight to do so, but the effort had been worthwhile.

The 2nd Jan saw me add six more to my total, included among those were mandarin, red-crested pochard and peregrine falcon, good quality again, and once more, all local. So far, I had hardly needed to get out of the car.

As the month progressed, quality seemed to be the name of the game. The pick were as follows: I had crossbills at Blithfield Reservoir of the 5th, the following day I saw black redstart, lesser redpoll, pintail and raven, also at Blithfield, and driving home a grey partridge at Woodmill. Blithfield again came good with tawny owl on the 7th, and travelling further afield, saw red grouse at Axe Edge Moor on the 8th.

Twite were seen on 12th, Blithfield once more, with a great grey shrike at Upper Longdon the following day. A little owl showed up at Whitemoor Haye with a long-eared owl putting in an appearance at Park Hall Country Park. On the 16th, a merlin gave me a fly-past at Whitemoor Haye, and I came home to be greeted by brambling in my own garden, three of them. Kings Bromley chipped in with a snow goose, Blithfield provided Mediterranean gull, Iceland gull and Caspian gull, all on different days I add, and the month ended with Siberian chiffchaff at Coleshill and great northern diver at Carsington Water. The month closed on one hundred and four, and with the exception of the red grouse, Siberian chiffchaff and great northern diver, all were seen within the county of Staffordshire. Plenty of effort, but not a lot of milage.

I was beginning to wonder just what sort of year lay ahead. This was the best start I had ever had, not just in number, but the quality of some of the birds seen. Was two hundred and fifty on?

I managed to complete my book by the end of the month, and I am pleased to say the publisher was happy with my work and it should be published late April/May. Wonderful news to start off a new month. Now, what would the birds do?

Things quietened down a little in February, but quality was still there, the best of which as follows. Whooper swans flying over the Alrewas Memorial Arboretum, mealy redpolls on Cannock Chase, a grey wagtail at Blithfield, this bird was actually in the Watery Lane car park, it obviously meant to be seen. Lamport in Northants sported a rough-legged buzzard, I was pleased a friend had told me about this bird, and on my return journey home I had Jack snipe at Whitemoor Haye. Blithfield was back on the scene with a smew on the 12th, this would have been Dorothy's birthday, a nice way to remember that. She had a liking for smews ever since she saw her first one at Slimbridge.

The month continued with dipper and hawfinch at Cromford. Short-eared owl near Alport, red kite at Caldecott in Leicestershire, and green-winged teal at Eyebrook Reservoir, also in Leicestershire. Kingfisher were seen at Marketon Park and the month finished with red-breasted merganser at Cop Mere. They helped me to reach one hundred and twenty-five for the year so far, but for many of those I had commenced to travel further afield.

On 3rd March we had a drake ruddy duck at Blithfield Reservoir, which we kept to ourselves in view of the persecution those ducks were suffering, plus a stonechat at Barton Pit. One final trip prior to Norfolk took us to Attenborough, where we had a Bahama pintail, an obvious escapee, the bittern put on a good show and several snipe were still to be seen. One hundred and thirty birds recorded so far.

Come Norfolk, fourteen of us ventured forth, full of expectancy, but Norfolk never lets you down, and it did not.

During the week we clocked up one hundred and ten species, and the pick of which were as follows:

Day One. Titchwell. We started off with an absolute cracker. A warden explained that a mega rarity was to be seen just down from the visitor centre, and the crowd of birders was quickly located. A Coues's Arctic redpoll was putting on a show. This bird is a North American variant of the Arctic redpoll and is a bird seen very rarely, and when it is, it is usually up on the Shetlands, a bird so far south was really special. You are unlikely to find reference to this bird in many field guides, so we were pleased we had been told about it and had the bird pointed out to us. Under normal circumstances we would just have classed it as an Arctic redpoll, we were very pleased to have been informed otherwise. Further new birds for the year were Cetti's warbler, avocet, ruff, marsh harrier, Brent goose, the dark bellied form, curlew and water rail. We then called in at Burnham Overy Staithe where we added barn owl and pink-footed goose. At the Raptor view point along the A149 near to Marsh House Farm, we saw Lapland bunting and hen harrier, and finished up at Salthouse for snow bunting. A very good start to the week, and I had now reached one hundred and forty-one species.

Day Two. Back to Salthouse, for scoter and turnstone. Then on to Cley Reserve where we had spoonbill, bar-tailed godwit and black-tailed godwit. On to Wells where we saw knot, grey plover and another top bird, an Hudsonian godwit, only my third ever. We finished off looking across the Cley marshes at a flock of white-fronted geese. One hundred and fifty-two.

Day Three. Hunstanton gave us fulmar, and on our way back we called in at Cley where we saw spotted redshank, velvet scoter and long-tailed duck. One hundred and fifty-six.

Day Four. This time we commenced on Cley beach where we had passing sand martins, with both red and black-throated divers, guillemot, kittiwake and gannet out at sea, and on Cley Reserve we clocked up Brent geese—the pale bellied variety, emperor goose, another escapee and bearded tit. One hundred and sixty-five.

Day five. Also a clear day, and on our final day, we added eider to the list. My 'year list' had now reached one hundred and sixty-six. Norfolk had done me and my group proud.

March was not finished. Middleton Hall Lake produced a garganey, Cannock Chase a woodlark, King's Mill Reservoir a black-necked grebe, Shustoke Reservoir a scaup and finally Blithfield Reservoir closed the month with green sandpiper and little ringed plover. One hundred and seventy-two. To say I was having a good year was putting it mildly, and I still had Scotland to come.

April arrived, this being the time of the year for our returning summer migrants to arrive back on the scene. I was beginning to wonder if I could reach the two hundred mark, before the end of the month. For me that would be some record.

Come with me and see how we fared, the race was on. April 1st, willow warbler at Blithfield Reservoir, 4th, wheatear again at Blithfield and a house martin at home. The 6th, swallow and osprey, Blithfield once more. A crane on the 7th at Radford Meadows, Stafford, Sarah also saw this bird, and on the 8th, Blithfield again, a yellow wagtail. On the 10th I travelled a bit further afield to see a barnacle goose at Carsington Water. The 12th and I was on Cannock Chase, this time for a tree pipit and the following day I was back at Radford Meadows for a lesser spotted woodpecker.

Croxall Lakes provided me with both common sandpiper and common tern on the 14th, and on the 18th, Sarah and I had the pleasure of a male redstart in our own garden.

Whitemoor Haye gave me an Arctic tern on the 20th, and the

following day Croxall shipped in with both reed and sedge warbler, whilst back down the Haye I clocked a garden warbler. On the 24th, back in Yoxall I had a whitethroat and a hobby gave me a fly-past. Whitemoor Haye saw both swift and little tern and Blithfield had black tern, this was on 27th. The 28th I found a little gull down the Haye, the 29th a Sandwich tern at Blithfield, and I finished the month on the 30th with a pied flycatcher on Cannock Chase. A bit of a chase around, and I died in the hole as they say, the month saw me out on one hundred and ninety-seven. I, at least, had given it a try. I hope you were not too much out of breath!

I came to a decision at this point, having reached nearly two hundred so early in the year, and with Scotland still to come, I would now make positive efforts to clear the two hundred and fifty mark. I might never have such an opportunity ever again, and I was finding walking easier than it had been for some time. I was definitely in 'twitch' mode!

May commenced with a bit of quality, a Dartford warbler on Cannock Chase on the 1st, a cuckoo, also on the Chase on the 2nd, and come the 4th, my two hundredth, a nightingale at Brandon Marsh in Warwickshire. The hard work was about to start.

On the moors I collected ring ouzel, this was on the 6th, and a wood warbler followed on the 10th, this time from Cannock Chase. On May 12th, my birthday as it so happened, I saw my first lesser whitethroat, this was at the Alrewas National Memorial Arboretum. That was number two hundred and three.

My book was published and this brought me two moments of fame. Well, a few minutes to be more accurate. I was interviewed on the BBC TV Midlands News, this was recorded at Croxall Lakes Nature Reserve, a very proud and interesting moment. Seeing myself on television was an experience I never dreamed of. Then came two book signing engagements, one at a book shop in Burton on Trent, the other in Derby. To have complete strangers coming up to you, buying your book and having it signed, was a completely new situation to me, but a thoroughly enjoyable experience.

May 20th, and we were on our way to Scotland. This time I took my own car up. One of my course members, Evelyn Syer, was a very keen and competent driver, and she agreed to share the driving. Once in Scotland she offered to do all the driving, this was a very good suggestion as it meant I could spend my time looking for the birds, instead of having to concentrate on my driving. The two, unfortunately, do not go well together.

Our programme was much as when up there last, so I will just mention the birds which were important to me. May 21st, Cairngorms—ptarmigan and at Avielochan, rock pipit and Slavonian grebe. May 22nd, Findhorn Valley, a goshawk.

May 23rd, was when it all happened. Firstly, in the Abernethy Forest we had spotted flycatcher, and then the bird we all wanted. Loch Mallachie this time produced the goods, thanks to Roy's observance. We had our crested tit. A 'lifer' for us all, and Roy, we thank you. The bird had not been easy to find, it was very active collecting food, obviously it had a nest nearby. The bird was not in posing mode, not that we cared.

At least when you do see a crested tit well, there is no mistaking it. The characteristic head markings, from where the bird gets its name, make it unmistakable, and the trilling call, described as 'prrululull', is distinctive to say the very least. This bird was very vocal for some reason, probably announcing its presence to the female on the nest. I could now breathe a sigh of relief, I had my bird at last. I may have seen them abroad, but this was my UK 'list'. Thank you, Scotland.

The 24th, the coast called. We visited Gruinard Bay where we saw great skua, razorbill, shag, and on our return journey near the junction of the A835 and A9 a small flock of hooded crows put in an appearance. Our final trip was to Lochindorb where white-tailed sea eagles had been reported. We dipped on those, but we had golden eagle as compensation. Those eleven species took me up to two hundred and fourteen. Over the week we saw ninety-one species, mainly thanks to Evelyn's driving.

I doubt if I will visit Scotland again, so the Scottish crossbill is unlikely to ever get on my list. Never mind, I did at least try, and I can always console myself by believing it to be a Scottish myth!

Back home, the month ended with a quail at Whitemoor Haye. This bird not only called well, it showed itself, which made it that more special. As game birds go, they are such a small bird, and if the vegetation is just inches high, they become almost invisible.

June commenced with a marsh warbler at Blacktoft Sands, a whinchat at Derbyshire Bridge on Goyt's Moss, a woodcock seen flying from the Whitehouse car park on Cannock Chase, and Croxall Lakes produced the bird of the month, almost the bird of the year, a red-footed falcon. A trip across to the Welbeck Park Raptor Site hit the jackpot with a honey buzzard, and calling in at King's Mill Reservoir on the return journey, gave me a grasshopper warbler. Come 15th June I was back on the Chase nightjar hunting, successfully so, and the 23rd saw me at Flamborough Head where rock dove, feral pigeon, puffin and Arctic skua were added to my list. Two hundred and twenty-six was now my figure.

Whitemoor Haye produced a wood sandpiper on 4th July, and on the 7th, I made a trip up to Anglesey where I saw black guillemot, chough and roseate tern, amongst fifty-one others. The 10th saw a bit of a 'plastic', five helmeted guinea fowl were in a field at Hoar Cross. How they got there I did not know, there were no farms or building close by, those had to be escapees. To compensate, a real bird was seen at Blithfield on 13th, a white-rumped sandpiper. You do not see many of those, they are a rare vagrant from North America.

The 26th July was time to visit Sutton Coldfield Crematorium once again, this is something I intend to do for as long as I am able. A moment of silent contemplation and wonderful memories, and as I said last year, no longer any tears.

Time does heal, as long as you let it. Slowly it may be, but it does.

I finished the month off with a greenshank at Blacktoft, this was on the 27th.

My total was now two hundred and thirty-three, I was rapidly approaching my highest number ever, that of two hundred and thirty-eight and I still had five months to go. Not that it was going to be easy, I would have to put the hours and miles in.

August started with a ruddy shelduck at Blithfield. On the 12th I visited a new location for me, Grimley gravel pits, in Worcestershire. A great white egret had been reported, so that bird had to be chased up, and it was done so, successfully I am pleased to report. Come the 26th, it was again pastures new, this time the Birstall Meadows in Leicestershire, where a spotted crake was the lure. After a lot of time and effort I managed to find the bird. That got me up to two hundred and thirty-six.

My first new bird for the year in September was a bird I will never forget. A sacred ibis had been reported from Stanwick Lakes in Northamptonshire. If that bird was still around, it was not going to be missed. It is a large white bird with a black head and neck with a very long curved bill, and a bird of that size would find it difficult to hide. They are an African species, although reports have been made of their now breeding in Europe. The purists are already claiming the bird to be an escapee, but if so, someone has been very careless.

Map reference obtained, and I was on my way to pastures new. I must confess when I arrived, I wondered if I was in the right location or whether the bird had gone, not another birder was in sight. I found a way into the quarry and, after a short while, had my bird. It was walking, very elegantly, through shallow water, continually stabbing with its long bill into the water, and on one occasion, came up with a frog. This was promptly swallowed. I watched the bird for several minutes before it vanished round a bend, and was not seen again. What a bird, that day will not be forgotten. As I was about to leave, I heard a purring sound, a turtle dove. This was quickly found, and I had now equalled my record number in a year, two hundred and thirty-eight. Come the 22nd September and I had set a new record. My two hundred and thirty-ninth bird was a little stint, seen at Attenborough. The following day saw me at Spurn Point, where the selection of birds was as normal, with three of exceptional value—sooty shearwater, Leach's storm petrel (here a 'lifer') and a cattle egret.

I was very fortunate with the Leach's storm petrel. I first picked up the bird way out at sea, thinking it was just a common storm petrel, as seen at Anglesey, but the bird turned shorewards and I had a very clear view of the bird. It was larger than the storm petrel and paler, close study also showed it to have a jerky flight and it continually changed direction, not the behaviour of a storm petrel. Flying in ever closer I also noted the rump was not very white, then it hit me, I had a Leach's storm petrel, as mentioned earlier, a 'lifer'. What surprised me most of all was the fact it was a solitary bird. My experience of petrels, limited though it may be, is they are birds which migrate in flocks, what this bird was doing on its own, I do not know, not that I am complaining.

The last day of the month saw me down at Slimbridge where a long-billed dowitcher was the star attraction. I ended the month on two hundred and forty-three.

October was 'lifer' time once again. On 5th, at Firsby Reservoir, near to Rotherham, a pallid harrier was seen. This was a bird not to be missed, so four of us went chasing the bird and we were successful. The pallid harrier, lives up to its name, being pale, and especially so on the underside of the wings, and unlike the hen harrier with which it is easily confused, the wing tips are not fully black. It has a black wedge which only covers part of the primaries, whereas the hen harrier has total black wing tips, all the primaries are black. Small differences, but they can be important at times. The bird was a rarity in the UK and should have been on its way down to east Africa from eastern Europe, nowhere near western Europe. I doubt if I will ever see one in the UK again. I was a happy man.

The remainder of the month proved to be very productive. We had a Greenland wheatear at Blithfield, a red-backed shrike at Burton Mere Wetlands on the Wirral, a grey phalarope at Carsington Water, black grouse at Worlds End, a lesser yellowlegs at Aldcliffe Marsh in Lincolnshire, finishing the month off with a bar-headed goose at Whitemoor Haye. That bird was mega, not in rarity, the fact that it was my two hundred and fiftieth bird of the year. My target was reached at last, and I still had two months to go.

Early in November a friend of mine came back from a couple of days' birding in Norfolk and he told me about two birds in particular he had seen, waxwings and a marsh sandpiper. Every birder wants to see waxwings and a marsh sandpiper was a bit special to say the least, so a quick day in Norfolk was called for.

I was off by 6.00 a.m., with Langham being my first destination, hoping the waxwings were still to be seen. Driving into the village I need not have worried, twenty or so birders were gathered staring intently at a row of trees. I found a spot and parked up. As I got out of the car, I could hear the waxwings calling away, and within seconds, I was seeing them clearly. It was a good-sized flock, they even outnumbered the birders watching them. A most enjoyable half an hour was spent there in the waxwings' company, before I departed for Thornham, marsh sandpiper hunting.

The tide was out and I had Thornham to myself, well from a birding point of view, a few walkers were passing through. I started to study each of the creeks where various waders were present, but not the one I wanted most. Crossing the dunes, I started to study the shoreline, and there, a very busy, long-legged, small wader caught my attention. Up 'scope, the bird was quite distant, but once in the 'scope I had no problem. It was a winter plumaged bird, a very pale, ashy-grey colour, with a long and slender bill. The legs were a greenish-grey, and when it flew, as it frequently did for short distances, the legs trailed well out beyond the tail. No doubt about this bird, I had my marsh sandpiper.

Late November saw me at Blacktoft where I picked up a water pipit, and December gave me Bewick's swans at Slimbridge and I finished the year off, on Christmas Eve at Blithfield, with a Christmas present of a red-necked grebe. Two hundred and fifty-five birds in the year. The purists would claim there were some 'iffy' birds amongst those, such as black swan, feral pigeon, helmeted guineafowl and even the sacred ibis. All I knew was they had not walked to where I saw them and all were capable of flight. Even if I discounted those, and I am not, I would still have broken the two hundred and fifty mark, amongst which were five 'lifers'—Coues's Arctic redpoll, crested tit, sacred ibis, Leach's storm petrel and pallid harrier. My top year without a doubt, and I doubted very much whether I could ever improve on it.

I was now also a published author, a dream accomplished, and more importantly, just before Dorothy died I had promised her I would try. Thanks to you my love, I have succeeded.

CHAPTER VI

2013 was now upon us, and how do you follow a year such as that? You do not try, you simply enjoy what you get.

The year started off with our usual bird race, Sarah and Martin versus me. I am sorry to report they beat me, I notched up forty-three to their forty-five, and my first bird of the year was a collared dove.

As the month progressed some quality started to appear, and all of it was local to Staffordsire and Derbyshire. The pick of those were waxwing, golden plover, ruff, little egret, great grey shrike, whooper swan, great northern diver, long-tailed duck, water rail, merlin, long-eared owl, glaucous gull, Caspian gull, hawfinch and short- eared owl. In total ninety-three birds were seen during the month.

February commenced with peregrine and yellow-legged gull at Hick's Lodge, and February 10th saw the Rosliston Birders off to Marshside and Martin Mere.

We called in at Marshside first and amongst the birds seen were pintails, pink-footed geese, knots and dunlins, a more than decent start to the day.

Martin Mere was, as is usual, very busy, it is a popular venue and here it was a question of splitting the wild birds from the collection species. Before we started, a coffee and a warm snack was called for, and Martin Mere has very good facilities.

Inner man sustained, we ventured forth.

The prime attraction here are the whooper swans, a large number over-winter having come down from Iceland and the near Arctic regions, and they did not disappoint. They are a very audible swan, unlike our native mute swan, their calls echoing out, and when you saw the number of swans the volume of sound could be easily understood. A noble bird if there ever was.

Large numbers of geese were to be seen grazing the meadows, grey-lags and pink-foots, and among them was a hunting barn owl. This ghost-like bird just drifted slowly over the heads of the geese before it dropped down among them. Job done, it flew off with some small creature—it had its meal for the day. I suppose the large number of grazing geese disturbed any animal feeding on the ground and the barn owl was able to capitalise on this. Owls are not classed as being among the most intelligent of birds without reason.

Another feature here at Martin Mere is the large flock of ruff which can be regularly seen during the winter, and very good views were obtained. A pair of red-crested pochards were also appreciated, these birds flew in so we had no problem in counting those. As well as seeing further dunlins and knots, we had several ringed plovers to add to the list. All in all, a very satisfactory visit, after which my 'year list' had reached one hundred and three. I was beginning to progress.

The remainder of the month saw me picking up some good quality birds. Amongst them were dipper, seen at Cromford, two in fact. A grey plover showed up down Whitemoor Haye, this bird was a beauty, it being in almost full plumage.

Croxall produced a small flock of seven curlews and in a meadow near the reserve a herd of seventeen Bewicks's swans were seen. Nearer to home, along my local river, a pair of grey wagtails were seen, these birds will hopefully be breeding shortly.

Chasewater provided us with a Slavonian grebe, this bird held on for several days providing good views. Red grouse were seen on the moors, a lesser spotted woodpecker entertained the Rosliston Birders on Cannock Chase and the month concluded with a drake hooded merganser over at Tamworth. 'Escapee,' the purists yelled! All one could say about this bird was the fact it could fly, and for the few days it was around, it did so frequently. The hooded merganser is a North American species and the odd bird has cropped up in a few places, but as it is a popular duck in collections, there is always doubt regarding sightings. It finished the month off well, and I closed on one hundred and sixteen.

March saw the group off to Norfolk once more, fifteen of us, needless to say The Pheasant was our destination. After the success of Evelyn's driving in Scotland, she again did most of the driving in Norfolk, freeing me once again to look out for the birds.

On our way we called in at two completely new locations. Eldernell saw us looking for cranes which proved very accommodating, a new bird for many of my colleagues, and then on to Houghton Hall. A mega rarity had been reported from there. For a week or two, a juvenile white-tailed sea eagle had taken up residence. That bird could not possibly be ignored, a 'lifer' for us all. I had only seen them in Norway.

We arrived to join a large crowd of birders, all eagerly waiting to see the bird. Initially, we did not and after an hour or so we began to wonder if it had moved on. A red kite did its best to cheer us up and a pair of buzzards appeared frequently. I spoke to a new arrival, he told me he had seen the bird earlier that morning further down the road past the entrance to the hall.

We decided to give it a try and drove down, we did not have to worry about the real spot, there were just as many birders there, not that any had seen the bird.

After several minutes a shout went up. "Here it comes," and gliding across the open parkland came our bird. We often describe it as a flying bedstead, its wings are certainly shaped like a bed. By our standards it is an enormous bird, which just glided in on outspread wings, the white tail from whence the bird gets the name very noticeable, to land in a tree. It sat for a few minutes before shuffling off into the tree where it vanished from sight.

We must have spent at least a further hour waiting for the bird to return, it did not, and as the weather appeared to be turning unpleasant, we made an early arrival at our hotel. No complaints, a great start to the week.

The following day saw us at Salthouse where the turnstones were still acting as car parking attendants, eventually letting us through. Additional to the turnstones, we had ringed plovers, redshanks and snow buntings. A bit of rain started falling so we quickly moved on to Cley where we had hides. The rain fortunately passed over.

Cley was at its best. Spoonbills, Brent geese, both dark and pale bellied races, two purple sandpipers moulting through into their summer plumage, avocets, black and bar-tailed godwits, greenshanks and dunlins. Bramblings were at the feeders squabbling with the chaffinches and, out at sea, gannets were moving through. Titchwell was next on the agenda. This too lived up to its reputation.

Amongst the sixty-three species seen, and additional to birds seen at Cley the previous day, the pick of the birds we added to our Norfolk list were water rail, Cetti's warbler, spotted redshank, knot, marsh harrier, great white egret, and red-throated diver. Calling in at Wells on our return we clocked up Caspian gull.

The following day, new territory again. We visited Sculthorpe Moor Reserve, where the pick of the birds seen were marsh tit, great spotted woodpecker, jay and a goshawk. As we were about to drive off a covey of grey partridge walked through the car park, seven of them. A bit of a special goodbye that!

The following day some of us had a day off, the remainder visited Cromer for a day's sea watching. Plenty of gulls, the odd fulmar, black-throated diver and black-necked grebe, were also noted. On the sea a large flock of scoter were seen, all common scoter unfortunately.

We finished the week off at Cley and Salthouse, where, apart from glaucous and Mediterranean gull, nothing additional was added. As Norfolk goes it had been a quiet week with only ninety-four species seen, but the sea eagle alone had made the trip worthwhile. The company was, incidentally, nae bad!

I came back with my 'year list' having reached one hundred and forty. The remainder of March saw me picking up on local species with the best birds being white-fronted geese at Doxey Marsh. White-fronted geese are not a bird we regularly see locally, they are a winter visitor from Siberia which are more frequently seen in the east of the country. A rough-legged buzzard was seen over Branston Water Park, only for a few minutes unfortunately, the bird was obviously just pasing through.

Blithfield Reservoir then enjoyed a bit of glory with sanderling, kingfisher, green sandpiper, little ringed plover and a little gull, not I hasten to add all seen on the same day, they were spread over ten days. The month finally closed with a willow tit on Canock Chase. I closed the month on one hundred and forty-nine.

April started with a bit of class near to home. I was walking up to my surgery to collect my prescription, when a bird of prey came flying across, initial thoughts being a female sparrowhawk. As it got closer, I realised I was looking at a male goshawk, what a way to start a new month. I will have to visit the surgery more often! Not a bad bird to reach one hundred and fifty with.

The Rosliston Birders commenced April with a field meeting up to Burton Mere, the bird of the day there being a male hen harrier, although a small herd of whooper swans were still to be seen, plus a few little egrets.

The remainder of the month saw the arrival of many of our summer migrants with a few vagrants and passage birds among them. I will list these by date order as it will give any newcomers to birding, an idea of what can be seen, and when, at this time of the year.

We commence on the 11th with swallow and sand martin, the 15th willow warbler and common sandpiper, the 16th a Jack snipe, the 17th house martin, yellow wagtail and wheatear, the 18th saw an Arctic tern, followed on the 19th by blue-headed wagtail and common tern. Come the 20th a tree pipit, followed on the 21st by passage Sandwich terns, a small group of seven. The 22nd saw the arrival of hobby, whitethroat. sedge warbler and a passage whimbrel, on the 23rd lesser whitethroat, white wagtail and spotted flycatcher. The 24th, probably the bird of the month, a passage whiskered tern, followed on the 27th by osprey and swift. The 28th saw garden warbler, the 29th cuckoo and wood warbler, finishing off on the 30th with reed warbler.

One or two of those were a bit special, so let us look at them in more detail. The Jack snipe was a winter visitor returning to northern Europe to breed, the whimbrel and Sandwich terns were on passage to their breeding grounds, probably in the northern UK.

Another three birds seen were very special, the blue-headed wagtail, whiskered tern and the osprey. The blue-headed wagtail is a race of the yellow wagtail, and is not regularly seen in the UK. I have seen them on the continent, mainly southern France and round the Mediterranean, so this was a most welcome addition to my 'year list'. Not a 'lifer', but I doubt I have seen more than four. A bird welcome at any time.

The whiskered tern, which was seen at Blithfield Reservoir, was only the second I had ever seen in the UK. My only other experience of them, has been in southern Europe, where they breed.

They are a member of the marsh tern group of terns, breeding on marshes and freshwater locations, none of the marsh terns breed in the UK, so they are always welcome sightings. The commonest marsh tern we see is the black tern which passes through the UK on migration. The whiskered tern, on the other hand is a vagrant, with just a very small number popping up in the UK.

The 27th saw the annual return of the osprey. For several years a bird has called in at Blithfield for a few days, in transit north, probably heading for Scotland.

A great way to finish off the month. I closed April with one hundred and seventy-nine species, almost twenty species down on this time last year. But that year was a bit special.

May commenced with a bit of fun. The group were at Croxall Lakes where we stumbled across a goose, foreign to all of us. It was no domestic goose and obviously was not going to be found in any of our field guides. The bird kept on nagging at me, I was sure I had seen the bird at Slimbridge in the collection and was an Australian species. Fortunately, I have a guide to the wildfowl of the world at home, and on my return, I quickly took it off the shelf. I was right about it being an Australian bird, it was in fact a Cape Barren goose. I would not argue with the purists on this one, there is no way this bird had flown halfway round the world. Someone, somewhere, had lost it.

Our annual visit to Bempton was made, with the usual results, with more concern over puffin numbers, they appear to be reducing annually. One bird I was delighted to see was the bridled guillemot, several of those were sitting out on the ledges. As I have mentioned previously, the bridled guillemot is not a species in its own right, it is just that occasional birds have a white eye ring and a white line behind the eye, hence the name 'bridled'. They are just a variant and will breed with an ordinary guillemot quite happily. That day saw me add eight birds to my 'year list'

The following day, at Whitemoor Haye, a honey buzzard graced the skies, very elegant and very welcome, although the event barely lasted two minutes.

Blithfield produced the goods on the 13th , a passage of little terns took place, fourteen of them were seen for a few hours before they moved on. In Stansley Wood redstarts and a pied flycatcher were seen, the first pied I have ever seen there, I can only presume it was passing through.

A day or so later a passage of black terns occurred at Blithfield, these hung around for a couple of days before they moved on. Then on the following day, a drake mandarin duck put in a brief appearance, but he was only seen for a couple of hours or so, I was very lucky to be there at the right time.

The 19th May produced a red-necked phalarope at Chasewater, this a male, brought the local birders in, and the month concluded with a pair of stonechats and a Dartford warbler seen on Cannock Chase. The month closed on one hundred and ninety-seven, progressing nicely. It looks as though I may have another very good year. Time will tell. June meant time for nightingales once again, and Little Paxtom did not let me down. I heard at least five males singing and saw three of them. The turtle doves took some finding and it was not until I was returning to my car that I heard one, and that was only briefly. Talking to a local birder he said they were rather worried as only one bird had been seen so far that year. Cuckoos had also been very vocal, a few of those were back at least.

An evening on the Chase went well. The nightjars performed as usual and the woodcock roded several times, much to my companions', the Rosliston Birders' pleasure. The hobby also put in a brief appearance, and two cuckoos were calling well. The only disappointment was the lack of owls, but you cannot win them all.

It was time for ring ouzels, and they certainly knew how to show themselves this year. I parked up on the layby and had only opened my door to hear the male calling. I got out, gently I may add, and peering over the stone wall, the bird was just yards away collecting food. I watched him fly off with this down into the valley, waited a few minutes, and back he came. This performance went on for a good twenty minutes before he failed to return. Judging by all this high activity the bird was obviously feeding young in the nest. It was great to know they had bred there again.

Driving back over Axe Edge Moor two red grouse greeted me with a fly-past, and as I drove off the moor, a wheatear was seen standing on the stone walling. This bird also had food in its bill but I could not stop to see where he went with it, a large van was following me and there was not room for me to pull in and allow it to pass.

The next piece of quality on my agenda was garganey. I had been told that it was believed a pair were breeding at Rutland Water, so armed with that information, I decided to pay a visit. As I have mentioned earlier, garganey are a summer migrant which breed here in small numbers, so the chance of seeing a breeding pair was too good to miss.

The birds were not actually on the reserve itself, and were best seen from the minor road to Upper Hambleton, in the North Arm. I knew the location well from previous visits. I duly parked up off the road, and made my way in and set myself up to view the bay. There was much activity on the water from cormorants, great crested grebes, mallards and black-headed gulls, but they were not what I was looking for.

I must have spent well over an hour searching the area with no luck. It was not that I was looking for a diving duck which could be spending much of the time under water, garganey are surface feeders. My problem was the fact that part of my viewing was obstructed by trees and bushes, but eventually my patience was rewarded. Sailing out from beyond a bush came the drake garganey, and in his summer plumage, he looked magnificent. I was able to enjoy him for almost half an hour as he just sailed round in the open water, only occasionally feeding. I did not see the duck at all, so if they are breeding, she was probably on her nest. My journey had been well worth it.

Potteric Carr was next on list. Black-necked grebe were breeding there for, I believe, the first time, well worth a visit. Potteric Carr is a very large reserve, but fortunately they allowed blue badge holders to drive into the reserve and park up near to some of the hides and café. I enquired about where the grebes were breeding and luckily the lagoon on which they were was close to a car parking area and served by good pathways.

I made my way round, enjoying a superb male redstart as I did so, and watching a spotted flycatcher taking food to its nest, which brought back memories of Weeting Heath. The hide was located and only two other birders were inside, they quickly mentioned the grebes and pointed out into the water in front. The male was out in front of the hide, constantly diving, and he certainly looked smart in the day's bright sunlight—I could almost have been back in Scotland. The nest unfortunately was not in view from that hide and it was too far for me to walk, so I did not have the pleasure of seeing the female or the nest. The male more than compensated for that, and I have seen them breeding previously. Another quality bird seen.

A bit of luck came my way later in the month, a common scoter had appeared at Chasewater, so a quick trip across put her in the bag.

The 23rd saw me back at Blacktoft. I understood the bittern had been rather active of late and the chance of a bearded tit was good. The day was bright and clear and almost the first bird I saw was a grasshopper warbler, and this was thanks to another birder. You by now know that the 'groppers' call has moved out of my normal hearing range, fortunately this birder mentioned the grasshopper warbler, he had just heard it and pointed out the bushes from which the sound had come. They were too far away for me to hear the bird even if it did call, but at least knowing where he had called from did give me the chance of seeing him. A nearby bench was quickly occupied.

A pair of birders came along, we spoke, I told them what I was hoping to see, and they joined me on the bench. They were much younger than me, I just hoped their hearing was good. It was. The bird started to call, or so they claimed! It had moved its location and was a little nearer, and then it showed itself. The bird popped out onto the top of the bush, gave a little burst, not that I heard it, I could just see its throat rippling, and was back in the safety of the bush. What a cracking start.

I made my way to the marshland hide. Avocets were plentiful, several sitting on their nests and having to keep marauding black-headed gulls at bay, which they appeared to be doing successfully. A water rail gave a brief appearance, it trotted out of the reeds for about two seconds, before dashing back into the reeds. Two male marsh harriers were out hunting over the reed bed, and the odd grey heron flew through. A couple of times I thought I saw movement in the owl box, but I could not be sure.

Time to move back to Xerox. I could not have timed things better. I quickly became aware of a feeling of excitement as soon as I entered the hide. A lady waved at me and pointed. There, right in the open, stood a bittern, this bird had just not read the book. Bittern do not do things like that, their aim in life is just to frustrate the birder, not entertain him. We were able to enjoy this bird for a few minutes, and I am sure we will all remember the day well.

To complete my day, I went down to the Singleton Hide. Here again it was marsh harriers and a few avocets, the odd reed warbler could also be heard and a reed bunting was busily collecting food, it no doubt had a nest nearby. I had mentioned the bittern to the birders in the hide, and they all decided to go and see if they could be lucky, so I now had the hide to myself. They should not have left when they did.

Barely five minutes after their departure, four bearded tits flew along the edge of the reed bed, the quick view I had of them made me think it was a family party. I did see a male bearded tit come out onto the edge of the reeds, but it was a solitary bird each time, no sight of a female or juvenile birds, but two of the birds originally seen did not seem to have long tails. I was more than happy with what I had seen. Another good day.

I finished the month with a whinchat, this was seen near to Dunstall. I was just driving through when the bird landed on a post along the lane. Talk about luck, a real right place, right time bird. You do win them occasionally, they just make up for the times you fail.

June closed with two hundred and nine species seen, no complaints with that.

July came in with quail once again down Whitemoor Haye, a cracking start to a new month. Mind you, that was almost it, if I had not seen a wood sandpiper at Blacktoft on the 19th, July would almost have passed by unnoticed, apart that is for my annual visit to the Sutton Coldfield Crematorium.

Since my visit, when I saw the robin, I have always taken some seed, most times I have just spread it on the ground for any bird to find. Not this time. I was sitting on the bench, deep in thought, when a robin arrived, landing close by my feet.

It obviously was not the same bird I saw a year or two back, they unfortunately do not live that long, but it was more than welcome. I managed to get the bag of seed out of my pocket without frightening the robin off, and spread this on the ground. This bird knew what it was all about, and promptly hopped onto the seed to eat its fill. I smiled and left it to it, my day was complete.

Things bucked up a bit in August. On the 4th a night heron put in a brief appearance at Kings Bromley, visible from the layby for less than half an hour. Only a few birders saw this bird, by the time I had emailed my colleagues, it had gone. A cracking bird to see locally.

As the month progressed, a little stint visited Blithfield Reservoir where it stayed for a few days, and the 23rd saw me off to some woodland near Sheffield where a large flock of crossbills had congregated, among which were three two-barred crossbills. I had not seen two-barred crossbills for a few years, so a trip up to Sheffield was called for. A friend had been able to give me a map reference, as the area was new to me.

I located the woods without any trouble and was pleased to see a goodly number of birders present, many pairs of eyes make light work, and so it turned out. A shout went up, we all glanced in the direction indicated, and there were a pair of two-barred crossbills feeding on the cones. We enjoyed the birds for several minutes before they shot off deeper into the woods. Although we saw many crossbills during the next hour or so, the two-barred were not seen again. Needless to say, I went home happy.

Later in the month Blithfield clicked again. A curlew sandpiper popped in for a few days, and it looked a very smart bird. It was an adult, presumably a male, and it still had a good proportion of its red breeding plumage remaining. Both a bit of quality as well as colour to end the month. Two hundred and sixteen was now my total.

September came in with a lesser Canada goose (cackling goose as it is now known), which was at Carsington Water on the 5th and a week later, the layby at Kings Bromley again featured. This time it was a cattle egret putting in a brief appearance, staying just long enough for Sarah to pop down and see the bird. That bird was the fourth rare heron/egret seen from this layby. Previously we have had little egret, great white egret and night heron, I doubt if there are many places in the country that could beat that record. The month was not yet over, ruddy shelduck, two of them, were seen at Blithfield Reservoir on 15th, a little crake at Belvide on 19th and the month finished off with a pectoral sandpiper at Blithfield on the 22nd. A few choice specimens there, and the month closed, on two hundred and twenty-one.

November produced a red-breasted merganser at the Staffordshire Wildlife HQ. Wolseley Bridge on the 3rd, and the month concluded with a twite at Chasewater. A quiet month but it found two pieces of quality, which also proved to be my last birds of the year. Nothing new occurred in December.

The year closed on two hundred and twenty-three. Not a bad total at all. I had not done the 'twitching' I had the previous year when chasing a record, so I was more than happy.

leave. It was also the opportunity to meet up with some old friends who had heard the news. The grapevine was working at full pressure with this bird.

I now just wanted the bird to stay on for a couple of more days so I could take Sarah across to see the bird. I put the news out to all my colleagues via the net and several managed to see the bird, and, best of all, it stayed put. Back again with Sarah, she now could enjoy such an exciting bird, and I saw it for a second time. It was quite amazing really, the bird was in the same small field as when first found a few days previously, and apparently, it flew the short distance to Chasewater at night to roost.

Brownhills had never been counted as a mecca for birders, but this bird had certainly put it on the map. Brownhills was now known to birders from many parts of the country.

A month which started off so quietly had produced a 'lifer', and what a 'lifer'. The month seemed to brighten up after that, and a few more interesting species came along. I had a lesser redpoll in my own garden, a long-tailed duck spent a couple of days at Croxall Lakes, little egrets off the layby at Kings Bromley (where else?), red grouse and hen harrier on the moors, and a lesser scaup at Tittesworth Water (they have dropped the word reservoir, Water no doubt sounds posher!).

Then came the 25th January, and news came through of a Hume's leaf warbler at Coleshill, a rarity such as this, and so close to home, had to be chased. Two 'twitches' in a month, unbelievable, and both so close to home. I had all the information required, so off I shot.

With a rarity of this value, you do not look for the bird, you just have to find the birders, and I quickly did so. Once again, with the bird being so local, I knew many of them, and the bird was quickly pointed out to me. Warblers are small, very active birds, and being insect eaters, they have to search away very diligently, especially at this time of the year when insects are not plentiful. This bird also had a few chiffchaffs in competition, but they all seemed to be doing fine. I was able to enjoy the bird for several minutes before it flew off, along with the chiffchaffs, four of them, and did not return. Half an hour later and I would have missed out on this bird, as it was not reported again.

The Hume's leaf warbler is listed as the Hume's yellow-browed warbler in some field guides, the reason being there is a school of thought which considers the bird to be a race of the yellow-browed warbler, as it does have certain similar characteristics. Having seen yellow-browed on one or two occasions, I feel that there are enough differences for it to be a separate species, call it what you will. Hume's leaf warbler it remains on my list.

After a slow start, the month had produced two superb birds and although I only totalled eight-six species in the month, it would go down as a special month, the glossy ibis saw to that, a bird I shall never forget.

Now how do you follow that? February tried. We commenced with a great grey shrike at Hopwood, in Worcestershire. I had no idea where Hopwood was, so once again, it became a map reference job. The bird was frequenting a lane of tall hawthorns, from which it had a very good vantage point for seeking out its prey. The bird was not difficult to find, the number of birders looking sorted that out.

Cannock Chase then came along with crossbills, a flock of twelve of them were seen from near to the Whitehouse car park. Staunton Harold Reservoir followed up with a Mediterranean gull, and Croxall Lakes, not to be outdone, had the bird of the month, an American wigeon, and surprisingly enough, I did not hear the 'purists' cry—escapee!

There is always a problem where waterfowl are concerned. Due to collections many foreign ducks are bred in captivity and sold on to new owners. In the majority of cases the birds are pinioned as the owners do not wish to lose the birds, due to the costs involved. Should a new owner only clip any birds which may be bred from captive birds, once new primary feathers grow, the birds will be able to fly, hence the fact many will consider that bird to be an escapee. All I know is that I managed to see the bird out of the water and it did not appear to be ringed, it goes on my 'year list'.

Blithfield followed on with red-necked grebe, an adult winter plumaged bird and totally unexpected. Whitemoor Haye saw two rock pipits, Cromford hawfinch, and the end of the month came with a merlin at Bromley Hurst. Those obviously were not the only birds seen, they were just the pick of the bunch. February closed on one hundred and seven species. Not as many as I would normally have expected by then, but decidedly up on quality.

March saw me climb up to one hundred and thirty, a slow climb, but once again a bit of quality therein. The month commenced with a goshawk at Croxall Lakes, this was followed the next day by a mealy redpoll at Middleton Lakes, and the first week in March concluded with a Caspian gull at Blithfield. My home patch, Yoxall, then produced a beauty, a red kite, only a hundred yards or so from home, nearly a garden bird that one!

When I think back to earlier days, I used to make special visits to the Elan Valley just in the hope of seeing a red kite. Thanks to the re-introduction programme carried out some years ago, they are now seen regularly in many parts of the country.

We do not know whether they have bred within Staffordshire borders, but they are beginning to be reported on a regular basis, and they have bred successfully in Worcesrtershire. It is only a question of time before they do breed locally, I am sure,

Cannok Chase would be an ideal spot for them. Birds have been seen on the Chase, I have had one myself.

The pick of the birds after that were scaup at Belvide, a superb drake, a bird well worth seeing, and it showed well, no mistaking this fellow. Blithfield then came along with probably the most unexpected bird of the month, a drake garganey. What this bird was doing so early in the year I do not know, they are a summer migrant which come here to breed. I do not think it was an early arrival, I think it had probably over-wintered, and this may well be a result of climate change.

If our winters are becoming warmer than in previous years, creatures which once needed to migrate to find food, may now be finding it here. If my thoughts should be proved to be correct who knows what lies around the corner. Many creatures which once needed to migrate may no longer need to, and other creatures will also move in as they expand their territories. Egrets are already doing this. Be careful of that lion at the bottom of your garden!!

On the 14th a passage of curlews occurred at Whitemoor Lake. I was there for about two hours and several small groups of curlews flew through. One small party of seven birds landed on the shores of the lake for about twenty minutes or so, but the remainder of the birds flew on. I would estimate over a hundred birds flew through that morning, quite a spectacle.

Blithfield Reservoir came up with the goods the following day. A small flock of five black-tailed godwits were seen, but the bird of the day was a rough-legged buzzard. I was parked up in the Admaston Reach car park as this bird flew through.

It came in low along the shore, flicked up over the causeway and continued on down Blithe Bay. I watched the bird for about three minutes or so before it drifted out of view, but what a few minutes. The grace of this bird was something special, at times you feel privileged to have experienced those moments.

Then on the 17th, a hint of summer. I had attended a meeting at the Rosliston Forestry Centre, and after this had completed I went for a short stroll. I had not proceeded far when I stopped, a chiffchaff was calling. There is no mistaking this little fellow, I love birds who shout their names at you, they along with the cuckoo make identification easy. I found him quickly, it is always better when you can both see and hear a bird.

On the 22nd, summer appeared even more closely. I was at Croxall Lakes when five sand martins flew in. They proceeded to hunt flies low over the water, and as it was a warm day, I hoped they were successful.

I visited Blithfield on the afternoon, and here too summer seemed to be in the air. On the dam were two wheatears, both males, they were eating small flies which were on the dam parapet, and along the shore near the sailing club a little ringed plover was found. That bird took me up to one hundred and twenty-five for the year, proceeding steadily.

The following day the little ringed plover's cousin appeared on the scene, well to be more accurate, two of them did. Ringed plovers were seen at Whitemoor Haye Lake, they were busily feeding along the shoreline.

It was time for a visit to Belvide Reservoir, especially as I had been told a velvet scoter had been seen. As I have mentioned previously, velvet scoters are not a common bird and few are seen so far inland. Some years none are recorded at all locally, so the chance to put one on my 'year list' could not be missed. I arrived at Belvide to find only another car in the car park, and I did not recognise the vehicle. Crossing the car park I stopped, a blackcap was singing close by, a very pleasant refrain, and I quickly located the bird, another summer migrant had arrived.

Approaching the hide a small bird flew across the path and vanished deep inside a holly tree, my initial thought was a goldcrest, but I wanted to make sure, and I was very pleased I had. After a few minutes the bird came out onto the outer leaves of the tree and I was delighted to see I was looking at a firecrest.

They are very similar in appearance to the goldcrest, but they are a much rarer bird, only a few, breed in the UK. This bird sat out for several seconds and I could clearly see the broad white supercilium, the goldcrest lacks this, so identification was made. This was a bird that had never been considered, we often joke that if you wish to see a firecrest you have to wait for it to come to see you, you will never find it yourself. This bird certainly had come to see me, and I thanked it!

On to the hide, which needless to say I had to myself. There were not all that many ducks on the water, which was a good thing really, it was mainly gulls and terns putting on a show. The odd pair of tufted ducks were seen, plus the inevitable mallards, but I was looking for a very dark duck. Fortunately, it was a drake, and hopefully the white patch near the eye would be visible, and if it should flap its wings the white patch, speculum, should show clearly. If the wings remained closed, the best I could hope for here was to see a white line on the wings.

I must have spent a good thirty minutes studying the birds, especially the coots, when the bird I wanted sailed into view. Scoter are great diving ducks, which at times seem to spend more time under water than on top of it, luckily for me, this fellow had not read the script. It just sailed by, quite happily, and after a short while tucked his head in his back, and went to sleep. I can but presume the bird had fed well and was now sleeping it off. Whatever it was doing, I was happy. Three new birds for the year, two of them being a bit special. Belvide had done me proud.

The final day of the month saw me at Cromford, where the dipper kindly put on a good show, so the month saw me out on one hundred and thirty.

April started off with grey partridge at Hoar Cross and a little gull at Blithfield Reservoir, and come the 3rd April, the bird we were all waiting for returned to Blithfield—the osprey was back. No bird is welcomed more, even the anglers appreciate this fellow, and he does not have to pay to catch his trout!

Be interesting now to see how our summer migrants, fare. We have had the odd few, chiffchaff, blackcap and osprey so far, let us hope the door is now open.

The 8th sees our next arrival, a willow warbler is singing happily in Fisherwick Woods, a delightful song it is too. A couple of days later, three yellow wagtails are seen chasing flies along the shore of Whitemoor Haye Lake, with barnacle geese out on the water, not that the latter are summer migrants. Two days later, Whitemoor Haye produces a common sandpiper and five swallows, is summer actually here now? I doubt it somehow. A whitethroat is heard at Croxall Lakes on the 13th, and two whimbrel pass through Whitemoor Haye two days later, plus a lesser whitethroat seen and heard at Croxall.

The 17th proves to be a memorable day. Things start off at Blithfield with the arrival of the common terns, seven of them and two Sandwich terns are among them, they will be quickly moving on, they do not breed locally. Then came the afternoon when it all happens at Whitemoor Haye. I met a very excited birder who had just seen a bird he could not identify, so I went with him the short distance to where he had last seen the bird. To say I was mighty pleased to have met him, is putting it mildly, his bird was a woodchat shrike, a real vagrant.

Woodchat shrikes are rare visitors to our neck of the woods, seen probably once every five years or so. I have only seen two locally, this one and one in Sutton Park some twenty years or so ago, so to have one on my own patch so to speak, was some record. Fortunately, I was able to enjoy the bird for nearly half an hour, you do not rush off from a bird of this quality. This bird should have been in the western Mediterranean region, where it is probably the commonest shrike to be seen, not so far west. I think it was safe to presume the poor bird was lost. This birder had found some bird, he should remember that day forever That was not the end of the day, looking over the lake I saw a small party of house martins, they helped to end a perfect day.

How do you follow a woodchat shrike? You do not try, enjoy whatever you see. Croxall Lakes came in with a reed warbler, a delightful calling male, followed two days later by an equally vocal sedge warbler. That day, which incidentally was the 21st April, also gave me a touch of winter, seven Bewick's swans were at Croxall, they needed to get a move on.

Cannock Chase came back into the picture on the 23rd, with two tree pipits down the Sherbrook Valley and a solitary wood warbler, singing well, at Seven Springs. In transit that afternoon I saw two Arctic terns at Blithfield Reservoir. For the next few days, it was all Blithfield. I heard and saw garden warbler in Stansley Wood, had a female whinchat on the dam parapet, and on the 27th, finished off with hobby and black terns. The black terns stayed at Blithfield for a further four days I was told, although I only saw them the once.

Come the 30th, I could officially say that summer was here. I heard and saw a cuckoo down Whitemoor Haye. The month ended in style, with one hundred and fifty-six birds on my list. Twenty-six of them added in the month.

May 4th gave me a male redstart at Blithfield Reservoir, it put on a good show, a most attractive bird, full of colour. The following day swifts arrived, only about a dozen of them, but what they lacked in numbers they certainly made up for with noise. Those birds were seen at Whitemoor Haye Lake.

The next four days passed by quietly, until on the 9th a small passage of little terns took place at Blithfield Reservoir. They are the smallest of the white terns and have a much faster wing action than other terns. They were likely to remain for a day or so, before moving on further north. They do tend to be a coastal breeding species.

May 11th brought some colour into my life. I visited Bradley Dam in Derbyshire and here I saw thirty-eight mandarins, that was some sighting. The drakes, twenty-one of them, were real glamour boys, being probably the most exotic looking duck to be seen in the UK. They may be the result of introduced birds, but they certainly have added colour to British wildfowl.

A few days later and Blithfield was back on the scene. Firstly, two green sandpipers called in down Blithe Bay, only staying for the day, and those were followed by a pair of black swans a day later. Someone had been careless here, I would imagine a pair of black swans would be expensive birds to buy. Those birds had full sets of primaries and were seen in flight on several occasions.

The 18th saw me on my annual pilgrimage for the nightingales and turtle doves, conditions however, were not good. I arrived in heavy rain. I visited the centre for a coffee in the hope the rain would either reduce or move on, it did neither, so it was a question of dress up and just get on with it.

The birds did not let me down. The nightingales and turtle doves showed well, and in the case of the nightingales, sang equally well! Being the breeding season, I suppose they just had to get on with it, irrespective of the weather.

They certainly brightened up my day. Hirundines and swifts were also out hunting over the lake, and reed warblers were busy in the reed beds. In the end the rain won, I was getting very wet, so time to call it a day. Fortunately, I saw the two birds I really wanted.

Then the 29th May hit the jackpot. I had heard of a white stork breeding at Thrigby Hall in Norfolk, so my photographer friend, Andy Toman, and I went down for a couple of days. The hall has its own collection of captive white storks, and it appears that two wild storks arrived and set up home. A large nest was on the roof of the hall, so obviously any birds building that had been able to fly, they had not climbed a ladder to get on the roof. Even the purists will have to accept those birds as wild. Needless to say, Andy took many photographs of those two. He also photographed a white stork walking down the middle of the road, stopping traffic.

This bird was one of the captive birds which had managed to clear the fence. We reported this, and the bird was ushered to safety. Seeing a white stork this close makes you appreciate the size of the bird. Whilst there, a bar-headed goose flew and joined the storks in their enclosure, that brought a most interesting day to its conclusion.

It also brought May to an end, I closed on one hundred and sixty-six.

There were still a few summer migrants I had not seen, which by now I would have expected to have done so. June 1st saw me chasing after the ring ouzels, Dane Bower again being my objective. The weather was fine, curlew could be heard calling and I had seen red grouse as I crossed over Axe Edge Moor, all I needed now was the ouzels.

It took me about half an hour before I struck lucky, and this was a very distant view. The bird at least showed for several minutes, so distant or not, he was recognisable. As I was about to leave a wheatear popped out on the nearby wall, and meadow pipits could be heard singing. I was more than happy.

Crossing Axe Edge on my return journey, I became even more happier. At my usual stopping place for the red grouse, which incidentally I saw again, I was delighted to see twite, three of them. I have now seen twite in this area on more than one occasion, I hope they are breeding there

The following day I was over at Seven Springs on the Chase where among the birds seen or heard, was a spotted flycatcher. As is usually the case with flycatchers they are invariably busily hunting, and this bird was no exception.

Blacktoft called. I had not visited for some while, it was time to get marsh harrier and avocet on my list, plus anything else which cared to oblige.

As I was booking myself in, a marsh harrier flew past the visitor centre, so that was a very good start to things. From the Xerox Hide I had very good views of a male bearded tit, which kindly sat out on the edge of the reeds, you can never ask for more than that. Marshland hide provided me with the avocets, several with young and the odd pair still sitting eggs. My two target birds were in the bag.

Walking back I had a special type of incident occur. I have mentioned frequently that the call of the grasshopper warbler is now almost outside my hearing range. I had sat down to listen to a sedge warbler, I can hear those, when I became conscious of a reeling type call from a nearby patch of nettles. I could not believe what I was listening to, a 'gropper' was calling just feet away from me, and I mean feet. I could not see the bird but the movements it was making in the nettle bed were less than six feet away from me. I was very pleased I had sat down to listen to the sedge, hearing the grasshopper warbler was the event of the day.

It was a further two weeks before I managed any productive birding. Then Blithfield came along with a sanderling, well three of them to be accurate, and a pair of oystercatchers had two large young, they were just about fledged and could flutter short distances. Given a day or two more and they would be flying.

As the month progressed my annual visit to Bempton Cliffs loomed. It was the 22nd June, one of the latest dates I have visited, but I was interested in having the opportunity of seeing young in the nests. I was not to be disappointed. The kittiwakes, gannets and guillemots in particular had large numbers of youngsters.

They breed on the open ledges so their nests are more visible than those of the puffins and razorbills, although the odd razorbills' nest could be seen.

The noise at this time of the year is quite deafening, the young keeping up an almost constant call for food. The anticipated birds were seen: gannets, kittiwakes, feral pigeons, razorbills, guillemots, rock doves, shags, puffins and fulmars, plus various gulls. The usual pleasant day expected at Bempton Cliffs. The weather too had been good.

The month concluded with common scoter, five of them, at Blithfield and a willow tit at Middleton Lakes. My total was now one hundred and eighty-five, and thanks to the storks, a memorable month.

July turned out to be its usual slow month of the year regarding new species. Many birds seen, and several family groups were on the wing. Only four new species added, but one, a drake ruddy duck at Blithfield was much appreciated, and kept quiet in view of what had happened to this bird. A greenshank also put in an appearance at Blithfield, with a stonechat on Cannock Chase and spotted redshanks at Blacktoft completing the month.

August made up for things in a big way and did it on day one. Blithfield had a small party of little stints on show, but the bird which excited us all was a Caspian tern. That was a bird you only dreamed of seeing, especially so far inland. The odd reports we get, which are few and far between, normally referred to records from the coast. A 'lifer' needless to say.

Caspian terns are a very large and heavy tern, the size of a common gull almost, with a large red bill. Our bird did not take to flight, so I could not see its tail or leg colour, I know one thing, I have never seen a tern this size previously. A visitor from the Baltic, no doubt a little bit off track.

Three days later, Belvide came up with the goods, two turnstones called in, and a few black terns were to be seen. Towards the end of the month the layby at Kings Bromley came back on the scene, as well as five little egrets, a great white egret put in an appearance, and very welcomed too. Blithfield finished off with two curlew sandpipers, both juveniles, a very dark lesser snow goose, what we call a 'blue phase', with a wood sandpiper being seen on the final day. The month closed on one hundred and ninety-six.

September is usually good for the odd special bird, and so it proved. The most unlikely sighting was near Junction 6, on the M18, where I saw a cattle egret in a field, but could not stop to admire it, obviously. Luckily the view I had as I passed by, slowing down as much as I could, was very clear, so no confusion with a little egret.

A black-necked grebe visited Shustoke Reservoir, a few days later, only staying for half an hour or so before it flew on. Luckily, I was there at the time. There was a sailing event taking place by the look of things with much noise and activity, the grebe obviously did not appreciate that, I did, I saw the grebe!

On the 15th it was Croxall Lakes which provided a good bit of quality. I was there with the Rosliston Birders looking at a small group of common snipe when one of my colleagues called my attention. She had found a small looking snipe tucked away in the grass. She had found us a Jack snipe, we were all happy she had picked up that bird, no one else had.

The 26th September saw me reach the two hundred mark. The autumn wader passage had commenced, several species were now to be seen at Blithfield, godwits, redshanks, greenshanks, plovers and sandpipers, but the bird of interest to me was knot. A small party of six knots were seen, one of which was still showing much of its summer colour, quite red in fact.

The month closed with the layby at Kings Bromley up to its usual tricks, a honey buzzard flew through. Unfortunately, it did not hang about, I doubt if I had the pleasure of its company for above two minutes, but I was grateful. The month closed on two hundred and one.

October produced the odd bird of quality, pink-footed geese at Burton Mere, a cackling goose at Tittesworth Water, a crane at Blithfield and finally brambling on Cannock Chase.

Towards the end of the month, an interesting movement of fieldfares and redwings took place. I was down Meadow Lane, looking for redpolls, which I had heard about, but did not see, when a large flock of thrushes came across. They landed in a meadow and I set myself up to try to count them. A tractor, however, came into the meadow, frightening all the birds off. The size of the flock and the noise they made, especially the fieldfares, was very impressive, and I estimated the flock size as being well into four figures, the largest I have seen for many a year. Most impressive, the pity being they did not return.

The final few weeks of the year saw me knock up smew at Blithfield, Iceland gull at Albert Village Lake, bittern at Attenborough, woodcock at Catton and I finished off with a glaucous gull at Albert Village Lake. I closed at two hundred and ten, down a bit on previous years, but I still managed a bit of quality. Three 'lifers', glossy ibis, Hume's leaf warbler, and finally, the Caspian tern. I never dreamed of those at the start of the year, and all so close to home. Just as a matter of interest, those three birds brought my UK 'life list' to 386. I had a dream of reaching 400, whether I would or not remained to be seen. I have already seen well over that number in the UK, but my UK 'life list' only includes birds accepted on the British List by the B.T.O/B.O.U.

CHAPTER VIII

Another new year rolled round. It is no doubt a myth, but the older you become, the faster the years seem to pass. 2015 arrived, and what would that hold in store? Only time would tell.

New Year's Day saw us have our customary bird race, and we did well. Sarah and Martin made the fifty mark, but I just eclipsed them, I reached fifty-two. Honour restored! It was a dry day and I must confess I really worked at it, including home I visited ten locations in total. My first bird of the year was a blackbird, and I had reached thirteen before leaving home. The pick of the birds ticked off were little egret, from the layby at Kings Bromley, redwing, tree sparrow and yellowhammer from Whitemoor Haye, green woodpecker and yellow-legged gull at Fradley Junction, raven and pink-footed goose at Blithfield and golden plover down Whitemoor Haye.

A very satisfactory start.

January 2nd included a willow tit at Freda's Grave on Cannock Chase, a peregrine provided me with a fly-past at Bishton, and Dunstall gave me a buzzard. This bird was soaring with its wings held in a shallow 'V', effortless.

On the 4th I visited JCB—Rocester, and here I saw a flock of twenty-seven barnacle geese, a drake mandarin, two Egyptian geese and several shelduck.

They were all free fliers, most of the other ducks were collection birds and were pinioned. Calling back at Whitemoor Haye, several fieldfare had joined the redwings I saw on day one.

I was down the Haye three days later where I saw a good flock of linnets. They were very mobile so difficult to accurately count, but they were most certainly into three figures. A small flock of seven stock doves I could count.

I had been told that a smew was being seen off the dam at Blithfield, so the following day I was chasing him, it was a drake apparently. The day was foul, a mixture of rain and sleet, I can only presume things were not to the smew's liking as I could not find him. I did, however, see a small flock of meadow pipits and two pied wagtails.

Going into Burton on the 10th I popped into Branston Water Park where among the ducks I saw my first shovelers of the year, so that gave my shopping run a bit more pleasure.

The 14th saw a bit of quality. I was at Blithfield Reservoir, when I met a birder who thought he had just seen fifteen white-fronted geese fly in and land down Blithe Bay. The way he described the birds made me believe he was right, so I drove round and proceeded down Admaston Reach.

Part way down I spotted a small flock of grey geese in an adjoining meadow, pulled in and focused up, the birder was absolutely right, they were white-fronted geese. The only problem was he could not count, there were eighteen of them.

I saw him later as I drove over the causeway, pulled in and told him he was right with his geese, the only thing I did not tell him about was his poor maths!

On the 15th, my own garden produced a bit of excitement. A sparrowhawk came in after a blackbird, which it chased into one of my holly trees. A lot of noise and movement came from the tree, but the blackbird lived to fight another day. I saw the bird flick out of the back of the bush with the sparrowhawk flying onto the fence nearby. Needless to say, after all of this there were no other birds in my garden, and it remained so for may minutes, even though the disgruntled sparrowhawk had left.

The next couple of days, saw me pick up a jay locally at Woodlane and a common gull at Whitemoor Haye.

On the 18th I managed to go a little further afield, Carsington Water, my first trip outside my home county of Staffordshire for the year. It was a poor day once again due to the weather, but Carsington has hides, so that would help, and as you know, it had a good café, which would certainly be used.

As I arrived the rain lessened, so I decided to make a quick visit to Sheepwash, it was not a long walk to the hide, and the walk down was through a wooded area, so you were sheltered from the elements to a degree.

The spit in front of the hide had many cormorants sitting out, with goodly numbers of teals and wigeons on the water. Of more interest were three common snipe feeding in the ditch and a solitary redshank feeding along the shore. They brightened up the weather somewhat.

I then drove round to the visitor centre, had a mug of coffee and a crispy bacon roll, which set me up nicely. I came out to find the rain had stopped, so a walk onto Stones Island was made. Not a lot happened until I reached the tip of Stones.

Looking out over the water, I was delighted to see a great northern diver, they have one here most winters, and I was able to study this bird for several minutes before it sailed out of view. It was an adult bird in winter plumage, and it had made my visit well worthwhile.

Turning to make my way back, I had a fleeting view of a bullfinch, just a flash as it flew across the pathway in front of me. Studying the dam, I picked up a small group of five swans on the water, quickly focusing up I was delighted to see they were whooper swans. Unfortunately, they took to flight and vanished down the reservoir, but I was happy. They were my fifth 'tick' of the day.

My day, however, was not finished. Driving through Cubley I had to stop to allow a covey of nine red-legged partridges to cross the road. They were probably very lucky it was me, a bird lover, as they did not attempt to fly. They brought the day to its conclusion.

The month finished off very quietly, all I saw was a song thrush at Branston Water Park and a marsh tit in my own garden. This bird did at least make several visits over a period of five days, and it brought my month's total to seventy-nine, the poorest January I have had for many a year. What was February going to do?

Well, it commenced very quietly. I had a wren at home on the 4th, a goldcrest obliged on the 12th and the 16th gave me an oystercatcher at Croxall Lakes. The 20th saw both corn bunting and mistle thrush both down Whitemoor Haye, and come the 22nd, a bit of quality at last. Albert Village Lake had a Mediterranean gull, a clean looking winter adult, and driving home through Whitemoor Haye a merlin kept me company for a minute or so. The following day it was Whitemoor Haye again. A black swan had joined the herd of mutes on the fields at Sittle's

Farm. That bird certainly stood out amongst about eighty white swans!

The month did however go out with a bit of a bang. The 25th came up with the bird of the month, a red-throated diver at Croxall Lakes, and down the Haye three bramlings were at the feeding area along with the tree sparrows and yellowhammers.

The following day Blithfield chipped in with a southern cormorant, and the month concluded at Cromford with hawfinch, five of them, a goshawk and a pair of grey wagtails. No complaints there. The month closed on ninety-three. As far as numbers are concerned, my slowest start for a long, long time.

March started off very well, was this a sign of things to come? On the 1st I was at the Central Forest Park in Hanley, Stoke-on-Trent, new territory for me. I was smew hunting. A duck had been reported the day previously. She did not take a lot of finding, the area of water was not great, so she was quickly in the book. The following day a quick trip across to Chasewater gave me a Caspian gull, and this was followed a day later, by a trip up to Derbyshire, Beeley Moor called. I was off to The Triangle, an area I have mentioned previously on occasion. The great grey shrike had been reported.

There were several birders looking for the bird and it did not disappoint. It flicked up onto the bare bush several times, it was not seen to catch anything, but was very active. Whilst there, red grouse could be heard and as I drove off a small flock flew across the road in front of me. A very satisfactory visit.

The good times continued. The 9th saw me at Belvide, and here I clicked for velvet scoter, scaup, water rail and a small flock of sand martins, my first summer migrants of the year, and a very early record. The water rail, incidentally, gave me one hundred for the year, a milestone reached at last,

The following day also produced a summer migrant, a drake garganey, this from Croxall Lakes. As I have mentioned before, it is suspected that a few garganey are now over-wintering, so whether this is a true summer migrant is open to question, all I know is that it is my first of the year.

It was back to winter birds next. The 12th saw Blithfield have two water pipits, both on the dam. They at least were seasonal, and one of them was beginning to look very smart, it was obviously a male moulting through into his summer plumage. A very welcome sighting.

It was back to Croxall Lakes on the 13th and amongst the birds seen here were a small flock of nine siskins, feeding in the hedge, and a pair of bullfinches made a colourful picture. Later, skylarks were heard and seen down Whitemoor Haye, they are always welcome.

The following day saw me visiting a new venue, Summer Leys Nature Reserve. Here, I was after a great white egret. You would think a large white bird would be easy to find, not this fellow. The reserve had dense reed beds and thick vegetation, and it was well over half an hour before the bird walked into view. More obliging was a drake pintail, he, at least was happy just sailing round on the open water. Walking back to my car a red kite flew through, some finale. I have a feeling I may well be back.

Back locally, two days later, I was looking over the Branston Gravel Pits, checking the gulls out, a glaucous had been reported. I drew a blank, but I was fully compensated. A greater snow goose swam into view, and for two or three minutes, I was able to enjoy this bird. To many it will go down as an escapee, but in one or two places they are now breeding, so you just never know. I was more than happy to see it, that was for sure.

Over the next ten days or so I had a very good run, and all locally. Lesser redpoll at Croxall, treecreeper at Branston Water Park, a kingfisher at Wolseley Bridge. Chiffchaff were calling at Kingsbury Water Park, Barton Marina produced a white wagtail, and Blithfield came up with a little owl. Then to bring things fully home, I heard a tawny owl calling during the night of the 28th. To finish the month, on the 29th, whilst visiting Carsington Water, I saw a Jack snipe. That brought me up to one hundred and seventeen species for the year. We are slowly getting there, but slowly is the operative word.

April turned out to be one of the best Aprils I have had, not necessarily for the numbers seen, but for the quality. I was not away on holiday at all, so the birding would be local or visits to my favourite locations, Blacktoft probably being the furthest I would be travelling.

Let us run through what I saw, and you can judge whether it was as good as I thought. We started off on the 4th at Whitemoor Haye where three little ringed plovers had arrived. The following day the Haye came along with a small covey of five grey partridges, they obviously had not commenced to breed yet as the birds were all adults The 6th saw a swallow at Croxall Lakes, no you cannot say summer has arrived, it takes more than one!! Whitemoor Haye chipped in with a wheatear the following day, and on the 10th, Ogston Reservoir came up with ringed plover and yellow wagtail, and calling in at Cromford on my journey home the dipper obliged.

The 11th was forecast as a very bright day so a trip further afield was called for, so Blacktoft Sands became my destination. I parked my car to the sound of a willow warbler singing, you can now say summer may be here! Some of the avocets were already sitting eggs and a small flock of house martins were busily hunting flies over the water. It does looks as though summer is here. I will say no more on that subject.

Marsh harriers were very active, three in the air at one time, two males and a female, Cetti's warblers were very vocal, as is their wont. A good flock of black-tailed godwits were in front of the Xerox Hide, many of which were looking very smartly dressed up in their full adult plumage, and two spotted redshanks were doing their best to compete, they were also in full plumage, both being males. Walking back to my car I was serenaded by a blackcap, as a goodbye, that takes some beating.

Blacktoft had been at its best.

The following day I was back at Blithfield. When I got back home, yesterday, I saw on the bird reports that the osprey was back at Blithfield, you do not miss out on this bird. I had to be patient, but this was eventually rewarded. The bird flew in and put on quite a diving display, before it caught a fish, which it promptly flew off with.

Fortunately, the bird has a favourite tree where it regularly roosted up, and it flew into this tree with its catch. The trout it had caught was not large, so it quickly consumed this and went off hunting again. Unfortunately, this time it flew round into Blithe Bay, which was not visible from where I was. To finish my visit off a common sandpiper flew in, no complaints there.

Blithfield called again on the 16th. A common scoter had been seen off the dam and a small flock of dunlins were being seen in Admaston

Reach. The chance to get a scoter so early in the year was too good to miss, so the dam, here I come. It was a calm day, the water surface with hardly a ripple, conditions for scoter hunting could hardly be better. They are a duck which dives frequently, so a smooth water surface is very helpful, and so it proved. I doubt if I was there above five minutes before I found my quarry, where I spent many minutes watching him go about his business, the bird being a smart looking drake. Now for the dunlins.

At this time of the year, they should be in full summer plumage with their black bellies, and so they were. There were seven birds in the flock and five of them were in full regalia. Not only had they the black bellies, their backs had a decided reddish-brown hue. Smart looking little birds, which were very active as they dashed about feeding. Whilst I was enjoying these, the osprey flew across to vanish into its tree, not carrying a fish this time. Some finish to a bit of birding.

I had heard talk of bittern breeding at Attenborough Nature Reserve, this had to be followed up, so the 17th saw me on my way. The usual species were congregated near the visitor centre, waiting to be fed and out on Coneries Pond three red-crested pochards were seen, two superb drakes and a duck. Years ago, you would have travelled miles to see one of these ducks, but thanks to escapees and released birds which have bred successfully, we now have a good population of wild birds.

I went into the visitor centre for a coffee and also to enquire about the bittern. The news on the bittern was good. They believed the bird was breeding, they obviously would not disclose exactly where, but a bird was being seen frequently on Clifton Pond. The coffee tasted rather good after hearing that news.

Making my way to Clifton Pond I stopped, common terns could be heard, screeching away from Tween Pond, a viewing screen overlooks this pond, so I made my way there. I was right about them being common terns, several were out hunting over the water, plunge diving in for small fish. Watching these birds in action, you could well understand why they used to be referred to as sea swallows, they have beautiful forked tails. Some bird.

Walking on down the track towards the kingfisher hide, which overlooks Clifton Pond, I heard the call of the whitethroat, so I stopped to do a bit of searching.

The bird eventually popped out of a bramble patch, then sat there for all the world as though it was sculding me, it certainly stared me out, before vanishing back into the seclusion of the bramble. A wonderful couple of minutes.

On to the kingfisher hide. As I was about to open the hide a sedge warbler gave me a burst, and sitting out on the top of a small bush sat this fellow, letting all the world know he was back and this was his patch. I like birds which announce their presence, and then sit out wanting to be seen. That was two on the trot, and was it a coincidence both were warblers.

On the pond were grey-lag and Canada geese, a good mixture of waterfowl including several very smart looking shovelers, gadwalls and a solitary goldeneye. I was very surprised he had not gone by now, it made me think it possibly could have been an injured bird, although I could see no evidence of it. Several grey herons were scattered round the pond and on the spit were three dunlins, two oystercatchers and two common sandpipers. Not a bad little selection. Time, however, to concentrate on the reed beds, bittern are rarely seen walking in open water.

I had come prepared to wait, bittern are not the most cooperative of birds, at times a brief view is all you get. If you seek bitterns, patience is the name of the game. Mind you, after over an hour my patience was beginning to wear thin, when a slight movement on the edge of the reeds caught my attention. Something was moving through the reeds and judging by the movement of the reeds it was not a small bird. My patience was rewarded, from the reeds stalked a superb bittern, and for twenty to thirty seconds stood out in full view, before walking back into the reeds.

Thank you, bittern. Although I gave it another half an hour or so, it did not return, so that ended my day, a wonderful day, shared with some wonderful birds. That is what birding is all about.

I should not have said that, particularly the piece about ending my day. I had hardly reached Tween Pond when the sound all serious birders love to hear, boomed out. The bird I had seen a short while ago was giving vent to his feelings, for a bird which is so secretive, it announces its presence with a conspicuous foghorn-like call, 'uh-booh'. For about thirty seconds, Attenborough echoed to the sound. Several people walking dogs stopped, saw me with my binoculars etc., and asked me what it was. I was only too pleased to tell them and also take out my field guide to show them. A final note concerning this bird, it is reported that the call can be heard up to five kilometres away. Some foghorn!

That did end a wonderful day, with five 'year ticks', I wonder which was the best?

I had a day out locally the following day. Calling in at Tucklesholme Quarry first, I had a fleeting glimpse of a green sandpiper as it flew though and was very pleased to see a pair of little ringed plovers displaying, they were obviously intending to breed there.

Moving on down to Croxall and Whitemoor Haye, I saw and heard my first garden warbler of the year, a very accommodating bird. It was very interesting here as just down the track a blackcap was singing, a good opportunity to compare the song of two birds which do sound similar. A chiffchaff and willow warbler were also in good voice. On to the Haye.

Sand martin activity had increased over the lake, forty to fifty were feeding away. A tern caught my eye, it was at a distance, but it did drift ever closer, and I finally got the view I wanted, it was a passing Arctic tern. Unlike the common tern which breeds locally, the Arctic tern breeds further north and is much more a marine species, so to us it is a bird of passage. That completed three new birds for the year.

Tree pipits are a bird which is causing concern in certain quarters. Over recent years their numbers appear to have declined, and I know from my own point of view, I see them less. Cannock Chase has hung onto a few in recent times, so a trip across to look for this specie was called for. Most of my recent records have been from the Seven Springs area, so that was my destination.

From the car park a nuthatch could be heard, he was really letting rip, with a blackcap doing his best to compete. The blackcap failed on volume, but won on quality of sound. A chiffchaff was also in good voice, I think things are slowly waking up as more of our summer migrants arrive back, the tree pipit incidentally being one of them.

I made my way along the track towards the stepping stones, not that I was walking that far. A short distance down the track the woodlands finish and on the left you have more open, hilly, moorland, with just the odd trees. Tree pipit favour the odd tree in these situations, which they use as a launch pad for their song flights.

Although called tree pipits they do not nest in trees they are a ground nesting species. They are named tree pipit due to their use of trees to roost and use as launch pads for their song flights.

Walking along the track I hear great spotted woodpecker drumming, and a green woodpecker gives me a very close fly-past, which was much appreciated. Further blackcaps are evident and I pause to watch a treecreeper climbing up a tree trunk.

I leave the trees and enter into open country. A raven is croaking away loudly from a small stand of Scot's pines, where in the past they have nested, and probably are again, if this bird's performance is anything to go by. In the distance a green woodpecker can be heard yaffling away, the Chase does very well with this bird, several pairs regularly breed here.

Proceeding slowly, I see a jay flash through and a buzzard can be heard mewing away, but it was the other side of a hill so I could not see the bird. A whitethroat gave me a burst from some nearby nettles, but he did not pop out to see me, it no doubt had other things to contemplate.

Rounding a bend, I picked up a small bird high in a tree, stopped to see what it was, and I need not have bothered. The bird soared high into the air, singing away as it did. So, I had my tree pipit. The song I quite distinctive, it commences with a series of trills, quite accelerated, and when the bird starts to drop down, this slows down into a series of drawn-out notes, frequently described as—'seea, seea, seeea, seeea, seeeeh'. All I know is that once you have heard it, well, you are unlikely to forget it. I almost think it has the quality of a skylark, and that is some comparison.

We have at least one tree pipit back, hopefully more will shortly arrive, and this bird's musical talents will be rewarded by his finding a mate.

The 22nd produces another warbler day. A reed warbler, well three of them is a more accurate statement, have arrived at Croxall Lakes Nature Reserve, and next door at the Alrewas National Memorial Aboretum a grasshopper warbler has turned up. I was very fortunate with this bird. I have great difficulty in hearing them and they are a very secretive bird, keeping well to cover. I met up with a birder I know, who told me about the bird and pointed out the bush the bird had been singing from, he had not seen the bird leave the bush. I had time, I could wait, and did. I watched that small bush for well over twenty minutes before I saw even a movement, and then minutes later, out popped my bird, only for a few seconds I add, but that was enough for me. I had my 'gropper', as we birders call them.

The following day another warbler was added to my list. This time down Whitemoor Haye, a lesser whitethroat showed well. The month had been very warbler productive, I have only the wood warbler of the regular species still to see.

Blithfield Reservoir came back into the picture on the 25th with a passage of black terns moving through, fifteen of them, and two ruff called into see us, one, the male, starting to look very colourful. In full summer plumage, a male ruff is a very colourful and spectacular looking bird, and they were, incidentally, my one hundred and fiftieth species for the year. The month ended on 29th, Blithfield again, with a swift, well a small group of them.

I think you will agree a very productive month, and if I had included all the birds seen, I would probably have broken the one hundred mark for the month. One thing which is most definitely certain, it will not come so easily for the remainder of the year.

To be fair, it looked as though May was going to try. The 1st of May saw a whinchat down Whitemoor Haye, and in the afternoon, I heard my first cuckoo of the year, and that was from my own garden, it cannot get much better than that! Blithfield followed on with a little gull. Not a bad start for day one of a new month.

On the 3rd Blithfield came up trumps with a hobby on this occasion. This bird caused consternation among the sand martins, and did in fact catch one for his dinner, the hobby being a male. To catch a sand martin on the wing you have to be some bird, but watching this hobby as it chased the martins you could see the skill and speed of the bird. Quite a flying machine

A couple of days later and Cannock Chase, Seven Springs again, completed my warbler list. I had very good views of a wood warbler, who also happened to be in good voice. As with the tree pipit the other day, I hope his singing produces the required results. Returning to my car I heard a drumming, and something about this caught my attention. It did not sound as though it had the intensity of a great spotted, and the bursts seemed to be lasting longer with a softer tone than that of the great. This had to be investigated, a chance here I was listening to a lesser spotted woodpecker, and you do not get many of those to the pound!

I made my way in the direction of the sound, which luckily continued, and stopped close to a tall old stump of a silver birch. There, right above my head, a lesser spotted woodpecker was working away. To say I froze is putting it mildly, I hardly drew a breath. It has been many a year since I had such good views of a lesser spot', I just stood still and enjoyed every moment of it. I certainly did not need my binoculars.

I was able to watch the bird for several minutes before it stopped, looked around, and was off. Thank you, *Dendrocopos minor* (the scientific name of the bird), for a magical few minutes, which will remain with me forever.

The 10th of the month saw me north of the border, off to Dane Bower, ring ouzel hunting. A layby lies on the A54, south of Buxton, from here an old chimney can be seen. For several years now ring ouzels have bred here. You will recollect I have visited here on previous occasions, would I be lucky now?

Initially things were quiet, a few meadow pipits and vocal red grouse. The grouse were distant and due to the many rises in the ground they could not be seen. A pair of pied wagtails were busily collecting food, they obviously had a nest nearby.

I was beginning to despair a bit, it looked as though a blank day was imminent, when a darkish looking bird flitted along the stream at the bottom of the valley. It was blackbird size, but here, so high and relatively bleak, it was not blackbird country. Luckily the bird flew again and this time landed on a grassy bank.

It was a male ring ouzel, I had my bird, even at this distance the white bib was clear, no mistaking this bird. It was very active and I presumed it was collecing food for either young or the female which could be incubating. It was only visible for a few minutes, but I was more than happy, minutes such as these are precious. Then, as if in celebration, two curlews flew through, calling as they did so, nothing can better that.

A perfect end to my trip out, and two 'ticks' in the bag.

It was back to Blithfield for my next bit of excitement. A passage of little terns was taking place, and they were almost in double figures. It had been a long time since I last saw little terns in those numbers. As with the Arctic terns, they are a bird more associated with the coast. These birds were probably in transit to north Wales. Wherever they were going, I wished them luck, they had made my morning.

Later in the day I picked up spotted flycatcher on the Chase, Seven Springs, the bird was visible from the car park. Birding made easy.

The next few days were all spent birding locally, with little stint at Chasewater and a redstart on the Chase, at Seven Springs once again. This was followed with a turnstone at Blithfield, this was a bit special as the bird was in full summer plumage.

Croxall Lakes Nature Reserve, not to be outdone, came in with a fly-through whimbrel, that was a real right place, right time. Ten minutes later and I would have known nothing about it. Blithfield again produced the goods with three Sandwich terns passing through, I doubt they stayed above an hour before they vanished.

The 22nd saw me at Coombes Valley, RSPB. I have an affection with this reserve as I spent a few days as a volunteer warden here and also had the opportunity of being the permanent warden, but having just started a family I turned the chance down. The living conditions were a bit bleak at that time. Back to the current, I was here for pied flycatchers, not memories, and after a few minutes they did not disappoint. I saw at least two separate males and heard another calling, the females were all no doubt sitting eggs. Other birds either seen or heard included chiffchaff, willow warbler, blackcap, garden warbler, wood warbler, chaffinch, spotted flycatcher and dipper on the narrow river which runs through the reserve. A very pleasant day, in fact.

With the month running out a couple of trips further afield were called for.

Firstly, Little Paxton, and by now you know what I visit here for, and I am pleased to say, saw them both. The turtle dove put on a very good display. I did not have to work for this bird, it was purring away from behind the visitor centre where it sat out on overhead wires. A superb greeting. As the morning proceeded it got even better. I had five separate nightingales, all seen as well as heard, and one in particular but on a vocal performance that was absolutely incredible. I was able to sit on a bench and watch this bird perform his complete repertoire, I doubt he was above twenty feet away, and completely visible. At times his throat was vibrating almost violently, the effort he was putting into it all. I trust a female somewhere was appreciating his efforts. All good things have to come to an end, and after several minutes of sheer joy, he was up and away. He may have gone, but the memory will remain, you do not forget such moments, unless you have no soul. A few cuckoos were also calling, a marsh harrier provided a fly-past, and other song birds were in good voice. I frequently believe that to hear real song the UK is the place. I have been abroad on many occasions, but I have never heard the amount of song we hear at home.

I finished the month of with a trip up to Bempton Cliffs, I would not consider I had been birding if I missed out on this. The birds were up to their usual high standards. Gannets almost shaking hands, they flew so close at times, the kittiwakes were as active and noisy as ever, guillemots and razorbills were sitting out as though enjoying the sun, which they probably were, and the puffin numbers seemed a little higher than previously, I hoped that was not an illusion. Fulmars were gliding past, effortlessly, the odd shag was out at sea and feral pigeons were active along the cliffs, but have you noticed something? No mention of rock doves. I did not see a single bird which fitted this category, I am sure some were there, just not seen by me. Also, no rock pipits, that too was a surprise. The usual gulls and cormorants were to be seen, another most pleasant day. The month closed on one hundred and seventy-six.

It was now the question of seeking out the more unusual and special birds, which meant I had to become a little more selective.

CHAPTER VII

2014 came in very damp and miserable, and the bird watching on day one was not a great deal better. We had our usual race and neither of us did well. I only clocked up thirty-four species with Sarah and Martin doing likewise, so we ended up with a draw. After a start like that, things could only get better, we hoped!

January proceeded rather quietly. I did have a few bits of quality, a tawny owl, a great northern diver, a peregrine and red-crested pochard, so it was not all gloom.

Then on the 10th of the month, it really woke up. Most birders have a hit list of the birds they most wished to see, and I was no exception. I had three birds which I first saw in Egypt all those many years ago, and they were the birds I most wanted to see in the UK. They were glossy ibis, bee-eater and roller. When I first saw those birds, they, more than any others, really set me on the road to becoming a serious birder. I can never thank them enough. But back to January 10th, 2014.

I received a telephone call from an old birding friend of mine, Chaz. He passed on the news to me that he had just seen a glossy ibis near an industrial estate in, of all places, Brownhills. He gave me full directions of where the bird was seen, and I was on my way. Within an hour of receiving the call I was standing watching a glossy ibis feeding, no more than twenty-five yards away. In all my years in Egypt, I had never been that close. It was in a small field with some horses which had churned up the earth, making it quite muddy in places, and the ibis was probing its long, curved bill into the mud. It was obviously finding plenty to eat, and it was not bothered by either the horses nor the number of birders watching it. Cameras were whirring away, but fortunately, due to the closeness of the bird, the birders had no reason to try to get nearer. You could have photographed this bird with a 'box brownie'.

Having waited so many years to see this bird I was in no rush to

Instead of just having a few hours out birding, it was now a 'quest for the best'.

June would illustrate this. On most of my excursions I shall be after just one or occasionally two species and this is how it worked out. June 5th, Blithfield a sanderling, a bit special this bird as it was in full summer plumage and should have been much further north breeding. What it was doing in Staffordshire I do not know, but I am not complaining.

June 7th, Cannock Chase came good with a woodlark from near The Ranges and a stonechat, a delightful male, form Anson's Bank. This bird just sat out staring at me for a few minutes, most friendly. June 10th, rough-legged buzzard at Blithfield, just a fly-through, I doubt I saw the bird for above thirty seconds, another right place, right time bird. June 16th, white-winged black tern, another bird which should have been breeding miles away in Europe and this was followed a day later by another unexpected species, a wood sandpiper. It also was miles from where it should have been. Blithfield was not finished, it followed those up with a crane. Since a breeding programme was started a year or so ago, these birds have become a more regular feature, with a bit of luck they will be as successful as the red kites have been.

It was not all Blithfield I am pleased to say. The 19th June saw me after nightjars and woodcock on Cannock, both seen well, along with hobby, green woodpecker and cuckoo, plus being almost bitten to death by mosquitos. A productive night for both birds and bites!!

I had not visited Brandon Marsh for some time, so a visit was more than due. So the 21st saw me off into Warwickshire. Brandon Marsh is the HQ of the Warwickshire Wildlife Trust, and is a well-appointed reserve with quality catering facilities, you do not need to take food. Being a member of the Staffordshire Wildlife Trust, entrance is free. Many wildlife trusts have these reciprocal arrangements.

After a pleasant coffee I made my way down the reserve. From the hide overlooking East Marsh Pool a little ringed plover is seeking food, which it unfortunately takes behind an island, so whether it is feeding young or not, is difficult to say.

Oystercatchers do have young, well one at least, which they noisily defend from a marauding gull, successfully I am pleased to report. Common terns are breeding on the rafts provided, as black-headed gulls appear to be on an island. Cormorants are also well accounted for.

I move on up to the hide overlooking Teal Pool, in which are two other birders. As soon as I settle down, they point out a duck to me and ask what it is. I look at the bird and for a few seconds I have to think, then it hits me. It is a drake fulvous whistling duck. The two birders look at me blankly. I tell them it is no good looking in their field guide, it is not in that. Fulvous whistling ducks are natives of Africa, South America and the Indian sub-continent, which as good as tells you this bird is an escapee. It has a full set of primaries so the bird can obviously fly.

Unexpected and unusual I think sums it up.

A very large number of sand martins are feeding over this pool and the swifts are not too far behind them, there is obviously a good supply of flying insects to account for this amount of activity. Seeing all this feeding makes me realise I am also hungry—the restaurant now calls.

I had a busy, few days, with no birding, apart from what visited my garden and there was nothing special there to report, but by the 26th, I was again free, and Blacktoft called. This was likely to be my last trip out this month.

The Montagu's harrier had been reported once again, so that was a bird well worth putting in some effort to see, and if not successful, Blacktoft always has plenty of other birds to see.

On arrival I learned the bird had made fleeting visits early that morning, so I at least had a chance. Initially I made my way down to the marshland hide, and had not proceeded very far, when I stopped, very smartly so. Right out in the open, trotting along the pathway in front of me, was a wonderful water vole. I knew they were seen quite frequently, but this was my first experience of them here. It has been some considerable time since I last saw water voles. You tend to think of voles as being small mouse-like creatures, but they are far larger than that, quite bulky in fact. I only had the pleasure of the voles' company for a minute or so, but it was magic moment as far as I am concerned, and whether I see the harrier or not, this mammal had made my day.

The lagoon in front of the marshland hide was very busy,

especially with avocet activity. Some were still sitting their nests, others had young birds to attend to, and avocets rarely do anything silently. They run a constant battle with marauding gulls, but their long bill does look a useful weapon at times. A water rail was moving through the reeds, occasionally popping into clear view, which is always welcome.

The black-headed gulls had young, some of which were quite large. A marsh harrier upset things a little as it glided in over the lagoon, most of the birds fleeing, the ducks included. What was interesting was the fact that the only birds which attempted to drive the harrier off, were the avocets. Well done, they succeeded.

Now round to the Xerox Hide, which I had to myself. Several teals, tufted ducks. pochards and a pair of gadwalls were on the water. The mallards had ducklings of various ages and sizes and the mute swans were escorting cygnets.

Whilst going through the ducks more seriously I had a very pleasant surprise, amongst them was a drake ring-necked duck, no one had mentioned this bird when I booked in, so to suddenly see it was completely unexpected. As I have mentioned previously, these are a North American duck which occasionally arrive on our shores, but normally you expect them to be seen much later in the year. What one is doing in June is anyone's guess. It may simply be the fact the bird has been in the UK since last year, vagrants from the American continent are unlikely to ever get back home. The 'purists' can always shout, 'escapee'! Me, it goes on my list.

I had not realised how long I had been in those two hides. So I made a quick visit down to the far hide, the Singleton Hide which overlooks the large reed bed area where the River Trent and Humber converge. At first, I wondered why I had bothered, just three grey herons and the odd duck. At least I had company in the hide, and one of these suddenly shouted, 'Harrier, coming in from the left.' We all swung round into the direction indicated, and we were very pleased we had. Gliding in, low over the reeds, was our Montagu's harrier. A superb male.

A young couple sitting next to me raised the question, 'Why is it not a hen harrier?' They explained they were newcomers to the hobby and to them this bird just looked like the illustration of the hen harrier in the field guides. Luckily, I could answer it for them, especially with the marvellous views the bird was providing.

'Just look at the wings, you will see a black wingbar on the upper wing surface and two on the underside, the male hen harrier does not have those,' I told them. The harrier, as if to emphasise the point, gave us a superb, close-up in fly-past. Some bird. Some finish to my day.

Two cracking birds to finish the month off, plus a water vole. I closed on one hundred and eighty-eight.

July came in steadily, Blithfield producing greenshank on the 5th, a nice early returning bird. Two family parties of little ringed plovers were also seen, they had bred successfully, and a little egret was walking the shallows. Not a bad reward for just a quick local hour.

The 11th saw me off to pastures new, Chatterley Whitfield Country Park in North Staffordshire, fortunately I had obtained the map reference for this spot. A red-footed falcon had been reported for the past two or three days, I had only ever seen two of those previously and they were fleeting views. Time to put that right.

I located the spot without any problems, there must have been at least fifty other birders there, some of whom I knew, and the bird just seemed to be enjoying the attention. As is to be expected in those situations, photographers were everywhere, and unfortunately, some did not have the bird's welfare in mind. No matter how large their lens, they always want to get that much closer. The bird flew into a nearby factory complex and a small group of photographers went in to chase the bird, a security officer challenged them and told them they could not enter for safety reasons. The security officer was Asian, and unfortunately, two of the photographers became very racist, to the extent some of us other birders told them what we thought.

The security officer phoned up the police on his mobile and a police car arrived within minutes, quickly followed by a police motor cyclist. The racist birders tried to hide away, but we were having none of it, and they were quickly pointed out to the officers.

The offenders denied all knowledge of the events but several of us were only too happy to give our versions of the events to the police, and the last we saw was the two main offenders being marched off. We were asked if we were prepared to give evidence in court if required.

We all said yes, but that was the last we heard of it.

The red-footed falcon was not at all disturbed by this, it just went on with its own business. An interesting follow up to this. Whilst we were enjoying the falcon, a black redstart suddenly arrived on the scene and promptly flew into the factory area.

Seven of us were invited in so we could obtain good views of the bird. I will say no more!

Whilst there I had one of those incredible moments. A birder walked up to and said, 'Excuse me, aren't you Brian George?' I obviously replied I was, and this birder then introduced me to his elderly companion who it turned out had bought a copy of my book, which they carried round in their car as a guide of where to go. It was his father, and I was asked if I would sign his book for him, I was only too happy to do so. I asked the birder how he knew me as he was a complete stranger to me, he remembered me from seeing me on the TV. All I can say is if he remembered me from a one-off few minutes on TV, seen over twelve months ago, he has some memory and was probably one hell of a birder. We live in a crazy world, but at times it is plain amazing. A day to remember that, in more ways than one.

On the 16th I visited Welbeck Park where there is a well-known raptor watch spot. Several birds of prey could be seen from there. I quickly notched up osprey, buzzard, goshawk, sparrowhawk and kestrel, but the bird I had really come for kept me waiting. Honey buzzard—a pair bred there. It ended up a two hour wait before a bird appeared, but as it performed for several minutes, the waiting had been worth it.

Later in the month I had a muscovy duck at Croxall Lakes, this is a bird which is being seen more frequently in a wild state, and although not on the British List, is supposedly up for consideration as many are now breeding in a wild state.

Time will tell. It was at least something a bit different.

The birding concluded with a bar-tailed godwit at Blithfield Reservoir, that was unexpected. One hundred and ninety-four is the total so far.

My month ended with my usual visit to Sutton Coldfield Crematorium. It was a very pleasant summer day, with the birds unusually active. Pied wagtails were flitting about along the shores of the small pool, the moorhen had three young on the water. A blackbird was going about its business, totally ignoring me I am afraid, even when I put some seed out. Although, as I walked on, I noticed a chaffinch came down to investigate, it was not going to be wasted that was for sure. A great spotted woodpecker also drummed briefly and a song thrush let forth a short burst of song.

All in all a pleasant day for memories, and there were plenty of those. All happy I am pleased to say.

The 1st of August saw me at JCB Rocester where I had bar-headed goose, Cape shelduck, another probable escapee and a ruddy shelduck. Then my birding ended temporarily. I went for a pacemaker check-up where it was decided I needed a more advanced model, so I was quickly booked in at Leicester to have my pacemaker replaced. Quick it turned out to be, I waited three days, that was all.

I was allowed to drive again very quickly, this surprised me greatly, but I was delighted, and I could not wait for the 23rd August to arrive. It duly did, and I took myself up to Blacktoft Sands as a celebration, and as events turned out, it was a celebration in a way.

The birds usually expected there at that time of the year were showing well. Decent numbers of black-tailed godwits, redshanks, spotted redhanks and dunlins were seen. Bearded tits had been reported, but I drew a bank on those. Fortunately, the avocets and marsh harriers were far more accommodating.

Whilst enjoying those, two birders came in the hide and told me they had just left First, and there they had seen a spotted crake, no need to say where I shot off to. The number of spotted crakes I have seen can be counted on the fingers of one hand, this was an opportunity not to be missed. I rapidly made my way to First.

Only three other birders were in the hide, and to my surprise they knew nothing about the crake, they had only arrived moments prior to my doing so. One consolation was the fact we now had four pairs of eyes looking for the bird, so we each concentrated our efforts on a single part of the reeds. It was several minutes before one of the birders commented on the fact he could see movement near the edge of the reeds, so we all concentrated our efforts on that spot. He was right.

After a short while the bird came out of the reeds and actually bathed in the water, a superb view for us all. I do not suppose we had the bird in view for more than two minutes, but what a two minutes, before, with a whoosh, it was back in the safety of the reeds, and it did not appear again while I was there.

My visit to Blacktoft had been well worth it, and when I got back home, my daughter, Sarah, told me a friend had phoned in to say he had seen crossbills on Cannock Chase, near to the White House. The following morning that was our destination. Sarah also had not seen crossbills that year. Time to correct that!

Crossbills are very active feeders and move on continually as they eat the cone seeds, so there was no guarantee the birds would still be there. It took us nearly half an hour to locate them. A rendition of, 'kip, kip, kip' was heard, and we looked up to see a flock of a dozen or so birds fly into the conifers. We had our crossbills, and enjoyed them for several minutes before they flew off again. We had a few other interesting birds, siskins, redpolls and a pair of bullfinches, so it had been a worthwhile trip.

The crossbills were my final new bird for that month, where I closed on one hundred and ninety-nine.

September was a very blank month, I only obtained one new species, that was a Greenland wheatear, seen at Blithfield on the 4th, that at least took me up to the two hundred mark. It was not the fact birds were thin on the ground so to speak, it was just that they were species I had seen previously.

Little egrets, for instance, had been popping up in various places, the Kings Bronley layby, for instance, had nine on one occasion, plus a great white egret.

Waterfowl numbers were building up well, good for winter viewing, and a peregrine falcon had been very active at Blithfield Reservoir, so it was not all bad.

October came in better. Blacktoft saw me again on the 2nd, and on that occasion the bearded tits were more cooperative. Several were seen and what was interesting was the fact I saw more young birds than I have ever done before, hopefully that signified they had bred well. You can never have too much of a good thing!

The barn owl was very active during the early afternoon, it was out hunting on several occasions. Once it came right in front of the hide I was in, just feet away, for a few seconds I had never been so close to a barn owl, and the silence of their flight was amazing. They frequently talk of the owl's silent flight, but this was one of the few occasions I have been close enough to an owl to really appreciate the fact. They are an incredible and beautiful bird, and this one will remain in my memory forever.

Curlew sandpipers had also started to move through, well four of them had, all juveniles in my case that day, but no one was complaining. That was three quality birds to add to my list. Blacktoft had done me proud that day, you can appreciate why it is one of my favourite reserves.

The following day Blithfield contributed a rock pipit, and I saw the peregrine falcon make a kill, taking a lapwing out of the air. A solitary bird flapping through when a peregrine was about was just asking for trouble. It had no chance and was obviously unaware of the peregrine's presence, until it was too late. The peregrine had his dinner that day, it being a male.

The 6th, of the month gave me the bird of the month, a red-breasted goose at Kedleston Hall. Although I have seen this species previously, they are a very rare bird, so this one was completely unexpected. Red-breasted geese are probably the rarest goose seen in the UK. They are a bird which breeds on the Siberian tundra, eastwards across the Taymyr Penninsular, and winter in south-east Europe, Romania, Bulgaria and north-east Greece. It begs the question, what is one doing in Derbyshire? The 'purists' will instantly shout, 'Escapee', but this bird was not displaying any rings and was behaving in a completely wild manner. They are a superb looking bird and the smallest goose we are likely to see, only fractionally larger than a mallard. I was happy, it goes on my 'year list'.

The 10th of the month and I was back in Leicestershire, this time visiting Eyebrook Reservoir, where a party of four spoonbills had been seen, and I was pleased to say, they still were. It was a family party of two adults with two juveniles, and it was suspected they were from the birds now breeding in Norfolk, none of the birds being ringed.

That saw the month out as far as new species were concerned, although the winter migrants and the usual birds of passage were either arriving or passing through.

I even had a few late swallows drifting through, they had better get a move on with November, nigh. The month closed on two hundred and six.

November was a total disaster, as far as new birds were concerned, not one. Winter visitors were arriving well and reports of fieldfares and redwings were coming in regularly. The odd waxwing was reported from the east coast, we keep our fingers crossed on that one. The great grey shrike had returned to the Chase, and I was lucky enough to see that bird on two occasions during the month, both of which were from the Coppice Hill area. Crossbill activity in that part of the Chase was also good, flocks of over fifty being reported, I saw several, but never in those numbers.

Whilst out looking for the crossbills, I had a memorable day, not with a rarity, but a local species. Jays are probably the recluse of the crow family, rare they are not, but seen infrequently. They breed on the Chase, and although you may hear them, see them you do not. Today, for some reason, they were intent on being seen.

They were spending much time on the ground and I have a sneaky feeling they were collecting fallen acorns. The past couple of days had been very windy, and the Chase being fully exposed, had probably felt the brunt of it, with many acorns blown from the oaks. Jays are well known for collecting acorns which they bury, many a mighty oak can thank the jay for its very existence.

Waterfowl had really arrived, both Blithfield Reservoir and Whitemoor Lake had large numbers of teals and wigeons in attendance, with tufted ducks not too far behind. The numbers of mallards had increased with the arrival of their continental cousins. Pochard totals, especially at Whitemoor Haye, were the highest I could remember for many a year, and gadwalls were not doing too badly. Mute swan numbers had increased greatly, Blithfield being well into three figures and Whitemoor Haye was not far behind. The Tame Valley, in which Whitemoor Haye lies, frequently has swan flocks of several hundred by mid-late winter. The local birders regularly study these flocks looking for the odd whooper and Bewick's swans, which may be tucked away, but it was a little early for them.

Waders were scattered round, with dunlins and ringed plovers being the two most frequently seen, with the odd curlew and green sandpiper being picked up. There was certainly much to be enjoyed, birding is not all about 'ticks'.

The question now was—how would December treat us? It certainly tried. The 6th gave me a black-necked grebe at Chasewater, this bird intended to be seen and gave a superb diving display just off the dam. The water that day was like a millpond and I was able to enjoy the bird for many minutes as it slowly drifted out further into the water. To complete things, a glaucous gull provided me with a very close fly-past, at this distance you could really appreciate the size of the bird. Not a bad trip out that, it had only been for a couple of hours, and the grebe had been a 'tick'.

Then, on the 13th, came a bit of a 'Twitch'. A hoopoe had been reported at Wall Heath, this bird was going to draw the birders in. A colleague from the Rosliston Birders had also heard about the bird and he picked me up to go across in the hope of seeing the bird. I had the details of where to go, so off we shot full, of expectancy. We need not have worried, we arrived to find a large number of cars parked up and were very fortunate to have a car depart as we arrived. It looked like the Gods were favouring us.

A large group of birders were congregated in a nearby field so we walked across to join them, seeing a flock of meadow pipits as we did so. We were quickly told where to look. The bird was flying in and out of the garden of a nearby house regularly, and was away at that moment, so it was a question of just waiting for the bird to return. After about fifteen minutes it did so, landing first of all on the garden fence, providing perfect views, before disappearing into the garden. Five minutes or so later, it came out of the garden and flew off. We stayed there for about two hours and must have seen the bird at least a dozen times. A well worthwhile trip.

This was to be repeated a few days later, my photographer friend, Andy Toman, came across with me in the hope of photographing the bird. The behaviour of the bird was much as previous, whatever they were feeding it on at the house I do not know, but they had certainly got it right. Andy managed to get a few photographs but they were all distance shots. A cracking bird for so late in the year.

It was not going to be my last good bird, December was on a roll. On the 23rd, and close to home, we had a male hen harrier. I say we because Sarah shared this bird with me. We had a quick visit down Whitemoor Haye, a break from Christmas preparations, and in the hour we had, we saw the harrier, four species of duck, the swan flock was now about two hundred and fifty, all mutes unfortunately, and a buzzard finished things off for us. Not a bad hour at all.

I managed a morning out on Christmas Eve, I think Sarah wanted me out of the way, so I popped over to Chasewater. I was not expecting a lot, nothing special had been reported, and hit the jackpot. Off the dam an Iceland gull was performing, harassing the black-headed gulls somewhat, they are quite an aggressive bird I have found. Whilst enjoying the gull a friend of mine came up to me, down by the power boat club a ring-necked parakeet was to be seen. Thanking him, and wishing him a Merry Christmas, I was back to my car and off.

A couple of birders were also there, they quickly pointed to a nearby tree, and there was the parakeet, this was birding made simple. He was a noisy fellow, well I presumed it to be a male, it had quite a pronounced black bib which I understand the female lacks. Either way it was a fine bird to see, and as it so happened, it finished the year off for me, on two hundred and eleven species. In view of what had gone on during the year, I was more than happy with that, and my new pacemaker was certainly doing the trick.

CHAPTER IX

The New Year, 2016, commenced with our usual bird race. We drew, forty- eight species each. I visited my usual locations for day 1, commencing at home, then on to the layby at Kings Bromley, next Whitemoor Haye, Croxall Lakes, Hoar Cross, Blithfield Reservoir and finishing up at the JCB Lakes at Rocester. A round trip of about thirty-five miles. Among the birds seen were several quality birds which were very welcome at the start of a new year. The prime birds being buzzard, whooper swan, tree sparrow, goldeneye, bar-headed goose, grey-lag goose, mandarin, Egyptian goose, ruddy sheklduck, red-crested popchard and finally goosander.

On the 2nd. Cannock Chase called, and here I added nuthatch, greenfinch, lesser redpoll and siskin. The 3rd saw me pick up long-tailed tit, these were in my own garden feeding on my seed containers, a delightful start to the day. During the rest of that day, I had jay and raven on the Chase, shelduck at Croxall and linnet down the Haye. The 4th saw me back at Blithfield Reservoir where I added great spotted woodpecker, wren, Caspian gull and grey heron to my list. The year had started well, long may it continue.

It was the 8th before I was next able to get out and a quick trip across to Blithfield gave a shoveler, and the following day, on another quick visit. I picked up fieldfare at Orgreave and golden plover at Whitemoor Haye

The 10th was the first time I managed a full day out since the start of the year, so I made my way up to the Staffordshire/Derbyshire Moorlands, mainly grouse hunting.

In transit, at Newchurch, I stopped to study a large flock of thrushes in a field. They were a mixture of fieldfare and redwings, there must have been at least two hundred of them.

On Axe Edge Moor the red grouse were most obliging, I saw several small groups, probably well over twenty birds in total, so that was most satisfactory.

Driving off the moor I stopped to study a small flock of pipits, nothing to get overly excited about here, they were all meadow pipits, but as they were my first of the year, I was more than happy.

I dropped down to Tittesworth Water, it was a rather chilly day and a nice mug of coffee would go down well, and it did! The usual waterfowl were to be seen, all of which I had seen previously, but three gulls drew my attention, and I was pleased they had, they were common gulls. As I have mentioned before, common by name, but not common in reality, well not in our neck of the woods.

I was looking at a group of cormorants on an island, when I stopped. One was smaller and slimmer necked, and showed a greenish tinge to the feathers—I had found a shag. This was a complete surprise, cormorants may be an inland species, shags are very marine, so what this one was doing in middle England is anyone's guess, you cannot be much further away from the sea. I was unable to ask it, just very happy to see it, a cracking bird to finish the day with.

The next day, the 11th, was going to be my last opportunity of any birding for a few days, I had work to get done at home, so a couple of hours locally, was all I could manage, so I decided to try the Chase once again. In transit, the Kings Bromley layby came up trumps once again. Five little egrets were busily feeding in the river. I enjoyed those for several minutes before moving on.

I pulled in on the White House car park and had hardly got out of my car before a green woodpecker commenced 'yaffling' away, as greetings go, that was not too bad at all. I walked from the car park, disturbing a bullfinch from the feeding area.

For several years someone has regularly provided seed here, and at times you can see some interesting birds, today the bullfinch filled that bill. There were also blue and great tits feeding and greenfinch could be heard. Walking further on a male stonechat popped out, and sat on the top of a small hawthorn. I stood completely still, and for a couple of minutes or so we stared each other out. The stonechat grew tired of the exercise, and flew off. In the space of less than half an hour I had experienced three of our most colourful birds. Time well spent.

Although being at home, a new bird for the year came and visited me, or to be more honest, my feeding station, a pair of collared doves. They were more than welcome, as they gave me the excuse to sit down and enjoy a mug of coffee.

On the 17th I was out and about once again, only for a couple of hours but during that time I saw a few birds, amongst them my first reed buntings of the year. It was a little group of five, three males and two females, a bird there was going to be unlucky in the breeding stakes. They were my seventy-fifth bird of the year.

The following day I had been to the Rosliston Forestry Centre on business and returning home I called in at Branston Water Park, and what a choice that turned out to be. I just pulled in on the car parking area which overlooks the lake, and had not even got out of my car. I was enjoying the birds, especially three diving little grebes, when a flash of blue flew over the water, to land on a nearby branch—a kingfisher. I was mighty pleased I had not been getting out of my car. The kingfisher dived into the water beneath the branch several times and eventually came up with a fish. It smacked the fish on the branch, no doubt to stun it, and then flew off down the lake with his dinner. Calling in here was the best decision I had made for many a day. Kingfishers may not be rare, but to have the view I had just experienced does not happen very often, and to think it was all seen from my car. I went home a very happy man.

Three days later I had a couple of hours free so a visit across to Blithfield would fit in nicely. The usual birds were to be seen, the cormorant flock was very large, it could have been approaching three figures, with great crested grebes not far behind, although they were well spread. It was early afternoon and the gulls were slowly drifting back in for their night time roost. A herring gull type landed on a buoy to preen, so I was able to concentrate on the bird. I was glad I had, it had yellow legs, this was no herring gull, it was a yellow-legged gull. I was very lucky there, if the bird had flown through, I would just have assumed it was a herring gull, landing on the buoy gave me the perfect view. You win some, you lose some, today I won.

On my return journey home, I won again. Driving down Whitemoor Haye I had a covey of seven grey partridge dash across the road in front of me. I doubt I saw them for above ten seconds, but that was sufficient, you do not mistake grey partridge when they are so close. A superb couple of hours, it is wonderful what you can see when you know your own patch. Also, as with my little grebes and kingfisher, I had not even got out of my car.

The 23rd saw me over the county border, into Derbyshire, hawfinch hunting, and hunting it turned out to be. In the places usually associated with seeing the birds, nothing doing. I slowly made my way towards the railway station at Cromford when I met up with a man walking his dog. We stopped to chat, he obviously saw my binoculars and asked what I was looking for. I told him, and much to my surprise he knew what I was talking about, and even more surprising, told me where he had seen some only minutes previously. I thanked him and was on my way.

The location was a large garden a little way further up the road, the birds were in trees. I easily located the spot, and he was absolutely right, there were seven birds seen, dropping down from the trees onto, I presumed, feeders in the garden. Unfortunately, a high fence ran round the garden hiding things from view. I was able to enjoy the birds for several minutes, until a road sweeper came along, with much noise, and the hawfinches flew off. Although I waited, they did not return. This had been one of the best sightings I had ever had of the bird, I owe that dog walker a vote of thanks.

Making my way back to the car I stopped again on the river bridge in the hope of seeing the dipper. I failed, but a stock dove put in a brief appearance, it was more than welcome.

Lunchtime was approaching, so Carsington Water now called. A bacon roll and a mug of coffee would set me up nicely for the afternoon ahead, and they did.

Walking onto Stones Island, the flock of barnacle geese were spread out along the shore and several cormorants were on the water. Duck numbers were very low, the birds were probably further up the reservoir.

From the tip of Stones a large flock of grey-lags slowly drifted past, and as they did so I became aware of a largish bird further out on the water. I found a more favourably viewpoint and was delighted to see I was looking at a great northern diver. For a few years now

Carsington has been a regular winter location for this bird, one year they had three there, one satisfies me, especially as the bird is an adult.

Light was quickly diminishing, so home called. A very successful excursion, with four birds for my 'year list', two of which were definitely quality.

The 24th saw me back a Blithfield. Sarah was with me on this occasion, and we celebrated with wonderful views of an almost tame black redstart. This bird was on the corner of the causeway and kept on popping up onto the wall, only feet away, giving the finest of views. The odd birder there with a camera was having the time of their life with this fellow, as it was a male.

Nothing else of too much excitement was to be seen, and the weather took a decided unpleasant turn in any case, so the morning was cut short, but thanks to the redstart, it had been some morning.

I called in at Blithfield on the 29th, as I had a few minutes. I visited the feeding station in Stansley Wood. Blue, great, coal and long-tailed tits were evident, and a pheasant was collecting fallen seed from under the seed containers. Walking back to the car I heard a call I did not instantly recognise. After a lot of searching, I located the bird, it was a treecreeper, not a bird you hear too often. I must try and remember that call for the future. You are always learning in this game.

The end of the month saw me back into north Staffordshire. A friend of mine had been up to Oakamoor where he had seen several dippers, a goodly reason to try it out. I combined this with a visit to Tittesworth Water, as there I could get a warm snack which goes down well on cold winter days, as it was that day.

Pulling into Tittesworth I saw a group of birders gazing very intently out onto the reservoir. I pulled onto the car park. In those situations, you are not shy, you walk up and ask, I duly did. One of the birders, with a smile on his face asked, 'Are you interested in a drake ring-necked duck?' What a stupid question to ask. 'Here it is in my 'scope.' No second bidding required. It was a fine-looking bird, and as it was swimming in isolation, it really stood out. I have mentioned previously about it being a rare vagrant from North America, and seven birders that day were very pleased he had made the journey. A cracking bird so early in a new year.

Lunch went down very well after that. I did not see a lot else, the birders had me told me things were rather quiet, so I did not waste any more time, Oakamoor called.

I had details of where my friend had seen the birds, so this was no problem to find. I parked and settled in to wait alongside River Churnett, a small car park being very appropriate. The Churnett certainly looked an ideal river for dipper, with many fast-flowing shallows and very rocky in places, and I did not have to wait long.

Hurtling along from under a nearby bridge came a dipper, its wings were almost a blur as it flew through, hardly a visit, more a bird of passage. Mind you as my first of the year, it will do. A short time later another came into view, this one being much more accommodating, landing on a rock quite close to where I was standing. So hardly daring to breathe, I stood stock still to enjoy the bird. It sat there for a good two minutes before dropping into the water to hunt food. I watched it progress up steam, as it popped out onto the rocks several times. The early bird may have dashed through, this one more than made up for things. A super end to a most enjoyable day, with two fine birds for my list, which had now reached eighty-eight for the month, not a great number, but certainly some quality.

February kicked off with a Muscovy at JCBs Lakes, it is not often you see one of these birds airborne. Mind you, it may have flown well, but it needed a few lessons on landing.

I picked up the news that a great grey shrike had appeared on Beeley Moor, so that was worth a trip out. You will remember my first great grey shrike of the year, last year, was also recorded on Beeley Moor. Be interesting to see if I can do it twice on the trot, so come the 5th, and I am off to find out.

The bird was last seen at The Triangle, an area well known to birders, and I was not on my own looking for the bird. Several pairs of eyes make light work, and the bird is quickly located and promptly puts on quite a display for us all. Two of the birders had never seen a great grey shrike previously, I doubt if they will ever get better views than this one gave us. For a good ten minutes the bird sat out with occasional drops onto the ground beneath. We were never aware of it catching anything, but it put on a show of trying. It then flew off and although I hung on for half an hour or so, it did not return.

As I had some time left, I called in at Cromford for a coffee and another look for hawfinches. This time they were found more easily, but did not provide the views of a few days ago. What I did see, however, was a song thrush, which was my first of the year.

It is amazing to think I was now into February and this was my first song thrush, it seemed only yesterday that I heard them back home. They nested in my garden regularly, if I see one now it is worthy of note. Their decline is frightening, and they are not on their own in that respect.

A quick look at the canal gave me a little grebe, moorhen, coot and mallards, the last three were chasing round after food. Some young children were having their introduction to the birds, and judging by the noise they were making, they were thoroughly enjoying themselves— long may it continue. A charming end to a pleasant day out.

A friend of mine gave me a call to tell me he had just seen a small flock of brambling on Cannock Chase, at Penkridge Bank, a good enough reason to have an hour or two seeking them out, so the 8th found me doing so.

Just off the car park is an area of shrub hawthorn and other small trees, and at times the birds seen here have been very good. I did not have to leave my car before a small party of fieldfares landed on a nearby hawthorn which still had a few berries. Not for much longer I thought. Walking on five redwings flew past, they were going in the direction of the fieldfares, was bush telegraph working? Three chaffinches had me going for a few seconds, I thought initially they were bramblings until I got a better view. But it all comes to they who waits, they do say.

A little further on, a small flock of birds flew into a tree, white rumps flashed, I had my bramblings. I counted eighteen birds, a mixture of both sexes, the largest flock I have seen for a few years. They stayed in the tree for a couple of minutes or so before moving on, and that was the last I saw of them. I was happy, they were my first of the year, and the male birds were most attractive. I drove home a happy man.

On the 10th I had a very pleasant surprise. I had gone into my kitchen and looking up the garden, a mistle thrush was strutting across my lawn. At a distance of less than twenty feet you can appreciate two things about this bird. Firstly, they are a smart and tidy looking bird, and secondly, the size of the bird. They are a powerful looking bird when seen this close, you would not confuse it for the song thrush, that is for sure. As it was also my first record of the year, I am very pleased it called in to see me.

The 11th saw me spending a few minutes down Whitemoor Haye, Sarah had seen ruff recently, so it was time for me to go chasing them. They did not take much finding, I am pleased to say. A flock of lapwings were in the field opposite the landfill site entrance, and as I parked up, they took to flight. Racing through the flock was a tight knit group of five smaller waders. I had the ruff. Unfortunately, they did not return, but I was satisfied, I had found them, five minutes later and I would not.

I was back down the Haye two days later, I had heard reports of a black-necked grebe being seen. If it was, it was not by me. As compensation I saw and heard a skylark, not yet in full voice, but it was working up to it. He took me up to ninety-five, my hundred was slowly approaching.

Blithfield Reservoir had me back on the 14th. Blithe Bay had a large mixed flock of Canada and grey-lag geese, well over five hundred birds I would estimate, and the mute swans were doing their best to compete. The pick of the waterfowl were goosanders, goldeneyes, and shelducks. A mixed flock of lapwings and golden plovers were on the shore and these made a spectacular display, completely unintentionally. A peregrine came flashing through and many of the birds departed in blind panic. The falcon showed interest in the lapwings and golden plovers, but they kept in tight formation and the falcon quickly gave up, leaving the scene. I wondered if it was really hungry or just out for a bit of fun? A wonderful few moments, as far as I was concerned, and it was not long before sanity was restored. The peregrine incidentally, was my first of the year.

The 18th saw me back down the Haye. I only had an hour to spend so I decided to go down the rough lane to see if any corn buntings were about. Corn buntings are another bird greatly in decline, and

Whitemoor Haye is their local hot spot, for several years now a few pairs had been hanging on. I parked up at my usual spot and was greeted by a small flock of tree sparrows. I had brought some seed with me so I walked a little further down the lane and put the seed on the verge, then back to the seclusion of my car to wait.

The tree sparrows quickly returned, as did a male pheasant. After a few minutes two male yellowhammers appeared on the scene, shortly followed by the bird I was after, and bird is right. A solitary corn bunting arrived on the scene, and this bird was very shy. It dashed in, picked up a seed, and promptly flew into cover to eat it, then darted out and repeated the operation. This went on for several minutes before it had eaten its fill. I was more than happy, I had my bird.

The 19th, and I was back at Blithfield, this time my destination was Stansley Wood. Little was going on at the feeding station, so I proceeded on to the Hide in Tad Bay. A good selection of waterfowl were to be seen, especially teals and wigeons, with the latter being well up into the hundreds I would have thought.

Amongst the geese were about a dozen barnacle geese, always a good bird to see at Blithfield, with many cormorants and great crested grebes on the water. A few lapwings and golden plovers were to be seen, the bulk probably still being down at Blithe Bay.

A loud call was heard, only one bird has this piercing voice, and down the bay flew two oystercatchers. These birds rarely do anything silently, they are not known as the wardens of the marshes for nothing. Their warning calls can be heard quite a distance away.

Making my way back through the wood I stopped, a chiffchaff was calling. This is far too early for it to be a returning migrant, the bird must have over-wintered, probably a visitor from further north. It could possibly be a Siberian chiffchaff, but as I could not locate the bird, a chiffchaff it will have to be. I was happy enough, I had now reached ninety-nine.

My one hundred was reached in a most fortunate way. I was on my way to a meeting in Swadlincote and as I drew near to the old Drakelow Power Station, I was held up by a very wide load, so I drew into the entrance of the station, to allow the load to clear. Knowing that road well I knew I would be unable to overtake the vehicle, so I pulled in to allow it time to move on.

It was a mild day so I had my window down and was, in fact, listening to a robin singing his little heart out. This suddenly stopped, the robin dropped to the ground, and landing on a telegraph pole nearby came a superb female goshawk. To say I was mightily pleased about the wide load was putting it mildly, this must be the closest I have ever been to a gos'. It is times such as this that really does make you believe in fate. If ever I was meant to see a bird, that was it. I enjoyed the hawk for three or four minutes before it flew off, the robin did not reappear. I drove on a very contented man, with my hundred in the bag. The wide load had also cleared. I did not meet up with it again.

Like a cricketer, once you have reached your one hundred the pressure is off, you can now relax and take whatever comes, be it runs or birds.

My next new bird came on the 21st, and this was at Croxall Lakes. Things were very quiet that day, just a few birds on the water so I had a stroll down to the River Tame which skirts the reserve. At first, I saw little, but a movement on a small spit caught my attention. It was just the flutter of a wing, but closer observation turned this brief flutter into five sitting snipes. If one had not lifted its wing I would probably have missed out on those birds, their plumage blended in so well with the background.

I then made my way down the Haye, and this proved to be a very good move. On the water's edge of Whitemoor Lake, a great white egret was slowly walking along, so I stayed in my car to study the bird. It was an adult bird almost in full summer plumage, the pale coloured legs and distinctive black bill were a good indication of an adult summer bird. These birds are certainly becoming a more regular sighting, they have to be breeding somewhere quite close I would think.

As with the little egret, I often smile to myself when I think of the journeys I made to see my first, now I have them just a few miles from home.

It was the 24th before I was out again, and Blithfield was my chosen venue. Plenty of birds to be seen, the only new species was a southern cormorant, mind you it was a very clear and well-marked specimen, a smart looking bird. No complaints from me that was for sure.

A friend of mine who lives in Tamworth, phoned me up to tell me he had just seen a small group of Bewick's swans at Alvecote. I had a couple of hours free so I needed no second bidding. I had the details, including the map reference, so I knew where I was going, and having worked in Tamworth for some years, I did know the area well.

The swans were easily visible from the road, all I had to do now was sort out the few Bewick's from the mute swans, fortunately this is not too difficult. The mutes are larger and the Bewick's have totally different bill markings. It only took minutes before I located the birds I wanted, seven of them in fact, and settled down to enjoy them. A couple walking a dog came past, and asked me what I was interested in. I told them, they were not birders and had never heard of a Bewick's swan, so I was able to show them the birds, loaning them my binoculars to enable them to do so.

Two dog walkers went home wiser people!

The final day in February arrived, the 29th in fact, it was a leap year, and I managed an hour or so on the Chase, visiting Seven Springs. Nuthatches were very vocal today for some reason, a great spotted woodpecker was hammering away at a nearby dead tree stump, and raven were calling from on high. Those birds I could not see due to the trees, but you do not mistake a raven's call. I made my way across to the Springs, and there I saw one of my favourite birds, a superbly plumed male grey wagtail. He was in wonderful condition, his yellow underparts were very bright, anyone only getting a glimpse of the bird could easily have mistaken it for a yellow wagtail, except they will not be arriving for a couple of months or so.

He ended the month for me. I have now reached one hundred and five. We are still progressing slowly, but I am not complaining. With the increase in daylight hours, I will now be travelling a little further afield, so I would anticipate my numbers building up more steadily. Time will tell.

I should not have said anything about ending the month, because it had not. I was in my study when I became aware of a commotion on my back lawn. I looked, two blackbirds were having a fight. Nothing unusual in that you may say, but these were two female birds.

Blackbirds are amongst our most aggressive birds, males will fight at any time of the year, especially now with the breeding season commencing, but normally it is only the males fighting each other. Although on occasion a male will drive a female away if he already has a mate.

This was the very first time in all my years of birding I had ever seen two female blackbirds fighting with such passion. At times they were holding each other firmly on the ground and pecking away at each other most violently, nothing ladylike with these two birds. What was also interesting was the fact a male blackbird was sitting on the fence watching it all. A complete role reversal.

I watched this for a minute or two and did something I rarely do, become involved. The aggression was such that I firmly believed the birds would injure each other, so I tapped my window, and off they flew, happily in opposite directions. What was also interesting was the fact the male blackbird followed one of the females, whether that was to congratulate her or continue with the attack, I do not know.

A most interesting, few minutes. Bird behaviour is fascinating, you learn something all the time, this is what makes bird study so special. And what is it they say about the female of the species?

It was the 4th March before I was able to do any birding, and that was only a quick stop on Cannock Chase as I was driving across. I had just called in at the Penkridge Bank car park for a few minutes to have a quick look around, I was on my way to Cannock on business. It proved to be a profitable few minutes, as I saw my first willow tit of the year. Willow tits are the scarcest of our local titmice, I have gone some years without seeing one at all, so that was a most fortuitous stop.

The following day saw me venturing further afield, a visit to Blacktoft Sands was much overdue. I clicked for a good day, almost springlike, and the pick of the birds seen were: Cetti's warbler, bearded tit, redshank, marsh harrier and jack snipe. The avocets had not arrived back yet.

The Cette's was as noisy as ever, but at least it did show itself, and more than once. The bearded tits on the other hand were just fleeting views as they flew through the reeds. The redshanks were very accommodating, they were feeding well and occasionally taking to flight where their bright white wingbars were clearly seen.

Marsh harriers were very active, and they all appeared to be males which made me think the females could by now be sitting eggs. The jack snipe was but a fleeting view, it walked out of the reeds and promptly flew back into them, a definite case of now you see me, now you don't. Fortunately, I did. A most satisfactory day in fact.

A couple of days later, I was at Attenborough Nature Reserve, many birds seen, the red-crested pochards were into double figures, with the mandarins and Egyptian geese not far behind. Walking down to the Kingfisher Hide I had very good views of a Cetti's warbler, this one had not read the book, and from the hide two water rails also put on quite a display. Both the warbler and the rail are frequently heard but not seen, today was a bit unusual and special. The usual waterfowl and gulls were seen, and the goldeneyes in particular were most impressive, two or three of the drakes were in display mode, worth the visit alone. The water rail had got me up to one hundred and twelve—things were moving in the right direction.

Come March 11th, the Rosliston Birders visited Rutland Water, little realising what was in store. We commenced our visit on the North Arm, where we clocked up Slavonian grebe, black-necked grebe and red-necked grebe, plus our native great crested and little grebes. For only the second time ever, I saw all our breeding grebes together at one location. It did not end there. At Lagoon 3, we had an American rarity, a long-billed dowitcher and a red kite flew over. Long-billed dowitchers are a North American species, similar in many respects to our godwits, not quite as large, but size at distance is not always easy to tell.

Finishing off at Lagoon 4, we had a drake smew and a duck scaup. Seven birds of real quality and all on the same day and at the same location, you would find that hard to beat. In total, we saw fifty-one birds, not a bad day out by any standards.

Back to more local birding. The morning of the 13th gave me a very pleasant surprise. On the feeders in my garden a blackcap put in an appearance, a smart looking male. He only stayed around for minutes, just ate enough sunflower hearts to fill himself up, and he was on his way. I was very pleased he had called in, he was my first of the year.

The afternoon went one better. I was back on Cannock Chase, at

Upper Longdon, after woodlarks, well one would do! For a few years now two or three pairs had bred over here, but as the young trees were now maturing it was a question of for how much longer would they do so?

I had good views of green woodpeckers, three of them, chaffinches were very vocal. Spring was definitely in the air, raven were calling from a distance, not seen, and a buzzard gave me a fly-past. Several minutes elapsed and I was beginning to feel I had made a wasted journey, when I heard what I had come for. A woodlark dropped onto a tall dead tree, sat there for about thirty seconds or so, and then took back to the air, singing as it did so. Over the next half an hour it repeated this manoeuvre several times. I was a more than happy man. Two cracking birds seen today, that was for sure.

On the 16th, down Whitemoor Haye, on a fairly quiet day in many respects, a merlin brightened up things considerably. I was walking down the rough lane, having enjoyed the tree sparrows and yellowhammers, when I stopped. Flying directly at me, at speed and zero feet above the ground, came a merlin. The bird was obviously not aware of me until the very last moment, when with a tilt of the wings the bird was up and over my head. I could have almost touched the bird it was so close. It was a superb male, and the speed he was coming made me very pleased he was not after me. What a few seconds, but these are moments you remember forever.

The 18th, and it was Middleton Lakes that called. I do not visit here as often as I should, it is a very large reserve, and unfortunately, I can no longer walk the distances required, but it has a heronry close to the car park, and that was the reason for my visit.

With the trees still quite bare, good views of the nests can be obtained from a nearby viewpoint. I was able to count twenty-one nests, although the warden had told me there were over twenty-five. The birds were breeding now and most of the nests appeared occupied, they are not the quietest of birds at any time, and at their heronry they are noisier than ever. The occasional heron flew in with food for his mate, and much activity was taking place.

The viewpoint is on the edge of a reed bed where coots and moorhens were very active, one coot was sitting tightly on her large nest. In a month or two reed warblers and sedge warblers will be in attendance, but today it was a more special bird that put on a show.

I had not been standing there for long before a squeal came out of the reeds. I froze, a water rail was calling. Time now for some real concentration. I had seen them at Attenborough a few days ago, but you can never have too much of a good thing.

The squealing appeared to becoming closer, and it was. Out into the open water walked the rail, and although I was in full view, completely still, needless to say, the bird was not the slightest bit interested. I was very lucky in being the only person there at that time, anyone walking through would have flushed the bird.

For a good five minutes the bird strutted about in the water, occasionally giving vent to its feelings, squealing away, at times sounding more like a pig than a bird. It slowly made its way back into the reeds, and that was that.

Time to concentrate on the feeding station nearby. Blue, great and coal tits were frequent visitors with an occasional marsh and long-tailed tit putting in an appearance. The odd tree sparrow was seen, and large numbers of house sparrows were regularly flying in, and two male pheasants were feeding on the dropped seed.

Then I had a most pleasant surprise, a lesser spotted woodpecker flew onto one of the feeders. It was full of peanuts, and it proceeded to hammer these. Bits were flying everywhere, much to the delight of the pheasants beneath. Although being a small bird, unlike his cousin the great spotted, it was still a feisty fellow, and any other bird which tried to land on the container was driven off. Woodpeckers obviously have strong bills, so discretion is much better than valour I would think.

The bird stayed put for a few minutes, but once off it did not return. A good 'year tick'.

My visit to Middleton Lakes had been most successful, now for home and I intended to do so via Fisherwick, I had not been there for some time. Driving through Fisherwick, I disturbed a red-legged partridge, which luckily just avoided my car as it flew off. A solitary bird highlighted the fact that the coveys had now broken up and the birds were breeding. A solitary bird it may have been, it was my first red-legged of the year, so I was more than happy. My second 'tick' of the day.

With March now running out I decided to go across to Albert Village Lake to have, what would probably be, my last look for wintering gulls. Then, if I had time, I would call in at Tucklesholme on my return journey.

Albert Village Lake was surprisingly quiet, just a few black-headed and lesser black-backed gulls, I had never seen such low numbers at this time of the year. The one consolation was the fact I had not many birds to go through, probably a couple of hundred at most. I had brought my 'scope with me, so I set myself up to work through the gulls. It appeared as I first thought, black-headed and lesser black-backed, but as I approached the last few birds, I had a pleasant surprise. A white-winged gull sailed into view, and this one had a bright black head, jackpot time. It was a full adult Mediterranean gull. As I have mentioned previously, the Med' gull as we know it, has a black head and the black-headed gull has a dark brown head, (birding can be a bit confusing). Well worth my trip across, and I now have time to visit Tucklesholme.

On my walk across the meadow, I saw a skylark, for once not vocal, could easily have been a female, and a large flock of Canada geese were on the River Trent which borders the area. Reaching the old quarry area, I heard ringed plovers calling, and a few lapwings could be seen. The lapwings all appeared to be paired off, which is understandable at this time of the year, but now for the ringed plovers.

After a lot of searching, a movement along the side of a small area of water drew my attention. I have a plover, the question now was which one, ringed or little ringed? Getting the view I wanted, there was no yellow ring round the eye, it was a ringed plover. The 20th March would probably have been a little early for returning little ringed plovers, but you have to make certain. Plovers are very nimble birds and this one was no exception, its little legs hardly kept still. Within a very short space of time, it had vanished from sight, but I was happy. Two 'ticks' on the day.

The month finished off with a quick visit to Blithfield Reservoir. Things had started to quieten down. Many of the gulls had moved on and the numbers of waterfowl were much reduced, they were now winging their way northwards to breed and we shall not see them again until late autumn.

I decided to try the dam in the hope an early wheatear could be passing through. It was not, but several pied wagtails were. It always pays to study pied wagtails at this time of the year, you never know what may be tucked amongst them, and so it proved. One of the birds had a very small black bib and a grey mantle, very little black on it at all. I had a white wagtail, the European version of our pied, although to put it more accurately—the white wagtail is the nominate species, our pied is a race, or subspecies.

I had time to call in at Whitemoor Haye for a few minutes on my return journey, and it was fortunate I did. A small party of twenty or so sand martins were flying over Whitemoor Lake, making that a perfect diversion on my way home. I ended the month on one hundred and twenty-nine.

The next two months are the months when it all happens, the return of our summer migrants, our breeding birds returning. I get really annoyed with people who call these birds summer visitors, they certainly are not, they are returning home, not visiting us. A swallow is a British bird and the only visiting it does is every winter when it flies to Africa, there it is a visitor. Anyway, let me climb down from my soap box!

Talking about swallows, on 1st April, Blithfield had the first of the year for me, five of them in fact. I know one swallow does not make a summer, five might!

We can live in hope.

Come the 2nd and Blithfield was at it again, this time in spectacular manner, the osprey was back. I say 'was back' because for several years we have had a bird stay at Blithfields for a few weeks prior to moving on northwards to either Scotland or Wales to breed. With the large number of trout in Blithfield, it could survive here quite easily, although the angling club would not appreciate it as much as we birders. They pay for their fish, 'Ossie' catches his for free. A wonderful bird, which as you will know, brings back many memories for me.

The 3rd April brought another returning migrant, this time down Whitemoor Haye, three of them to be accurate, two males and one female, yellow wagtails.

Magnificent birds, and their name sums them up, especially the male, yellow he really is. Wagtails are very elegant birds I think, and the yellow particularly so. Hopefully they will stay and breed down the Haye, a few have most years.

Blithfield now called. I had heard of a new location for a little owl, this time near the Angling Club. I had an hour to spare, so what better to do? I arrived to find a couple of my friends there on the same hunt, three pairs of eyes are far better than one. This quickly proved to be the case, the owl was sitting out in an oak tree, on a bare branch, providing perfect viewing conditions. 'Scopes were not required for this one. It sat out for many minutes before flying off, and it twice came very close to where we were standing, giving us wonderful views. Little owls are probably the most diurnal of our owls and are seen frequently during daylight hours. They are big insect eaters, and many of the larger insects are found during daylight. A perfect end to another good day.

The following day, things became rather exciting. An unusual wagtail was being reported among a small flock of yellow wagtails, seen on the dam, and a couple of my colleagues asked me to join them in looking at the bird. Various suggestions had been made, the most repeated being a juvenile female blue-headed wagtail.

Should that prove to be correct, it would be a good 'year tick'.

Prior to my going to see the bird, I did some checking up on the net. I had remembered reports of a Channel wagtail being seen in Warwickshire some years ago. The Channel wagtail is a cross between the blue-headed wagtail and the yellow wagtail, and the female is very difficult to separate from the female blue-headed, a bit of genning up was required before I went out after this one.

I met up with my friends at Blithfield, where about twenty or so birders were congregated, the majority known to me, among whom were two or three very experienced birders. The bird in question was quickly located, and first impressions were very much in favour of it being a female blue-headed, but I was not convinced.

Having experienced blue-headed wagtails on several occasions on my travels, something about this bird was not quite right. I explained this to my experienced friends and they agreed with my thoughts. One of them then produced a sheet of paper, it was a printout from his computer, this was about the female Channel wagtail, and this confirmed the thoughts I was having. I was very pleased I had read up about the bird as I am convinced this is what we were looking at. We expressed our opinions to the other birders on site, and left them to draw their own conclusions.

It has gone down on my records as a Channel wagtail, and was obviously a 'lifer'. I later learned that one of the county recorders was also of a similar opinion, so whether the bird would go down on the county list remains to be seen. Not that it mattered, it was on mine!!

As the month was slowly progressing, more retuning migrants were being reported, hopefully I was going to catch up with many of them.

Blithfield jumped in once again, on 8th April. I was on the dam hoping to see the wagtail again, I did not, but as compensation two wheatears were active along the dam wall, both were males and they were looking rather smart and crisp. One thing birders do like about wheatears, is the fact they are not shy, they sit out to be seen these two certainly did

Two days later, Blithfield had the first common terns of the year. Three birds were skimming the water just off the causeway, putting on their usual display of aerial skills. Very agile and attractive birds terns, it was great to see them back again.

The afternoon saw me on Chase, near to Freda's Grave. I was initially listening to a chiffchaff calling when I realised a more melodious song could be heard in the background. A willow warbler was trilling away, that to me was the real sound of summer approaching.

The following day, 11th April, I was back at Blithfield. A steady drive down Admaston Reach saw ringed plovers, oystercatchers and common terns, now in double figures. I stopped in my usual spot, and my timing was perfect. Two small plover flew in and started walking the shoreline towards me. Very accommodating of them. As they got nearer, I picked out the detail I was after, clear bright yellow eye rings, I had my little ringed plovers now. I hope, as in the past, they breed successfully once again

A couple of days later and I am again back at Blithfield. A small number of little gulls had been reported. These are birds of passage, unlikely to hang around for long, so it was strike while the iron was hot. They had been reported from off the causeway, so that was where I headed. A few other birders were to be seen, more eyes, and it was not long before two were picked up. There had been five yesterday I was lead to understand, so three of them had departed already. Very smart little birds, almost tern-like in their flight, and as the name implies, they are the smallest of our gulls seen regularly.

As I had time, I called in at Branston Water Park on my way home. Willow warbler and chiffchaff could be heard, and a couple of common terns were also in the air, but what interested me the most, was a singing garden warbler. This bird was right by the car park and it did not take long to seek him out. I had the pleasure of his company for about five minutes before he decided he had better things to do, and flew off. A more than decent conclusion to my day, and I had now reached one hundred and forty.

A couple of days later and I was back at Blithfield Reservoir. I only had an hour or so available on that occasion so I went straight to the hide in Stansley Wood.

No one else was in the hide, and as I opened up one of the viewing slits, the noise flushed a common sandpiper which had been feeding just below the hide. Fortunately, the bird did not fly far so I was able to obtain good views.

Further out in Tad Bay a solitary tern caught my attention. At this time of the year a solitary tern should always draw the birder's attention. The common terns which have now arrived in reasonable numbers, congregate with each other, a single tern may well be another species on passage. Fortunately, I had my 'scope with me and after a short while the bird had drifted in closer. I was able to pick out the detail I required. The bird had a black tip to the bill, enough to convince me I had an Arctic tern, common terns have a completely red bill. This bird was cooperative, it landed on a nearby buoy, and now all the confirmation detail was visible. The bill was rather short, it hardly seemed to have any legs, they were so short and the final point as far as I was concerned, the tail streamers extended beyond the wing tips. On the common tern the bill is longer, the legs are longer and the tail does not extend beyond the wing tips. You need to see the bird at rest to pick up all of this, that day I was lucky.

Time had flown very quickly but it was not all over. As I was about to leave, a bird flew into some shrubbery in front of the hide, what it was I had no idea. I studied the bush and detected a movement, this continued and the culprit finally popped out, a superb male whinchat. What a climax to my visit, a bird I had not even thought about seeing, and as with the Arctic tern, another bird on passage. Whinchats no longer breed locally, they used to on Cannock Chase, but I have not been aware of any for a few years now. I usually have to go up onto the moors in the hope of seeing one. To have one come to see me. I am more than happy to accept that. A great hour or so.

Mid-April, it was time to go ring ouzel hunting. I only had an afternoon available so it was just a 'twitch' in many aspects. Fortunately, I had already seen red grouse, so it was a case of just spending as much time as available looking for the ouzels at Dane Bower. They are worthy of a little effort, they are a bit special.

It was a bright day and several cars were parked up on the layby, not birders, walkers, some of which were visible and, unfortunately as far as I was concerned, vocal. In these wild places sound does seem to carry, I just hoped the ring ouzels had become used to it. If birds breed in an area regularly disturbed by walkers, you presume they have become accustomed to it. That theory is being put to the test.

A few small birds were putting in an appearance, two or three meadow pipits were seen and a wheatear was strutting his stuff on a nearby wall. I have a feeling he was displaying slightly, probably a female was about, or he may just have been practising for the big day when it came. Either way, he impressed me.

Then the sound I love above all others, the true sound of the wild open moors, curlew could be heard. The hairs on my neck rose, some call and what a bird. Three of them came flying overhead, calling loudly. I am sure they tipped their wings to me, I certainly gave them a wave back. For a few moments I completely forgot what I had come up for, curlew do have that effect on me.

After their passing the world seemed strangely quiet, although not for long, a party of walkers soon brought reality back. Concentrating back on ouzel hunting, I brought my 'scope into operation. Down the bottom of the valley is a small stream with the occasional short grass patch, almost like lawns, and these are favoured places for hunting ring ouzel. After much concentration I was beginning to think I was not going to have any luck, when a dark-looking bird landed on a rock. White bib flashed,

I had my ouzel. It bobbed its tail a couple of times, and was off. Ten seconds possibly, and that was that. Not another peep from him, but I had got him, and as if in celebration, in the distance curlew were again calling. A wonderful climax to my trip out, two cracking birds, one, the curlew, magical as far as I am concerned.

Three more summer migrants put in an appearance on 17th April. Common whitethroat, a very vocal bird, and two male reed warblers had arrived back at Croxall Lakes. Driving through Dapple Heath I had my first house martins, things were decidedly warming up.

On the 18th a trip across to the Chase was called for, it was time for tree pipits, hopefully. That year I had a change of venue. I had been told that the previous year an area of the Chase near the Shooting Butts had been cleared with just a few isolated dead trees left standing, and tree pipits had moved into the area. Worth investigation. The news was correct about the area, it looked pipit perfect. I settled in to wait, and this did not take long. A tree pipit came swooping down and landed on one of the dead trees, and for the next twenty minutes or so, repeated the operation. If I had been a female tree pipit he would have convinced me, that is for sure. Mission accomplished.

Two days later, I had a phone call from a friend. He was at Whitemoor Haye Lakes and he believed he was looking at Sandwich terns, was I free. For a Sandwich tern, most definitely.

I met up with him and he pointed out the birds he had seen. He need not have phoned me for confirmation, he most certainly had Sandwich terns, five of them.

I am always happy to receive telephone calls of that nature. Sandwich terns are a bit special as I have mentioned previously, and we only see them occasionally on passage. Plus the fact, those birds were my one hundred and fiftieth of the year.

We are very fortunate in the fact that hobby have been breeding on Cannock Chase for a few years now, so it was time to track one down. They are a summer migrant bird of prey and I had heard that a pair were back in territory down the Sherbrook Valley. If they were the birds from last year, I knew exactly where to see them, it looked like they were.

I had hardly walked down from the Whitehouse car park before a hobby came flashing across. Hobby, do nothing by halves, they are almost as fast and agile as a peregrine, and are big insect eaters, dragonflies especially. Any bird which can take a dragonfly in the air is a bit special. I did not see my hobby catch anything that day, it just seemed to be enjoying itself in the sunshine of the day. I am convinced birds of prey do fly for pleasure, they spend so much time on the wing they surely are not hunting all the time?

Come the 24th, time to return to Blacktoft to see the avocets. It dawned a little damp but as I drove east it cleared and became a very pleasant day. I booked myself in, accompanied by the call of a sedge warbler. As greetings go, that was very acceptable

I made my way down to the Marshland Hide, usually the best hide for the avocets, and I was not to be disappointed. Eleven were to be seen, none appeared to have commenced to breed as yet, they were mostly standing still or wading through the water on their long legs and probing deep with their equally long bills.

The avocet is a real success story. They were lost as a breeding species in the UK many years ago, but fifty or sixty years ago a few returned and commenced to breed once again on the east coast. Thanks to the efforts of various bodies such as the RSPB and county trusts, they are now breeding in many parts of the country. Even in the Midlands where I live, we have them breeding locally.

Round now to the Xerox Hide, and as I walked in, the screeching of swifts was clearly heard. Zooming across in front of the hide were the swifts, and it was a surprisingly good number of them, hence the noise. They may not be the most musical of birds, but their call is most certainly a sound of summer, as well as being a sound of speed. No bird was more aptly named…

Leaving the hide I paused, I could just about hear a grasshopper warbler calling. As I have mentioned previously, their call is almost outside my range of hearing, so when I can hear a bird, it has got to be fairly close. I located roughly from where the call was coming, and as I got closer, I saw a movement in a bush, and there he was. Fleeting glimpses was all I had, but where 'groppers' are concerned, that was enough for me.

Down at the Singleton Hide marsh harriers were putting on quite a display, which unfortunately was not appreciated by the birds expected to be seen, they were noticeable by their absence. I wonder why? Almost hiding away on the reed bed fringe, were two spotted redshanks, they no doubt were keeping their heads down until the harriers departed, a most sensible thought.

During the day I saw forty-seven species, as well as the best reported above, reed warblers were very active, the water rails were letting rip, but not showing, common terns were feeding well and the odd dunlin and oystercatcher popped up. A very satisfactory day, and I closed the day on one hundred and fifty-six.

Cannock Chase called on the 28th. I went summer migrant hunting with the wood warbler being my main objective. Their numbers have reduced greatly in recent years, but Seven Springs has produced the odd pair fairly regularly.

On arrival I was greeted by a male redstart, he was actually making his way across the car park, providing very good views. That are, after all, a bright coloured bird.

Walking on I heard what I had come for. Above my head in a large ash the wood warbler was singing away. They invariably sing from on high, they are a treetop bird, so a bit of neck craning is required for these fellows. He may have been vocal, but he was intent on remaining invisible, or so it seemed, then I had a bit of luck. The bird shot out from a branch to chase a largish fly, whether he caught it or not I did not know, but knowing where it landed, I at least enjoyed seeing it for a few seconds at least. That however, was it. The bird did not sing or show itself again.

Further on I saw tree pipits, they are regular down here most summers, and then I heard the sound all of us recognise, birders or not, a cuckoo called. Summer is here!

It was some time before I located the bird, but it kindly gave me a fly-past before landing on a tree where it commenced to call again. The bird was quite close, and through the binoculars you could see the throat quivering each time it called. No mistaking this fellow! The Chase had done me proud.

The month finished with a lesser whitethroat at Croxall Lakes, and I closed on one hundred and sixty.

May commenced well with a passage of black terns through Blithfield. I counted nine on the 5th, the way they were skimming the water surely meant an emergence of insects was taking place. There was also swift activity, and they too were flying low over the water. It was an interesting comparison on speed. Black terns are no slouches, but the swifts were flying through as though the terns were standing still. Swifts are speed merchants of the top rank, why else are they so named?

It was back at Blithfield two days later. Waders had commenced to pass through in small numbers. As well as the ringed and little ringed plovers already in, dunlins had arrived on the scene. Unlike the plovers which would remain to breed, the dunlins were on passage further north, but many of them were showing off their bright summer plumage, a few black bellies were to be seen. The odd curlew was heard, and two, darkish backed little waders appeared from behind a ridge. These birds had a reddish tinge to head and back and very white underparts. For a second or two I wondered what I had, then it hit me, two sanderlings in full summer plumage—wonderful. Sanderlings may not be rare, but we see very few locally, the odd birds appear on passage each year. Like the dunlins they will quickly move on, and if we are lucky a few will pass back through come the autumn.

Cannock Chase came up trumps on the 5th, Seven Springs being my venue once again. I had very good views of the wood warbler who had tormented me previously, the cuckoo was letting vent to his feelings and at least two tree pipits were now singing. Making my way back to my car I stopped. A small brownish bird had flicked out of a tree to take a flying insect. There is only one bird, so colourful, which hunts in this manner, the spotted flycatcher. I settled down to watch, a comfortable tree trunk was handy. After a few minutes the bird repeated the manoeuvre, yes, a spotted flycatcher it was. I enjoyed the bird for several minutes before time caught up with me. A most pleasant couple of hours that had been.

I then had a busy time, I did not even manage to get out on my birthday, the 12th, but on the next day I was finished, so I managed a couple of hours at Blithfield, and I was pleased I did. The usual birds were about, common tern numbers had grown well and activity was going on at the tern rafts, hopefully some of the terns were breeding on those. Several broods of mallards were seen, one had five very large ducklings, they had been hatched some time ago looking at their size. To get five to that stage she had done very well. A male hobby put in a fleeting visit, but there were not many martins or swallows about that day, so he did not stay for long.

I moved on down to the dam to see if any yellow wagtails were on the grassy embankment, they had bred there on occasion in the past. Three were there, not on the embankment, they were feeding on a patch of small flies which were on the dam parapet. Whilst watching those a couple came up to me and said, 'Are you an expert bird watcher?' I hate that word, you meet so many so-called experts. I answered no, but could I help? Further along the dam they had seen a small white tern and did not know what it was. I had not noticed the bird being more interested in the wagtails, so I looked up the dam. I was very pleased I had met those two birders, the bird was a little tern. Another bird only seen on occasion, primarily being a bird of passage. They are also one of the more unusual British terns, nowhere as common as the Arctic and common terns, and are very much a coastal breeding species. I was very pleased I met up with those two birders, I may easily not have seen the little tern being so interested in the yellow wagtails.

Two days later I was down the Haye, I only had an hour or so to spare so it was a quick visit down the rough lane. Tree sparrows were well accounted for and the odd yellowhammer put in an appearance, those were all males which may be a good sign that the females were on the nest. To my great joy, I must have heard at least ten or so different skylarks singing in the area, the sound was beautiful, almost as though they were competing with each other, which at that time of the year they may well have been doing. Whilst listening to those I had a smile on my face, in my mind I was musing on the fact that I wondered if Vaughan Williams had enjoyed such a day, which was why he wrote his piece, *The Lark Ascending*? Us birders do have other interests.

Whilst listening to the larks I became conscious of another call, this time it was a soft 'pit, pil-it', being frequently repeated. Only one bird sounded like that, it was a male quail calling. It was calling from the meadow on the opposite side of the lane, here the vegetation was a bit taller than where the larks were, and the chance of my seeing the bird were slim indeed. Although I gave it as much time as I could, I did not see him. In those type of circumstances, an audible record would have to suffice. I was more than happy.

It was a further four days before I was able to get out again, although I had experienced one piece of good fortune at home. A marsh tit made several visits to my feeders, this only lasted one day, the 18th as it so happens, but I was very pleased to have seen him. 'Year ticks' in your own garden at this time of the year, are very welcome.

Time to visit Bempton Cliffs drew nigh, and on the 19th I was on my way

The day was bright and clear with little or no wind, not perfect in one respect. No wind meant that birds out at sea would not be driven closer to shore, but there is normally more than enough going on at Bempton to keep you occupied.

With the calmness of the day the kittiwakes could be heard calling from the car park, and as you approached the cliff tops, they came into sight. Gannets were winging their way majestically along the cliffs, what a bird, and feral pigeons were busy on the cliffs. Guillemots and razorbills were on the ledges and large numbers were on the sea, rafts of them in places. Birds which had all the credentials to be rock doves were more plentiful than the last time I was here. Fulmars also seemed up, these birds just gliding past, silent but elegant, hardly a flap of their wings as they came past, masters of the air. A few rock pipits were busily flying up and down the cliffs, and finally, the bird we all come here to see—the puffin.

Several were sitting out in the sun, one was very close and it looked almost as though he was studying us the way he turned his head to follow people's movements.

One young fellow was so excited by this bird; his parents had almost a struggle to keep him from climbing after the puffin. I spoke with his parents, commenting that I thought a future birder was here, from their reply it was obvious it was not the future, he loved them already. Good luck to him.

A most pleasant day as is usual, species numbers were down due to the calmness of the day, no shags, cormorants or terns out at sea, but I was not complaining, it had been a most enjoyable day which gave me nine 'year ticks'.

The bug had bitten, so a little more excitement was called for, this time it would be Litle Paxton, and excitement it really was. I arrived to be told a great reed warbler had arrived the previous evening and was providing good views. This bird may not be a 'lifer', but I had only seen two in the UK previously. I found out where the bird was to be seen, as I should have expected, it was at the furthest reaches of the reserve, so I had some walking to do. Fortunately, I had arrived early so I had a full day to accomplish things, and the reserve did have plenty of benches!

Making my way down, the nightingales were very vocal, I felt they were putting on a show, because of the rarity's arrival, this was their home and they were not going to be outshone by an alien. Two nightingales in particular were singing away very close to each other, most certainly either a battle over territory rights or a female was taking place. Whatever the reason, it was beautiful to hear.

Continuing on my way, the terns were out over the water, diving in for food most spectacularly, the herons had young in the heronry and many cormorants were sitting tight on their nests. Reed warblers were singing from the reed beds, but these were nowhere near the volume of the great, he has some voice. He will be heard quite a time before he is likely to be seen.

Turtle doves had been rather elusive, but finally one came in and landed nearby, purring away most delightfully, and luckily a bench was close so I could see and hear him in comfort.

Moving on down by the river which skirts the reserve, I had a great surprise. A bird of prey came gliding towards me which I at first took to be a buzzard, but as it got closer, I realised it was a honey buzzard. I had not been aware that one of these birds was on site. As it flew almost directly overhead, the small size of the head was very noticeable, no mistaking this bird. To use an old expression, 'You do not get many of these to the pound.' A real bonus.

Cuckoos had been calling frequently, judging by the sound there must be several on the reserve, always a delight to hear, they are nowhere near as common as they once were.

I rounded the tip of the reserve and met a group of birders. They had just seen the great reed warbler and they were able to tell me exactly where it had been. They did also say I would not have to look too hard, about fifty birders were up there in any case.

The birders came into view, and as they did, the bird could be heard. Some voice, some distance. How far it carries I do not know, but I was quite a distance away. I arrived to see I knew one or two of the birders and I settled in to wait to see the bird. There was no problem regarding where the bird was, not with the voice he had, it was just a question of waiting for him to pop out of the thick reeds.

The wait was not long, ten minutes of so, before he flew out and landed on the top of the reeds. He was quite a sturdy bird, hence the name great. Certainly larger and heavier looking than the reed warblers I had seen earlier that day. He did not stay out for long, back into the reeds he went.

A bench was handy, no one was using it, so I sat down and for half an hour and enjoyed the occasion. Who knows whether I shall ever have the opportunity again?

That brought a delightful day to the perfect end. One hundred and seventy-nine birds seen so far this year, and included amongst those is some quality.

The warbler, however, was not the end of things. Later that evening Sarah heard a tawny owl hooting, so we went outside to see if I could hear it. I was not to be disappointed. Hoot he most certainly did, and for several minutes. He really wrapped up a delightful day as he was my first of the year.

I was out on business the following day, coming back via Walton on Trent, and as I had a few minutes I pulled off to have a look over Tucklesholme. I walked across to view the wet area, a couple of little ringed plover were working the shore and a pair of lapwing had young. A dark little bird was also running along the shore, and here I hit gold. It was a Temminck's stint, a full adult, what it was doing here in late May I do not know. That bird should have been hundreds of miles north of us, they are not a UK breeding species. I shall never know the reason for its presence, but I was very pleased to have seen it.

The 27th saw me at JCB, Rocester. Not a lot was happening, a pair of red-crested pochard were on the water and a mandarin gave a short flight, he at least had a full set of primaries. Then a large duck came flying down the lake which I did not instantly recognise. It banked in front of me and landed on the lake. I was very surprised to see it was a drake Cape shelduck, somebody had been a bit careless and not pinioned this bird, it was an obvious escapee, but a smart one to see.

My final trip out for the month was up to the Staffordshire Moorlands, and Bearda Hill in particular. Here I was after the pied flycatchers, and they did not disappoint. I was only there for about half an hour but I heard birds singing and saw at least three males. The hanging woodland in which those birds breed has several pairs, plus redstarts, willow warblers and chiffchaff, and all obliged.

Driving back over Gun Moorlands I saw a small greyish looking bird perched on a wire fence. Luckily a parking spot was to hand so I was able to pull in. I was delighted to see the bird was a twite, a bird whose numbers have reduced considerably. A few years ago, I could have visited the moors and almost guaranteed seeing twite, not any more, so this bird was a bit special. It also gave me my second 'tick' of the day. May closed on one hundred and eighty-four, and among the birds seen during the month, there were several of real quality. You cannot ask for more than that.

June commenced rather quietly, but on the 4th Blithfield came up trumps. giving me a drake garganey. As I have mentioned previously, garganey are a summer migrant, and of our breeding ducks, they are among the rarest. Some years I do not see them at all, so it was pleasing to see this bird. They are one of our most attractive looking ducks, so I was more than content.

I made several trips out locally, the summer migrants were now well in, but due to my walking capabilities, I have now had to miss out on a regular venture—nightjar and woodcock hunting. The pathways on the Chase are fine in daylight conditions, but not recommended in the dark, so those days look as though they are over. I've had my moments, so I am not complaining.

On the 16th, the scene changed quite dramatically. A great skua was reported from Westport Lake in Stoke-on-Trent. Bonxies, as birders call them, are not seen very often this far inland, and a June record especially is rather special, so this one had to be chased down.

I was quite surprised to arrive at Westport Lake to see no other birders in attendance, had the bird departed? I settled in, after a warm coffee, to study the lake, and after several minutes I was delighted to locate the bird, but something about the appearance of the bird worried me. It was a bonxie all right, but the bird looked unwell, it just drifted round aimlessly, even suffering the indignity of being attacked by a black-headed gull. Under normal circumstances any bird attacking a great skua was dicing with death.

I departed, feeling rather sad, and later my fears were founded. The bird was captured and taken into care, but tragically died. A very sad outcome for such a marvellous bird. I never did find out what killed the bird, I suspect poison of some sort, the amount of plastic waste being put into the sea, it is surprising any sea creature survives….

Moving on to happier news. Two days later I was back at Blacktoft, the Montagu's harrier was being reported frequently, another bird not to be missed. The regular birds were to be seen, the avocets had several young, although with the marsh harriers out hunting, how long they would remain is anyone's guess.

A few early returning black-tailed godwits were to be seen, those still in their summer plumage, and not to be outshone, a very smart green sandpiper was also to be seen. Those were two birds I had not expected to see so early in the year.

The bearded tits had also had a good season, or so I was told, and although I did not see many, I certainly heard them. Having young, they were no doubt staying secure deep in the reeds.

From the Xerox Hide I saw the bird I was really after, the male Montagu's, who for three or four minutes put on quite a flying display, well worth the visit on its own. Harriers are superb flying machines at the best of times, and this fellow did not disappoint. That was three 'ticks' on the day. Blacktoft rarely disappoints.

June had been quiet in one respect, lack of new birds, but it had produced some quality, and on the 25th it surpassed itself. Old Moor called, a little bittern had arrived on the scene, a bit special this one. 'Twitch' mode I think you may call it.

I was not the only one seeking out this little beauty. I only just managed to find a parking spot, but if I was fortunate enough to see it, it would be a 'lifer', hence my interest.

I made my way round to the bittern hide, where else, and just managed to get in, one seat remaining. According to what I heard, the bird was only being seen fleetingly, when it flew short distances before landing in the reed bed.

Things progressed very slowly, although I was delighted to see a bittern walk out of the reeds, this was my first of the year, so my trip was already worthwhile.

After a long spell a shout went up. 'Here it is.' You did not have to wonder what 'it' was, flying directly towards the hide came the little bittern, and when you compare the size with that of the bittern seen previously, little it really is. I doubt it was larger than a moorhen. The bird was probably only seen for a few seconds before it vanished over the roof of the hide. A mass exit of the hide took place, most of the birders rushing off in the direction the bird had taken. I did not follow, rushing I cannot do, so I took the opportunity of finding a more suitable seat from which to bird watch.

I had only repositioned myself for a minute or two, when the bird returned and landed in clear view, not twenty yards away, I could not believe my luck, somebody, somewhere, certainly loved me! The bird proceeded to feed away, slowly moving off into the reeds, but I must have had it in full view for at least three minutes. Three minutes for a 'lifer', is plenty of time. The hide filled up with returning birders, who had not seen the bird when they raced off, they were not very amused when I told them what I had experienced. They did ask, I would not have told them otherwise. I do not like to 'grip' people off intentionally, that is not kind. Old Moor had hit the jackpot that day. The little bittern brought up one hundred and ninety-one for the year so far. Both bitterns on the same day and at the same place was some record, which is unlikely to be repeated.

From now on, new species would have to be really worked for, and living, as I do, well inland, we do not get the number of species seen moving along the coast regularly. So let us look at each species, one by one, as they occurred.

July 2nd, a crossbill at Thornton Reservoir. To say a crossbill, is not strictly true, it was more like twenty, and they put on a wonderful display for many minutes. A peregrine also came dashing through, not that it disturbed the crossbills, they were so busy feeding I doubt if they knew of its passage. On the shores of the reservoir were two little egrets and on the far shore several grey heron were feeding, whilst over the water, tens and swifts were very active. The crossbill was my 'year tick'.

A week later and I was back at Blacktoft, spoonbill hunting. A friend of mine had been up a couple of days previously, and told me about the spoonbills, five of them, a family group apparently. The weather was very good, warm and clear, so I made my way down to Marshlands where the spoonbills had last been seen.

I arrived in the hide to find it deserted, not a good sign as there had been several cars on the car park. I settled myself down, put my 'scope up, and started to view. The anticipated ducks and waders were visible, one or two of the juvenile avocets were now almost as large as their parents, which was a good sign and a pair of water rails were feeding along the fringes of the reed bed. Three little egrets were standing still, almost like white statues, when a marsh harrier flew across, flushing most of the birds, but in doing so did me a favour. I watched her, it being the female, as she flew across in front of the owl box, and as she did so, I became aware of movement in the box entrance. A barn owl was sitting in the entrance hole, almost as though it was enjoying what was going on, obviously not concerned about the harrier.

I could so easily have missed out on this bird had the harrier not arrived on the scene.

I moved on to the Xerox Hide, now there was so little to see at Marshland. Initially all saw was a spotted redshank, mind you, it was in full summer plumage, a bird not to be sniffed at, and a great white egret was strutting his stuff further down the lagoon. A few ducks were on the water, one an early wigeon, which did surprise me, then, delight of delights, from behind an island walked a spoonbill, closely followed by four others. I could not help but agree with my friend, it was indeed a family party.

I enjoyed those birds for several minutes, watching them sweeping their spoon-like bills sideways through the water, as they busily fed. The three juveniles had learned their trade well, emulating the movements of their parents. All good things must come to an end, and they slowly moved back into the reed bed. I was more than happy, two more 'ticks', the owl and the spoonbills.

The following day and Blithfield was back on the scene. Waders were starting to filter through. Ringed plover numbers had increased, the odd common sandpiper was seen and a curlew paid a brief visit, but the bird of the day was on the causeway slope. A turnstone, in almost full summer plumage, was busily foraging away. It was difficult to see what it was eating I can only presume flies were basking on the warm concrete slope, but whatever it was, the turnstone was happy, and so was I.

Five days later and I was back at Blithfield again. It was only a fleeting visit as I was passing through coming back from Cannock, but my luck was in. I spotted a couple of birders I knew in the Admaston Reach car park, busily gazing through their 'scopes. Needless to say, I pulled in. Before I could even ask what they were looking at, I was called across to look through one of the 'scopes. Three drake common scoter were to be seen, my luck was most certainly in. The birds did not hang around, they quickly drifted off down Blithe Bay. I had no complaints, they had made my day.

My last trip out in July was to Carsington Water. I was interested to see if any waders had dropped in there. There were a few redshanks, ringed plovers, two early dunlins, both adults flashing their black bellies, and two, family groups of oystercatchers. I moved onto Stones Island. More ringed plovers and a common sandpiper, and as I was walking round, a clear whistling 'tchew-tew-tew' was heard, oft repeated. Only one bird sounds like that, the greenshank, and seconds later, two came flying past, their long green legs dangling, as they came into land.

I was quite well hidden as it so happened, so I was able to watch those birds running through the water, probing their long, thin bills into it. I have often said that I consider the greenshank to be our most elegant wader, and watching those two going about their business, I am convinced I am correct in that belief. Those two were quite well marked, obviously adult birds.

A good bird to finish month with, closing on one hundred and ninety-seven. I am having a decent year, I just hope it carries on.

August sees me back at Blithfield on the 5th. I had a call this morning telling me whimbrel were being seen in Blithe Bay, three of them, and they could be seen from off the causeway. I had an hour or so free, those were too good to miss. We do not have many pass through, some years I see none at all.

Arriving at the Admaston Reach car park I met three birders I knew well, asked them the obvious question, and to my surprise they knew nothing about the birds. To be fair they had not been concentrating on Blithe Bay, they had been studying other parts of the reservoir. Needless to say, Blithe Bay now became the focal point. Within a matter of minutes, the whimbrel had been located, and the three birds were still feeding together.

Whimbrel are a smaller edition of the curlew in many respects, and at distance could be easily confused. They have the same curved bill as the curlew, and colouration is very similar, but we were close enough to pick out the minor differences. My friends were very pleased I had arrived on the scene, they may easily not have picked the bird up. When you know a bird is there, it is much easier to find, you know what you are looking for.

Two days later and it was Blithfield yet again. This bird I had no pre-warning about. I was in the hide in Stansley Wood, casually surveying the far shore where greenshanks were sporting about, when a small wader landed on the shore, right in front of the hide. I could not believe my luck, it was a wood sandpiper, and this bird had flown in to see me!

Wood sandpipers are longer legged than the common or green sandpipers, and look a more delicate bird. This bird still had much of its summer plumage, it had a slate-grey hue to it and dirty-white spots on the back. The legs are greenish which could cause some confusion with the green sandpiper, but it lacks the latter's white rump and belly. Of the three sandpipers mentioned here, it is the least common, and a quality bird to reach one hundred and ninety-nine with. What would be two hundred?

It was to be another sandpiper, and Blithfield had done it yet again. This time it was a curlew sandpiper, a small sandpiper with a curved bill, from where the name originates. As with the wood sandpiper seen a day or so previously, this bird also had much of the summer plumage remaining, and in consequence was looking quite red. Not a bad bird at all to celebrate two hundred, that was for sure.

I finished the month off on the 27th at Blacktoft. I only wish at times I lived nearer to this reserve. It was all action that day, the marsh harriers had young fledged.

There was much experimental flying taking place, which disturbed many of the ducks and waders, so there was not a great deal to see. Having said that the marsh harriers were putting on quite a display, even if the juveniles were not that accomplished.

Things eventually quietened down and the odd bird returned. I was watching two common sandpipers feeding when a smaller wader came into view. I was very pleased it had, it was a little stint, and my first of the year. They are aptly named being the smallest wader seen regularly in the UK. No complaints now, not that I had been complaining in any case.

Passing through Ousefleet, I pulled over in surprise. On a field were seven helmeted guineafowl, those obviously had to be escapees, but where from? There was not a building in sight, house of farm, so where they had come from was anyone's guess, but it brought an interesting conclusion to my day out.

The 3rd of September saw me back up in Humberside, this time North Cave called. For two or three days a spotted crake had been showing well, so that was worthy of a bit of effort, plus the fact I had not visited North Cave for some time.

Waders were showing well, common sandpipers, a green sandpiper, redshanks, a spotted redshank, avocets and curlews. Not a bad collection. Five little egrets were also to be seen.

There were several birders in the hide and one of them picked up the crake. It was not the most cooperative of birds, providing just fleeting views, but a herring gull did us a great favour. The gull landed almost where the crake had hidden, flushing the crake out, for a few seconds, and it was a few, the bird could be clearly seen. I waited for many minutes in the hope it reappeared, it did not, so that was that.

I was happy though, I had seen the crake—just! Not a bad start to the month. Then on the 10th, real excitement. A purple gallinule (some new field guides now call this bird the purple swamphen), had been reported from Alkborough Flats, an area I had heard of but never visited, I now had a very good reason to put that right.

Alkborough Flats lies in north Lincolnshire, and is the area where the rivers Trent and Ouse meet to form the Humber. Much of the area has been artificially formed or so I have been informed, to help prevent flooding, and this has produced an outstanding area for wildlife. A friend of mine, who had been up to see the bird, was able to give me the map reference for where he last saw it, that would be my starting off point.

In almost perfect conditions I arrived at the allotted location and was a bit disappointed to see so few cars, only five. I would have expected far more than that for such a mega bird. I scanned the area, not really looking for the bird, it was not going to be on grassland. I was looking for birders, and eventually I saw a small group gazing through their telescopes out over the marshland. I made my way down to them, and on arrival a cheery soul said, 'Here mate, have a look, he's in my 'scope'. I did not need a second bidding.

The purple gallinule was a bird which had always avoided me. I had been to places round the Med', where the bird bred, and never had a sniff, to now see one finally, and in England, was a wonderful experience.

The bird was out in the open feeding away on the mud, probably after rotting vegetation as I understand its principal food is plant material. It would find plenty of that round there. Although the bird was at least one hundred yards away, it showed up well, especially through a 'scope. They are a large bird, domestic chicken size at least, and its dark colouration showed why it was so called. It behaved very much like our native moorhen, even to the extent of cocking up the tail where the white under-tail clearly showed. I was able to watch the bird for several minutes, sometimes through the 'scope of my 'new' friend, before the bird moved back into thick vegetation, not to be seen again for the next hour or so I remained. You cannot help but think I was meant to see that bird, if so, 'thank you, someone!'.

Many waders were out on the flats, dunlins and redshanks in large numbers, but the birds which I was pleased about were the bar-tailed godwits, my first of the year. Alkborough Flats had been well worth the journey, I shall probably never see a purple gallinule ever again. A 'lifer' I had only ever dreamed about, never expected to see.

The month ended on two hundred and six with a pintail seen at Blithfield. This bird was a smart looking drake, and it put on quite a display for the watching birders.

When it upended in the water you could really appreciate where the name pintail originated from. They may not be the glamour boy of ducks, the mandarin probably has that title, but they are certainly the neatest looking of our waterfowl. A bit of quality to end the month on as far as I was concerned.

October commenced with a 'twitch', and not for a 'lifer', just a very special bird to me. A glossy ibis had been reported from Lound Gravel Pits, so the chance to see another one of those was not going to be missed, and it was not. This bird was very flighty and moved around a lot, but it gave very spectacular views, and I had a pleasant hour or so studying the bird. This bird was an adult, and you could understand where the name 'glossy' came from.

Depending upon how close the bird came it almost changed colour. At distance it just looked a brownish-black bird, nothing special at all. When it came close it showed beautiful glossy green and pink highlights to the feathers. Very well named. This was most definitely the bird I had seen in Egypt for the first time, those many years ago.

Little egrets were in double figures. On one of the pools a great white egret was stalking along the shore, and scattered over the reserve were many grey herons. It had been a long time since I saw so many great black-backs at an inland water, here they were well up into three figures. A very satisfactory day.

The layby at Kings Bromley came back into focus on the 6th October. I was on my way back from Lichfield, when I pulled in, I rarely drive straight past, and I had chosen well. In a meadow alongside the river, I saw a rather hunched up egret, something about this bird told me it was no little egret. I got out of my car to get a better angle on the bird, and as I did so, it turned its head and I saw the short, stout and pale bill. The little egret does not have a bill this shape and colour, theirs is long and black, this bird was a cattle egret.

The bird moved closer providing very good views. I was very pleased I had pulled in, and so was somebody else. Sarah was at home, a quick phone call and she too was able to enjoy the bird. I passed the information on to my Rosliston colleagues, so quite a few others enjoyed it too.

The following day Blacktoft called, probably for the final visit of the year. Pink-footed geese had been passing through regularly, a good enough reason for my visit.

I must confess that I had my doubts on why I had bothered. The M1 was almost stationary in places, and it was not until I reached the M18 that things improved. A journey time of two hours exceeded three that day, and I arrived in rain.

Fortunately, Blacktoft has several hides and with one exception, they are close to each other. When booking in I was told pink-foots had been reported that morning, so I was in with a chance.

On my way down to the Marshland Hide the heavens opened, so I made a quick dash into Xerox Hide, and here I hit lucky. Running round the edges of an island were two knots, a 'year tick' with almost the first bird of the day. It cannot get much better than that.

Little egrets were dotted round and I quickly counted eighteen of them. Their numbers are most certainly increasing, it is almost as though wherever there is water, little egrets are in attendance. Not to be outdone, a great white egret was also on view, they too are becoming regular sightings, with more reports of their breeding.

A few waders were on view, but I understood the tide was out so many had moved across into the Humber. There were black-tailed godwits, spotted redshanks, redshanks and two greenshanks, so the story was not one of gloom.

The rain stopped so onto Marshland. This provides a different view of the reserve, it points westwards whereas Xerox points north. Wader numbers here were very small, two dunlins and a further knot

Over the reed bed the odd grey heron was to be seen and a female marsh harrier was very active, this probably accounted for the fact few waders were to be seen. Two bearded tits gave fleeting views, but that is always better than none at all and the odd small group of swallows were still moving south.

A large skein of geese were coming in, low over the reeds, could these be my pink-foots? As they got closer, I could hear them calling, no they were grey-lags, so I calmed down. I then had a disappointing moment. I was watching a large cargo vessel sailing on to Goole, trying to identify the flag, when I caught a glimpse of a white bird dropping into the reeds. Something about the bird was not egret-like. I waited for it to reappear, it did not. I believed I had missed a spoonbill,

Finally, patience was rewarded. A small skein of grey geese came across, only twelve of them, but they were not grey-lags. The underside of their wings was dark, the grey-lag shows grey, and they are a larger bird. As they got closer a shrill 'kayak, kayak' could be heard—I had my pink-foots. Blacktoft had done it again, birds brilliant, weather unfortunately abysmal, as the heavens once again opened up. I decided enough was enough, at the next break in the weather I was up and away.

The remainder of the month saw me making local visits, plenty of birds enjoyed, nothing new added. The bird which interested me the most was the great white egret, on my 'travels' I saw eight of them, and all within half an hour from home. I started off with two at Doxey Marsh, one at the Staffordshire Wildlife Trusts HQ at Wolesely Bridge, another at Blithfield Reservoir, one at Tucklesholme, two down Whitemoor Haye and the final bird at Croxall Lakes. Those birds were spread over a period of five days, I have to smile when I recollect seeing my first, I had made a round trip of nearly two hundred miles to see that one.

November 5th saw me at Tittesworth Water, not expecting any fireworks there. I had been upon the moors first looking at the red grouse, they had not disappointed, plus a raven put on quite a flying display. Approaching Tittesworth, I had to slow down to avoid running over a covey of red-legged partridge which looked as though they were eating grit.

I went in for a coffee and a snack and whilst in there I met up with a birder I knew from the distant past. We had quite a chat about old times, and then he mentioned the fact had I come up to see the purple sandpiper? I had not, I was not even aware one had been seen. He told me where he had seen it an hour or so before, so I quickly had lunch and was on my way.

The bird was down by the dam, so I had a bit of a ride round and walk when I arrived. He told me where to best park and a public footpath was nearby which went down near to the dam, and the bird was to be seen from there.

His directions were smack on. I quickly spotted three other birders gazing intently along the shore. I joined them and the bird was pointed out to me. It was an adult bird in winter plumage, very dark looking, a general dark grey with probably the most striking feature being the yellow legs. Those really stood out against the dark plumage, in summer the legs are much darker. They are a dumpy looking bird, heavier than dunlin, and a bird not seen all that often so far inland, being very much a coastal species. More than a satisfactory compensation for the lack of fireworks!

November had things still in store. Westport Lake called, you will remember my seeing a great skua there back in June, today, the 19th, a duck drew my attention.

A drake long-tailed duck had been seen. They are a mountain and tundra breeding species which winters at sea, not seen too often inland, so the opportunity was not going to be missed.

I was not the only birder to be interested, several were spread round the lake and one near to me received a call on his mobile, his friend had located the bird so we moved off in the right direction

Fortunately, the bird was an adult drake and still had his long tail, so he was fairly easy to pick out. I had my 'scope with me so I did not have to walk far. I often think this duck is more attractively plumed in winter, when he has more white in his plumage, which combined with the long black tail makes it a striking bird. This bird had obviously fed well as all he did was drift round, lazily, on the calm water. A superb view.

The month finally closed on the 26th, Chasewater being my destination. A red-breasted merganser was showing off on the dam. They may not be as rare as the long-tailed, but they had avoided me all year, I had chased after them, and failed.

This was going to be my last chance.

I arrived to find I was going to have to do it the hard way, not another birder in sight. I made my way to the dam, seeing goldeneyes and goosanders as I did so. I also saw a pair of pintails, they are always welcome, I have only seen one this year, the Blithfield bird, back in September.

On reaching the dam I saw several cormorants and great crested grebes, and whilst studying those I noticed two black-headed gulls dive-bombing a duck which was diving to escape their attention. The gulls gave up, the duck surfaced, and I had my red-breasted merganser, which I was pleased to see was a drake. I was able to study the bird for several minutes as it slowly drifted out in the reservoir, diving frequently. Another successful one bird day.

December arrived. I was now standing on two hundred and thirteen species for the year, what had the final month in store for me?

It started well, Chasewater once again. The 5th saw me velvet scoter hunting, a drake had been reported. Velvet scoter are not seen that frequently so far inland so they are worthy of a bit of effort. Unlike the day of the merganser, several birders were after this fellow, and I knew most of them.

The bird had last been reported from off the dam, so we all made our ways there. Approaching the dam, we were very pleased to see the merganser was still *in situ*, he had now been at Chasewater for over a week. A long time for a marine duck to stay so far inland, and today we were after another sea duck.

It was a very dull day, grey and overcast, looking for a very dark duck on dark waters was not the easiest of tasks, especially for a duck which seems to spend more time under water than above it. But that day eight pairs of eyes were searching for it, all experienced birders, and we found it, well one of us did. The bird was constantly diving but

I eventually had the view I wanted, the white spot on the face and the white wingbar, were just visible. I was more than happy.

It was a several days before I was able to do any serious birding. I made a quick visit up to the JCB Lake at Rocester, and there I saw, what I had not seen for many a year, a free flying Hawaiian goose. Obviously, an escapee, but nevertheless an interesting bird to see on the wing. Whenever I see those birds, I remember the work done by Peter Scott at Slimbridge which saved this bird from extinction. If a few colonised the UK, they would be more appreciated than Canada geese, that is for sure.

The year ended on a marvellous note. I had received information that waxwings were being seen regularly at Frogatt in Derbyshire, that would be a wonderful bird to finish the year on, it was, after all, the 31st December. I managed to get the map reference for the location, so off I set, full of expectancy.

I arrived to find I was not the only birder interested, several cars were parked up. Fortunately, the road had a broad grass verge alongside it. What interested me was the fact the birders were widespread, a returning birder explained why. Apparently, the waxwings were split into several groups as the few remaining trees still with berries were also widespread.

I started to move in the direction of the nearest group of birders when I stopped. A flock of waxwings flew directly over my head to land on a hawthorn just feet away from where I was standing. What a view, their chatter was almost deafening, it had been a long time since I was so close to waxwings. I was able to count them, and in this one tree were fifty-eight birds. When you consider how many groups of birds were in the area, there were several hundred waxwings there. Not that I went chasing them, I had my own flock.

I have seen waxwings on several occasions, and seen them close, you will remember my experience of them on Cannock Chase, but never in such numbers.

Frogatt will remain in my memory forever, and what a way to finish a year, where, incidentally I closed on two hundred and sixteen, which included three 'lifers'.

CHAPTER X

The New Year, 2017, came in wet and miserable, at times very heavy rain, not good from a birding point of view, but you can only make the best of what you have got. We decided to attempt to have our usual bird race, come what may.

Things at home were quieter than usual. My first bird of the year was a woodpigeon, and prior to going out I had made my way up to twelve, not a very good start. During the day I visited Kings Bromley, Croxall, Catton Park, Whitemoor Haye, Barton Water Park, Branston Water Park, JCB Lakes, Blithfield Reservoir and finished off at Woodmill. Due to the weather, all my birding was done from the car, and I chalked up thirty-nine. Not a great number, but in the circumstances, I thought not bad.

As things turned out, our bird race was a washout, excuse the pun. I just hoped that things would improve tomorrow. As far as the weather was concerned, improve it did, the day was bright although very cold. I visited Blithfield Reservoir again, there were hides there should they be required.

Here I saw a further twelve species and included among those was some quality. Nuthatch were busy and vocal, several grey herons were along the shore, goosander, gadwall and shoveler were the pick of the ducks, a grey wagtail showed up well in front of the hide in Stansley Wood, and a raven made frequent flights over the wood. On my return to the car, the bird of the day put in an appearance. A male brambling landed in a garden opposite, they had a feeder out and the bird was visiting this. He was worth the trip out alone, and he took me up to fifty-one.

I had things to attend to on the 3rd and come the 4th I was at home all day, but I did add a wren to my list. It was seen in my back garden, and he kept me occupied for a few minutes, I know one thing, wrens are rarely still, they are a very active little bird, always seeking food.

I was again out on business the next day, but driving back through Croxall I saw two mistle thrushes feeding in a field, and I was able to stop and watch them for a few minutes.

The 6th dawned damp and gloomy and remained so for most of the day. I did, however, manage a couple of hours serious birding. I firstly visited Cannock Chase where among the birds seen were kestrel, a male bird, two bullfinches, a party of nine long-tailed tits and many fieldfares. On my return journey I called in at the layby in Kings Bromley, and here I was delighted to see nine little egrets. I felt things were starting to click.

The gloomy weather continued on the 7th, but it was at least dry, and I had more time available, so I decided on a ride round the Chase, JCB and Whitemoor Haye.

Things were surprisingly quiet on the Chase, even the feeding station at the Whitehouse car park was strangely deserted. The odd blue and great tit popped in and the most exciting bird seen was a male bullfinch. He at least brought a bit of colour to a drab day. Venturing onto the Chase I had fieldfares and a pheasant, and as I made my way back to the car, a small flock of lesser redpolls landed in a silver birch tree. They certainly brightened up things and I was able to enjoy their company for a few minutes before they moved on. Back at the car a buzzard flew overhead, so that brought things to a positive conclusion. What has JCB got to offer?

Plenty of noise and activity, the ducks were being fed, and ducks never do things quietly. Moving away from the maddening throng, a bar-headed goose flew in. This bird has been here for many months now, and the resident pinioned bar-heads regularly chased the bird off, it looked as though they resented its freedom. One thing I had noticed in the past is that when the collection bar-heads came up for food, the free flyer did not. The Egyptian geese looked as though they have already paired off, they are an early breeding bird and the population here, did seem to be slowly increasing.

A drake red-crested pochard was in the distance, but I could not get a clear view to see if he was one of the collection birds, or a wild species. I had time so a quick drive round Whitemoor Haye could be fitted in.

The lakes were busy, wigeon and teal numbers high, the odd goldeneye and goosander were on the water and the far shore had a large Canada goose flock and six little egrets were scattered round the shore.

Nipping down the rough lane I saw tree sparrows and had a spectacular encounter with a female sparrowhawk. She came in so low I expected her to collide with my car aerial. Had I been outside my car, I would most certainly have felt her passing. I have had some close moments before with sparrowhawks in my own garden, but this bird was literally only inches above my car roof. An exciting conclusion to my trip out.

The 8th was again overcast, and although not actually raining, it had a very damp feel to things, but I decided to go out, Cannock Chase being my destination.

I pulled in onto the Penkridge Bank car park, and was greeted by a flock of redwings. Unfortunately, they did not stop, they flew on further into the Chase. I have had worse welcoming parties that is for sure! I had barely got on the Chase when I heard yellowhammers calling, I had to smile to myself as when young we always referred to this call as 'a little bit of bread and no cheese'. A little bit further on I saw two males, probably having a verbal battle over territory rights.

Deeper in the Chase, I stopped, I could not believe what I was hearing. Close by, were waxwings, but where? I moved off the track and a short distance away I saw them, seven of them in fact. They were chattering away as waxwings do and for a few seconds I just stood there watching them. It did not last long before they were up and away, and that was that. There may only have been seven, and I know just a few days ago I was looking at hundreds, but this is a new year, they are my first of it, and could easily be my last. I am a very happy man.

The weather was not improving, again being damp, cold and very grey, and I was driving across the Chase on my way home, when a bit of colour came into my life. A jay flew across the road in front of me and landed in a bare tree on the side of the road. I was able to stop and look at the bird for a few seconds before another car came and I had to move on.

The 10th came in, once again wet and miserable, not a day for birding, but as I had to do my weekly shop, I was not too concerned. I was on my way home, being held up somewhat by a trundling tractor and muttering away to myself, when I saw a bird, at first presumed to be a buzzard, gliding over an adjacent meadow.

Something about the flight of the bird made me stop. The bird glided in with a definite kink in the wing, buzzards on the other hand glide on flat looking wings. As the bird came in closer, I saw it had a white tail with a dark terminal band, only one buzzard had that. It was a rough-legged buzzard.

Some bird to get and so close to home. This species breeds in the tundra and is a rare vagrant to the UK in the winter. The few we see are usually northern or east coast birds, so far inland they are most unusual. In all my years of birding I doubt if I have seen this bird more than ten times, a cracker to get and so local. I will never moan about tractors again!

The weather at last changed. Very windy but at least bright and clear, a day for a bit of serious birding. I visited Blithfield, and to escape the wind I went down to the Stansley Wood Hide. Here the wind was coming in from the north-east and was hitting the back of the hide, so viewing from out of the hide was no problem.

Waterfowl numbers were high, the pick being goldeneye, goosander, pochard, gadwall, shoveler and shelduck, with good numbers of wigeons, teals, mallards and tufted ducks. Cormorant numbers were high and great crested grebes were scattered over Tad Bay and I counted sixty-four of them. There were more no doubt, they do spend much time under water.

On the meadow at the bottom of the bay were many Canada and grey-lag geese, with a solitary little egret among them. There were many lapwings also on the meadow as well as on the shores of the reservoir, and whilst looking at those I picked up a small group of golden plovers, seventeen of them. I was pleased I had brought my 'scope as I was able to study those birds well, especially as they were a 'year tick'.

Turning my attention back to the water I spotted three small waders running through the water, up 'scope, they were dunlins, another first. These birds were dashing about as though their very lives depended upon it, constantly probing the water with their bills, easy to see why they were called 'waders'.

They were my sixty-ninth bird of the year, and Blithfield that day gave me forty-four in total. Not a bad day out.

The following day was most miserable, rain and sleet with snow expected. I went out for a short drive down to Whitemoor Haye, more to escape boredom than to see birds, but I was lucky. Not a lot to be seen but I did click with a small flock of stock doves, they were most welcome, and well worth the trip out.

The snow came but fortunately it did not come in heavy, and the rain on the 14th cleared what was left, so a day of birding was possible. I thought it would be interesting to visit the moors after such weather, with snow about the red grouse should stand out well.

Before I started out I had a bit of excitement back home, a song thrush appeared in my garden, only momentarily, but I was lucky enough to see it. They are not as common as they once were, and as I have mentioned previously, they are now worthy of note.

Driving across Axe Edge Moor it was quite spectacular, the snow had drifted deeply in places, it was very much a white world. I was thankful I was driving a 4 x 4, I would not have fancied driving a standard vehicle in those conditions. I managed to park in my usual spot, wound the window down slightly and settled down to both watch and listen.

I had not been there long before two ravens caught my attention. They had obviously found something dead in the snow and they were arguing over it. When raven argue it is not kids' stuff, they really meant it and eventually one flew off leaving the other to enjoy its meal. At least whatever had died, it was not being left to waste.

It was getting rather chilly so I put my engine on and started to run the heater, it was not going to be long before I would have to move on. It was only a matter of minutes when five birds came flying over a ridge to land, rather ungainly in the snow—red grouse. I was right, they certainly stood out against the snow. They vanished behind a mound so I decided to move on, a warm coffee and meal at Tittesworth now called. Driving off the moor I slowed down, a buzzard was sitting on a stump, but unfortunately, as I approached it took to flight. I had only seen three species and eight birds in total, but they were all sheer quality.

Tittesworth was very quiet, few cars were parked up and I think they were rather pleased to have a customer in the restaurant. To help them to make ends meet, I actually had two coffees with my snack.

The light was reducing rather rapidly, and up over the moors it was going very dark, rain was imminent, so I drove down to the car park which overlooked the reservoir, where should the rain arrive, I at least could view from my car. It was not long before the rain did arrive, well to be more accurate, sleet. I did at least manage to see a marsh tit on the feeders and eleven barnacle geese were on the water. Time to go, the elements had won.

As I approached home it cleared and driving back through Hoar Cross I was most fortunate to spot a merlin flying low over a field. I do not suppose I saw the bird for more than a few seconds, but I was happy with that.

Not a bad day at all. Including the song thrush I had seen five new birds for the year, and I had now reached seventy-five, and I am only halfway through the month.

The poor weather continued, so the next day I just had a run out in the car to brighten the tedium, and drove across the Chase. I pulled in on the Whitehouse car park just as the rain lessened, so I was able to have a short walk. My luck was in. A green woodpecker was calling, this continued for several minutes, and I eventually caught a quick view as it flew off. Fieldfares and redwings were seeking out the remaining berries and a mixed flock of titmice gave me a fly-past. The weather then took a hand, so I turned back towards the car park. Rain or not, I stopped. A loud drumming had started, and from nearby. On an old tree trunk, a great spotted woodpecker was hammering away, and the chips really were flying. Blow the rain, I just stood there for three or four minutes watching the bird's activity. The muscles they must have in their necks and the strength of their bills to work like this, is just amazing. I certainly got wet, but I would not have missed a second of it.

The following day was even worse, rain, cold and patchy mist, January so far has been a very poor month, so it was another day to birdwatch from the car. I popped out locally, calling in at Croxall Lakes initially, and what a start. I had hardly switched my engine off before a flash of blue hurtled across the lake—a kingfisher. I only had the bird for a few seconds before it vanished into the mist, and went round a bend in the lake, but what a few seconds. A kingfisher is a bird to brighten up any day, even one as poor as today. What a start, and from my car.

Not a lot could be seen due to the gloom, so I drove on down to Whitemoor Haye Lakes. Conditions here were no better, the odd duck on the water and Canada geese could be heard but not seen thanks to the mist. A chaffinch was doing his best to liven things up, but his singing attempts sounded very half-hearted.

I decided enough was enough, so one last glance around and I would be on my way. That did not happen. A male reed bunting popped up in the hedge and sat there staring at me. This face to face went on for several minutes before the bunting decided he had seen all he wanted to see, and my birding was completed.

The 18th brought in similar weather, so it was watching from the car once again. With the mist I did not consider it worth bothering with water watching, so I just had a drive down the rough lane at Whitemoor Haye, taking some seed with me for the tree sparrows.

The seed was not required, someone had beaten me to it, and the tree sparrows were thoroughly enjoying it. A few yellowhammers and chaffinches were also to be seen, so I just sat in my car, nice and warm, watching it all. A pheasant arrived on the scene and the seed started to reduce quickly, and two jackdaws did not help matters. I spent half an hour studying it all, and before I drove off, I replenished the seed stocks.

The 20th dawned, bright and clear after overnight frost. On the bird news I had noticed that bean geese were to be seen at Whitmoor, the day looked perfect to chase after them, Whitmoor is not to be confused with Whitemoor Haye. Whitmoor is in north Staffordshire, an area I visit infrequently, but it does have a very good record for the rare geese, and bean geese are probably the rarest geese we see in Staffordshire, worth a bit of effort. Which it was.

Driving into the lane which lead to the meadows where the geese were last reported, I had to proceed with caution, the entrance to the lane was flooded, and it looked deep. I know I have a four-wheel-drive, but it is not a boat. As I sat there a Land Rover came the other way, the driver was obviously a local and he drove through without hesitation. Once he had gone, I took the same line through the water and I was on my way.

The meadow which had the geese in was party flooded, and I had not realised that a large party of pink-footed geese were also to be seen. I had brought my 'scope so I set myself up to go through the birds, well into three figures. I slowly worked my way through them and I was approaching the end when I picked up my first bean goose. This turned into eleven, a very good number and it was interesting to see them among the pink-foots where the differences could be noted. The bean is slightly larger than the pink-foot, had a larger bill and probably the most important feature, leg colour, the bean has yellow legs, the pink-foot obviously pink. Two 'year ticks' together cannot be bad.

Many gulls were on the meadow and I was pleased to pick out several common gulls among them. A very satisfactory day, and as it was getting cold, home I went, remembering my way through the flood!

The cold weather continued although it was not so bright. I decided to have a crack at the hawfinches at Cromford, finishing off at Carsington Water where a warm snack would be available. You have to think of your creature comforts, especially in this weather.

For once, Cromford was very obliging, the hawfinches came to see me, well almost. I may have mentioned the fact before, near the car park I use there is a very large horse chestnut tree in which I have, on occasion, seen the odd hawfinch. The hawfinches had decided to have a party, and nine of them were to be seen. What a sight, I doubt I was thirty yards away from my parked car. I was able to study the birds for several minutes before they moved on, a car parking right under the tree saw to that. I now had more time for Carsington, where an early coffee would not go amiss.

Coffee enjoyed I took myself off to the public hide, which I had to myself. Things were rather quiet, a few ducks, geese and gulls, so I turned my attention onto the island. Here there was more activity. Several lapwings and five golden plover were to be seen, and in the shallow water a solitary redshank was feeding away, a single bird it may have been, but it was my first of the year. Time now for another coffee and a warm snack and then for Stones Island.

The afternoon saw a distinct change in the weather, rain had come in, making my visit to Stones short. Walking down an oystercatcher gave me a fly-past, a very vocal one as is their wont. On the water were several cormorants and great crested grebes, plus a large group of mute swans, there must have been nearly fifty of them.

The rain intensified so I turned back. Rounding the corner, I stopped. On the water's edge was a group of common snipes, eight of them, so rain or not, these had to be studied. I managed a bit of shelter under a tree, but being leafless this was not much use. After a few minutes the rain won, the snipes waterproofing was obviously superior to mine.

A damp ending to a very good day's birding, which had increased my total by four. I am still progressing well.

Conditions on the 23rd were still unpleasant, cold and misty, visibility in places very poor, but I took a chance and visited Chasewater. The velvet scoter I saw last month has reappeared, the chance to get him out of the way so early in a year had to be taken.

I was lucky in one respect, the mist was not as bad as it was at home, although it certainly was not 'scope conditions. As I walked towards the dam, I disturbed a small group of ten or so meadow pipits, so that was a good start. On the dam I met up with another birder whom I knew. He had been there for an hour without any luck, and he was about to depart. Meeting up with me he decided to give it another half an hour or so, and he chose well. I doubt we had been there together more than ten minutes, before, sailing out of the mist, came our bird. Unlike when I saw him last month, he spent far more time on the surface so we could enjoy him to the full. He concluded a very satisfactory visit.

As a change, the 25th was clear but cold, it is still January after all. So I decided to give Blithfield a go. It was a calm day with no wind and Blithfield was like a millpond. Duck numbers were very good, there seemed to have been a movement in of goldeneyes and goosanders particularly and shelduck numbers were also high. With the rain we had experienced of late I did not drive round the shore, I just did all my viewing from the Watery Lane and Admaston Reach car parks and had brought my 'scope for doing so.

The cormorant population just seems to increase every time I visit, they cannot all be local birds, although we do have at least three colonies locally. Many of those seen must be winter visitors from the coast. Great crested grebe numbers are also high which is also a good sign, and whilst working my way through those I hit the jackpot. A scaup pops up, I was just in the right place at the right time to see him, it being a drake. Had he not surfaced at that very moment, I may well have passed through without being aware of him. I regularly say that birding is ninety per cent luck and ten per cent knowledge, today has proved that. The scaup has helped me reach ninety for the month so far.

The cold weather continued as did the cloud. On the 26th I was passing through Barton-under-Needwood, and as I had a few minutes available I went into the water park. This turned out to be a good decision, among the birds expected, a pair of little grebes were diving close to the shore. That was five minutes well spent.

January was certainly proving to be a miserable month, but you cannot give in to it all the time, so, come the 28th, damp and overcast as it was, I visited Blacktoft. As I have mentioned on several occasions, the hides here are ideally situated, just minutes apart.

I was informed that water levels were very high, that was no surprise, and the majority of the waders were out on the Humber as it was currently low tide. That being the case I decided to have an hour or two in the singleton hide instead of starting off at marshland as I usually do.

Birdwatchers were few, the locals were no doubt aware of the water level situation and were elsewhere, and, most unusually, I had the hide to myself. Although it was early in the year, the odd marsh harrier had not migrated south, and a male did its best to keep me entertained, but to attack a grey heron was not a successful manoeuvre. Hopefully the harrier learned a lesson that day, a heron's beak is a powerful weapon.

I must have been in the hide for about half an hour before the real quality bird of the day performed. A male hen harrier came sweeping across the reeds, this, put up birds I had not even been aware of which had been hidden among the reeds. Included among these were three water rails. I had two 'year ticks' at the same time. Now that cannot be bad.

The excitement died down, peace was restored. I moved down to Townend Hide to finish my day off, the cold was beginning to bite. For some reason the water level there was lower and three redshanks were feeding away, and several common snipes were sitting out on a small island. Water rails were again seen, five of them on this occasion. A movement in a nearby bed of reeds drew my attention, and after very close scrutiny I picked out a jack snipe, a superb bird to finish my day on. The weather may have been most unpleasant, but I had chalked up four 'year ticks', so no complaints. I was just thankful my car had a powerful heater....

From a birding point of view, the month closed on the 29th. Heavy frost overnight, was followed by rain. I had a couple of hours free so it was going to be a case of birding from the car.

My first destination was Blithfield, and here conditions were most unpleasant. Due to the rain, visibility was very poor, although I had brought my 'scope with me, it was useless. A few ducks were scattered on the water, the inevitable cormorants were to be seen and several gulls were passing through. One of these, very obligingly, landed on a nearby buoy, an adult winter plumaged Caspian gull. It most certainly brightened up the day.

As I still had time, I decided to drive home via Croxall Lakes in the hope conditions were better there. They were not, if anything they were worse, but I clicked for a cracking bird. In the field opposite the reserve's entrance were several swans. Studying them closely I was delighted to see they were all Bewick's swans, eighteen of them.

The weather may have been vile, but two birds had made it all worthwhile, which is what birding is all about. The month closed for me on ninety-seven, just failing to reach the magic number of one hundred.

My first trip out in February, on the 3rd, was again in wet weather, although it was at least milder than a few days ago. So it was another occasion for birding from the car. I only had a short time available so I chose Blithfield. For a change I drove down to the dam and crossed over towards the angling club car park. Part way across I stopped, a herring gull type was sitting out on the parapet. Raising my binoculars, I was delighted to see the bird had yellow legs, it was no herring gull, it was a yellow-legged gull. My last two visits to Blithfield had produced two of the rarer variants of the herring gull. the Caspian and now the yellow-legged.

Arriving at the angling club a pleasant surprise awaited me. Sitting out, in the rain, was a little owl. What it was doing in those conditions I have no idea, and as I repositioned my car to obtain a clearer view, it flew off.

Not a lot else was to be seen, a few gulls were drifting through. Tufted ducks and mallards were on the water, but the gull and the owl had made my trip out well worth it. February started well. I am now on ninety-nine, what will be my century bird?

The 4th came in crisp and clear after a heavy frost. It was afternoon before I could get out to seek my one hundred, and Whitemoor Haye was my destination. I briefly called in at Croxall, not a lot doing, although the Bewick's were still to be seen.

I then pulled in at Whitemoor Lakes and straight away I had my hundred, and in a way, it was a disappointing bird, it was a black swan. Nothing wrong with a black swan, it is a superb bird, it is just a bit 'plasticy' as we birders claim. But nothing can change the fact it is my 'century bird'. The pressure is now off.

Turning to drive home I had to stop, I could not really believe what I was listening to. A skylark was in full voice, and looking up I saw him, high in the sky, singing his little heart out. What on earth it was doing so early in the year I do not know, unless it was just celebrating the fact it was a dry and bright day! He brightened my day that is for sure.

The 5th was bright and clear once more and birding was not really on the agenda. I had been across to Swandlincote on business and on the way home I stopped for a quick look over the lake near to Barton Quarry. Not a lot initially, then a large white shape appeared moving through the reeds, and to my delight, a great white egret walked out into the water. Providence had certainly come to my aid. I watched the bird for many minutes before it walked out of sight, a totally unexpected.

sighting.

Another frosty and misty day followed, but I decided to have an hour out so I drove across to Branston Water Park. Ducks and gulls were having a great time as several people were feeding them. I know it was only bread, but on a day such as this the birds certainly appreciated it.

I took a short walk down the lake, enjoying a pair of bullfinches and several chaffinches, but not a lot else was seen. Walking back, I heard a soft call coming from an ivy-covered tree, stopped to see if I could locate the bird, and was pleased when a goldcrest flicked out. It was a crisp looking male, and he was my first of the year. A more than welcomed sighting.

Over the following few days, we had frequent snow showers and no birding was done. Come the 11th, we had sleet and rain which at least cleared the snow which was still about, and I managed a drive out. A quick visit down to Whitemoor Haye was all I had time for, and it was going to be watching from the car, the rain had increased in intensity.

Nothing unusual on the lakes, and the skylark certainly had nothing to sing about today. Continuing down the rough lane, a few tree sparrows were eating seed and two pheasants dashed off at my approach. As I turned the bend, a small bird flicked out and sat on the top of a nearby bush, and he was a real beauty. It was a male stonechat. Even in the dull conditions of today his bright colours stood out. Attractive birds, and they do seem to like to show themselves, they do not hide away. If you have it, flaunt it! A more than satisfactory end to my quick visit.

The 12th was again a drab day, persistent rain combined with poor visibility. Another day for birding from the confines of a car, if at all.

Early afternoon, the rain lightened so I decided on a quick drive out and called in at Blithfield. As far as the weather was concerned it was not a very good decision, the rain came back, and with a vengeance. No matter how I parked up I had difficulty in lowering a window so I could view out, it was a question of running my engine and using my wipers. I was not going to be there for long, that was sure.

I was able to pick out the odd bird, cormorants were well spread as usual, the odd great crested grebe was seen and a few ducks were scattered on the water, but it was mainly gulls. They are probably more used to this type of weather than many other birds, and with the weather as it was, they were coming in early for their night time roost.

One gull came in close which I at first thought was an adult black-headed gull, but as it passed by, I realised the head was black, not brown, and it had no black on the wings. My trip out had paid dividends, it was a Mediterranean gull in almost full adult plumage. The rain no longer mattered. A miserable day had ended brightly.

Poor weather continued, and combined with work at home I did no birding for almost a week. I had one piece of good fortune, however, a small party of siskins passed through my garden, stopped for several minutes on my feeders, before moving on. Another bright interlude in the middle of all the rain.

Come the 18th and for once it was a dry morning, grey and overcast, but at least dry. By midday it had actually brightened up and I managed a quick drive across to Blithfield, where I actually did my birding from outside my car. Amongst the birds seen were two southern cormorants, both looking very smart, and in the brighter conditions they really stood out amongst their companions. This is a bird which is becoming more regularly seen, as with the yellow-legged and Caspian gulls, birders report them more frequently.

The dry weather continued for another day, still overcast and grey, but I decided to make a quick trip up to Cromford, friends had told me the dippers were showing well. That being the case an hour or two there would not be wasted.

My friends were right. I had only been on the bridge over the Derwent a matter of minutes before a dipper came through. It whizzed under the bridge and quickly vanished downstream. A few minutes later and back it came, well I presumed it was the same one, to quickly disappear upstream. Over a period of half an hour or so I saw dippers on several occasions. I also saw goldcrests in the yew trees in the churchyard and had a fleeting view of an hawfinch. Well worth the visit.

It was another few days before I was able to get out, and when I did it was accompanied by strong winds and showers, with gales forecast for later in the day. Not a day for walking far, so I drove down to Whitemoor Haye, here I just had a slow drive round the rough lane.

The birds had been fed and tree sparrows were enjoying themselves along with a few yellowhammers. A male kestrel was hovering nearby and was experiencing great difficulty in holding his position due to the strength of the wind. A few lapwings were flying over the meadow, although it was more accurate to say, being blown over the meadow.

Continuing down the lane three red-legged partridges walked across the lane, they were in no hurry which was rather surprising, and as I continued on my way a buzzard was blown through. Stopping near Whitemoor Lakes I saw goldeneyes, teals and wigeons. Considering the conditions that was not a bad little haul, especially as the partridges were my first of the year.

The gales duly arrived and for a day they battered us about a bit, but they passed through quickly and the following day came in bright and clear. I had been told that the Cetti's warbler was calling again on the corner near to the National Memorial Arboretum at Alrewas, so as I had an hour or two, I went out to see if I could find him.

I knew exactly where to park up and listen, having done so on a few occasions over the past months, and fortunately, they do call throughout the year. They have a very loud call, so if one is nearby there will be no problem with hearing it. For the size of the bird, the volume is impressive.

I parked up, window wound down, and settled back to listen. Blackbirds were vocal, a robin was doing its best to add some melody to the occasion, and a chaffinch was almost in full song. A wren livened up proceedings, he has got some voice, and a skein of Canada geese came honking across. Plenty of sound, but not what I had come for.

I must have sat there for well over half an hour before my patience was rewarded. From a thick tangle in the hedge the Cetti's burst forth, and he meant to be heard. I would not claim the bird to be musical in the sense of a songbird, but they most definitely are vocal. I spent several minutes trying to locate the bird, without success, when the little fellow obliged. He flicked up onto the top off the tangle, gave me a burst of his call, and then vanished down, and did not appear again. I was happy, I had both seen and heard what I had come for.

My final birding trip for February took place on the 25th and Attenborough was my destination. My birding actually commenced before I arrived. Driving through Toton on the A53 I was able to pull over. A common crane was flying over some open ground, heading in the general direction of Attenborough. What a bird to start my day with.

When I arrived at Attenborough I asked if anyone had seen the bird, but it had not been reported. The usual birds were to be seen, although I was disappointed not to see any red-crested pochards, they are usually guaranteed there. Egyptian geese on the other hand were showing well, and a small group of them was causing great excitement to a party of young children who were feeding the birds.

Walking down to the Kingfisher Hide, a Cetti's gave me a burst, but he did not put in an appearance, but two bullfinches did. From the hide it was the usual birds, and I was pleased to note that the gadwall numbers were high. Many cormorants were on the islands and grey herons were stalking the shore. Two little egrets flew in and whilst watching those I had a pleasant surprise, a drake mandarin swam into view. He was not on the sightings board, so I certainly had not been expecting him.

A distinct change in the weather had been taking place so I decided to make my way back to the visitor centre for a warm lunch, and I just beat the rain to it.

Whilst in there I had an interesting chat with one of the wardens who wanted more information on the crane I had seen earlier. Apparently, someone had mentioned seeing an unusual bird with long legs fly over the reserve, and when checking the time I saw the bird, presumed it was the crane.

An interesting enough day, with two 'ticks'. I have now reached one hundred and twelve.

March came in dull but dry, and I manged a quick visit to Croxall Lakes. I was lucky, although things were quiet on the bird front, two ruff were to be seen on the island, they were greatly appreciated. A pair of great crested grebes were on the water and the male was displaying well. They almost look as though they are walking on water at times, they are a very special bird.

The 3rd saw me visiting Blacktoft, but I arrived in heavy persistent rain, with very poor visibility. Bird numbers were also low, I think the rain had even driven them to cover. A few ducks were on the water and the odd common snipe was to be seen, and that was about it. I decided to call it a day and made my way back to my car. In transit I heard the call I love, curlew were about, rain or no rain, those had to be found. I was lucky, they found me. A flock of fourteen birds came swooping, low overhead, calling as they did so, to vanish in the direction of the Humber. I only saw them for seconds, but that was time enough to appreciate their beauty and vocal capabilities. They brought a gloomy day to a magical conclusion.

The following day saw a change in the weather, bright and clear with a breeze. I had a full day available, so Carsington Water called. As you by now know, it is not only the birds which draw me there, food is plentiful!

I called in at Sheepwash initially, and this proved to be a good decision. On entering the hide, a birdwatcher already there, pointed and said, 'If it is the diver you are after, it is right out there.' I was not, I did not even know one was there. You cannot beat introductions such as that. A great northern diver was majestically drifting past, and for once staying on the surface, not constantly diving as is their usual wont. For several minutes I was able to enjoy this bird before it drifted round a point and vanished from view. My timing had been perfect, and the bird was an adult just starting to moult out of its winter plumage. Two redshanks and a ruff were also to be seen from the hide, and after a chat with the birder, I moved on to the visitor centre—a coffee called.

After coffee and a snack, I moved on down to the visitor hide, and had this to myself, no one there to point out birds. I now had to find them myself, that was not difficult, there was much to see.

Many ducks, mallards, tufted ducks, shelducks, gadwalls, pochards and a scattering of goldeneyes were quickly seen, plus cormorants and grebes. Moving to the shore, more redshanks, two oystercatchers, a dunlin, two curlews and eight barnacle geese. Not a bad haul.

It was to be a week before I was able to do any further birding, and that was only a quick drive round Whitemoor Haye, where just the usual were seen, but instead of driving back by my normal route, I chose to go via Elford. As I drove through, I saw a lady using a pair of binoculars, so I stopped and asked her the obvious question, and I was pleased I had. She was searching for a chiffchaff she had heard calling. Four eyes are better than two, so I joined her. After a few minutes the bird called again, this time much closer than she had heard it previously, then to take the pressure off, out he popped. The bird sat in the open for a minute or so before returning to the safety of the undergrowth. My first summer migrant, was summer that close?

It could be. The following day dawned bright and mild, and as I had the full day at my disposal, I visited the moors. My initial location was Merryton Low.

Here I saw meadow pipits and heard curlews, but the bird that really had my attention was a short-eared owl. This bird was flying low over the ground, just an occasional flap and a long glide as it searched the ground beneath. I thought to myself the meadow pipits had better keep their heads down, but they were safe. The owl dropped silently onto the ground, and emerged carrying a small mammal, it had its dinner, and the pipits need not worry for at least another day.

Moving on to the Chimney, ring ousels had been arriving in the UK, although it was probably too early for them to have come so far north, you do have to give it a try. I failed but I did see curlew, two of them and a raven was very vocal. Returning over Axe Edge Moor I saw a small group of red grouse, all males, and driving off the moor, two golden plovers put on an aerial display. A very good day that.

The pleasant weather continued and I had a couple of hours on the Chase, visiting Seven Springs. Here I heard two more chiffchaffs, had a buzzard fly overhead and watched a great spotted woodpecker fly into a hole in a tree. Obviously, it had its nest there and was probably taking food to a sitting female. Not wishing to disturb the bird, I moved on. Further on I spotted a bird working its way up a tree trunk, a treecreeper. I stopped to watch this bird's progress. It was obviously seeking food, and judging by its actions, finding some. I was able to watch the birds progress for a minute or so, before it flew deeper into the woods. I was more than happy, it was my first of the year.

The mild weather held on and a couple of days later I managed an hour down at Croxall. Nothing of great interest on the bird front but I did see a female brimstone butterfly, she was more than welcome. As I still had time, I drove round to the corner near the arboretum, parked up, window down. I was listening for the Cetti's warbler, but what I heard was a complete surprise, a common whitethroat was calling. I was even lucky enough to see the bird aerial displaying, I think he was being a little premature there, but they do say that practice makes perfect. Just to finish off the day, the Cetti's did give me a burst. When I got home and was writing up my notes for the day, I realised the common whitethroat was my earliest ever record. The 15th March is now a date in my records.

Three days later I was back up on the moors, this time Swallow Moss was my destination. A great grey shrike had been reported. This bird was obviously on passage and was not going to stay for long, so if I hoped to see it, time was the essence.

The weather could not have been worse. After the bright and milder previous weather, it was now heavy rain and misty. But needs must, and I had my car for shelter. Due to the weather, I had Swallow Moss to myself, and in the conditions of that day, it was a bleak spot. I had my windows down slightly just in case I could hear anything, and this paid dividends, I heard red grouse on a couple of occasions. I also had a wren keep me company for a minute or two as it searched beneath a nearby bush.

The odd carrion crow flew over and the chatter of a magpie was heard, but apart from those it was relatively quiet.

My problem was I did not know where exactly the shrike had been seen, so I drove on to a local spot where I had seen shrike previously, a shrubby area about half a mile away. I had chosen well. Four cars were parked up with 'scopes and binoculars pointing out of the windows. I joined them, looked in the direction their optics were all pointing, and there was the shrike, sitting out on the top of a stone wall. I was very fortunate, it only sat there for seconds before it flipped over the wall, and although I stayed for over half an hour, it did not reappear. As I have said before, some days you win, some days you lose, that day I won, but only just! Mind you, I did not get wet.

The following day the weather had improved, it may have been dull, but it was at least dry and mild. I had seen reports of the return of the avocets to Middleton Lakes, an afternoon there may be worth it.

My first stop was by the heronry, and the noise coming from here was quite something. They are an early breeding species, and judging by the sound, some birds already had young in their nests. There was a lot of aerial activity with birds flying in and out of the heronry.

The feeding station was quiet, just the odd titmouse and chaffinch, so I proceeded on my way down the woodland trail, the avocets were probably down near to the canal. I stopped at the viewing platform which overlooks a lake, and here I hit lucky. I heard avocets calling and three birds flew into view and landed in the shallows of the lake. I stood stock still, I was in clear view, hardly daring to breath.

I did not even lift up my binoculars, not that I really needed to, for fear of frightening the birds away. This went on for three or four minutes as I watched the birds feeding, and then two other people walked onto the viewing platform, and off the avocets went.

Those three avocets had saved me a longish walk, so I was very grateful to them. I walked a short distance on to have a look at the rookery, as with the heronry, plenty of noise there too, and made my way home. A happy man once again.

I had a busy time at home and did not manage any birding, until the 24th of the month, then it was a fleeting visit to Blithfield Reservoir and Whitemoor Haye. I visited the dam at Blithfield hoping to pick up an early wheatear, one had been reported, but I drew a blank. At the angling club car park I was compensated.

Among the pied wagtails on the car park was a male white wagtail, it was an ideal opportunity to compare them both. The pied being a definite black and white bird, the white on the other hand being mostly grey and white. Pleased as I was to see the white wagtail, I think our pied out-smarted him.

Due to time, I drove straight down to the rough lane, not stopping at the lake.

Tree sparrows were busy feeding, the odd yellowhammer flicked in, and a male bullfinch put in an appearance, that is a bird always welcomed. Driving further down the lane I was delighted to see two corn buntings feeding on the verge. I managed to stop without disturbing the birds, and enjoyed their company for a few minutes. We are very fortunate down the Haye as we still have a few pairs of corn buntings, a bird not seen all that often. They, along with the white wagtail, gave me two 'ticks', a very pleasing run out.

The 26th was a lovely day, bright and warm, and I decided to check up on the peregrine falcons, to see if they were back at their breeding site at the Swains Park Industrial Estate at Church Gresley, they were, the pair showed well. A buzzard came drifting across, the bird obviously meant no harm, but the female peregrine was having none of it. She proceeded to have a real go at the buzzard and on one occasion she actually struck the buzzard and a couple of feathers drifted down to earth. After this the buzzard flew off fast, and I mean fast. Peace returned. Learn a lesson here, never hassle a female peregrine!

The 30th saw the first sand martins of the year, these being at Blithfield Reservoir, and here again a buzzard was in trouble. There were only seven sand martins, but two of them were brave souls, they persistently dived at the buzzard.

Being small and fast fliers, there was little the buzzard could do about it, apart from fly on, which it did.

The end of the month and a sign of summer's approach was noted. A swallow was seen at Whitemoor Haye lakes along with several sand martins, they were well into double figures. Just be careful, however, they do say one swallow does not make a summer!

The month closed on one hundred and twenty-six.

I have always considered April to be the month when it all starts. Our summer migrants begin to arrive, and most of our resident birds have broken into song, and many birds are already breeding. Some of our birds have two and occasionally three broods a year. It is a busy time for them. Birds breeding further north are also on passage, so the odd unusual species is likely to pass through.

The month commenced with a visit to Blacktoft, on a bright and clear day. Duck numbers were down, many of the winter visitors had departed for their breeding grounds, but other birds were already taking their places. As I arrived, I was entertained by a blackcap, he was in very good voice, and two or three chiffchaffs were calling. I booked myself in listening to one chiffchaff calling from right outside the visitor centre, enough to make one think summer had really arrived.

I made my way down to the Xerox Hide, and as I arrived a birder was just leaving and he gave me the news a garganey was on the water. Garganey are a summer migrant duck, and they are not a common species at all, so the chance of seeing one was most welcome.

What he had not told me was the bird was a drake, so I was more than delighted to find the bird. They are a very attractive duck, and this one was quite happy to just drift about enjoying the warm day, I was happy just to see him. Two new birds already and I had only been here minutes, not a bad start.

After half an hour or so I moved on down to Marshland to have a look at the avocets, and I was pleased to see them in double figures, but I was more pleased to see two other wader species. I counted nine black-tailed godwits, most in summer plumage, and they really stood out, these birds would be moving on soon. The bird which surprised me the most, was a green sandpiper, I would have expected it to have departed by now. Not that I was complaining, it and the godwits were new birds for the year.

Two broods of mallards were on the water, the ducklings being just bundles of fluff, they were only days old. Marsh harriers were active over the reed beds, I counted three in the air on one occasion, and a water rail was heard, but not seen. I notched up four new species on the day, not a bad start to a new month.

Blithfield saw me the following day, another bright and warm day. Sand martin and swallow numbers were growing, although these scattered when a peregrine falcon flew through, not that it was interested in them, it was just on passage. The martins and swallows quickly returned.

I drove across the causeway and parked up on the Admaston Reach car park, took out my 'scope and commenced to work the causeway slopes. Two small black and white looking waders were dashing along, fortunately coming in my direction. They were obviously a ringed plover species, but I needed a closer look to see which.

The birds were very obliging and kept on coming nearer. I got the view I wanted, no yellow eye ring, which combined with their bright legs, meant ringed plovers.

I moved on to Stansley Wood. A few titmice and chaffinches were on the feeders and as I walked down towards the hide, I heard a willow warbler singing. After a lot of effort, I located him, summer may well be here after all! My visit had been short, but I collected two more new species.

The decent weather continued and several days later I was back at Carsington Water, this time with the Rosliston Bird Study Group. We called in at Sheepwash first, and here we saw a pair of oystercatchers and a redshank, feeding in the shallows.

Several cormorants, including one well marked southern cormorant and a few great crested grebes were on the water. Sand martins were flying over the water in small groups, and as we walked back through the wood, we both saw and heard chiffchaffs and willow warblers.

We then drove round to the visitor centre and visited the hide. A large flock of Canada and grey-lags were on the water, with tree sparrows on the bird table.

A male reed bunting also made regular visits to the feeders, and to our amusement, a mallard also landed on the bird table, not very elegantly I am afraid. A friend drew my attention to a small wader which suddenly appeared on the island, I was pleased he had, it was a summer plumaged turnstone. He had found us the bird of the day. Leaving the hide, we heard another chiffchaff, but could not locate it. Another very pleasant day.

The following day I was back on the moors, still hoping for ring ouzel. Once again, I drew a blank, but as I drove back across Axe Edge Moor I stopped to watch a flock of red grouse, and whilst so doing a bird of prey flashed across. This bird was not interested in the grouse, they were much too large for it, a pigeon was its prey. The bird banked, and I was pleased he did. I had at first thought it to be a female sparrowhawk, I am pleased to say I was wrong; it was a male goshawk. Whether it caught the pigeon I do not know, they both vanished behind a rise in the ground, but the hawk was certainly gaining on the bird, so I think it may. An exciting few seconds, to finish off my day.

By the 14th the weather had changed, overcast with scattered showers, so I made Blithfield Reservoir my destination, and as things turned out, it was a good decision. On the causeway I saw two common sandpipers from the Watery Lane car park, and walking a little way down Watery Lane, I saw a lesser whitethroat.

Driving round to the angling club I had very good views of a wheatear, a superb male which seemed intent on being seen. I then drove to Newtonhurst Lane to have a final look at the bottom of Blithe Bay. An Egyptian goose was on the meadow and many sand martins were feeding over the water. A large bird took off from a tree, I had not noticed it before, the osprey was back. For two or three minutes I watched this majestic bird fly and glide over the reservoir, it did not dive for fish unfortunately, but it put on quite an aerial display. A super finish to my visit, on which I had seen four 'year ticks'

The following day saw me back at Blacktoft. The birds were much as seen a few days ago, apart from the green sandpiper appeared to have moved on and the godwit numbers had increased. Marsh harrier activity was high, although it was mostly males I saw. Several avocets were now on their nests and the water rails were vocal. The barn owl was also showing as it sat in the entrance hole to the nest box, and curlews were calling in the distance

Moving on to Zerox, I was delighted to see five spotted redshanks, all in full summer plumage, and they looked a treat. The best way to describe them was a sooty black bird covered with small silver stars, some bird.

Sand martin numbers were high and swallows had commenced their build up, summer is approaching. Little egrets were also on the increase, and shelduck numbers were good.

Unfortunately, the weather took a turn for the worse, so my day was curtailed somewhat, but it had nevertheless been enjoyable, the spotted redshanks had seen to that.

The 16th came in cloudy and with many showers. I only had an hour or so at my disposal, so a quick drive across to Blithfield was all I could manage, and the causeway would be my objective.

I pulled in on the Watery Lane car park and was greeted by several house martins. These birds were skimming low over the waves, in company with both sand martins and swallows, our three hirundines had now all arrived. They appeared to be welcoming summer even though the weather was not! Which is right, I wondered?

Crossing over the causeway to Admaston Reach a common sandpiper flew off the parapet, flashing across the road in front of me. Arriving at the Reach I saw ringed plover species in the bay—concentration time. There were nine birds to sort through, fortunately they were fairly close in. I got the view I wanted, two had distinct yellow eye rings, so I had seven ringed plovers and two little ringed plovers. I was more than happy with that.

Turning my attention to the reservoir I saw the osprey out fishing, a few abortive dives were made, before the bird gave up and returned to its roost. Whenever I see the osprey now at Blithfield, I remember the last time Dorothy and I saw one together, our last trip out. Memories are wonderful things, even when recalling sad times. That brought my quick trip out to an end, a pleasant hour's birding even if the end had a hint of sadness,

The 20th saw me off ring ouzel hunting once again, my third attempt, would it be third time lucky? Crossing Axe Edge Moor I heard red grouse, but did not see any, the heather had started to grow tall again so the birds were secluded from view. I sometimes think the call has an almost human tone to it, a true sound of the moors, as is that of the curlew.

I just managed to park up at Dane Bower, it looked as though a walking club was trekking the moors. A wheatear greeted my arrival, hopping up onto the top of a stone wall, and a skylark was singing away, not that I could find him.

I settled down to survey the valley in front of me. I had brought my 'scope for this purpose, as on occasion the ouzels have been very distant. A further red grouse called, but he was some way off and a pair of raven were sporting about, high in the sky. A small bird down in the valley caught my attention, it turned out to be a meadow pipit.

I had been studying the valley for well over half an hour, patience is not a virtue in this game, it is a necessity! Three sheep were grazing one of the grassy areas, lawns as we call them, and they disturbed a black bird, only one black bird lives up here, the ouzel. Blackbirds are found at lower altitudes. I eventually got the view I wanted, the white chest really showed up well, even at this distance. I had my ring ouzel, a male bird, the heat was now off. I enjoyed him for a few more minutes before I had to depart. Job done.

Two days later I had more time at my disposal, so I visited Carsington Water. I called in at Sheepwash where blackcaps were singing, two of them in competition, almost a duet. Walking down to the hide I was serenaded by willow warblers, there was at least four of those, and as I approached the hide, I heard a bird with a slightly different tone to that of the blackcap. A garden warbler was expressing his feelings, and very melodiously so. I hoped there was a female close by which was as impressed as me.

In front of the hide an oystercatcher could be seen sitting her nest, and working the shore was a green sandpiper. This bird did surprise me I would have expected it to be well gone my now.

Instead of visiting Stones Island, and not requiring the café today, I had brought my own supplies, I decided to go back home via Blithfield Reservoir, it had been producing the birds of late.

I arrived at Blithfield to a complete change in the weather conditions. Carsington had been bright with an odd shower, Blithfield was damp and very windy, so I drove down to the dam where it would be more sheltered. The hirundines did not seem too worried about it, they were active over the water, and two wheatears were feeding along the dam roadway. A common sandpiper briefly landed on the dam slope, but quickly departed up the reservoir.

A number of common terns were over the dam, well into double figures, and whilst watching these perform, one of them started to hover before diving into the water. The duration of the hover caught my attention, common terns do hover, Arctic terns on the other hand hover much longer and more frequently, which this bird was certainly doing. I approached more closely, and was delighted to see the bird lacked the black tip to the bill which indicated it was an Arctic tern. My trip to Blithfield had paid dividends, added to the garden warbler seen earlier, I now had two new 'ticks'.

I can now safely inform you of when summer arrived, it did so on the 23rd April, and how do I know, I hear you ask, I saw and heard my first cuckoo! To be more accurate, two of them. I had called in on the Chase for a few minutes, at Penkridge Bank, and I had hardly got out of my car when I heard a cuckoo calling. I managed to locate him quickly on a nearby tree and was impressed with the effort he was putting into his calling. As he flew off another one started to call from behind me, this one was not so cooperative, but I did at least see him fly away.

I was back on the Chase the following day in the hope I would again see and hear the cuckoos. I failed, but there was plenty of other birds to both see and listen to.

I drove round from Penkridge Bank to Seven Springs and was greeted by blackcaps and willow warblers singing away. I made my way in the direction of the Stepping Stones, here I saw the chiffchaffs and garden warblers, obviously a day for warblers, that was four of them I had seen and heard.

Walking on larger birds took over, a raven was calling and occasionally taking to the air, a buzzard came across, unusually for them, silently. I wondered if it was in hunting mode, not wishing to announce its presence. A green woodpecker also gave a burst, accompanied by a short fly-past. All very interesting, but I was after pipits, well one would do.

I reached the open area of the Chase where in the past I have found my tree pipits, and I am pleased to report, they were back. At least two males were seen performing their aerial song flights, they were quite a distance apart, so they were not exactly in competition, I was just pleased to see them again. I sat and enjoyed them for several minutes before setting off back to my car.

In transit I had another pleasant surprise, a cuckoo burst forth, so I got one after all. The distance I was from Penkridge Bank I think it is safe to presume this is a further bird to the two I had the previous day. A great finish to my trip.

The 26th April commenced, interestingly enough, in my own back garden. I have mentioned previously about a small rookery that has been set up near to my home. It currently has eight nests occupied, and the birds on those nests can see clearly into my back garden. They have things weighed up well, and when I go to put out scraps for the larger birds, they watch me, and as soon as I have vanished indoors, down they come. Things turned out differently on this occasion.

I was scattering the food on my lawn and before I had finished, there was a thump on my fence, there sat a rook, just feet away from me, watching my every action. Its eyes were just staring straight at me, almost as though it was challenging me, and as I started to move off, down it came, gathered a beak full of food, and flew off towards the nests. The bird no doubt had young to feed, and it made sure it found some. Within seconds the garden had several rooks squabbling away over the food, no doubt my friendly one being in amongst them. The confidence of wild creatures at times is quite amazing.

I had an hour free, so the afternoon saw me making a quick visit down to Croxall Lakes. I was interested to see how the warblers were faring. Blackcaps, garden warblers, chiffchaffs and willow warblers were very vocal, and I thought I had a brief view of a grasshopper warbler, but it was very distant and too far away for me to hear it. Turning my attention to the reed beds I was pleased to hear reed warblers calling, there were at least two males singing, and further along I thought I caught a sedge warbler. Unfortunately, it only sang the once, so I could not be sure. I now at the very least had a reason to come back in a day or so, both for the sedge and the 'gropper'.

The following day I was returning from Uttoxeter where I had been on business, and just called in for a quick look over Blithfield Reservoir. I was pleased I had, the first of the returning common terns had arrived, five of them as it so happened. There may have only been five, but they were making a lot of noise as if celebrating their safe arrival. Popping in for a minute or two had paid dividends for me.

The 29th was a typical mixed April day, bright with many April showers, but at least it was not cold. I decided to go back to Croxall Lakes to see if I could find the sedge and grasshopper warblers. I had no trouble at all with the sedge, he behaved perfectly, sitting out in full view, calling away. They are more accommodating than the reed, which usually sings from deep in the reed bed, the sedge on the other hand perches on low bushes and shrubs near to the reeds, and sings from those. I do like birds which cooperate! The grasshopper warbler I am afraid did not.

As I still had a bit of time, I drove across to Blithfield, and here the weather took a decided change, no longer showers, but persistent rain. I just parked up on the Watery Lane car park, window wound down, and stared through the rain.

Common tern numbers had increased, now well into double figures, and I was delighted to see a few swifts hurtling through, low over the water. When you see them like this you can really appreciate why they are so called, swift they most certainly are. Two flew close to my car and I could really hear their screeching, they are rarely silent when in flight. Rain or no rain, I was very happy, they were my one hundred and fiftieth bird of the year.

I finished the month off with a trip up to Bearda Hill, pied flycatcher seeking, and this was successful. I heard several and saw at least four different males, so the breeding numbers there seem to be holding up well. Willow warbler, blackcap, garden warbler, chiffchaff and common whitethroat were also singing well as was a tree pipit. These hanging oak woods are a paradise for woodland species, and as long as I am able to park my car, I am quite happy to just sit and listen. Thanks to the pied, I ended the month on one hundred and fifty-one.

The weather on May Day was very drab, overcast and damp, another day for birding from the car or close to it, so once again I chose local, starting off at Whitemoor Haye, and I chose well. Opposite the lake a small bird was busily feeding in the hedge and it took me a few minutes to get the view I wanted. It had been worth the wait. A superb male whinchat was seen, a most unlikely bird to be seen at this time of the year in this location. By now it should have been upon the moors breeding, but I certainly was not complaining, whinchats were not birds I expected to see there.

Turning my attention to the lake, Canada geese were in goodly numbers, common terns were in the air and black-headed gulls were as noisy as ever. Five little egrets were feeding round the shore and whilst enjoying those a long-legged wader walked into view. The whinchat had been a wonderful surprise, what I was looking at there, was even more so, a bar-tailed godwit. We get black-tailed godwits regularly enough on passage, but bar-tailed are far more unusual, they are a coastal bird of passage, only very occasionally seen so far inland. This bird was not showing much colour, so I presumed it to be a late juvenile, a first-year bird. Whatever it was, I was delighted to see the bird, two crackers within minutes of each other.

A quick call in at Blithfield was now as much as I could manage, but I was interested in seeing how the swifts were doing. In the matter of a couple of days their numbers had really increased, probably up into three figures now. Common terns were also building up nicely, so we may have good breeding numbers this year.

Whilst enjoying the terns and swifts I became conscious of three small dark looking terns flying through, fast and low—black terns. The swifts were not the only birds enjoying the emergence of flying insects that day, the black terns were doing likewise. Unfortunately, the terns were only seen for a few minutes before they flew under the causeway bridge to vanish up into the northern reaches of the reservoir.

I was happy, thanks to them I had seen three new birds for the year, a good start to the month.

It was the 5th before I managed a trip out, and this was also going to be short, so I chose Blithfield once more. This time I concentrated my efforts on the dam. It was a brighter day, although rather breezy, but much activity was taking place on and over the dam. Swifts, hirundines, all three species and common terns were much in evidence. As I drove across the dam a wheatear sat out on the dam parapet and watched me drive by. Parking up on the angling club car park a further wheatear was seen, this time a female, and glancing over the adjoining meadow I was delighted to see a small party of yellow wagtails, five of them, three males and two females. The day being bright made the male yellow wagtails look almost like long-tailed canaries, wonderful little birds, and so elegant. Not a bad selection seen in a little over an hour.

A couple of days later, I was back on the Chase, this time near to Upper Longdon. I had read reports of woodlarks being seen in the area, this required investigation.

A few years ago, woodlarks could be guaranteed in one or two locations on the Chase, but as newly planted conifers gained in height, this changed the habitat and made it unsuitable for the woodlarks. I thought this had occurred at Upper Longdon, so I was surprised to see the report.

The day at least was suitable, bright with only a slight breeze. I had the area to myself, apart that was, from a lady riding a horse. My first impressions were not favourable, the young conifers which had been planted there, were all ten feet or more tall, and as they were all planted quite close to each other, conditions did not look very suitable. I was fortunate, however, a male redstart was calling from a small group of silver birches and I was able to locate him without any trouble. I shared a few minutes with him before he flew off. I was happy, my first of the year.

I spent a further hour looking out for the woodlark, without success. Had it not been for the redstart, it would have been a very quiet day, as I saw and heard little. I have my doubts regarding the accuracy of the woodlark report, so I do not think I will return to look for it.

The 12th May arrived, my eighty-fourth birthday. Once again time was limited and the weather was not that brilliant, but I had to celebrate somehow. A quick ride across to Blithfield, and if I had time, I would drive round near to the Branston Gravel Pits, where I understood a black-necked grebe had been seen.

The common terns were now well in at Blithfield, but the black terns had passed through. The osprey put on a good display for me, actually catching a fish, which it flew off with, being pursued by two lesser black-backed gulls, but it managed to avoid them. The swifts and hirundines were enjoying themselves, obviously plenty of insects about, and two yellow wagtails were busily chasing flies along the causeway slope. Three terns out over the reservoir caught my attention, they were not flying as gracefully as the common terns, and they looked larger. Eventually they came closer and I was delighted to see they were three Sandwich terns, not a bad birthday present that. Time now for Branston.

I parked up in my usual spot near to Dunstall, from where I could view the main area of water at Branston Gravel Pits. There were many birds to be seen, principally geese and cormorants, and a pair of mute swans who had five small cygnets.

Common terns were very active, as were black-headed gulls, both breed there. The odd great crested grebe sailed into view, but not the grebe I was after.

Due to the weather, I had not brought my 'scope out with me, and I was beginning to regret the fact. A birder I knew drove up and asked me about the grebe, and he mentioned he had seen the bird earlier in the day, and pointed out the area of water the bird had been favouring. This was quite distant, but he kindly got his 'scope out and scanned the water for me. He quickly located the bird and I was able to have very decent views of it, and I was pleased to see the bird was an adult male in summer plumage, a real cracker in fact. That was the perfect end to my birthday trip out. A malt will definitely be required tonight, to complete the celebrations.

The time for nightingales and turtle doves was nigh, so the 13th saw me off to Paxton Pits. It was a dull day and very breezy, not the best of days for expecting nightingales to sing, but we have no control over the weather.

Luckily, the weather at Paxton was not as bad as back home. I could have had better conditions, but the sky at least had brightened up considerably. I checked in at the visitor centre, where a mug of hot coffee was most acceptable. Nightingales were in, five males had been heard singing that morning, but only one turtle dove had been seen, and that had been two days previously. Things did not look all that good, but all you can do is get on with it.

I had the locations of two of the singing nightingales, and made my way in those directions. Many common terns were flying over the lake, cormorants and herons were busy in their nesting colonies. With swifts and hirundines feeding low over the water, there was plenty to see and enjoy. At least two cuckoos could be heard calling in the distance, and several little egrets were scattered in the shallow waters.

I slowly made my way down to the first nightingale area, listening to several warblers on the way. Chiffchaffs and willow warblers were plentiful, plus odd blackcaps and garden warblers. One area of reed had quite a number of reed warblers chuntering away, and the odd sedge warbler was seen.

Reaching my destination, where a bench was available, I settled in for nightingale listening. A common whitethroat was the first bird to be seen and heard, and for several minutes he entertained me well, then the bird I had come for burst forth. Pleasing though the whitethroat had been, there is nothing to compare with a nightingale, and this bird went through his full repertoire, not once but several times.

Here was a true virtuoso. I hoped that tucked away somewhere nearby, was a responsive female, he deserved one with that performance. He enthralled me that was for sure.

Time to move on, and not far. A red kite came gliding over, they have become a regular feature here in recent years as they have slowly spread over England. Their re-introduction has certainly paid dividends, they are no longer a rare bird. The days I used to travel to Wales in the hope of seeing a bird have long since passed, I have even seen the odd one near to home.

The weather conditions were deteriorating, so I turned back, stopping briefly to listen to the nightingale, he was back singing. Obviously, that bush was his favourite singing post, and whilst listening to him I had to smile to myself. Several people walked or jogged past me, and few stopped to listen to the bird, had they no soul?

I stopped at the top of the lake to watch two mute swans having a bit of a tussle, and as I was doing so, the sound I had waited for was heard. The soft purring of the turtle dove. I swung round just in time to see the bird fly off from a silver birch to vanish in the distance. That was that, in total no longer than ten seconds, an eternity compared with no time at all. Brief though it may have been, I now had my turtle dove. Many birds, good views of most, serenaded by many, and three 'year ticks'.

A good day by any standards.

It was a week before I manged any serious birding, and the day was miserable and wet. Friends had mentioned to me about a spot in Derbyshire, Cutthroat Bridge, where ring ouzels were showing well. This needed investigation. A new location for ring ouzels would be most useful for the future.

I knew where it was, I have driven through it before, but never stopped to birdwatch, so armed with the actual map reference for the birds, I was on my way.

I pulled in at the Ladybower Reservoir, did not see a lot, but mused about the famous *Dam Busters* who did many of their low level practice flights here, and turned off along the A57. A short distance along this road is a largish layby on the right, overlooked by the Hordron Edge. Birds could be seen and heard from here and also on the opposite side of the road on the Highshaw Clough, my informants were not wrong.

I had barely got out of my car before I heard a male singing from upon the edge, some improvement from my previous efforts at Dane

Bower. I crossed the A57 as I had seen a bird flick up in the heather, and was delighted to see a male ringy, this was birding made simple. I spent well over an hour at Cutthroat Bridge and I saw at least five separate male ring ouzels. If they all had mates that was five breeding pairs.

I have a feeling this will not be my last visit. To complete things, curlews were also calling, and a red grouse flew in.

The following day saw me at JCB Rocester. Sarah and Martin had been over the previous day and had spotted flycatchers near the HQ building, good enough reason for me to visit. I needed spotted flycatchers for my 'year list'. It did not take long to pick up a bird, it was hunting flies right in front of the building. It was showing no concern at all for passers-by nor people leaving or entering the building, this bird had one thought on its mind—food. I was able to enjoy the bird for several minutes before it flew off, no doubt it had eaten its fill.

On the water the pick of the free fliers were barnacle geese, bar-headed geese and Egyptian geese, with, infuriatingly, a red-crested pochard which I was again unable to get a clear view of, so I had no idea whether it was a free flier or a captive bird.

A few days later I was able to have a few hours at Blithfield Reservoir and the Chase, and the weather had also taken a move for the better. It was bright, clear and warm, actually reaching twenty-five degrees. Summer at last.

Blithfield was relatively quiet apart from the common terns, swifts and hirundines, and the osprey appeared to have moved on. His return come the autumn will now be awaited.

Driving across the causeway a small tern flew over, I hoped I would be able to see the bird from Admaston Reach as I believed it to be a little tern. My luck was in, the bird had remained in the area, and it was a little tern, the smallest of our white terns. It may have been only one, but one will do.

My destination on Cannock Chase was the Stepping Stones, and the bird I was after was the wood warbler. For a few years now we have had the odd pair near Seven Springs and the Stepping Stones. For the first time in many a year I had drawn a blank at Seven Springs. Today may be my last chance for seeing one this year, so I was prepared to have to put time in.

Walking up from the car parking area I had heard and saw at least two cuckoos, a male redstart had watched me pass by and various warblers had been singing away. Buzzards were also active, I just think all the birds were enjoying the weather, as with the heat, many insects were on the wing.

Near the Stepping Stones I saw a spotted flycatcher fly into a nesting box and heard a tree pipit, but could not see the bird. I settled down in the area previously favoured by the wood warblers, prepared for a long wait. I am delighted to say, this was not necessary. I had only been there a matter of minutes before I heard the bird singing. It has a very distinctive song, best described, and here I quote Lars Jonnson from his book, *Bird of Europe*, as a silvery series of ringing 'zip' notes which accelerate and merge into a metallic shivering trill. The bird was singing from high above my head and it was some time before I managed to see the bird, but see it I did.

Mission accomplished.

The 27th came in overcast and very showery, still pleasantly warm, hides were obviously going to be required, so Blacktoft called.

Several of the avocets had young, and reed warblers were very vocal, as were the sedge warblers. As I approached the Marshland Hide I stopped, I could not believe my luck, I heard a grasshopper warbler calling. I have mentioned the fact before that the call of this bird is almost outside my hearing range, so to actually hear one, it had to be very close, and he was. The bird popped out, only momentarily, to sit in full view, only feet away. Binoculars were not needed for this one, and whatever follows, this was going to be my bird of the day.

From the hide several avocets were seen, and as mentioned above, many had young. Marsh harriers were out hunting over the reed bed and the barn owl was sitting in the entrance hole to the nest box.

The rain decided to take a turn for the worst, so I made my way down to the Singleton Hide, and this proved to be a master stroke. Rain does not worry many birds, especially water birds, and I had only been in the hide a matter of minutes when out of the reeds stalked a bittern. You never expect to see bittern, the best you hope for is to hear one booming. I doubt in all my years of birding whether I have seen ten in total, and to see one in the open like this bird, was simply amazing. It is now questionable as to which was my bird of the day, I will give it a draw! (Just as an aside, when I checked my records, the bittern was my thirteenth.)

The rain eased slightly and the odd harrier came out, and among them was the Montagu's harrier. This bird is almost a regular here during the summer, it being a migrant harrier. It just has to be breeding locally, and where hopefully remains a closely guarded secret.

He bought my day to a close, four superb 'ticks', which brought May to an end. My 'year list' now stands at one hundred and sixty-eight.

June commenced with my annual pilgrimage to Bempton Cliffs, as with the nightingales at Little Paxton, if I did not visit, I would require a 'fix'!

The day was bright and clear, with a slight breeze coming in off the sea, perfect for birding, and the birds performed. The pick of the birds seen were gannet, kittiwake, puffin, razorbill, feral pigeon, rock dove, guillemot, fulmar, shag and rock pipit, all 'year ticks', plus a barn owl and tree sparrows. On the day I had thirty-seven species, and the puffin numbers did seem to be holding up well. Bempton had done its stuff once again.

On the 4th I just had a ride round Whitemoor Haye, and here I spent an interesting few minutes, watching a song thrush deal with a snail. The snail was quite large and the thrush was using a piece of concrete as an anvil. The power of the bird as it smashed the snail onto the concrete was most impressive, apart from the snail's point of view. After the song thrush had flown off, I went across to look at the concrete, judging by the amount of snail shell to be seen, this was not the first time the thrush had used it.

I drove home via Barton Marina and there I saw a hobby swooping among the hirundines. I did not see it make a kill, but it certainly scattered them.

It was the end of the month before I did any more serious birding, the 29th in fact. I managed a couple of hours at Blithfield, and here I was pleased to see a few waders were starting to move through, the pick of which were two greenshanks. I have always considered them to be the most elegant of our waders with their long legs and long slim bills. They are the classical wading bird. More than a bit special today as they are my first of the year.

Then the month did end, and the 30th June 2017, became a day I shall remember for the rest of my life.

East Leake, Nottinghamshire, was a place I knew, having travelled through it on occasion, I never thought of it as being a mecca for birdwatchers. The end of June 2017, changed all of that.

Unknown to me at the time, bee-eaters had been reported there and Sarah had happened to see this reported by the BBC, she brought it to my attention needless to say. I think I have mentioned previously that the bee-eater had been on my most wanted list for the UK for more years than I care to think about. I had seen them for the first time when serving in the RAF in Egypt, and on a few trips abroad. the UK, never.

East Leake looked only an hour or so's drive away, so that chance had to be taken. A quick check on my maps, route decided, I was on my way by 8.30 a.m. I was right about the time, it did just take over the hour, a little over thirty miles away. Parking up, and paying my fee of £5.00, half for the farmer and half for the RSPB. I was on my way.

The walk was a bit of a struggle, but to see that bird so near to home, I would have climbed a mountain! Birders returning from looking at the birds were full of it, apparently five at least, were flying in and out of an ash tree and had been doing so for some time. It seemed no doubt I was going to see my dream bird at last.

There were about fifty birders at the viewing spot and as I looked across at the tree, I saw a bee-eater sitting out on a bare branch. I had my bird at last, sixty-six years after seeing my first in Egypt, that brought back some memories.

I joined the throng and was told that a total of five birds had been seen roosting up at the same time, and they occasionally took sorties out as they chased a passing bee or the like. I had not brought my telescope as I knew the walk was not that good for me, but a birder called me across to have a look at them through his 'scope. I needed no second bidding.

As I have mentioned before, they are a most colourful bird, a technicoloured swallow I always refer to them as, and although the light that day was rather drab, the yellows and blues could be clearly seen. One of the birds actually flew out and caught a passing bee, and on its return to the perch, tossed the bee up into the air and deftly caught it again. I can only presume the bee-eater was turning the bee so as to avoid being stung. That brought back memories of my seeing bee-eaters in Egypt, stroking bees to remove the stings. Nature is simply wonderful, and they do not need computers!

I spent a good hour enjoying those birds, you do not rush off from a bird you have waited that long for. Whilst watching them I became conscious of a further two bee-eaters sitting apart from the five, we had seven birds. I pointed those out to my friend who had loaned me his 'scope, and he agreed, seven it was. I also saw one or two of my old birding friends who had come across to see the bee-eaters. All in all, it was a great day.

I only wish I could have shared this occasion with Dorothy. When in Mallorca many years ago, she had seen her first bee-eater, and like me, fell in love with them. To have shared today with her would have been wonderful, but you cannot turn the clock back, unfortunately.

My 390th species seen in the UK, although if I count birds not on the British List, escapees and birds still being considered by the BOU, I have now seen 424 free flying birds. My first 'lifer' of the year, would I have any more? I doubted it.

I later heard that at least one pair had bred at East Leake. It will now be very interesting to see if any return next year.

June certainly ended on a high, the bee-eater being my one hundred and eighty-first bird of the year. What would July do for me? It tried.

On the 3rd I had whimbrel on the Burton-on-Trent Washlands, or to be more accurate, over the washlands. I was out on a field meeting with the Rosliston Birders, on what had been a very quiet morning, and as we were returning to our cars one of my colleagues stopped, pointed and asked, 'What have we here?' I turned to look and he had really turned our morning round. Five whimbrel were flying over, as they past they started to call, making a perfect ending to our morning. A few of my friends went home with a 'lifer' that day.

I was back at Carsington Water on the 7th, I was hoping a few waders were passing through, in view of those seen at Blithfield. I only had time for a couple of hours at Sheepwash, but I was not to be disappointed. A small party of little ringed plovers were seen along the shore, two oystercatchers were flying through, two redshanks were wading and the bird of the morning flew in, and landed right in front of the hide. If ever a bird intended to be seen, that wood sandpiper was it. The bird slowly moved along the shore, feeding in the shallow water, until a cormorant touched down close by, and the wood sandpiper flew off to vanish in the distance. It had made my trip worthwhile, being my first of the year.

For the rest of the year, it was probably going to be a case of chasing up the odd bird, so my remaining trips would have that in mind. Obviously, I will see many other birds, but my reporting will concern mainly the special birds.

July 9th saw me back at Blithfield, the odd knot had been reported, so there was a bird worth chasing after, and it was not very co-operative. I drove down Admaston Reach well into Blithe Bay with no luck. Plenty of other birds about, including a few common sandpipers, ringed plovers and little ringed plovers, that was until a hobby came flashing through and most of the smaller birds vanished.

Back to the causeway and my luck changed. Whether knot had been among the birds flushed I did not know, all I did know was the fact two were running along the causeway slopes, and that was enough for me. They were both adults and still showed some of their red summer plumage, a very pleasant sighting.

It was a further week before I managed another trip out, and this time, Shuttington, near to Tamworth, was my destination. Sanderling had been seen, hence my interest. I managed to park in a spot which overlooked the lake the bird had been last reported from. I set up my 'scope to scan the lake shores, although I made several passes and spent many minutes looking, no sanderling was to be found. The only birds along the shore were grey herons and little egrets.

I now concentrated my efforts on the water, sanderling being off the agenda. Common terns were well accounted for, it seems to have been a very good year for them, and interestingly, a pair of black swans were on the water. To see a pair in a wild state was a little unusual, the odd escapee was the normal, someone here had been very careless. Working my way through the gulls, I picked up a smallish gull with very dark underwings, excitement time. Only one gull has this feature, the little gull. I quickly got back onto the bird and watched it for several minutes. It was a classic, feeding on insects it was taking from the surface of the water, behaving in many ways as would a black tern. The fact I had not found the sanderling, no longer mattered, the gull was more than adequate compensation.

The 22nd saw me back in Derbyshire, and although I saw nothing new, I did see a few quality birds. Carsington Water provided me with a Caspian gull, two little ringed plovers, two common sandpipers and a white wagtail. Driving home passing Bradley Nook Farm I saw a red kite. Needless to say, I quickly pulled in to enjoy that bird, which brought a pleasant day's birding to an end.

That brought my birding for July to an end, closing on one hundred and eighty-five species.

My only remaining venture forth was my annual pilgrimage to the Sutton Coldfield Crematorium to spend some time, sharing memories with Dorothy, and this time a robin did join in. I was pleased I had brought some seed for this bird, one of its kind helped me greatly some years ago.

August started off with a grey partridge at Branston Gravel Pits, this was on the 4th. It had taken me nearly eight months to see my first for the year, but better late than never.

The 7th saw me back at Blithfield, on a rather dull and chilly morning. For a change I decided to enter the reservoir from Watery Lane and drive the shore to the dam. I started off with a very pleasant surprise. In Watery Lane Bay two avocets were wading. Those birds were a complete surprise, they were not a bird regularly seen at Blithfield, so I sat in my car and enjoyed them for a few minutes. Also in the bay were several common terns, they seemed to have found a shoal of small fish as they were diving into the water constantly. A most satisfactory start to the day.

Driving through Portfield Bay a large gull sitting out on a buoy drew my attention. I had my 'scope for such an occasion, and focused up to find I was looking at a fully plumaged adult Caspian gull. I had seen quite a few of those birds this year, they are obviously becoming a regular feature at the larger waters such as here and Carsington. Along with their close relative, the yellow-legged gull, they are very much becoming a British gull and no doubt breeding. Whilst enjoying the gull a common sandpiper came dashing through. Rarely still that bird.

Into Mickledale Bay. I at first thought I had caught up with the common sandpiper again, but when it turned sideways on, I realised I had not. The bird lacked the bright white underparts and the distinctive white wedge visible in front of the wing-bend. This bird was a more generally brown looking bird with dark legs. It also had a dark streaked breast which ended with a sharp edging to the dirty-white breast.

Then it hit me. I was looking at a pectoral sandpiper, a vagrant from across the pond.

I had heard nothing about this bird, so it was a complete surprise to me, and to make it even better, it was the first time I had ever seen one which I found for myself. My few previous sightings had been thanks to other people or at least being told where it was. It was almost as though I was seeing the bird for the first time. Needless to say, I enjoyed the occasion for several minutes, a perfect end to a great day.

A week later and it was Blithfield once more. This was to be a very quick visit, I only had an hour to spare. I was in transit to business in Stoke. I called in at the Admaston Reach car park and had a quick look down Blithe Bay, nothing special to be seen, so I turned my attention to Tad Bay. This was also quiet, and then a large bird of prey flew across—our osprey was back. It glided towards me before it banked and flew back to its roosting tree. A lovely sight of a bird which will always bring back memories.

I then concentrated on the causeway slopes. Two common sandpipers and a knot were quickly picked out, and common terns were feeding in the calm water off the causeway. I crossed over to look down the other side and picked up a small wader running in and out of the water which was softly lapping the slope—it was a sanderling, a juvenile bird. The markings on the back were quite distinctive as were the white lower chest and belly. Stopping off at Blithfield had been a good decision, the bird I missed out on at Tamworth a short while ago, was now in the bag.

The end of the month saw me back at Blacktoft, spoonbills had been reported, a good enough reason for a journey to Yorkshire.

The day was bright and warm, a perfect summer's day as far as I was concerned. All I now needed was the birding to match. On checking things at the visitor centre, I was pleased to learn the spoonbills were actually a family party of five, two adults and three juveniles, and they had been seen well from the Xerox Hide.

No need to ask where I made my way to.

Walking down to the hide I heard Cetti's warblers, but did not see any, and a lesser whitethroat popped out briefly. I was surprised to enter Xerox and find the hide empty, I would have thought that five spoonbills would have drawn the crowd.

The first birds I saw were black-tailed godwits, those were in double figures, birds which had bred further north were now commencing to move back through the UK, on their migration southwards. The odd avocet was in the lagoon, and whilst I was enjoying those, a birder came in the hide and told me the spoonbills were now being seen from Marshland Hide. Sorry avocets, I was off.

There were certainly a few more birders in Marshland, I only just managed to fit myself in. One thing about spoonbills is the fact you do not have to search for them, if they are there, you see them. Five large white birds plodding through the water, swishing their wonderful bills sideways as they do so, are not difficult to see.

It was not obvious what they were catching, but watching their necks, they certainly were swallowing something, and not just water. A magnificent bird, we are very fortunate that they have retuned back to the UK to breed once again.

More black-tailed godwits were to be seen and a water rail made a brief excursion out into the open water. The usual marsh harriers were out over the reed beds along with grey herons, and the avocets were busily feeding, some now having very large young birds. Time was now catching up on me, so I made a quick visit down to the Singleton Hide and here I saw several common snipes and a green sandpiper, plus a distant harrier which I thought may have been the Montagu's. Having seen the bird on previous occasions, whether it was or not was not too important.

That visit brought August to an end, and my yearly total had now reached one hundred and eighty-nine.

September was a disaster month from both a health and birding point of view.

I suffered pain with my leg which meant both driving and walking was most difficult, and the month passed me by. I did at least have one new bird to add to my list, I heard tawny owl calling on two or three occasions, although I did not see the bird.

My problem sorted itself out, the nerves in my leg apparently had caused the problem. The only snag was it could return again, and at any time. Growing old is great!

Back to birding. Early October saw me back at Carsington Water, friends had seen a green-winged teal down Sheepwash. I had a morning free, so a few hours sorting this fellow out, it was a drake apparently, would, hopefully, get me back into the swing of things. September had been a sabbatical, which I had no wish to repeat.

As I arrived in the hide a couple were just leaving, and they had not seen the teal, although I got the impression, they were not experienced birders and the similarities between the bird and our teal do make things a bit difficult.

I settled in to work the area and had brought my 'scope with me. A few teals were to be seen, plus tufted ducks and the inevitable mallards. Curlews were heard and two redshanks came running along the shore before they took off. I had spent many minutes going through every bird I saw and was beginning to give up hope, when round the tip of the spit sailed my bird.

Green-winged teals are a North American species, a rare vagrant to the UK. I have only seen a few. The main difference between this bird and ours is that the drake has a white vertical stripe down the side of the breast. Without this feature, splitting the birds would be very difficult. That day's bird, luckily for me, was a well-marked bird, and needless to say, a 'year tick'.

Although my leg felt fine, I had decided to take things easy for a week or two, so my birding would be done either from the car, or close to it, when hopefully a hide would be convenient, as had been the case at Carsington.

It was back to Blithfield a week or so later, and a drive round the reservoir shore was called for. Between the Watery Lane entrance and the sailing club, a grey phalarope had been reported. As I have mentioned earlier, phalaropes are not regularly seen so far inland, being very much a bird of the sea, so this was a challenge which had to be undertaken.

The southern end of the reservoir was very quiet apart from gulls, as I slowly drove myself round. I did see a common sandpiper and a redshank flew past, its bright white wingbar flashing. No problem on identification there.

Driving into Mickledale Bay I spotted a small bird on the surface of the reservoir, and as I stopped the bird commenced to spin round. No problem here, it was the grey phalarope. I think it was at Eyebrook Reservoir a year or so ago, where I last reported seeing a grey phalarope doing its spinning routine. Bird behaviour is as good an identification feature as plumage or voice, especially when seen at the distance away this bird was.

Two days later a cattle egret was the star attraction, this bird had been reported from Ammington, near Tamworth, by the 'Pretty Pigs'. Not a direct reference to the well-known Tamworth red pigs, it is the name of an inn, behind which is a large lake.

Having worked in Tamworth for some years I knew the area well, so I managed to find myself a suitable parking spot without any trouble, which provided me with a good view of most of the lake and adjoining meadows. The meadows being the likely place for the bird to be, they do not wade as frequently as their cousins, the little egret.

I quickly found a little egret, which I hoped had not been confused as a cattle egret and watched it go about its business for a few minutes, before turning my attention back to dry land. The bird was living up to its name. Walking among a herd of cows, doing exactly as it should be, was the cattle egret. Searching for insects disturbed by the grazing cattle. Unfortunately, there was a rise in the meadow and the egret chose to go behind this, and that was the last I saw of it.

As I had some time still, I drove up to Polesworth, just a short distance away, here I saw three more little egrets and a great white egret. That gave me our three white egrets all within a mile of each other. How things have changed. To see just one of those some years ago you would have travelled miles, as I had, here close to each other, and only ten miles or so away from home, were all three.

Come the end of the month and I decided to make a visit to North Cave. I had not been there for quite some time, and it does get some very good birds. It also has the advantage that you can drive right up to the hide.

Part way up is another hide, and a quick visit in saw a drake garganey, you do not get many of them to the pound. A couple of avocets were also busy and a marsh harrier was flying over. A flock of grey geese came flying in. I was hoping they may be pink-foots, but as they got nearer, I could hear their call—they were grey-lags.

Never mind, skeins of geese of any species are impressive.

I reached the top hide and two birders were leaving as I arrived. I asked the obvious question, the reply to which was no. I entered to find on one else in the hide, as I have suggested many a time, empty hides are not a good sign. At least I was able to pick the best spot in the hide to sit, so it was not all bad.

I set up my 'scope and commenced to pan the lagoon, and it was not all doom and gloom. I counted nine little egrets, four curlews were feeding in the shallows and seven black-tailed godwits were scattered round the lagoon. Shelduck numbers were very good and I was pleasantly surprised with the number of gadwalls to be seen.

Scanning further down the lagoon a large number of lapwings were seen, a few hundred of them, so I slowly started to work through those to see if anything else was tucked in amongst them. Part way through I stopped, I had a few plovers and they did not look like golden plovers. I needed another angle to get a better view, at least I had plenty of choice!

Focusing up once again, I was delighted to see they were grey plovers. They may have been nothing to local birders, they were a bit special for me. There were sixteen of them and a few were still looking very smart with much of their summer plumage remaining. Two or three were juvenile birds, so it was an interesting mixed flock, and importantly for me, a 'year tick'. They closed the month for me. I now have one hundred and ninety-four, the two hundred mark is slowly approaching.

Early November saw me returning to Blacktoft, I had heard that skeins of pink-foots were being seen. Although I have seen them previously, they are a wonderful sight with a mystical call, well worth a visit even if I see little else.

The pink-foots greeted me almost as soon as I arrived. A large skein flew over as I made my way down to the visitor centre, calling as they did so. Talking to a warden in the centre he told me the geese were feeding on a meadow just a short distance from the reserve entrance, and were clearly visible from the road. Additional to this news, I was informed that a white-rumped sandpiper was also on the reserve and was showing well from the Singleton Hide.

White-rumped sandpipers are a rare vagrant in the UK, a North American species, which I have only seen very rarely. Should I see the bird, choosing Blacktoft today was great stroke of luck. Needless to say, I made my way straight down to Singleton's.

I was surprised to find only two or three birders in the hide, for a bird of this rarity I would have expected the hide to be full. Talking to a local birder he told me the bird was only seen late the previous evening, and the report of it had only been released an hour or so ago. The crowds would be arriving soon.

Back to the bird. It was regularly wading out in shallow water on the edge of a small island, which was pointed out to me, so it was just a question of patience.

This was not required for long, the bird appeared within minutes of my arrival and for the next three or four minutes proceeded to feed, fully in the open. Without a doubt, this bird gave me the best views I had ever had of the species. It was a juvenile bird which had been blown across the Atlantic. They are a small wader, slightly smaller than our dunlin, and unlike our commoner small waders, the primaries extend beyond the tail. The back has prominent white edging to the darker feathers, almost white V's, and a distinctive white supercilium. As if wishing to confirm who or what it was, it gave us a short fly-past when the white rump was clearly seen. A most accommodating bird.

I remained in the hide for about an hour, fully enjoying seeing the bird so well, and set off to return to my car for a quick snack and then on for the pink-foots.

Part way down the track I stopped. A male blackbird was behaving most peculiarly. It was calling loudly and kept flying up into a large bush, and then returning back down to the ground, repeating the operation several times. I approached slowly to get a better view, and had a most pleasant surprise. Roosting in the bush was a long-eared owl, the blackbird had obviously found the bird and was doing its best to drive the owl away. The blackbird eventually won, the owl decided enough was enough, and off it flew. I was delighted to have not only seen all of this, the owl was another 'year tick' to add to the sandpiper. Bird behaviour is a fascinating subject in its own right.

Snack over, I drove round to look for the geese. Three or four hundred geese in a field take little finding. What was growing in the meadow I have no idea, possibly winter rape, but whatever it was, the geese were happy enough. Slowly working my way through the birds, I realised they were not all pink-foots, tucked in amongst them were several grey-lags. The geese brought my day to an end, a very enjoyable day too.

The following day, Bonfire Night as it so happened, came in clear and bright which augured well the night time festivities. I went north to Tittesworth. Before calling in at Tittesworth I had my regular drive over Axe Edge Moor, red grouse hunting. They took some finding, but my patience was rewarded when a parry of seven launched themselves from the heather and flew quite close to my parked car.

They at least had escaped the gun.

Driving back down to Tittesworth I saw further grouse plus a pair of ravens, and pulling in to have a look over the River Churnet bridge I caught a glimpse of a dipper, for no more than a couple of seconds I hasten to add.

A coffee, and something warm was called for, and enjoyed. As I walked out, I had a pleasant surprise, meeting up with two birders I knew well. We compared notes, they shot off grouse hunting. I went swan hunting. Off the point, near the centre, they had just seen a herd of sixteen whooper swans, finding them would make my day. They would be my first this year.

You are unlikely to miss sixteen swans, and so it turned out. They were lazily drifting about on the open water, six adults and ten first year birds, no doubt three family groups. A few pairs do now breed in Scotland but the chances were, those birds had come from much further afield. Whatever their origins, I was just delighted to see them, and enjoyed them for many minutes.

Duck numbers were good, especially teals and wigeons, and shelducks were not far behind. Gulls were also plentiful, although those were the expected kind, nothing special as far as I could see.

A very pleasant day out. Time for home, daylight hours in November are not that good.

The 10th was also another bright and clear day, but on this occasion I only had a couple of hours available, so a quick trip across to Cannock Chase would have to suffice.

Driving by the Glacial Boulder, a flock of thrushes flew across and landed in some hawthorns which still had berries on them. I pulled over to see them more clearly, they were a mixed flock of fieldfares and redwings, which were enjoying the berries. I then drove on to Freda's Grave, in the hope something interesting was at the feeders.

The feeders were well stocked and a good selection of birds were in attendance. Long-tailed tits were in double figures and blues, greats and coal tits were not far behind. Two marsh tits caught my attention as they made fleeting visits back and forth, and then I realised my mistake. One of the birds had a pale panel on the wings and a distinct black bib. That bird was no marsh tit, it was a willow tit, a 'year tick', and I nearly missed it. You can never take things for granted in this game.

My trip did not conclude there. Driving back across the Chase a red kite glided past, now that was quite a send-off!

The clear and bright weather continued, so not wishing to miss out on that, I visited Attenborough. For some reason it was very busy, so I just decided to have a quick trip down to the Kingfisher Hide and then I would move on.

The hide was peaceful enough and a goodly selection of ducks were to be seen, and I was working my way through those when I spotted an upturned duck with a long pin-like tail. There is only one surface feeding duck which looks like this—the pintail. It bobbed back up and it was a magnificent drake bird. They are a superb looking bird, not as exotic as say a mandarin, but in the glamour stakes they take some beating, and as that bird was my first for the year, it was more than a bit special.

I managed to get a warm drink and something warm to eat, and as I still had time, I decided I would call in at Blithfield on my way home, just for a quick scan from the causeway.

I arrived to be greeted by very cold weather, so I just sat in my car with the heater running and glanced across the reservoir. The gulls were starting to come in for their evening roost, the usual mixture of black-headed, lesser black-backed, herring and a few great black-backed gulls. Two gulls caught my attention, they were squabbling over the rights to perch on a buoy. One, a lesser black-backed lost, the victor landed on the buoy and I realised it was a large gull, showing no black at all.

Fortunately, I had my 'scope with me, and quickly focused up on the bird. In the UK we only have two large gulls which do not have black primaries, both usually only seen during the winter. The Iceland and the glaucous gull, the largest of those being the glaucous. This bird was large, great black-backed gull size at least, I had dropped on a glaucous gull, what a stroke of luck. They are not a bird I see each year, they are very sporadic, and this one was very special, it was my two hundredth bird of the year. This bird brought back happy memories of cruises off Iceland and Svalbard, where in a day I saw more than I ever would in total in the UK.

A great bird to end my day on.

It was a week before I was able to get out again, and when I did Ogston Reservoir was my destination. A red-throated diver had been reported, and I could come home via Cromford for a bit of hawfinch seeking.

The bright weather had continued, although once again it was rather chilly. It was a very calm day with hardly a ripple on the water, conditions could not have been better,

Duck numbers were not high, but the range was not bad: teals, wigeons, pochards, gadwalls, tufteds, shelducks and the usual mallards. Several great crested and little grebes were to be seen as were cormorants, but where was the bird I was after?

I had my 'scope with me and I brought this into operation. A bird caught my attention over towards the dam, it was diving constantly, and the way it dived, it was no cormorant. After a few minutes I got the view I wanted, it was my red-throated diver. If ever birds were aptly named it is these. I can never accept the American name of loons which some UK field guides have now started to use. My trip up to Derbyshire had been well worthwhile. What would Cromford have on offer?

Cromford on that day was very good. On the large chestnut tree in the car park, four hawfinches were sitting out, it looked like they were thoroughly enjoying the sun, not that I would have sat out, the day was not that warm. Bird's feathers are probably better insulation than any clothes we may wear.

I moved over to the river bridge. A drake goosander was swimming upstream on the Derwent and two grey wagtails were on the adjoining meadow. I could hear goldcrests calling from the yews at the church, not that they were keen to show themselves. High above Willersley Castle two buzzards were soaring, they rose steadily in the sky until they were mere specks, they certainly were not hunting, they were just enjoying themselves. To finish things off on a high, the dipper put in an appearance, it landed on a nearby rock in the river and made several sorties into the river. Quite a display for a few minutes. It ended a most enjoyable day.

My final November birdwatch was a brief visit to Blithfield. I only had an hour or so to spare, so I headed for the dam. It was just before mid-day, so not many gulls were to be seen, they had not started to return for their evening roost. Not a lot was to be seen on the water either, just grebes, cormorants and mallards, so I took a short stroll on the dam.

Here pied wagtails were busy working the parapet and I was also surprised at the number of meadow pipits seen. I was not aware of any insects, so whether the sun was warm enough on the concrete to bring ants out, I do not know, I certainly was not going to investigate and frighten the birds off.

Whilst slowly going through the pipits I noticed one of the birds had very pale underparts and a distinctive pale supercilium, no meadow pipit has those features, but water pipit does. A cracking bird to end the month on, an unexpected 'year tick'.

December commenced with my 'year list' standing at two hundred and two. Was there anything else to find? As events turned out, just one.

On the 2nd I had a trip to Far Ings, on the Humber. I had not been here for some time, so another visit was overdue. As things turned out it was a very quiet visit, not a lot was seen apart from one real piece of quality, a red-necked grebe. They are a large grebe, only the great crested is larger, and they are solely a winter visitor to our shores, when a few cross over from the continent. I always consider it to be the rarest of the grebes seen regularly in the UK, so I was very pleased to see one.

My birding for the remainder of the year was very limited due to one or two problems on the health front. I will not bore you with details.

The year closed on two hundred and three, not a great number, but some real bits of quality, and that is what matters the most. Just to remind you of a few—waxwing, rough-legged buzzard, bean goose, hawfinch, velvet scoter, scaup, great white egret, crane, short-eared owl, great grey shrike, garganey, osprey, bittern, Montagu's harrier, bee-eater, pectoral sandpiper, spoonbill, green-winged teal, grey phalarope, cattle egret, white-rumped sandpiper, long-eared owl and the red-necked grebe mentioned earlier. Enough there to keep the most serious of birders happy.

Next year sees me complete my eightieth year of birdwatching, which will also be the final chapter in this book. Come along and join me as I see what this last year has in store. We will take each bird as it comes, the commonplace and the rare, they will all get a mention.

CHAPTER XI
THE FINAL YEAR.
EIGHTY YEARS OF BIRDING JOY

The previous pages in this narrative have all been memories in a way, talking of things that have happened, recalling memorable moments, of both sadness and joy.

Now let us look at the present and see it as it actually happens.

Before we start, Happy New Year. We are off on our annual bird race, Sarah and Martin have sorted out their route, I have done my own. But before we move off, what did we see in the garden. My first bird of the year was a rook, followed by blackbird, magpie, long-tailed tit, dunnock, starling, woodpigeon, carrion crow, blue tit, great tit, coal tit, chaffinch, robin, greenfinch and bullfinch. Fifteen in total. A good start there I think.

Now I am off, and down to the layby at Kings Bromley, you have heard mention of here on many an occasion. Today I have mallard, black-headed gull, mute swan, buzzard and jackdaw. Moving on to Croxall Lakes I pick up great crested grebe, and driving on to Catton, collect a pheasant, this one a bit special, it is a full albino. Whitemoor Haye is next and here I have coot, tufted duck, Canada goose, great white egret (that's a bit special on day one), raven, lesser black-backed gull, golden plover, another bird of quality, lapwing and wigeon. Blithfield adds goldeneye, cormorant and teal and Dunstall signs off with grey-lag goose. Not a great start with numbers, only thirty-five birds seen, but two were of quality, the great white egret and specially so. I beat Sarah and Martin by one.

All of those birds were seen within a ten-mile radius of home, which just emphasises the fact you do not need to travel miles to see birds. You never know what you may find on your own doorstep, unless you look.

I am at home all day on the 2nd, but I add goldfinch and house sparrow to the list, and on the 3rd, I manage to call in at Barton Marina where I pick up moorhen and pochard.

My next free day is Friday 5th January, I have a couple of hours available here, so come with me. Calling in at Barton Marina again we see a little grebe, driving down to Croxall we have a mistle thrush and Whitemoor Haye comes up with yellowhammer, tree sparrow and song thrush. We then drive on to Blithfield, calling in at the Kings Bromley layby first, here we see three little egrets, Blithfield coming up with a great black-backed gull.

The weekend lies ahead so we can go further afield, and Saturday takes us to Blacktoft. Unfortunately, the water levels are very high and waders are non-existent, but we pick up a wren, grey heron, Cetti's warbler, shelduck, marsh harrier and Bewick's swan, and we also break the fifty mark—fifty-two in fact. It had been my intention to go into Derbyshire on Sunday but a telephone call changes all of that. An adult, winter, great northern diver is at Chasewater, you cannot miss out on a bird like that so close to home. Chasewater, here we come. It does not take long to find the diver, it is just off the dam and showing well. We also have goosander and herring gull, so it is well worth the visit.

Monday 8th January, sees me out with the Rosliston Birders, we are at Blithfield, and the prime birds seen are nuthatch, shoveler, oystercatcher and little owl. On the 9th, as I drive into Burton-on-Trent I see collared doves at Woodhouses, and on the 10th, whilst out on business, I see a kestrel at Alrewas, and a gadwall at Barton Marina.

On the 12th I have a free afternoon, come and join me at the JCB lake in Rocester, bring some bread if you wish to feed the collection ducks. On the wild front we see a good flock of barnacle geese, twenty-three of them, a ruddy shelduck flies in, no argument about him being an escapee, it was a drake, and two common gulls join in the fun.

On getting home I learn of a large flock of hawfinches being reported from Darley Dale, in Derbyshire. There has been a large movement of hawfinches into the UK this winter, a much greater influx than for many a year. These birds have moved down from Scandinavia, where conditions must have been very bad. Although I see hawfinches most years, to see a large number together is an event not to be missed.

The 13th sees me off to Darley Dale, the birds have been reported from the churchyard, so if that is where they remain, I should have no difficulty in finding them. About a dozen birders are congregated by the church and I quickly learn the birds are being seen frequently, and at times they are well into double figures. I am used to seeing them singularly or at best in lower single figures.

I quickly pick up the odd bird and it is not long before a flock flies into a nearby yew tree, vanishing into its thick foliage. After a short time they emerge, and I am able to count sixteen birds, that single group probably exceeds the total number of hawfinches I have seen in a single year. I remain at Darley Dale for a good hour enjoying these birds, and a great spotted woodpecker also appears regularly. A very good morning that.

The 14th and I am driving through Dunstall where I see a small flock of linnets, and a merlin flies across the lane in front of me.

The 15th, and I am back out with the Rosliston Birders, well three of them, the numbers are reducing rapidly. I am beginning to think we have come to the end of the road. At Whitemoor Haye we have a small herd of whooper swans and at Catton Park we see stock dove and redwing. Whilst here we see several totally black pheasants, not one, several, I would be most interested in learning the whys and wherefores of this. I have seen single black or very dark pheasants, but never eight, as this turns out to be. This illustrates the fact that it is not just the rare that is of interest, the unusual is equally so.

Come the 19th and Tittesworth calls, where an adult Mediterranean gull gives a good display and a small flock of redwings are active on some bushes which still contain a few berries. Not for long I think, judging how the redwings are going at them.

The following day, I travel further afield, North Cave in Yorkshire being my destination. Things here are very quiet, although I do manage to get green woodpeckers, three of them, a small flock of bramblings at one of the feeders, and a solitary redshank flies across. On my way home, I call in at the Doncaster Services on the M18 and add pied wagtail to my list, which incidentally, has now reached seventy-eight. I am back local on the 21st, seeing fieldfare at Catton Park.

For the next five days I do no birding being otherwise engaged, but on the 26th I have a quick trip out to JCB at Rocester where I see four red-crested pochards, two pairs and all fully fledged. I have no idea where they have come from, just happy to see them. The following day I am driving through Checkley and have a very pleasant surprise. A peregrine falcon is sitting out on some overhead wires, and we just stare each other out for two or three minutes before the falcon becomes bored with it all, and flies off. The 28th sees me on Cannock Chase where I see another bird of prey, this time a sparrowhawk. She, it being the female, is not as interested in me as the falcon had been, she just flies through. January ends up on eighty-two, not a great start.

On the 1st February I am back at JCB, Rocester, where a small flock of five Egyptian geese are parading. The 2nd sees me on Axe Edge Moor red grouse hunting, successfully I am pleased to add, followed by a male hen harrier at Swallow Moss later in the day. Whilst driving to visit friends on the 3rd, a jay flies across the road in front of me, this is at Drakelow, and I duly thanked him.

The 8th produces some real excitement. For a few days a pair of cattle egrets have been seen near to Newton Solney. I get hold of the full details, and know exactly where to go. I drive across and find a parking spot by a gate into a field, which is only the matter of a few yards away from the meadow in which the egrets have been regularly feeding among a flock of sheep. The sheep are there, many of them, but where are the egrets? After a few minutes I move my location slightly which brings me by a track which runs down the edge of the field. It has a small hedge running along it, and there are the two cattle egrets. Thanks to the hedge they were not visible from where I had originally stood, they are now. I stand still so as not to disturb them, and they carry on feeding, eventually making their way through the hedge and back into the field amongst the sheep. They slowly make their way across the meadow until they vanish over a brow, and that is the last I see of them. I am more than happy with that, I have seen them for a good quarter of an hour.

I may have mentioned this before, if so, bear with me. Cattle egrets are being seen on a more regular basis, not common by any means, and the first few pairs have commenced to breed in the UK. That now means our three white egrets, the little, great white and cattle, are all breeding here, no doubt this is due to climate change, our winters are warmer and shorter, birds which were once only visitors to our islands are now able to survive as a resident species. This is fine in one respect, new creatures always attract interest, the only problem is native species are having to move north, and we will lose many much loved species. If this was just due to evolution, it would be acceptable, unfortunately it is not, it is solely our influence which is causing these great changes. Are we too late to alter things? I believe we are.

The 10th sees me at Attenborough, which is remarkably quiet. A few birds already seen this year, but one bright spot does occur. From the Kingfisher Hide I see water rail on three or four occasions, very accommodating for a secretive bird.

The 11th and I am back at JCB where the free flying cape shelduck, puts on a good display, the barnacle geese flock are also here today, and to cap things, a pair of mandarins fly in.

It is almost a week before I see anything new, and this was not thanks to a birding trip. I was driving through Draycott-in-the-Clay and had to slow down, a covey of red-legged partridges, were crossing the road, seven of them, and they were in no hurry. Luckily for them, neither was I!

The following day it was back to serious birding, and Albert Village Lake was my destination. I parked up where I could see the gulls flying in from the local landfill site. I got out of my car just as a birder walked up from the lake. 'Are you after the diver?' he asked. I was not, but I sure am now. A black-throated diver was on the lake, so I was very pleased I had my 'scope and tripod with me, it really was serious birding now.

From my position I am looking down on the lake, quite a distance below in fact. Many gulls were on the water, the usual mix I at first thought, not that my interest was directed at them specifically. The lake has an island which obstructs your view somewhat, but today it was no problem. After a matter of just minutes, from beyond the island swam the diver, and for several minutes it provided perfect views thanks to having the 'scope. It dived on a few occasions, did not appear to catch anything, and slowly returned behind the island, not to be seen again.

Back to concentrating on the gulls. The usual black-headed, lesser black- backed, great black-backed, herring and a few common gulls were to be seen. Whilst casually glancing at these, a large gull flew towards me, which I initially thought to be a herring gull, but as it flew overhead, I realised it did not have black primaries. A herring gull it certainly was not, it was an Iceland gull. I watched it continue its journey to the landfill site. It gave me two superb birds for the day, both of which were complete surprises.

My next two trips out were local and these gave me meadow pipits down Whitemoor Haye and a southern cormorant at Blithfield.

The 24th and I was back to the serious stuff, and Blacktoft again called. I had been told that the first of the avocets had returned, so that was a good enough reason to visit.

When I arrived and spoke with a warden, the news was not accurate, but I was there, so let us see what I could find. Walking down to the hides I was pleased to hear goldcrests calling and quickly located five of them. They may not have been avocets, but they are a delightful little bird, little being the operative word, They are the smallest bird breeding in the UK.

As I approached the Xerox Hide rain started to fall, and it quickly commenced to fall heavily. Fortunately, it was sideways on to the hide so it did not come in through the viewing slits, so I could birdwatch without rain on my optics. Not a lot was happening, however. Teals and wigeons were roosting up on the islands, a few gadwalls, pochards, shelducks and mallards were on the water, and that was about it.

The rain appeared to be easing off so I moved onto the Marshland Hide. Here things were more interesting. I had not been in the hide long before two bearded tits flew along the edge of the reed bed and a water rail called. I was very pleased to see the bearded tits as last year I drew a blank on them. Two little egrets were also on the edge of the reeds and a grey heron flew in to join them.

The weather started to change for the worst once again so I decided to call it a day. Walking back to my car, the bird of the day as far as I was concerned flew over, well eleven of them did to be accurate, calling as they flew—curlews. As you know these are my favourite bird, and vocally there is no other bird which can compete, rain or no rain, I stood and watched their progress. They gave me three 'year ticks' for the day, the avocets can wait another day.

The month ended with my seeing four siskins in my own garden, always a delight to see and a skylark seen down the rough lane at Whitemoor Haye, and he gave me my one hundredth bird of the year. Not a great total, but it did have some quality among it.

I am at Blithfield on March 2nd and here I get a good start to the month. I am standing on the dam as a large gull landed on the dam wall, an adult yellow-legged gull, and a smart looking bird it was too. Adult gulls are normally tidy looking birds, I suppose it is the amount of white in their plumage, and spending so much of their time in water obviously helps them to stay clean.

A couple of days later I am near the National Memorial Arboretum enjoying listening to the Cetti's warbler, when I happened to look over the arboretum. A large bird of prey was gliding across, first thoughts a buzzard. As it got closer, I began to get more excited, the bird had a decided kink in its wings, could this be a rough-legged buzzard? As it banked slightly, I could see the tail clearly, only one buzzard had a white tail with a dark terminal band, it was most certainly a rough-legged buzzard. This is a bird never on your anticipated list. They are a scarce winter visitor to the UK from Scandinavia, a most definite case of the right time, right place bird. I wished it well for a safe journey home.

It was another week before I was able to do any birding, and this was just a quick call in at Whitemoor Haye, but it turned out well worth it. I was standing, looking over the lake, when the call all birders recognise, and wait to hear, rang out. A chiffchaff was calling, my first summer migrant of the year was letting me know it had arrived. I slowly made my way towards the piece of hedge he was calling from, I wanted to both see and hear my first migrant. After a few minutes I did, he kindly hopped out and sat on the top of a bush, called a few notes, and vanished again.

Thank you *Phylloscopus collybita*, I am showing off a bit here, only because it is one of the few scientific names I know!

Six days later and I am back at JCB. Not much change on the water front, but I did see the mandarins and red-crested pochards again, you can never have too much of a good thing

Driving back from Rocester, I picked up a bird of prey flying low over a field, and I managed to pull in at a gate. I was very pleased I had, the bird was a red kite.

We are seeing these birds more frequently, although I have not had all that many in Staffordshire. As I have said before, they are a wonderful flying machine and I was able to enjoy this bird for several minutes before it vanished in the direction of the Uttoxeter Quarry.

From Uttoxeter I made my way up to Tittesworth Water to both have my lunch and see what was about on the bird front. The lunch was, as normal, very pleasant, but unfortunately, whilst having it the weather changed and down came the rain. Birding was now off the agenda, but I did manage to have a few minutes near to the bird feeders, where there was at least some activity.

Titmice were busy, mainly blues and greats, and the occasional chaffinch came in, but not a lot really. I was thinking of moving on when I had a pleasant surprise, a marsh tit flew in. It did not hang round for long, and although I waited for many minutes, it did not return. I was happy, thanks to it and the kite I had two 'year ticks', and the weather cannot take that away.

A week later and I was again visiting Blacktoft, the avocets were back, or some were. The weather was pleasant too, so I may get a full day in. As I approached the entrance to the reserve, I spotted a small group of partridges in a field, and was able to draw in to have a good view of them. I was pleased I had, it was six grey partridges, they obviously had not commenced to breed yet. A perfect start to my day.

I confirmed the news regarding the avocets, they had commenced to return and were best seen from the Marshland Hide. I made my way straight there, just stopping to listen to a Cetti's warbler which had no intention of showing itself.

From the hide I saw nine avocets, some of which were busy feeding, probing their long bills deep into the water. The odd redshank was to be seen and the usual little egrets were dotted about, five of them to be precise, and a scattering of ducks were on the water. Grey-lag geese could be heard from deep in the reed beds, but were not visible

Moving on towards the Singleton Hide, I paused, a bittern was booming. For a few seconds the sound echoed round, no mistaking this fellow. Even if I do not see him, to just hear it is a wonderful occasion.

There are four birds where the sound is sufficient, they are the bittern, Cetti's warbler, nightingale and nightjar, all with distinctive voices, and heard more often than seen.

I arrived in Singleton just in time to see a male marsh harrier flying off with a catch, a moorhen by the look of things, his mate was going to have a good lunch that was for sure.

Two birders in the hide mentioned the bittern, apparently it had called from the reed bed in front of the hide, but had not been seen. I had time, so I settled in to wait. A couple of avocets landed in the lagoon and strutted their stuff for a few minutes, and a small flock of curlews flew across. Grey herons were feeding in the lagoon and two little egrets were squabbling over something, what it was I have no idea. It could have been two males having a territory dispute.

A marsh harrier came in and landed in the reed bed and this bird did me a great favour. He landed where the bittern had obviously been hiding, making the bittern run out of the reeds into open water, providing a wonderful view of the bird.

It only lasted seconds before it was back, and hidden away, amongst the reeds. I was happy, as were my fellow birders.

The odd few pink-foots had been flying over the reserve, so after lunch I drove down to the corner from where I saw the pink-foots recently. Today it was not pink-foots, a flock of swans were in the field, and these birds were very straight necked, they were whoopers, thirty-three of them. It will not be long before they are on their way north to breed. Whooper swans are the largest migrant bird we see in the UK, and it is claimed they fly non-stop from places such as Iceland to the UK. For a bird of their size and weight, that is some accomplishment, they are the jumbo jet of the bird world. They brought a great day's birding to its conclusion.

The following day a quick visit to Blithfield was called for. A friend had phoned in the information a little stint was showing well in Watery Lane Bay, definitely worth a few minute's effort.

I did not park up in the Watery Lane car park, I drove into the reservoir as I had taken my 'scope, which I could use from the car. Two redshanks were in the bay and a large flock of grey-lags were also in and around the bay. No chance of getting out of the car with the geese being so close, they would instantly fly off, taking everything else with them. Fortunately, I had my windows wound down, so I settled in to work the shore line.

Little stint are the smallest wader we see regularly in the UK and they cannot wade in deep water, they are a shore bird in every sense of the word. A movement in a small pool caught my attention, and there it was, the little stint. That had not taken much effort, so I was able to just sit and watch it go about its business. It fed very actively, frequently dashing off after some flying insect or other. I enjoyed the bird for several minutes before driving off. Not wishing to disturb the birds, I carried on round the reservoir to the dam, and exited from there. I saw little as I drove round, but the stint was more than enough.

The final day of March saw me at Eyebrook Reservoir, in Leicestershire. I had heard that a drake smew had been there for a few days, they are a scarce winter visitor to the UK. They breed in the far north in boreal forest areas, apparently using tree holes and the old nesting holes of the black woodpecker.

They are a superbly marked bird, and although being only black and white, an artist put them together, a diving duck, and a member of the group of ducks known as sawbills. This is due to the fact their bills have a tooth-like cutting edge which enables them to grip their prey easily. Another bird fit for purpose.

Anyway, let us get back to Eyebrook. No birders were seen so I was having to do it all myself, but my luck was in. I pulled in at the car parking area at Stoke Dry and almost the first bird I saw was the smew, it was as though the bird had come to see me. It is not often you see your target bird so easily and quickly, and was he active! The smew was diving and moving through at speed. I doubt I saw it for more than five minutes before he vanished round a point in the reservoir, never to be seen again. Had I arrived ten minutes or so later I would never have known the bird was still there. They do say you win some, you lose some, I had certainly won.

I drove down the side of the reservoir towards the bridge over the Eyebrook, and here I spotted some waders on the edge of a shallow pool. I pulled in and was pleased to see they were common snipes, a tidy flock of sixteen birds. A flock of that size at this time of the year probably meant they were on passage further north to breed. Our local breeding snipe would have been paired up by now I would have thought.

I had a quick drive round to Rutland Water to see if the ospreys were back, if they were they were not showing, and made my way home. A very successful day, and the month closed on one hundred and eleven.

April sees the commencement of the arrival of our summer returning migrants, plus the odd bird of passage travelling to destinations further north, and not necessarily in the UK, some of these birds are Arctic bound. Come with me as we chase these down.

The 1st, at Tittesworth Water, we see a scaup, a superb-looking drake. He is on passage, probably off to Norway where they breed. You will probably recollect my talking about them on cruises to that country. I wished him luck on his travels. My prime reason for visiting Tittesworth had been the fact an osprey had been reported, if so, he was not here now.

The 3rd produces a corn bunting down Whitemoor Haye, they are a resident species of course, but over the lake are some true migrants—sand martins have arrived—about twenty of them. Summer approaches, not quite here, sand martins are among the earliest birds to return, I often joke you cannot talk about summer until the cuckoo arrives.

The 6^{h} and the bird most local birders await, the osprey, is back at Blithfield Reservoir. For several years now we have had at least one pass through on its way to Scotland, although who knows, now they are breeding in Wales the bird could well be Welsh, not Scottish. Either way, it is more than welcome. Today I did not see it fishing at all. It flew round on one occasion, the remainder of the time it just sat in its roosting tree, where very good views were obtained. The weather was good so the bird was probably quite happy just sitting out in the sun, especially if it had fed earlier.

Come the 7th, Summer may well be closer, a swallow, note a swallow, not swallows, is down Whitemoor Haye. What is it thy say about one swallow does not...

Making my way from the Haye to Croxall I walk into real excitement. For some reason I walk across the road to look into the meadow in front of Broadfields Farm and cannot believe my eyes. Striding across the meadow is a white stork, looking for food in the various puddles lying on the meadow. A quick phone call is made, Sarah is at home and I am sure she would like to see the bird, she does, and quickly arrives on the scene. Storks move very elegantly on their long, thin legs, and we enjoy this bird for many minutes, watching it going about its business, before Sarah has to leave. I enjoy the bird for a little longer before I go on my travels.

Blithfield is my next call. Not a lot going on today, although I hear and see my first blackcap of the year, so that is worth the visit. On my way home I stop by Hoar Cross church where I see a treecreeper working its way up an old oak stump. Not a summer migrant, they are residents, but it is the first of the year for me.

The 8th and two more migrants are seen, a willow warbler at Croxall Lakes and a house martin down the Haye. I have a particular affection for willow warblers, delightful little birds always full of song, you hear them more frequently than you see them. They are a true sound that summer is imminent.

The following day sees me at Carsington, and here things are very quiet which does surprise me. The feeders by the hide, however, compensate me somewhat. A willow tit is a regular visitor to the feeders, so I am able to sit down and thoroughly enjoy it. Willow tits are the scarcest of the titmice found in England, so to be able to enjoy one for so long is well worth the trip on its own. On my return journey I call in at Blithfield, a few sand martins and swallows are feeding over the water, and on the dam embankment I see a white wagtail. They are very similar to our pied wagtail, but are a European species, and are the nominate species, our pied being a sub-species, which is normally only found in the UK. When you holiday on the continent and believe you have seen pied wagtails, they will have been white wagtails. The bird I see would, hopefully, make its way back over the Channel and join its true companions.

Down Whitemoor Haye on the 12th, I have a very pleasant surprise. I am studying a herd of mute swans feeding in a field, and as I slowly pan through these I suddenly find myself looking at a crane. Needless to say, I promptly stop. The bird is slowly moving across the field, continuously probing with its powerful bill into the ground. Even though swans are large birds, the crane with its long legs and neck is towering above them. Some bird.

Over the past few days, we have hit the jackpot locally. A white stork at Croxall and now a crane down the Haye, these two very special birds have been seen less than a mile apart with only five days separating them. I certainly have not driven miles to see these two wonderful birds.

The 13th sees me back at Blithfield. Where I see yellow wagtails, seven of them, plus my first little ringed plover of the year, and the crane is still down Whitemoor Haye.

The following day my daughter receives call from my photographer friend, Andy Toman, he could not believe his eyes, he has just witnessed a stork flying over his home, and was phoning in to let me know about it. Sarah is able to tell him he was not imagining it all, we have seen one recently down at Croxall, the bird is obviously still in the area, as Andy only lives a short distance away. Whilst all of this is going on I am at Dunstall where I am enjoying watching a lesser spotted woodpecker going about its business. They are very active little birds who spend their time high in the trees, so this was a rather neck straining operation, but worth the 'pain'. I see very few lesser spots a year, so when I do, I try to make the most of it.

The 15th and I am at Tucklesholme watching a Caspian gull harassing the local black-headed gulls, they do not appreciate its attention that is for sure. The gulls had commenced to breed so I presume the Caspian gull is egg stealing.

A day on the moors is called for, so the 16th sees me chasing pied flycatchers and ring ouzels, will I be successful? Come and join me to see. My first port of call is Bearda Hill Woods, here the pied flycatchers breed, have they arrived this year? After about fifteen minutes—yes, they have, well at least three males have. I hear them calling initially but eventually, thanks to not a lot of leaf cover as yet, I pick out three separate males. They are busily feeding away, chasing after early flying insects, they are not called flycatchers without good reason! On now to Dane Bower for the ring ouzels.

Driving through Blackshaw Moor I am accompanied for a short

distance by a goshawk which is flying in the same direction, and at over forty miles an hour according to my speedometer. I think this bird was a racing goshawk. Quite a spectacle, pity it only lasts briefly.

I pull in at the Chimney layby, having it all to myself, and settle in to wait. I quickly hear ring ouzel calling, but cannot locate the bird. Whilst looking I see meadow pipits and red grouse, and hear skylarks, so I have plenty to occupy my mind. Then, a dark bird flits across some open ground and lands on a grassy bank. I have my ouzel, a superb male which starts to hunt for insects on the short grass. I can only but presume he is lucky as he shortly flies off and vanishes into the hillside, probably off to feed his mate.

A very successful trip, and crossing Axe Edge Moor I see a merlin flash through and two buzzards are circling up on high, not a bad conclusion to a cracking day out. Hope you think so too.

The 18th sees me back at Blithfield again, and a bit of a passage is occurring. Several Arctic terns are seen during the morning, a single little gull puts in a brief appearance, a definite case of 'now you see him, now you don't', and three common sandpipers are racing along the shoreline, which is how they normally behave.

Yellow wagtails are in double figures and one white wagtail is seen. In Stansley Wood several willow warblers can be heard, plus a solitary chiffchaff.

The following day I am back at Blithfield where the first of the common terns has arrived back home. Unlike the Arctic terns, which just pass through on their journey further north, the common terns do breed here. The first ringed plovers of the year have also arrived, a day or so later than their close relatives, the little ringed plovers, which have been here now for a few days. I think I had better mention the date, the 19th April, because summer has arrived!

That afternoon I am on Cannock Chase when I hear my first cuckoo of the year, but not just one. I actually see and hear at least three, the best day I have had for cuckoos for many a year. Hearing them calling is my favourite sound of summer, a nightingale may be more musical, but a cuckoo heralds summer, and three of them may mean a cracking summer. Time will tell on that one.

Astronomers have had a good time. Venus is showing bright and clearly in the night time sky at present, I was even taken out to enjoy it myself. Sarah and Martin are keen. But back to my love—the birds.

The 20th sees me down Whitemoor Haye seeking out warblers, and I do well.

Along with willow warblers, chiffchaffs and blackcaps already seen, in the space of less than twenty yards and a time of five minutes, I have both whitethroat and lesser whitethroat showing themselves. It is not often that happens. The afternoon sees me back at Blithfield where three little terns are to be seen and in Stansley Wood I hear and see my first wood warbler, he being my one hundred and fortieth bird of the year.

The remainder of April sees me picking up sedge warbler at Attenborough, black tern and swift at Blithfield and I end the month with garden warbler on Cannock Chase. April has not been a bad month, I close on one hundred and forty-four. Now May, what lies ahead, apart from my becoming eighty-five years old, but more of that when it happens.

Before becoming involved with May, I would like to talk to you about bird behaviour. On the 12th April I became conscious of a male blackbird attacking my study windows. I did not think much about it until a few days later when I realised it was a daily event, and repeated several times a day. I will not comment on the state of my windows, I am just pleased I have a window cleaner.

This continued for a fortnight, and then a female blackbird appeared on the scene, and within two days the male stopped attacking my windows. I began to think about this and I am of the opinion that the male blackbird had chosen my garden as part of his territory, and seeing the reflection of himself in the windows, attacked this believing it to be another male bird, and competition. Once a female arrived and the bird had her all to himself, no other bird competing, the attacks stopped. I was pleased about that, so was my window cleaner, but I was disappointed that after all of this, the birds did not nest in my garden, my garden has just become their larder!

The month commences with my calling in at Croxall Lakes where I am pleased to report the reed warblers have finally arrived. Always a cheerful bird to hear, you rarely see them, but they are quite vocal fortunately. The afternoon I am on the Chase and here I see and hear one of our most attractive migrants, the redstart, a very colourful, small bird. I then journey over to JCB at Rocester where I pick up a bar-headed goose.

The 5th sees me on a bit of a 'twitch'. Dotterel have been reported near to Blacktoft Sands, so I call in at Blacktoft to ascertain their exact location. Whilst there I see a grasshopper warbler, I would have loved to have said I also heard it, but they have moved out of my hearing range. I often joke that to hear one again I would have to be standing on it whilst it screamed for help! I can see this bird's bill going, but cannot not hear a sound. I think they call it age! I have a bit of luck as well. The Montagu's harrier also flies through, normally if you wish to see this bird you have to be prepared to spend some time, it is rather nice to think the bird has come to see me. Back to dotterels. They are in a field at Swinefleet, right on the side of the A161, so finding them should be no problem, and it is not.

Five cars are parked on the side of the road and several birders have their telescopes pointing into a field. I drive up and walk across to them, one quickly calls me across to his 'scope, and there they are. Some are looking distinctly summery as they are moulting through into their summer plumage. Dotterel are similar to phalaropes in the fact the female is more attractively plumed than the male and the male is responsible for incubation and care of the young. If you believe in an afterlife, and you are male, do not come back as a phalarope or dotterel! There are fourteen dotterels visible, and this one group is larger than all the dotterels I have previously seen added together. I spend a good half an hour enjoying these birds, I will never see so many again. What a day!

Dotterel, when seen in England, are usually birds of passage. A few may breed in northern England on occasion, but the few British breeding pairs are mainly to be found in Scotland. These birds today could easily be travelling even further north than Scotland. The near Arctic. I am just pleased they decided to spend some time in Yorkshire.

The 12th May arrives, my eighty-fifth birthday. After opening cards and gifts, to help celebrate, I take myself off to Little Paxton where I hope the nightingales and turtle doves will join me in celebration. They are in no rush to, but eventually a nightingale breaks the silence, and that wakes one or two more up, so I am able to sit and enjoy their refrain. Some songster. Their power and clarity is unsurpassed, well among our birds most certainly. The turtle doves however, are not in celebratory mode, but cuckoos certainly are. I do not know exactly how many cuckoos I hear and see, many could just have been repeats, but I thought I had done well on the Chase, Little Paxton is in another league. Garden warblers and blackcaps are also very vocal, and in goodly numbers too. As I am making my way back to my car a dove flies across the pathway, vanishing into a thick bush, but starts to purr away—I have my turtle dove. I may have only seen him fleetingly, but he puts on a good vocal performance. Not a bad birthday at all, and I have a bottle of malt at home, this having been one of my birthday presents!

The next day I am back to local birding, on Cannock Chase. Warblers are very vocal, blackcaps and garden warblers especially so. We have good numbers in, and a cuckoo is also letting vent to his feelings. A bird of prey comes flashing through, a hobby, and its arrival quietens down things for a while. The bird, a male as it so happens, sat in a tree for a few minutes, much to my pleasure, but not the local small bird population.

Thinking of the cuckoo. A non-birding friend of mine recently commented on the fact I frequently referred to a singing bird as him, why not her? A good point, but with the very odd exception only the males sing, they do this to either attract a female or to announce they are holding territory and other males beware. Male birds will fight over both territory and females, but most of this is show or vocal, although in a few cases fights can end in serious injury or either death. Robins, which are the most territorial of birds, are one of the few which sing all year and will fight fiercely.

Female birds, on the other hand, have a range of calls as their means of communication, which males also have, they do not only sing.

The 18th sees me over at Stauton Harold Reservoir. Just off the dam are a large number of hirundines, sand martins especially so, and the common tern population is good. The bird which draws my attention is a male grey wagtail. This bird is collecting food and flying off towards the dam with it. Mid-May is probably a little early for it to be feeding young, but it most certainly could be feeding a female on the nest. Either reason, the bird is working hard.

On the way home I call in at the Kings Bromley layby, and here I really do hit the jackpot. A kingfisher flies past and lands on an overhanging branch, from where it proceeds to dive into the river. After four or five dives it came up with a fish which it hammers on the branch to stun, and then flies off with it. As with the grey wagtail earlier, food was being taken to a nest I presume.

Time for my annual visit to Bempton, and the 19th was an almost perfect day weatherwise. Although my journey up is trouble free for a Saturday, on my arrival I find Bempton to be very busy indeed. Fortunately, when I show my blue badge I am shepherded round to a parking area nearer the shop and café, so my walking is reduced somewhat.

I slowly make my way down to the cliff tops, glad of the benches provided, and settle down to study the birds. As I have said previously, this is a bird city, and you do not have to walk miles to see most of the species. You can if you wish, for the nimbler, enjoy a pleasant cliff top walk and you frequently meet walkers who have little or no interest in the birds.

Let us run through the birds in the sequence I see them. Firstly, are the gannets, these wonderful birds just come gliding past like a white glider, hardly a flap of their wings, a truly amazing sight. Kittiwakes are everywhere, their call 'kitti-wak, kitti-wak', rings out, you do not need to ask where their name originates from, and the cliff ledges are full of their nests. Puffins, I am pleased to say, seem more plentiful this year than recent times, and talking to a volunteer warden, he confirmed that numbers are higher this year. Long may that continue. Razorbills are sitting out on the ledges, looking very smart in the day's sunlight. A few shags are out at sea, mainly single birds, their mates no doubt incubating on the nests. Fulmars are just gliding past showing their complete mastery of the air, and guillemots are lined up on their nests along the ledges. Rock doves are flying along the cliffs as are many feral pigeons, at times making identification very difficult. Sandwich terns are out at sea seeking food, they do not breed here at Bempton.

Finally, a couple of rock pipits are having a bit of an argument, over what I have no idea, but they look as though they mean it, two males obviously, probably arguing over either a female or territory rights. Eleven new species seen, and many thousands of birds in total. I did call it a bird city. A great day, hope you also enjoyed it, and like me will want to return.

The 25th saw me back at Attenborough, where the bird of the day for me was a greenshank, my first of the year. Little ringed plovers were very active and they looked as though they may be feeding young. Egyptian geese certainly had young, five goslings were on the water, and a drake red-crested pochard graced the scene. Common terns were on the tern rafts, where nesting was obviously taking place.

On my return journey home, I called in at Blithfield. Here a large number of swifts were to be seen, all flying low over the surface. An emergence of flies had obviously taken place and the swifts were not going to miss out on this. They were flying that low their wing tips were barely missing the water. Some sight.

My final bird watch was on the 26th, and I thought it was about time I got the dipper on my list. I decided to visit Cromford, and if need be, wait until I saw one.

The day was bright and warm, so any waiting would be comfortable. I arrived at the bridge just in time to see a drake goosander fly off downstream, and a male grey wagtail was chasing flies on the river bank, and he seemed to be doing well. Eventually he flew off with a beak full, some young birds had their breakfast in transit.

I did not have to wait long for my dipper, a bird came flying down the river to land on a rock near to the bridge. For a few seconds I watched the bird bobbing and then it dropped into the water, came out shortly afterwards with something wriggling in its bill, and off it shot. As with the grey wagtail, some birds were about to be fed.

I gave it another ten minutes or so, the dipper did not return, so, as I had plenty of time available, I decided to go back into Staffordshire and visit Tittesworth and Bearda Hill.

Tittesworth Water was my first stop, initially to feed the inner man, prior to a stroll down to the River Churnet. The walk down was most pleasant, warblers were very vocal, and on the river, I saw my second dipper of the day, albeit rather fleetingly. A bullfinch caught my attention, and apart from enjoying him, he also brought me a bonus.

A small bird flicked out of the tree above his head, caught a passing insect, and was back in among the foliage of the tree—a spotted flycatcher. A bench was conveniently placed, so I spent several minutes watching the bird going about its business. It flew from the tree several times, not always successfully, but his catch ratio was very good. This bird was no novice. My second 'tick' of the day was in the bag.

Now for Bearda Hill. I am normally here for the pied flycatchers, but as you will remember, I saw those here, last month, not that a repeat will go amiss. The drive to Bearda was uneventful, a buzzard and a pair of ravens being the pick of the birds seen.

The wood at Bearda was full of song, including a wood warbler, this was only the second I had heard or seen this year, that alone was worth the trip. Pied flycatchers were very active, and it was very noticeable I only saw males, the females were no doubt otherwise occupied.

I dove down to where the woodland is more open, and here I heard a tree pipit singing. I quickly located him, and for several minutes enjoyed seeing and hearing him. Pipits work at their song, they do not just sit out and warble. A cuckoo called a couple of times in the background, but he was not seen.

The pipit brought the day to its conclusion, three 'year ticks' obtained and the month closes on one hundred and seventy. We are progressing steadily.

June comes in bright and warm, the forecasters are promising a warm summer, I could have told them that, remember my cuckoos in April? The only disappointment is the fact the bee-eaters have not returned this year, so it looks very much as though last year's visit was a one off. Fortunately, I saw them and enjoyed every moment, they cannot take that away.

On the 1st Blithfield kicks off the month with a black-tailed godwit, this bird is looking very bright as it is in almost full summer plumage, very reddish,

The 9th sees me conducting a bird walk at Rosliston Forestry Centre. This is an annual event I do for them, where, for a nominal amount, which helps the centre,

I take them on a two-hour walk looking for the local birds. Today the birds are not very cooperative, with the heat I think they are staying in shelter, but we see and hear enough to keep everyone happy, and the butterflies compensate to a degree.

That afternoon I go for a drive round the Croxall/Whitemoor Haye area and whilst looking at the black pheasants once again, near to Catton Hall, a honey buzzard gives me a fly-past, talk about being in the right place at the right time. I do not suppose I see the bird for more than thirty seconds, but that is enough, an eternity when compared with not at all.

Many years ago, they were believed to be breeding on the Byrkley Park Estate, but when a large proportion of the estate was taken over by the FA as the training ground for the English football team, the birds appeared to have moved on. I must admit, I was one of the objectionists to this, but our pleas were ignored. As we are right in the breeding season, could a pair be back locally? We live in hope.

This will be the first year I have not gone after the nightjars, walking over uneven ground in the dark is not recommended, so that is a pleasure I will no longer have. Friends who have been after them have had very good views so the numbers seem to be doing well, which is what is important.

I intend to visit Blacktoft on the 16th, come along and join me. The day turns out to be a scorcher, summer is here with a vengeance. The avocets have young and the marsh harriers are very busily hunting, they no doubt too have young to feed. A small number of returning spotted redshanks are on view, and some of these, look absolutely magnificent A sooty coloured bird covered with silver stars is the best way to describe them, they are a wonderful bird in this plumage state. A drake garganey is also on show, he is a bit spectacular too, and a black-necked grebe also puts in an appearance. Seeing the last two at this time of the year, are they breeding locally, no reason why not. Little egret numbers are good, certainly well into double figures, these birds are obviously breeding locally, and I hear the bittern was seen briefly earlier on, not by me needless to say. All in all, a most satisfactory day. Three 'ticks' at this time of the year, that cannot be bad.

Whilst at Blacktoft I go into reflective mood. I am watching a reed warbler busy hunting insects and it suddenly flies off further down the reed bed. Watching the bird depart I thought how fast the wings were beating. The amount of energy the bird was using up to stay airborne is amazing, no wonder small birds seem to be constantly seeking food, they need to.

This made me think a little. The larger the bird becomes the less energy it seems to require. Flight is not so hectic, for the really large birds a flap and a glide covers a considerable distance, and larger birds tend to roost up regularly. They eat less frequently, although they do consume larger prey when they do eat, and they live far longer. A warbler is lucky to make two or three years, and to compensate for this they raise many young birds and can have up to three broods a year. Take a golden eagle for instance. It is several years old before it first attempts to breed and when it finally does manage to successfully, it will only raise one or two young. To compensate for these low numbers, they can live thirty years or more. Nature is quite amazing, so if you come back as a bird, be very careful which you choose!

The remainder of the month sees me going local. Blithfield has started to see a few returning waders, the pick of which was a green sandpiper seen on the 21st.

The following day I do have quite a surprise. I am at Upper Longdon. You will remember my mentioning the height of newly planted trees affecting the woodlarks. I was there today in the hope of seeing a stonechat which had been reported, I did not, but whilst there I heard a woodlark singing. After spending several minutes trying to locate the bird, I saw it fly on to the top of a tall old tree stump, from, where it did its song flight. I was never more pleased to have been wrong with my thoughts.

My final trip out in June was back to the moorlands. Axe Edge Moor gave me red grouse and meadow pipit. The red grouse were particularly active, several fly-pasts. The meadow pipits were sitting out on the fence posts just enjoying the sun, or so it appeared.

Down at the layby curlew were very vocal, and there appeared to be at least two pairs of ring ouzels. Skylarks were still singing and red grouse could be heard calling.

Back down to Tittesworth for a snack and then off for a quick visit across to Swallow Moss. I was greeted at Swallow Moss by raven calling, here on the open moors the sound of them is so fitting, like the curlew, they do belong here. Red grouse were also showing well, it looked as though they may have had a good breeding season.

A movement on a stone wall caught my attention, a male whinchat was sitting out. This particular area was a regular haunt for whinchats a few years ago, but not any longer, so seeing a bird back here, and in the breeding season, leads me to hope they have returned.

He was my final 'tick' for June, where I now stand at one hundred and seventy-eight.

June apparently was the warmest on record since 1945, my cuckoos certainly had it right, and no respite is anticipated. We Brits moan about the poor weather we have, but after a few days like these experienced at present, we have had enough. The problem is not just the heat, it is the humidity levels. When I was in Egypt I experienced temperatures far higher than those current, but it was a dry heat, little or no humidity. Anyway, back to birding.

July has obviously come in warm, well hot to be more accurate, and day one sees me on Cannock Chase. I heard of stonechat being seen near the cadet camp, so I am off hunting those. After much searching and fly swatting, I see a male sitting out on the top of a gorse bush. Thank you, stonechat, you are a little beauty, and he sits out for quite some time, which is most obliging. A 'tick' to start off the month. I was also pleased to see a woodlark sitting on some overhead wires, it was using them as his launch pad. Further on a tree pipit could be heard, but it was too far away for me to see. No complaints, three very good birds, including a 'tick'.

The 4th shows Blithfield doing its stuff again. I was in the hide in Stansley Wood when I had a most pleasant surprise. Walking round the shore came a spoonbill, this bird had not been reported and I certainly was not looking for it. We birders get a tremendous pleasure when we find special birds on our own, with no assistance from anyone else. We are looking at a bird no one else has seen, we have found it, there is some personal satisfaction in doing that.

I was able to watch the bird for several minutes as it swung its bill from side to side searching for food. There is one thing about a spoonbill, you are not going to confuse it with anything else.

Two days later and I am back at Blithfield. This time, looking for a bird I have been told about, a wood sandpiper seen in Blithe Bay. The weather is still very hot and near to water flies are a nuisance, not that the hirundines and swifts are complaining, finding food for their young has never been easier.

Along the shore a few small groups of waders are seen, ringed plovers, little ringed plovers mainly along with a few common sandpipers and dunlins. My wood sandpiper, however, is proving rather elusive. After an hour of seeking it, when my eyes are getting rather strained due to the glare from the water, a small, rather dark looking wader runs into view. My time and effort have not been wasted, the wood sandpiper has finally come into view. Fortunately, it spends some time feeding close to where I am parked, before it flies off across the bay to the far side. I was happy, I had found him, or to be more accurate, it had found me.

The following day I am back at Blacktoft, be interesting to see how the wader movement is getting on there, and one point about Blacktoft is the fact you will always see birds.

I have Blacktoft almost to myself, not usually a good sign, but things turn out very pleasantly. To start off I chalk up another 'year tick', this time a ruff, well several, many with much of their summer plumage still on show. I will list the other prime birds seen, to give you some idea of how good things are. Two spoonbills, an adult and a juvenile, a little egret, black-tailed godwits, several of those still showing much of their summer plumage, spotted redshanks, many of those also sporting their summer regalia, redshanks, common sandpipers, two green sandpipers, four snipes, two greenshanks, several avocets, an occasional bearded tit and marsh harriers, and in front of the Xerox hide, a reed warbler feeding young. Not a bad haul I think you will agree.

On the 14th I visit Derbyshire Bridge, on the Derbyshire Moorlands, where after much searching, I finally find myself a wheatear. I have been looking for this species for several months, I usually tick them off before the end of April, not wait until July. Still, better late than never, and it is a male. During the remainder of the month, I see little, the best birds being a red kite flying over the A515 near to Ashbourne and a great white egret at Tucklesholme Quarry. Birds of quality at least.

Whilst enjoying my wheatear a thought occured to me. Anyone new to birding and having a current field guide could, depending upon which guide they are using, have difficulty in deciding which wheatear I am talking about. Some guides will refer to my bird as the northern wheatear.

Since I first started birding, many names have changed and some current field guides are now using the international names, not our long-standing common names.

Birders of my generation, tend to use the names they always have, Bewick's swans will never be tundra swans, and nightingales will never be common nightingales, I only wish they were common! So to avoid any possible confusion, at the end of this narrative I will list the most frequently used name changes.

Later this month and I am back at Sutton Coldfield Crematorium. It is now ten years since Dorothy died, and this was my tenth visit to the crematorium. I still remember the robin which came to see me on my first visit, and the subsequent robin seen a year or so later—they did their job. My visits now are no longer sorrowful, they are full of happy memories, which is how Dorothy would have wanted it. Time is a great healer, if you will let it. It cannot bring things back, but it makes the memories more precious.

July incidentally, also sees records broken for heat, and although the first day or so of August sees a drop in temperature, it is only temporary.

August 1st and I have a couple of free hours, so I take myself down to Croxall and Whitemoor Haye. Things are quiet, although a passing hobby brightened things up for a few seconds, so I decide to go and have a look at the sand martin colony in the new quarry workings. I have taken you there before. No sand martins are seen, not that I expected them. By now the young will have left the nest and they are probably feeding themselves up over some nearby water, in preparation for their migration south. They are one of the earliest species to arrive, and one of the earliest to leave.

Whilst surveying the remains of the colony I become conscious of a small wader working its way along the shore, and the bird is showing a little red in its plumage. My initial thoughts are sanderling, but on focusing up my binoculars I am delighted to see it is a curlew sandpiper. A 'year tick' on day one of a new month, now that cannot be bad. It still has a small amount of red in its plumage, not fully moulted out yet, and as it makes a short flight, the white rump is clearly seen. No problem with the identification of this one. A good start to a new month, long may it continue.

Friday. 3rd, sees me off to Carsington Water. I have heard of a turnstone being seen, so that is worth a bit of a 'twitch'. The day is dull and overcast, which is not bad for a day's birding. At least I will not get burned by the sun.

I make my way to the Sheepwash Hide from where the last reports of the turnstone came from. I have the hide to myself, which as you know from previous comment, I do not consider to be a good sign. As events turn out, it is rather mixed.

No turnstone, but whilst searching away I come across a very small Canada goose, this requires careful study. I eventually get the view I want. The black neck has a white ring round the bottom of the neck, a good indication that I have a lesser Canada goose, or to give it its new name—cackling goose. I am more than happy with that.

I move on to the visitor centre, enjoy a coffee and then go onto Stones Island, to look for the turnstone. No joy, the island is very busy, especially with children as the schools are now closed. Walking back however, I have a stroke of luck. I hear waders calling, do not instantly recognise the call, which is usually a good indication that they are not a common species and they are not. Five whimbrels come sweeping overhead and vanish on the far side of an island, away from the maddening throng. Although I wait for several minutes, they do not reappear, but I am happy. Two cracking 'ticks'.

Turning to walk back, my day is not over. Two large gulls swim past, they both have very dark eyes, and I am surprised to find myself looking at two adult, Caspian gulls. They may not be a 'tick', but two in this plumage state are a bit special to say the least, and that is not the end of it. Walking the shore, completely oblivious to the noise come a great white egret, another most interesting bird.

Carsington had done well today.

As I have time, I call in at Blithfield Reservoir on my way home, and here it is 'jackpot' time. Do you believe in fate? I now do. In Admaston Reach I see three little ringed plovers and whilst watching these, a dark little wader rushes into view, a turnstone. Unbelievable. I travel to Carsington in the hope of seeing one, a round trip of over sixty miles, and here I am, seven miles or so away from home, looking at a turnstone. That is birding, you win a few and lose many. Today, I think I can safely say I won. Three 'year ticks' on the day, and all relatively local.

Common terns are also very active today. I am pleased to say there are several juveniles flying amongst them, learning the tricks of the trade before they commence their migration southwards in a few weeks' time.

Tomorrow I am going further afield, I am visiting Old Moor Reserve, near to Barnsley. It is a first-class reserve, with good catering facilities, so come along with me, and you do not need to bring your lunch, we will dine in style!

The journey up to Old Moor is very comfortable, traffic light, and I do the distance of a little over seventy miles in just over ninety minutes. On booking myself in, I enquired about what had been seen recently, not a lot really although the bittern has been showing well.

I make my way down to the Family Hide, which I have to myself. The expected waterfowl are seen and five little egrets are actively feeding. The only waders to be seen are lapwings, so I make my way to the Wath Ings Hide, here there is a little more activity on the bird watching front. Two black-tailed godwits, a ruff and a snipe can be seen from this hide, with seven more little egrets. The main interest for the birders in the hide is a garganey which has been reported, unfortunately, it did not show itself whilst I was there.

I then move on to the Field Pool Hide, here again I have things to myself, four additional little egrets are seen, that makes a total of sixteen. A movement near the hide catches my attention. A green sandpiper is feeding along the pool's edge, and whilst enjoying this bird

I become conscious of a small, darkish looking bird feeding along the edge of a narrow spit of land stretching out into the water. My initial thoughts are meadow pipit, so I concentrate my attention back on the sandpiper.

This bird moves out of vision, I then return to seeking out the pipit. I am glad I do, now that I have a clear view of the bird, I realised it is no pipit, it is a stint.

Stints are our smallest waders, being no larger than a pipit, and they are a similar colour at first glance. Time to concentrate. We see two species in the UK, the little stint being the commonest, and the Temminck's stint being the most unusual.

This bird is uniformly dark, and this gives me the clue I want, I am looking at an adult Temminck's stint. The little stint is much paler on the breast and belly. This bird being an adult does me a great favour. Most of the Temmincks I have seen in the past have been either juveniles or winter plumaged birds, to see an adult bird is almost like seeing a new bird. Mind you it is a new bird for the year.

With one small bird, Old Moor has suddenly woken up, my trip up north has definitely been worth it, hope you think so too. And the lunch was not bad either!

The Staffordshire Bird News on the net catches my attention, Blithfield Reservoir has some very interesting reports. A passage of waders has obviously taken place, plus reports of other interesting species, one of which most definitely gains my attention. Four common scoter have been seen off the dam, they are a species which has been illuding me, time again to chase them up. So the 8th August and I am on my way, almost in 'twitch' mode.

Today is a breezy day, the water is looking quite rough as it splashes up against the dam, not perfect conditions when looking for small dark ducks, which dive persistently. There are also a number of anglers out on the water, and they are close in to the dam where there is some protection from the breeze. Conditions could have been better, but we have no control over that.

There are many gulls out on the water plus a few terns, but nothing of special interest amongst those. The antics of a lesser black-backed gull drew my attention. It is constantly diving at a small group of birds on the water, which promptly dive to avoid its attention. Concentration time.

The gull eventually gives this all up, and flies off, the ducks returning to the surface, and I am very pleased they did so. It is the four drake common scoters which have been reported. As is their wont, they were constantly diving, in unison, searching for food. I believe I have mentioned before how they do this. Synchronised diving at its best. When seen doing so it is one of their best identification features, especially when seen at distance, such as on the open sea. I enjoy them for several minutes as they slowly drift further out on the water. At last they are on my 'year list'!

I have not been down to the dam for some time, so I drive off there, not that I am expecting a lot due to the wind. Several gulls are gliding over the dam, two or three great black-backed among them, the wind does not worry these birds. Several great crested grebes are swimming just off the dam and three grey herons are standing on the dam slopes, looking quite unhappy as the wind blows into them, ruffling up their feathers.

Going onto the dam several yellow wagtails are to be seen hunting away in shelter from the wind. As I slowly approach where they were feeding, I can see a lot of ant activity, so I retreat, allowing them to get back to their feeding, which they quickly do. There are eleven of them, five of which are juveniles. A very nice little group.

Further along the dam are two meadow pipits, they too are feeding well, an emergence of ants has certainly occurred, much to the pleasure of these birds. I am not so sure the ants are happy.

To finish off, a large flock of Canada geese fly in, as noisy as ever, and they disturb a small number of cormorants, crash landing right in their midst. The times I see Canada geese do this to birds already on the water, makes me wonder if it is deliberate!

Having time, I decide to drive across to Dunstall to see if anything of interest is in the quarry. It is not, but as I drive back towards Dunstall I quickly stop and pull over. A small party of pheasants have dashed across the road and race through a fence into the adjoining field. When looking in the field it is 'full' of pheasants, I have never seen so many together before. I settle down to count them, and I count sixty-eight birds, many of which are juveniles.

As they are in such a tight group I can only but presume they are captive bred birds which have been released only recently. The pheasant shooting season commences, I believe, on 1st October, so these birds had better learn quickly, otherwise their lives will be short.

I am frequently asked the question about my thoughts on shooting, and I must confess it is a most awkward question to answer. My basic thoughts are that no wild creature should be shot or hunted for that matter, but on the other hand, without shooting some of these creatures would no longer be with us. Red grouse are a very good example of this.

The countryside is forever changing, and quite naturally so, it evolves and the creatures and plants decrease or increase accordingly. Grouse moors have to be maintained, if not they would slowly vanish as stronger growing trees and ground vegetation takes over, with the result being the grouse will no longer survive. Moor maintenance is a costly business, and although there are a few societies such as the RSPB, and the county trusts, who do their best, without the money from grouse shooting, most of the moors would by now have vanished. So if you wish to see grouse, the only way you will is if people pay for their breeding and pay to shoot them. Fortunately, many survive for our pleasure.

The same can probably be said for pheasants and partridges, especially the red-legged partridge (our native partridge, the grey partridge does not breed easily in captivity, they are truly wild). Although moors are not part of this equation, the fact they are bred in such large numbers means many survive and add to the wild population, so it is safe to say their numbers are increasing, thanks to shooters. No one is going to breed pheasants and partridges without some monetary gain. It is not very pleasant I know, but without the guns we would not have the numbers of game birds we do. As I have said, on several occasions, it is a hard world out there, all we can do is help it.

The 10th of the month sees me at Blithfield Reservoir. After a visit to the surgery for a blood test, I am off on a chase. Two sanderlings have been reported from Blithfield and this bird has become a bit of a challenge this year. Normally I knock them off without any trouble, this year they have begun to haunt me. Wish me luck, I feel I might need it.

The reports, unfortunately, do not say where at Blithfield they were seen. I often think that reports of this nature are not worth anything, Blithfield is a large reservoir, its shoreline is about eight miles I have been told, so to find two small birds in such an area is not easy. All the reportee needs to say is where it was seen, the name of the bay or nearby farm, other birders may then have a chance.

Finding today's birds is going to have a bit of luck, plus my own experience of where this type of bird is most likely to be found, and I have put my money on Blithe Bay and Admaston Reach. I drive part way down the reach, park up, and erect my 'scope. This is going to be needed today.

The water level is very low and the bay has dried out considerably, sheep are grazing where water usually lies. Dunlins, little ringed plovers, ringed plovers, redshanks and three curlews are easily located, as are seven little egrets. A small flock of five common sandpipers fly in, these causing a bit of excitement as two of the birds looked smaller, but it is an illusion. A green sandpiper flicks past, always a bit of quality, but not today I am afraid, I am in 'twitch' mode.

After a little over an hour, I turn and drive back to the causeway, to concentrate my efforts on the causeway slope and the end of the reach. A few ringed plovers and lapwings are feeding along the shore, plus another green sandpiper, this could quite easily be the same bird as the one just seen, as this bird flew in.

Time now to concentrate on the causeway slope. Common sandpipers are again seen, three of them this time, and the odd black-headed gull and tufted duck are also sitting out on the causeway slope. Two pied wagtails fly through and they do me a great favour. They land on the slope near the water's edge, and in doing so, flush a small wader I have not noticed.

Fortunately, the bird flies in my direction and the bold white V-shaped wingbars can be clearly seen, as can the white on the tail, thank you, pieds, I have my sanderling. After nearly two hours I only see my bird thanks to the intervention of two other birds. Birders have an expression they use frequently when talking about birding and it is

'Birding is ninety per cent luck and ten per cent knowledge'. I cannot argue with that, without the assistance of the pied wagtails today, I may not have picked up the sanderling. You win some, you lose some, today I win some! I think a drop of malt is called for tonight, care to join me?

I have decided to visit Far Ings, a reserve in Lincolnshire tomorrow. When up here last year I had a red-necked grebe, what will this visit bring?

One hundred and fifteen miles away, and just over two hours journey time, and I pull in at Far Ings. Nothing special has been reported, so I will have to find things myself. Initially a mug of coffee is required, and then I will be off on my travels. The reserve incidentally, is overlooked by the Humber Bridge, which dominates the area.

The visitor centre lies on the shores of the pursuit pit, and very good views can be obtained of this from the viewing gallery in the centre, and from here I pick up a large white goose, which just does not look right for being a domestic goose. I need a better viewpoint for this bird. I leave the centre and make my way to the shores of the pit where a far better view is obtained. I am right with my first thoughts, this is no domestic goose, it is a snow goose. The black primaries are very visible, and this bird has a full set, it obviously is a free flier. An unexpected 'year tick'. Large numbers of both Canada and grey-lag geese are very evident, and I am most impressed with the number of gadwalls to be seen, they are not the most common of our ducks. A brief sighting of a marsh harrier is seen over the distant reed bed, but it is just a fleeting view, and the bird does not return.

After spending time here and at the ness pit, where a flock of redshank were actively feeding along with three common sandpipers, I drive down to Chowder Ness which overlooks the Humber Estuary. The tide is partly out and the shoreline is exposed, plenty of mud being visible, ideal for waders, I hope.

Hard as I work, all I can find is the odd lapwing and a solitary curlew, even gulls are at a premium. I have just about decided to call it a day when a small flock of waders fly by, and land on a small pool which has appeared where the tide has retreated. I quickly focus up on these birds, seven of them, and am delighted to see they are knots, two of them adults and still showing some of their red summer plumage. (Some new field guides now call them the red knot, a name used in America for years.) My patience has been rewarded with my second 'year tick' of the day.

A most pleasant day, and as I journey home, I listen to the test match against India, we are doing well, that adding to my pleasure. One thing I have forgotten to mention is the fact that entrance to Far Ings is free, whether you are a Lincolnshire Wildlife Trust member or not.

I intended to go crossbill hunting today, the 12th August, but the morning has come in very wet with steady rain falling, after a night of almost continuous rain.

Not that I am complaining about this, after the weather recently experienced, we really do need the rain. The rain has now changed my thoughts for the day. I do not mind getting damp, but I have no desire for my optics to get soaking wet, they may be waterproofed, but you cannot see well through rain covered lenses. So I have decided to do something I have thought about for a long time.

Rain and birding do not go together, when raining you really do require shelter, and this is where hides come in. I have long considered one of the best hides you can have, is your own car, so today I am, as an exercise, going to do it all from my car. Not only will this be an example of what can be done in poor weather conditions, it will also illustrate that birding can be done easily by the disabled. I am a blue badge holder myself, and I frequently do all my birding from the car, as you well know.

The principal requirement when birding such as this, is to know your patch, you need to know where you can park and view. Today I have planned my route to cover Blithfield Reservoir, JCB Lake at Rocester, Dunstall, Croxall Lakes, Whitemoor Haye and the layby at Kings Bromley. A round trip of about forty miles and all the locations are free parking and no membership of societies is required.

My first stop is in Watery Lane at Blithfield, and here I see great crested grebe, cormorant, black-headed gull, lesser black-backed gull, herring gull, common tern, coot, mallard, carrion crow, swallow, yellow wagtail and meadow pipit.

Crossing the causeway to Admaston Reach I add lapwing, dunlin, sanderling, ringed plover, little ringed plover, oystercatcher, redshank, tufted duck, gadwall and great black-backed gull to the list. Next stop Newtom Hurst Lane. Here in Tad Bay I see Canada geese, grey-lag geese, raven, grey heron, kestrel, blackbird and blue tit.

Total so far twenty-nine.

JCB provides moorhen, little grebe, mandarin, red-crested pochard, barnacle goose, shelduck and a cape shelduck, this bird being a free flyer, and pied wagtail.

Total now thirty-seven.

Dunstall gives me pheasant, great tit, starling, buzzard, great spotted woodpecker, wren, song thrush and great white egret. Total forty-five.

Now for Croxall. Little to add here although magpie and jackdaw obliged, we reach forty-seven.

Whitemoor Haye starts off with house sparrow, followed by yellowhammer, tree sparrow, rook, sparrowhawk, corn bunting, chaffinch, bullfinch, red-legged partridge, common whitethroat, woodpigeon, collared dove, mistle thrush and a coal tit. Total now sixty-one.

Kings Bromley layby. Here I add little egret to my list and also see a further great white egret. The little egret gives me sixty-two species for the day, a very good return for just forty miles or so and a little over four hours' time spent. This I believe really does emphasise getting to know your patch, and I did not step out of my car once.

Today, the 14th August, I have a day working at home, and over a coffee I am enjoying the birds in my garden. Having restocked all my bird feeders etc, there was a fair amount of activity, especially with the starlings which were devouring the fat balls at a rate of knots. I happen to glance up at my neighbours' roof to see a long row of small birds sitting out. A pair of binoculars are always to hand, so I quickly pick them up and am delighted to see eighteen house sparrows sitting on the roof. This is the largest group I have seen locally for quite some time, and the pleasing thing is ten of them are juvenile birds. Four pairs of house sparrows have raised ten youngsters to a free flying state, absolutely wonderful. I frequently say to people that homes and gardens without house sparrows and starlings, are deserted places. They are both welcome in my garden, any time.

If I have had one real disappointment this year so far, it is the fact that the bee-eaters did not return to East Leake. Having bred there successfully last year I really did expect some to return. From reports I have seen, there have been few records of the birds being seen in other parts of the country. With the summer we have experienced I really did think we had a good chance of their returning. No such luck, as I have said before, you cannot win them all!

It is the 17th of the month before I am able to get out for a bit of birding, and bit is the operative word. I have a medical examination due mid-afternoon, so any birding will have to be local and of short duration, so I am having an hour or so at Blithfield Reservoir.

Driving down Admaston Reach into Blithe Bay I pick up a few waders, both ringed plovers, black-tailed godwits, dunlins, ruffs, a green sandpiper and two ravens fly overhead, quite vocal, a wonderful sound, very guttural and one which I always think suits the bird so admirably. As I round the bend into the bay I see the great white egret feeding away, this bird has been present for several days now, and I am most certainly not complaining. Scattered around the shoreline are several little egrets, well actually eight of them and when you compare the size of these two species, you can understand why they are called great and little respectively!

Driving back, I stop in the Reach. When I first drove down only a few gulls were here, but now I have five common sandpipers and three oystercatchers. Also, several common terns are feeding in the water, very noisily as is their wont as they plunge dive, bill first, into the water. They certainly do nothing by halves!

Nothing new to report, but a very pleasant hour or so, time now for my medical appointment.

As I drive back through Hoar Cross, things turn most interesting. I have pulled in on the layby opposite the church. I regularly do this when passing, and I have had the odd interesting bird in the past, but today is jackpot time. I have the windows wound down so I can listen for any birds when I become aware of a commotion overhead. Looking up I see two carrion crows chasing a tawny owl, which is having great difficulty in escaping their attention, the crows being far more agile than the owl. After a few seconds the crows are happy they have driven the owl off, so peace returns to the countryside.

I can only presume the crows have stumbled upon a roosting tawny owl, and promptly attack the bird. No owl is a predator to a bird as large as a crow, but crows are very territorial and they would not welcome any bird of prey or similar, in their patch, as the tawny found out. I frequently see them attacking buzzards in a similar way, tough nuts the crow family.

It had been a most interesting few minutes, not for the owl, for me, and to top it all, the tawny owl is a 'year tick'. I cannot remember when it last took me nearly eight months to chalk up my first tawny of the year. Thank you, corvids. My medical incidentally, was also fine. The end to a perfect day.

I have just heard that a buff-breasted sandpiper has been seen at Blacktoft, so my plans for tomorrow are made. If I see this bird, it will be only the second occasion I have seen one. They are a rare vagrant from North America, a bird worth some effort. Why not come and join me, for a bit of excitement.

The journey up is uneventful, but when I arrive, I am very surprised to see only two cars on the car park, not a very good sign. When I book myself in it is to receive the news that the buff-breasted sandpiper had moved on two days ago, my information had not been entirely accurate. Still, I am here now so all I can do is get on with it.

I usually start off by going west and visiting the Marshland Hide, but I have been informed that work is being carried out at the Ousefleet Hide and this is disturbing the birds at Marshland, so little is being seen. Today it is a case of going east, I walk to the furthest hide—Singleton.

There is much activity here, a large number of waders are to be seen. Dunlins, ruffs, ringed plovers, little ringed plovers, black-tailed godwits, lapwings, redshanks, golden plovers, and the odd curlew and turnstone, a very good selection. I am also impressed with the number of gadwalls to be seen, plus an eclipsed state drake garganey, these are always a bit special.

Moving on to Townend Hide. Not a lot to report from here, just five black-tailed godwits and three snipes, and these birds quickly depart when a marsh harrier flies over.

First prudces little apart from a fleeting view of two water rails, always a bird worth seeing, even if only momentarily.

Lunch approached, so this is partaken, and I decide to go home and listen to a local football match on the radio. Driving through Reedness, which lies alongside the Humber, I spot two cargo vessels making their way to the docks at Goole. I pull up to watch their progress, you do not see many ocean-going vessels on the Trent in Staffordshire. One looked as though it was flying a Russian flag, the second I could not make out.

Whilst watching their slow progress, I become aware of some birds calling, obviously waders, but I have no idea which. They quickly fly into view, three of them, keep on coming, and they look large, they obviously are not curlews, I know their calls only too well. As they approach, I can see they are godwits, the question now is which. They flash past me. Problem solved. Bar-tailed godwits, a 'year tick' to boot. In flight the principal differences between our two godwits are that the black-tailed has a broad white wingbar, easily seen when in flight, the bar-tailed lacks these completely and these three had plain wings. The day has ended up brightly, I get myself a 'year tick', even if it was not the one I hoped for. Do you think I need to do more ship watching?

The 19th has dawned grey and damp. Not a lot has been reported locally so I decide to take myself upon the moors for an hour or so. Here, if the conditions still remain miserable, I can at least view from or near to my car.

Driving up onto the moors I am beginning to think my decision is not quite right, I am running not only into heavier rain, visibility is becoming very poor, foggy almost. I pull onto Axe Edge Moor and realise that birding is well-nigh impossible, so I turn back and head for Tittesworth Water.

The light at Tittesworth is much improved, although the rain is still falling. After a coffee it is time to start birding. The water level is very low and most of the mud has dried so waders are not in evidence, that is apart from an oystercatcher and a few lapwings.

Looking back up to the moors, the fog is most certainly clearing, so I decide to go back and visit Swallow Moss, here I hope I may come across a short-eared owl. But before I drive off a gull flies in and lands just in front of me. I have said before how good a hide the car can be. Time for a bit of excitement. The gull does not have any black on the primaries, this is no common species of gull. Focusing up, I quickly realise the bird is an adult Mediterranean gull, moulting out of its summer plumage, and having just the odd dark blotch on the head. They may not be the rarest of gulls, but they are a bit special, and make my trip out worthwhile.

Driving up onto the moors I spot a bird sitting on the top of the 'Winking Man' and I am able to pull off the road. The 'Winking Man' is a famous landmark, being a superb rock formation in The Roaches which resembles a face. Back to the bird, it is a raven, so it is probably a good job it is a rock formation and not a real man! I must confess a smile crossed my face as my mind mused on.

Approaching Swallow Moss, I flush a flock of small birds from off the road in front of me, they are linnets, no doubt collecting grit from the road surface. You will frequently see seed eating birds collecting grit, it aids their digestion, helping to grind up the seeds in their stomachs. I stop a little down the road, and within minutes the linnets return, this is obviously a popular spot.

Swallow Moss is very quiet, and although I spend many minutes there, no owls, no anything!

The weather may have been poor, the birding not great, but I have three memories—a Med gull, my raven on the 'Winking Man's' head and the linnets, well worth the effort.

As August has progressed it has become a very pleasant month. Rain which was so much required has come on occasion and many of the days have been overcast with the temperature in the lower twenty degrees. A pleasant change from temperatures in the high twenties and reaching into the thirties on occasion, in previous weeks. Fine for the sun worshippers, not for me.

Tomorrow, the 24th, I am meeting up with three friends of mine, who were members of the Rosliston Birders, we are visiting Croxall and Whitemoor Haye. It will be very pleasant to catch up with them once again. As a preparation for tomorrow, I am having an afternoon's birding at Croxall and the Haye to see what we are likely to find.

I have not the time for going into Croxall Lakes Nature Reserve, so my viewing is from the car parking area. A large mixed flock of Canada geese and grey-lags are on the water, cormorants are plentiful, mallards, gadwalls, tufted ducks are also evident and a few common terns are in the air. Down now to the Haye.

On the lake are a pair of pochards, a few great crested grebes, many coots, some of which are juveniles, more cormorants, the mute swan flock is building up, thirty-seven here today, with both black-headed and lesser black-backed gulls. A goldeneye had been reported, but I cannot find him, something to look for tomorrow.

As I drive down the Haye, two small birds flick out of the field and land on a hawthorn bush, sitting out in full view. I manage to stop before I get too close, they are a pair of corn buntings, and for about a minute they sit out in full view. I just hope they will be as accommodating come tomorrow. Several tree sparrows are also in the area, they keep on flying in and out of the hedge. They appear to have done very well this season, I have seen reports of flocks in excess of seventy, which is very good news.

I turn my car round and slowly make my way back. I suddenly stop, it is a good job not many motorists use this road! Seven partridges are strutting across the lane in front of me. I rapidly raise my binoculars and am delighted to see I am looking at a covey of seven grey partridges, two adults and five juvenile birds, a wonderful sight. I have mentioned before that grey partridge are our native species, unlike the red-legged which was introduced from the continent for shooting purposes.

They continue to feed on the verge for a short while, before two carrion crows come down to investigate what they are after. With a whirring of their wings, the partridges are off, and that is the last I see of them. The crows are certainly not friends of mine on this occasion!!

When coming home from work yesterday, Sarah had spotted four little egrets from the layby in Kings Bromley, so as I return home, I call in. Three little egrets are instantly visible as they feed in the river, and when compared with a grey heron nearby, you quickly see where the name 'little' originates. These birds are all adults, the long plumes down their necks being still partially visible. Watching the way they are plunging their long bills into the water so actively, they obviously have plenty of food available.

If I can find any of those birds tomorrow, plus what may be at Croxall as we will go into the reserve proper, we may be in for a good day. You are welcome to come and join us.

It looks as though our trip out today may be rather damp. After a bright clear early morning, the clouds are coming in and I have been informed rain is likely. Fortunately, Croxall has hides, so we should at least get some 'dry' birding in.

As things turn out, the weather is an irrelevance, although rain it does. For some reason my friends do not turn up and I also become involved in an unusual accident. I open up the gates to drive in, the gates being heavy wooden structures, and as I drive through, a strong gust of wind blows and catches one of the gates. The net result is much damage to my front offside, and tomorrow I now need to take it to the car repairers for appraisal. Then I await my insurer's acceptance before work can proceed. This, fortunately, could be in six days' time as long as no special parts are required.

The repairer is in Ashbourne, so as long as the car is legally drivable, and it seems fine, I can at least have a few hours birding in Derbyshire, as compensation of a kind. No one has ever said birding is easy!

My insurance appraisal carried out, I now await confirmation for the work to be done. It is anticipated the work will take two weeks to complete, but fortunately, a hire car is available under my insurance policy.

I am only a few minutes away from Carsington Water, so I make my way there. A coffee will go down well, and it does, before a bit of birding commences. I go into the nearby visitor centre hide initially, and I have this all to myself, I must admit, I have found Carsington Water very quiet, considering it is a Bank Holiday weekend. Here I am, talking people, and I am not complaining.

Many geese and waterfowl are on the reservoir, nothing special is tucked in amongst them. Working the shoreline, I pick up three ringed plovers, and whilst enjoying these, a greenshank is heard. Within seconds the bird glides in, calling away, as if it was announcing its arrival to all and sundry. I am more than happy with its appearance.

Nothing else of excitement occurs, so I go round to Stones Island and here I am very disappointed. A large amount of windsurfing is taking place, the participants being young children whose noise level is even greater than their excitement. I do not expect to see a lot here. Walking round to the eastern side of Stones Island I am pleasantly surprised. A flock of ringed plovers, eleven of them, are feeding along the shore, three dunlins are amongst them and a snipe is tucked away in the vegetation.

Noise does not affect these birds I am pleased to say.

Walking back a large bright looking duck swims past. I stop, a magnificent drake ruddy shelduck is out on the water. It may not be a 'year tick', but they are a bit special, you do not see many in a year, last year I saw none.

After a quick lunch I decide to drive across to the Staffordshire Moorlands, see how the red grouse are going on now the 'Glorious 12th' is here. Not glorious should you be a grouse!

From the point of view of grouse, it is not worth the effort, I see nor hear any. They have probably quickly learnt to keep their heads down, stay still and you may survive, fly and you will not!

Little is to be seen today, just the odd carrion crow, lapwing, meadow pipit and the occasional flock of linnets. The latter have certainly started to flock up early this year.

Driving across Axe Edge Moor, a flock of linnets land on the wall, and for some reason I stop to look at them more closely. The old quote of 'Somebody, somewhere, loves you baby' comes to mind. There are only seven birds in the flock, and one of them looks decidedly streaky and small billed. I am pleased indeed that I have stopped, the bird is a twite, and it is the first I have seen this year. I could so easily have driven past those birds, just presuming them to be linnets. I am a lucky lad! The day finishes on a high note, the damaged car almost forgotten about.

Sunday has come in very damp, with rain forecast for most of the day. It is on days such as these that make you glad you are retired, when you are working your days are precious, when you are retired one day is much like the rest, and you can choose what to do with it. My choice today will be a drive round my local spots where I can bird watch from the dryness and comfort of my car.

My first stop is JCB at Rocester, where I have the car parking area to myself. The rain is pouring down and I cannot lower any windows, so my birding is limited through the windscreen with my wipers working—not the best of conditions, but needs must. A few shelducks are on the water, two of them a little agitated with each other so there is much wing flapping, both have full sets of primaries, these are countable. The collection birds are looking rather remorseful, no one to feed them today. A large duck comes flying down the lake, and as it passes, large white wing patches are clearly seen. An Egyptian goose, it brightens the gloom up a bit. Now on to Blithfield Reservoir.

It is not often I have Blithfield to myself, especially on weekends, today no day-trippers nor the ice cream vendor, just me. Watery Lane is mine. Fortunately, plenty of birds about, especially gulls and swallows. The latter are in the largest numbers I have seen this year, well into three figures, as they hurl themselves across the reservoir surface, wings almost flicking the water. There must be a good emergence of insects to account for so much activity. A yellow wagtail, a female, is busily chasing after insects on the causeway slope, she seems to be doing very well. The swallows are not having it all their own way.

I drive across the causeway, and due to lack of traffic, I am able to stop for a few seconds to admire a superb looking great black-backed gull, which is sitting out on the causeway wall. A magnificent looking bird and at this close proximity the expression is certainly not friendly, this bird has the eye of the killer.

Admaston Reach has two ringed plovers in attendance, rushing along the shoreline searching for food. Three oystercatchers are on the water's edge, one of which is a juvenile, as large as its parents, but not quite the full plumage. Several common terns are feeding away, plunge diving into the water, and further out over the reservoir, three dark looking terns catch my attention, and I am pleased they do.

They are black terns, and as with the swallows, they are skimming low over the water catching insects. I have mentioned before, that black terns are what we class as marsh terns, and they are great insect eaters. The white terns predominantly eat fish.

Today I think is bonanza time for all the insect eaters.

I now move on to Whitemoor Haye. Things initially are very quiet, the rain if anything is falling heavier, but as I drive through Whittington it slackens down.

Driving out of the village I see two small birds sitting on some stone walling, they look rather plump little fellows. I stop, this time I can wind down one of my windows, and I am delighted to see they are corn buntings, a welcome sight at any time. A quality finish.

Well not quite. Driving through Kings Bromley I pull in onto the layby, and my three little egrets are feeding away in the river. They will do as my grand finale.

It may have been a damp and miserable day weatherwise, but I certainly cannot complain about the quality of the birds. Nothing new, but some happy memories.

The bank holiday Monday has dawned grey and dull, but at least, unlike yesterday, it is not raining, well not yet. I only have a couple of hours available this morning for any birding, as at lunch I am meeting up with my proofreader, Evelyn.

You will remember Evelyn as our driver on group bird study tours, but she also works extremely hard in keeping me on the straight and narrow, especially where grammar and spelling are concerned. If reading your own work these errors are not always picked up, you read what you wanted to say, which is not necessarily what you actually typed.

Locally, Blithfield Reservoir still appears to be having the birds of interest, so I will spend my morning there. From the Watery Lane car park, as with yesterday, gulls and terns are plentiful, nothing special amongst them. From Admaston Reach the ringed plovers are still to be seen, and two black terns are plying their trade, one down on yesterday. Cormorants today are much in evidence. One flock, sitting out just off Beech Tree Point totals fifty-seven, what this is doing to the trout population is anyone's guess. Somehow, I just feel I would not like to be a trout, well not today!

I drive on down to the dam. Here many swallows are again feeding away, skimming low over the waves as they gulp down their prey. How many hundreds of flying insects they must eat in a day is impossible to judge, but just think, if we had not the swallows and other insect eating birds, life would almost be unbearable. A big thank you is due.

Whilst musing away, I hear Canada geese coming in, they rarely do things quietly, and amongst them is a large white goose, time to concentrate. As they bank on coming in to alight on the water, black tips to the white goose's wings are clearly seen. I have a snow goose. My second snow goose in just over two weeks, you will remember I saw one when up at Far Ings earlier in the month. At the distance away I am, if the bird had not shown its black primaries, I would just have had to presume it was an escaped domestic, we have a small flock of those on the reservoir at present.

Whilst all of this is going on a pale gull has landed on the dam embankment, a quick glance, and this time the lack of black primaries is important. We have a Mediterranean gull. I have mentioned previously that the Med' gull is a white winged gull which is a great help in splitting it from the black-headed gull which has black primaries. Small details such as these can make bird identification a little easier.

Time is rolling on, one last scan over the reservoir prior to my departure leaves me looking at a very dark looking duck, which is continually diving.

Eventually, it stays on the surface for a few seconds, and I am pleased it does so. I am looking at a duck common scoter. As if saying you have had your chance, she is back to her diving activities, and I drive off to my meeting with Evelyn in a very contented state of mind.

The meeting with Evelyn goes fine, not too many corrections to make to my manuscript I am pleased to say, so I will soon be back at my birding.

Wednesday is here, and a dull but mild day it is. I have heard that two whinchats and two wheatears have been seen at Blithfield. Although I have seen both this year, they were not local records, so my plans for this afternoon are made.

Both birds have been reported as being seen from the angling club car park, so a drive across the dam is required. Nothing of great interest is seen on the dam, just a few swallows flying overhead, but as I draw onto the car park, a surprise awaits me.

As I get out of my car a swift comes screaming overhead, a bird I have not seen for some time of late. Their numbers have been causing me concern this year, normally I have seen them in large numbers, this year not so. I wish this one well on its travels.

Now for the birds I have come for. They have been seen sitting out on a fence which runs up the field, so I hope they behave the same today. I am here for many minutes before two birds flit out onto the fence, one landing on a post, the other on the wire. My view is not good, they are some distance away, but as they flit down onto the ground their white rumps flash. I have the wheatears, not for long though, they quickly fly away.

It is some time before the whinchats put in an appearance, but they at least are much closer, these are a female and a juvenile, and they are very active feeders.

Continuously flitting down from the fence onto the ground beneath, I have a feeling they have located some ants. These perform for a few more minutes before they too fly off. I am happy, job done as they say, wheatears and whinchats are now on my local list.

As I am about to move off, a birder I know drives up. He has just returned from Frampton Marsh in Lincolnshire, where he has had a wonderful, few hours. He has seen a long-billed dowitcher and a stilt sandpiper, two mega North American species. Apparently, they have both been there for a few days now, if they remain for the weekend, I will have a crack at them myself. I have seen dowitchers before, only twice, but a stilt sandpiper, never. A chance of a 'lifer' looms!

I have my route worked out, according to Google maps, a distance of ninety-seven miles, so that is not quite as far as I thought. I now await checking up Friday to see if they are still there, if so, come Saturday I will be on my way.

Friday duly arrives and the news on the net looks good, both the stilt sandpiper and the dowitcher are both seen this morning, plus a few grey plovers. If those three species can be seen tomorrow, I am in for a very good day. At least I now know where I am bound for tomorrow, come and join me on a 'twitch', see if we can get an adrenalin rush?

Before thinking about Frampton, I have a tyre to change. Sarah had noticed a bad cut in the wall of one of my tyres, so this had to be remedied before I drove any real distance and at speed. My tyres are heavy duty as I frequently off road, and were not a stock item, but at last my garage had contacted me, my tyre was in.

Tyre fitted, a quick visit to Blithfield is called for, and I can now drive down the bays. With the time available today, I can only do Blithe Bay, but this is very productive.

As I drive into Admaston Reach I see eight little egrets and two great white egrets, as a start you cannot complain about that. The water level is rapidly reducing so it is not necessary to drive down the bay fully, so I park up in a suitable spot, already have my windows wound down, and survey the scene. My car has not upset many of the birds, and the waders, which are the birds I am really after, are too busy feeding on the exposed mud, to worry about a parked-up car. If I get out the story will be very different!

Many ringed plovers are visible, I would estimate at least forty, all very actively feeding. Five curlews are striding through the shallow water probing their long bills into it. A flock of seven greenshanks are dashing along in the water, feeding at a feverish rate. The odd ruff is dotted about, one of the birds still looking very colourful, obviously a male. Single green and common sandpiper are among the mix as are two snipes. Not a bad selection of waders at all, and there are, needless to say, many lapwings.

Turning my attention to the open water I see ten goosanders, four Egyptian geese and many Canada and grey-lag geese, with two barnacle geese tucked in amongst them. As I prepare to drive off, seven yellow wagtails flick in, a very attractive end to my visit. The month closes with me on one hundred and ninety-five.

The question now is, what will tomorrow bring? I could have three 'year ticks', one a 'lifer', or I could see nothing at all. Time alone will tell!

I commence my journey to Frampton Marsh rather concerned. The 1st September has come in rather misty, with visibility down to under one hundred yards.

No real problem for driving but, if it continues, birding will be rather difficult. As I drive across country things begin to improve and by the time I reach Grantham, it is blue skies and bright sunshine. I reach Frampton in a little over two and half hours, a journey of just under one hundred miles.

To say Frampton is busy is putting it mildly, they have had to open up an overflow car parking area. This, hopefully, should mean one thing, the birds are still here. I book myself in at the visitor centre and find out where the birds were last seen. The grey plovers were seen out on the shore, so I can write them off, I cannot walk that far, but more importantly, the dowitcher and sandpiper are on the reserve, and are very close to the centre. A crowd of birders is clearly seen just down the pathway, and birders do not stand in groups just to talk!

I approach the birders, ask the obvious questions, and the sandpiper is pointed out to me. I have my 'lifer' within minutes of arriving, and do not have to work for it. One of the birders invites me to have a look at the bird through his 'scope, an offer quickly accepted.

The stilt sandpiper is standing in rather deep water so the length of leg is not visible, but the markings on the bird are clear, plus when compared with four greenhanks standing close by, whose leg length I am familiar with, I quickly appreciate this bird's legs' length.

Being a 'lifer' and my first of the year, I stay to enjoy the bird, before moving off to find the long-billed dowitcher. I am informed by some birders that the bird has flown over to the 360 Hide (so called because the hide has all round viewing), and I slowly make my way in that direction, being very grateful for the odd bench along the route. Part way there I meet some more birders who inform me the bird has flown off and is believed to be by the East Hide. That hide is much too far for me to walk, so I make my way back to studying the sandpiper.

As well as the sandpiper, a very large flock of black-tailed godwits are to be seen, several hundred of them, probably even reaching four figures, the largest number I have seen for some time. Many of which are looking rather red as they still have some of their summer plumage. A decent number of dunlins are also in attendance, and small numbers of curlews, redshanks and ringed plovers are also to be seen.

Back to enjoying the sandpiper. It has become very active and is feeding away almost vigorously, stabbing its bill into the water repeatedly. It has certainly found something here to its liking. Whilst enjoying this a shout suddenly goes up.

'It's back.' No need to wonder what 'it' is. The long-billed dowitcher flies in and lands in the water right in front of us. No bird ever received a warmer welcome! To have a bird call in to see you, especially such an unusual species, is birding at its best!

Today I have been very fortunate.

The dowitcher does not hang about for long, ten minutes or so at the most, and it is off again, but it left a group of about thirty birders very happy.

Time is rolling on so I make my way back to the visitor centre for a coffee, and whilst sitting down, enjoying this, a volunteer warden walks up to me and points at the water in front of the centre. I look and I cannot believe my eyes, the stilt sandpiper has just landed, no more than twenty yards away from the centre, and its legs are certainly visible now. No wonder it is called the stilt sandpiper, its legs are almost stilt length when compared with the size of the bird. It is only visible for seconds before it dashes out of sight, but I have never enjoyed a mug of coffee so much in all my life. A perfect end to a memorable day, when two rare and exciting birds both called in to see me!

As I am getting into my car to drive home, I see a familiar face. A birder I know has just pulled in. We obviously have a few words, and he tells me to drive very carefully through Frampton village, he has just seen five turtle doves in the village. Needless to say, I heed his information, and as I slowly drive through, no traffic about fortunately, I see three turtle doves sitting out on some overhead power cables connected to a cottage. I am able to enjoy these birds for several minutes before they fly off. They bring the day to an end, and what a day!

Now how do you follow that? Today I only have a couple of hours at my disposal, so I visit Whitemoor Haye and Albert Village, the latter in the hope the passage gulls have started to arrive.

The Haye is very quiet, just a small party of tree sparrows, so I park up down the rough lane and commence to survey the new quarry workings. At first just a few rooks and jackdaws, but my attention is drawn to a broken-down old oak tree. This tree is still remaining standing amongst the quarried landscape, and it has a very large branch, partly broken off by gales in the past. A bird is perched on the branch, I focus up and I am delighted to see it is a tawny owl sitting out. The tree is very gnarled and has several holes suitable for nesting, so this tree needs to be studied more closely come next year.

This is only my second tawny of the year, and unlike the last one which gave me a fly-past, I am at least able to study this one closely, and whilst doing so I realise it is not one, I have two. Hunched up near to the main trunk is another tawny owl, this tree will most certainly have to be investigated further next year.

Driving on to Albert Village I make a slight diversion and call in at the Swains Park Industrial Area, and here I hit the jackpot. Sitting out on one of the Tarmac Industries' towers, is a peregrine falcon, a superb-looking tiercel, the male of the species.

The sunlight has come out fully by now, and is really highlighting this bird's plumage, an absolute cracker. That gives me two totally unexpected sightings, not 'ticks', just birds of quality.

The gulls at Albert Village Lake are low in number, just a small mixture of black-headed, lesser black-backed and a few herring gulls. To make up for this, along the shore a small flock of yellow wagtails are feeding away, nine of them, more than adequate compensation for the lack of gulls.

A very productive two hours, which produced three birds of quality.

September has commenced well.

The last couple of days have been rather dull and I have also been busy, so today, Wednesday, is my first opportunity to get out for an hour or two, so a quick trip across to Blithfield will fit the bill.

Stopping at Watery Lane there is little to see, apart from the gulls and cormorants, so I drive across the causeway to the Admaston Reach car park. Here things are a little better. Several great crested grebes are on the water, the odd common tern is out hunting and a solitary black tern is off Beech Tree Point. Whilst enjoying the black tern I become conscious of a large bird circling high overhead, the osprey is out and about. For several minutes the bird has to avoid the attention of lesser black-backed gulls which are harassing it, before it plunge-dives into the water beneath. It hits the water feet first, sending spray high into the air, before it reappears, unfortunately, without a catch. It repeats the manoeuvre three or four times, all unsuccessfully, before it flies off. A very special, few minutes.

Two little egrets fly in and proceed to hunt very actively in the shallow waters of Admaston Reach, with what appears to be far more success than that of the osprey I can only presume they have found a shoal of small fish judging by all the activity.

I turn my attention back to the reservoir, and off Beech Tree Point a great white egret is seen, it was not there a few minutes ago when the osprey was about. Even at this distance it is easy to see just how big they are, no mistaking this bird.

At this moment a friend of mine drives up. I show the great white egret and black tern to him, in return he tells me about two spotted flycatchers he has just seen along Watery Lane. That is a fair exchange. Off to Watery Lane I go.

He had seen the birds down towards Concrete Bay, so I park up and slowly make my way down. A small bird catches my attention which vanishes into a thick hawthorn bush. This is not the flycatcher, it is a warbler of some kind. After much effort I locate the bird, partly hidden by the thick foliage, it is either a chiffchaff or willow warbler, but as the bird is silent, it is not helping. After a few minutes the bird hops out onto the end of a branch and I have a decent view, although only momentarily. Fortunately, I manage to see its legs clearly, they are dark—it is a chiffchaff. The willow warbler's legs are much paler, minute detail, but helpful to obtain correct identification.

Back to spotted flycatcher hunting. Near Concrete Bay is a small wooded area, just four or five shrubby trees, and I concentrate my efforts on these. There is no activity taking place although I can hear a chaffinch calling, a feint 'fink, fink' can be heard.

I reposition myself so I can view from a different angle, and this is rewarded. A bird flits out, takes a passing insect, and vanishes back in the tree. Although chaffinches will do this, it is no chaffinch. A chaffinch has a bright white wingbar, this bird looked just a 'little brown job', it is the spotted flycatcher. I wait a few minutes before it repeats the action, another passing insect meets its doom. It is not much fun being low down in the pecking order!

I spend a few more minutes, and see the bird three more times, before it is time to leave. A very productive and enjoyable hour or so, nothing new, but several birds of quality seen, and all so close to home.

Friday morning is here, time for a bit of perusal on the net to plan my next few days' birding. Blithfield I see has a pintail reported, so that is this afternoon's birding sorted, and Blacktoft Sands has red-necked phalarope and spotted crake on the agenda, plus pintail as a backup should I fail today at Blithfield. Subject to no changes at Blacktoft, that is tomorrow arranged. Over the next thirty-six hours or so I could reach my two hundred for the year. Come and join me for a bit of fun, and who knows, it could even be excitement, phalaropes and crakes are a bit special, and pintails are not that common.

A thought has occurred to me. We are rapidly reaching the end of this narrative, the conclusion of my eightieth year of bird study, so in a way it is rather a special year, certainly for me. The birds we are seeing this year have most definitely been special to me, so I will list them all, in sequential order, and where seen, as an appendix to this book. For those of you new to the hobby, this may prove useful as a guide to when certain birds may be seen.

At Blithfield, I make my way directly down to the hide in Stansley Wood, as it is from here the latest reports of the pintail came. I have the hide to myself, so I set things up for scanning the bay ahead. The water levels are very low, and instead of the hide overlooking water, it is now dry with grass having grown, so water is much further away than I thought it would be.

Many birds are to be seen on the water, but in today's conditions they are all in silhouette, this is not going to help matters. Before concentrating on the pintail, I work the shore and find two curlews feeding away, and energetically so. A black-tailed godwit is in the distance, a little egret is dashing about in the shallows, it looks to be having a great time, and three shelducks are sitting out. Now for the water.

Seven great black-backed gulls are slowly drifting by, several black-headed and lesser black-backed gulls are on the water or circling above, and there are good numbers of both teals, and wigeons. A solitary Caspian gull flies in, not that anything takes any notice of it, and swallows are active today, skimming low over the water. A group of thirty-four great crested grebes are assembled in the bay, with the odd lapwing and ringed plover flying through, but no pintail.

Whilst all of this is going on, the hide is slowly filling up, more birders are pintail seeking. We now have seven pairs of eyes looking for the bird, they do at least find me two ruffs which I had missed.

I give it an hour and decide to move off in to Blithe Bay. As I am leaving a great white egret appears round a corner in the bay, so that is a decent send off!

I drive round into Blithe Bay, there are far more duck on the water here. Mallards especially so, with just the odd tufted duck and pochard. There are also many teals and wigeons, here they are on the water, in Tad Bay they were sitting out on the shore. They are not going to help me.

Before I start to work, there are a further five little egrets and a great white egret in the bay along with a small group of black-tailed godwits and about twenty ringed plovers, among which are tucked in four dunlins. Not a bad little selection really, but not what I am after.

Back to scanning the water. After many 'nearlies', I spot a bird frequently up-end to feed, a characteristic of pintails, so I focus up on this bird. The light, if anything, has deteriorated somewhat, and picking out any colour is nigh impossible. Fortunately, the bird stops up-ending for a short period, and I can see the bird has a longish neck. Pintails probably have the longest neck in relationship to body size of any of the duck and the head looks very rounded. It commences to feed again, but luckily for me its angle has slightly changed and I can now see the bird has a decided pointed tail. I am happy now. Combining neck length, rounded head and pointed tail, I have my pintail, the only thing I am not certain about is the sex of the bird. In this poor light it just looks generally brown so it could be either a duck or drake in eclipse, or even a juvenile for that matter. All that really concerns me is the fact I have a pintail at last, and today I believe I have earned it. Now let us see what Blacktoft has in store for us, come tomorrow. See you there.

Last thing I did tonight was check up on the birds at Blacktoft, and I am sorry to say neither the phalarope or crake has been reported for over twenty-four hours. It very much looks as though they have moved on. I will still visit Blacktoft, there are always other birds to see so the day will not be wasted, and as the weather forecast does not look too good, a reserve with hides may be beneficial.

At least the weather forecasters have it right. I arrive at Blacktoft in moderate rain with heavier rain forecast. A quick check up on booking in, confirms the news regarding the phalarope and crake, they are no longer to be seen on the reserve, so what has Blacktoft got on offer?

I make my way to Singleton Hide where I understand the best birds are to be seen. I have never been to Blacktoft and seen the water levels in the lagoons so low, they have almost dried out with the odd bit of soft mud and water, and the numbers of waterfowl and waders very much reduced in consequence.

Although the numbers of waders are low, there is a decent spread of species.

Dunlins, curlew, sandpipers, black-tailed godwits, lapwings and curlews are seen, just a few of each, but as I have said before, one is always better than none. A good number of both pied and yellow wagtails are to be seen, a passage is obviously occurring, and a marsh harrier is out hunting over the reeds. The waders do not hang around for long, a sparrowhawk comes flashing through, and that is that. I move down to Townend Hide, and the rain now means it.

Things are quiet here, water levels again very low, but I do at least have a green sandpiper and two snipes, so it is not all bad. A water rail also comes out of the reeds for a few seconds and a group of swallows fly through, probably over fifty of them, but they were not stopping.

Whilst in the hide a birder comes in, he is a local man from Scunthorpe, and I have seen him on several occasions previously. We are the only people in the hide so we have our usual chat, and the phalarope is obviously part of this. He surprises me, and tells me where the bird has moved to. Apparently, the local birders are keeping the information as secret as they can as the area where the bird is being seen is down a very narrow lane and if many cars tried to travel down it, problems are very likely.

Vehicles would have great difficulty in passing each other, and parking is also rather limited. I had helped him in the past and he was only too happy to give me the location. It was Chowder Ness, on the banks of the Humber near to Far Ings, and I know the place well. No need to ask where my next destination is.

We say our goodbyes, I return to my car for lunch, and drive off to Chowder Ness, where he was right about the narrow lane. I meet up with two cars and it took a bit of shuffling round so we could pass safely. I arrive on the small car park, accompanied by a Cetti's warbler calling away, a very cheery greeting indeed. The tide is still out on the Humber, not that I am interested in that, the phalarope has been reported from one of the lagoons adjacent to the shore, Ness Lake.

Fortunately, there are not many birds on the water, and I quickly locate my quarry, spinning round like a top in the water. Phalaropes feed in this manner frequently. They stir up small food particles, such as plankton and insect larvae from the water, which they take in and expel the surplus water, similarly to how some whales feed. Although they will probe in soft mud for food, this spinning is a very good way of identifying them as a phalarope. Your only problem then, is which?

The red-necked has the longer and more slender bill, the grey phalarope has a shorter and more stouter bill.

I enjoy this bird for a good half an hour, before it eventually 'spins' out of sight. I am very pleased I met the birder at Blacktoft, I will have to thank him profusely when I see him again. This bird is number one hundred and ninety-nine for the year. A day that commenced quietly has ended rather special to say the least.

I have no plans for any birding today, Sunday, I have some business to attend to. On my way back home, I call in at the layby in Kings Bromley, I rarely pass this by, and I am pleased I do. Nine little egrets are to be seen, this is the largest number I have seen here for several months. Their success in colonisation in the UK, England especially, has been most impressive, and they are slowly being joined by great white egrets and cattle egrets, both now breeding in small numbers. Results of climate change?.

It is Wednesday before I am able to do any birding, and this will just have to be a quick visit to Blithfield Reservoir after I have gone into Lichfield to have my hair cut and visit the bank. In transit I call in at the layby in Kings Bromley and here I am greeted by five little egrets, four teals and a grey heron. Not a bad little greeting that.

Haircut and bank business completed I drive across to Blithfield. I call in at Watery Lane first, not that a lot is seen from here, so I proceed across the causeway to Admaston Reach. Things are livelier here, with two coots providing much of it.

Coots are notoriously aggressive birds, they will tackle anything, even larger birds such as mallards if the mood takes them. Today it was coot versus coot, and these birds really meant it. They were attacking each other most fiercely, continually holding each other under the water whilst pecking away, it looked as though they were trying to drown each other. After a few minutes of aggression one of the birds decided enough was enough and managed to break free and fly off down the reservoir.

The reason for this fighting, I do not know, I may have expected it during the breeding season when birds fight over territory rights, but at this time of the year I have no idea. Whether it had started over food, one bird had something the other wanted, I do not know, but it is possible.

There was also much gull activity, lesser black-backed and black-headed principally, and the odd common tern is still evident, not for much longer. Two oystercatchers are in the Reach and three little egrets fly in to join them, and further round the bay a small group of five ringed plovers are feeding away. A small bird is busily flitting along a nearby fence, and when I eventually get a good view if it, I am pleased to be looking at a very smart male wheatear. A welcome sighting at any time.

Turning my attention to Tad Bay, two great white egrets are feeding along the shore, due to their size they stand out even at this distance. Moving onto the osprey's tree, it is sitting high up in the tree, showing quite well against the trees forming a dark background, the amount of white on the bird helps in these situations. For how much longer the osprey remains is open to question, but it is normally here until at least October, one year we actually had a bird locally early in November, a very late record.

Swallow numbers are now reducing, many will have already departed as they commence their migration southwards. Some bird facing some journey.

My time has now run out, off home I go. A pleasant hour shared with some interesting birds, that is what it is all about. And it is not often you see a battle royal as I had with the coots.

Thursday has dawned bright and clear, if it remains so, I may manage an hour or so out this afternoon, as long as I get on well with one or two things I must do at home. This I do, the day is still bright and clear, so where to go? It is a toss-up between Blithfield and Whitemoor Haye, and Blithfield wins. It is going to have to be a quick visit, with viewing from near to where I park, I have not time for going into Stansley Woods, or walking far.

My first stop is Watery Lane, very quiet on the bird front, although the ice cream vendor seems to be doing well. Across to Admaston Reach, here things are a little more interesting. Two little egrets are feeding in the Reach and a great white egret is just about visible down Blithe Bay. Gull activity is high, many black-headed gulls in particular, plus lesser black-backed and four great black-backed gulls, no terns to be seen, however. A greenshank is heard, but cannot be located. I am just about to move on when a birder I know drives up. He has only been birdwatching for a couple of years, since he retired, and as he says himself, still very much a novice.

He comes over to me and asks am I going down to the dam, he believes he has just seen a water pipit, but could not be absolutely certain. I ask him a few questions about the bird and he picked up three details which confirm what he has seen. The bird was a bit greyish looking, had a pronounced white eyebrow, and the clincher was he saw two distinct white wingbars. As a novice he had done darn well to note all this. I told him so and also confirmed he had in fact seen a water pipit. It is wonderful when you meet a novice who actually makes notes, and does not just rely on his field guide. This birder will go far, and so do I, well off to the dam anyway. I thank him, point out the great white egret, and shoot off.

Time is now at a premium. I pull up on the sailing club car park. He had seen the bird on the dam slope, so that is where I concentrate my efforts. Although the day is bright and clear, a very strong breeze has now blown up, and waves are crashing against the dam slope. Not the best of viewing conditions, but my efforts are rewarded. A small bird is dashing along on the edge of the waves, definitely a pipit, but which? Keep on coming, and it does. I get the view I want, confirm the details given to me, and I have a water pipit.

This sighting brings a sigh of relief really. I was sure I had seen one earlier in the year, but it was not down on my records, so I would never be absolutely certain I had, now I have, so the problem is solved. My two hundredth bird of the year, the pressure is now off. I can now drive home a happy man, and I have a beginner to thank for it. Next time I see him, thank him I will.

On my return journey home, I make my customary stop at the layby in Kings Bromley, and today I have six little egrets on view. The numbers here are holding up well.

Friday looks a dull day, showers are promised, but as midday approaches things clear up a bit and as I have completed my few chores, a drive round the local area will not go amiss.

I have not been over to Alvecote for some time, so I will include that in my agenda. Driving through Kings Bromley I, needless to say, call in at the layby and today seven little egrets are on show. On now to Croxall Lakes, and here, as well as about two hundred Canada geese, we have a further three little egrets, that gives me ten in the first half an hour. As all my locations for today are water based, for a bit of fun, let us see just how many little egrets we may see. That, of course, has put the kiss of death on things!

No, it has not. Pulling in at Alvecote Pools, two more little egrets are quickly spotted, along with a pair of garganey which are both in moult unfortunately, the drake just showing a little colour. Working my way round the shore a further three little egrets are seen. We are on a roll here I think, that takes us up to twelve.

Next stop will be Whitemoor Haye, and here as a change, the first birds of interest I see are not water birds, they are game birds. Driving slowly along the rough lane, I spot a group of partridges up ahead. I stop, wondering if they are the grey partridge, I saw a short time ago. Not this time, they are a covey of seven red-legged partridges, two adults and five juveniles, the latter being almost as large as their parents, but lacking the plumage. I have obviously disturbed them as they swiftly run through a gap in the hedgerow and vanish in the field beyond. As I proceed along the rough lane, I see a small flock of tree sparrows and a solitary yellowhammer.

I pull in at a spot which overlooks Whitemoor Haye Lake, which is rather peaceful today, no water activities taking place. This at least leaves the birds in peace and a goodly flock of grey-lags are on the water, along with small flotillas of teals and wigeons, plus three pochards. Along the water's edge are two more little egrets, both sitting there, just hunched up, obviously well fed.

We will now finish up at Blithfield Reservoir. No water pipit on the dam today, it has no doubt moved on. I was very fortunate yesterday. To make up for this, a little egret is feeding in the corner and another is standing out on the dam wall.

They are mounting up, that is the sixteenth seen so far.

On to Watery Lane. Very quiet here, just a few gulls in the air and a flock of cormorants out on the water, but towards Concrete Bay I see a speck of white, focusing up, a little egret. It is well worth the stop.

Admaston Reach calls, and here things take off on the egret front. Initially two great white egrets are seen flying down Blithe Bay, and as they glide in to land, several white birds are on the shore, far too tall to be gulls. Concentration time. I re-position myself for a clearer view, to find I am looking at five more little egrets, standing in a group on the shore, they take us up to twenty-two for the day so far.

They prove not to be the end of it, slowly walking along the causeway slope come two more, which take us up to twenty-four. When I think back to my first ever little egret, you will no doubt recollect my talking about it as a group of us drove all the way to Anglesey to see it, and today I have seen twenty-four of them, all within a radius of ten miles or so from home. Plus, most of the views I have had today were vastly superior to my first. Is there a moral in all of this? This concludes a most enjoyable day. No rarities, no 'ticks', just interesting birds, and that is what birding is all about.

On browsing the net in the evening, I was most interested to see that a scarlet rosefinch (or rosefinch as they are now known), had been recorded at Spurn Point for three or four days. I have not visited Spurn for some time nor seen a rosefinch for several years, so tomorrow I will put that right—hopefully!

An early start is called for, and I am on way by 07.30 a.m. The journey is not too bad and I arrive in a little under three hours, my mileometer telling me I have driven just under one hundred and forty miles.

Before chasing up the rosefinch I spend some time sea watching, and this was an almost complete waste of time and effort. Due to an off-shore wind birds, the few I could see, were all far out at sea, making identification very difficult. The only birds I could be certain of were a small group of four common scoters and the odd gull. I now hope the rosefinch will be more accommodating!

The bird was last reported from an area known as the canal, and I manage to park close to this. A small party of birders are walking back along the canal. We stop and talk, they confirm the bird is about fifty yards or so down the canal, and there are other birders there still looking at the bird, so I should have no problem. I have heard that comment on many an occasion, and it has not always been accurate.

I quickly spot the birders and they tell me the bird keeps on popping out onto a small tree, providing good views. That sounds very hopeful, and so it proves.

I doubt if I have been here ten minutes before the bird obliges, and out it pops. Their name is a little misleading, the amount of red in their plumage varies with age and sex, but the bird's pronounced forehead and hefty bill, combined with the two narrow wingbars, help in identification. No problem with this bird. I stay for half an hour, seeing the bird on five more occasions, before moving on

When I drove in earlier, I had noticed a nature reserve at Kilnsea, this was not here when I was last visiting, so I call in. It is the Kilnsea Wetlands Nature Reserve and is being developed to help compensate for the land loss that is occurring on Spurn. Coastal erosion has occurred at a rapid rate in recent years.

I make my way to the hide which overlooks a newly created lake, and it has many birds in attendance. A large number of gulls, black-headed, lesser black-backed and the odd herring and great black-backed gull, and whilst making my way slowly through these, I pick up a herring gull type which has very dark eyes. A Caspian gull is tucked away, herring gulls have very bright, hard, yellow eyes.

Moving on to the waders, which too are plentiful. Redshanks are in large numbers, several hundred are spread round the shores of the lake, probably reaching four figures. Curlews calling, but I cannot locate them, dunlins are plentiful and several knots are busily feeding. Black-tailed godwits are in goodly numbers, and a few ringed plovers and golden plovers are seen. A very silvery/greyish looking bird emerges from behind a mound, and I am delighted to see I have a grey plover. This bird has been avoiding me all year, at long last I have it on my 'year list', my second 'tick' today. The bird still has much of its summer plumage, and stands out well.

A passage is obviously taking place, birds are on migration. Several groups of yellow wagtails are flying through, as are pipits. The pipits are flying quite high, so all I can do with these is presume they are meadow pipits. Small parties of swallows are also on passage. I wish them all luck on their journey southwards.

As I have time I will pop down to Sammy's Point, an area which overlooks the Humber, as the tide is now going out a few waders may be in. I have the Point to myself and just the birds. The waders are not as plentiful as I had hoped, a few curlews are feeding on the newly exposed mud, accompanied by dunlins and knots, with the most numerous waders being ruffs, and these are certainly in three figures.

Gulls are also moving in to feed, small flocks of those drifting in, so it is a scene of some activity and not a little noise. A great white egret can also be seen on an area of the salt marsh, these birds are popping up everywhere now.

I return to my car and before driving off I spend a few minutes studying the meadows adjacent to the Point, and what a decision this turns out to be. A short-eared owl is out hunting, and it slowly moves backwards and forwards over a stretch of meadow. Their flight is effortless and very graceful, the perfect flying machine.

Today the owl goes hungry, I see it catch nothing as it slowly drifts out of sight, a super ending to a perfect day. My third 'tick' of the day, at this time of the year that takes some beating. A lot of miles and over six hours of driving, but well worth the effort, and the cost for that matter. You only live 'ONCE'. Unless you are James Bond!

After the excitement and effort put into yesterday's birding, today I think a quieter day is called for, so I will visit Shustoke Reservoir and the lakes at Coton, both in Warwickshire.

In transit to these two destinations I go through Kings Bromley, and I need not tell you where I end up. My car almost automatically turns into the layby, and once again I am not disappointed, seven little egrets are to be seen, their numbers are certainly staying good.

Arriving at Coton, I am very surprised to see the entrance to the car parking area is closed off, no access at all possible. The reason for this I do not understand as the car parking was used by both fishermen and birders, there is even a hide for the birders. I can only presume some vandalism or fly tipping has taken place. I am going to be at Shustoke earlier than anticipated.

I have a feeling I am not in for a good day. A sailing event is taking place at Shustoke and this is accompanied by regular sounds of a loud horn, no doubt of benefit to the yachtsmen, not for me.

The few birds which are in attendance are at least up near to where I am parked, but not a lot of excitement amongst them. Canada geese, mallards, coots and moorhens are about, plus the odd grebe. I turn my attention to the few gulls which are about, these regularly take to the air when the horn sounds, and one of them catches my attention. It is a smallish gull, showing black on the underside of the wings, and there is only one gull of this size, so marked, that is the little gull.

Concentration time. The birds alight back on a buoy, so I can study it more closely. It is almost in full summer plumage, the black head almost still completely black. The black-headed gull which it closely resembles, has a brown head and it only covers approximately half of the head, whereas the little gull has a complete black head. Come the winter they both lose their head colouring, and then the black underside to the wings becomes the best identification feature, although if seen together, the black-headed is the larger of the two.

Little gulls are not common by any means, especially inland, so although I have seen the odd one or two, I am more than happy to see this one. It justifies my trip out to Shustoke. I watch the bird take flight on a few more occasions before deciding to move on.

As I now have more time than anticipated I will make a quick visit to Blithfield, and as I pass though Kings Bromley on the way, I, naturally enough, end up in the layby. Since I was here earlier, the little egrets have been breeding! We now have nine in view, all busily feeding away in the river. Wonderful birds.

Blithfield is birdwatcher less, well at least the two areas I visit. Not a lot of activity on the bird front either. Four little egrets are visible in Admaston Reach and two great white egrets can be seen in Tad Bay, which plus two buzzards flying through, are about it. The rest are gulls.

Nothing mega, but a pleasant enough three hours, and the little gull at least was unexpected, bringing a bit of quality to the scene.

It is now Wednesday and this provides me with the first opportunity I have had of any birding for a couple of days. I only have two hours or so available, so I will have a quick trip across to Blithfield Reservoir. I may even manage some time down Stansley Wood, we will see.

It is a windy day and the wind increases in strength as the day progresses. Driving across to Blithfield the sky is darkening and as I arrive at Watery Lane, the heavens open, and down comes the rain. It absolutely cascades down, reducing visibility as though fog was descending. I cannot open any windows, not that it really mattered, due to lack of visibility, I can see little.

The stormy conditions last for over half an hour, before things slowly improve, and when they do there is little to be seen. A few birds are on the water, cormorants, ducks and grebes, but all the gulls have flown off and just the odd swallow is flying through.

As I have some time left, I decide to pop across to Croxall and Whitemoor Haye, and I arrive here in perfect conditions. The roads are all dry, no rain obviously fell, not that the birding is any better. I have not seen Croxall so quiet for some time, two great crested grebes and a coot, very exciting!

The lake at Whitemoor Haye improves matters slightly. The local flock of Canada and grey-lag geese are in attendance, and the numbers of teals and wigeons are building up well. The cormorant flock is over thirty and a mixture of gulls is evident. Down the Haye it is much quieter, just a small flock of tree sparrows and a buzzard sitting out in a tree, but that is better than nothing at all.

Driving back home through Kings Bromley, I, naturally enough, call in at the layby, and I am rewarded by six little egrets. These are all out on the meadows and the way they are mingling with the cattle you could be excused in thinking they are cattle egrets—they are not. They are however, a bright conclusion to my afternoon's trip out, so I am not complaining. It is now a question of what does the remainder of the week hold? Only time will answer that question, and if the weather is anything like that forecast, it will not be answered tomorrow!

Home provides me with some interest. Due to the wind of late my fat ball stand had swung round and one of the containers was now directly over a small conifer. A rook had quickly learnt that it could stand on the top of the conifer and reach the fat ball container. Watching this bird, I realised that as it attacked the container it moved the position of it, and to compensate for this the bird moved its position to feed which returned the container almost back to its original position.

What fascinated me was the fact this manoeuvre was carried out several times before the bird had eaten its fill. I know I frequently talk about the intelligence of the members of the crow family, this rook certainly illustrated this fact. You can learn a lot by just watching the birds in your own garden.

The forecasters have it right, the weather is very damp and birding is really on the back burner. I do however, manage to feed the birds and in doing so need to replenish my sunflower hearts stock, so a visit to my supplier in Kings Bromley will be called for later in the day.

On my journey down to Kings Bromley, I do, obviously, call in at the layby, here little egret numbers are reduced, only two are out in the bad weather. Egrets may be water birds of a kind, but it looks as even though they are happy enough to walk and feed in it, they are not so keen to be out in it. A duck goosander swims through, he obviously does not worry about the weather, and a grey heron is also seen. It, on the other hand, looks decidedly grumpy standing hunched up in the elements. An interesting few minutes or so, well worth pulling in for.

I duly collect my supply of sunflower hearts, hopefully it will keep my birds supplied for another month or so. I no longer work out what I spend on the birds, if I did, I would probably have to stop. The pleasure they bring me is worth every penny I spend, except it is not pennies, or should I say pence?

Whilst I am at the farm I hear raven, two fly overhead and circle round for a few seconds. Considering the weather today, the few birds seen have all been quality.

If the weather forecasters are to be believed, the next few days look rather damp and windy, more gales being likely, not that our current one has fully left us yet, we still have a 'yellow' warning locally. If I am to do any birding over the next few days, I am going to have to be rather selective, especially when the weekend arrives. I shall be spending some time on the net, that is for sure.

Friday has at least commenced dry and bright, although rain is promised for later. Locally, the best selection of birds appears to be at Carsington Water, in Derbyshire, so I will give it a try. This has the advantage of having hides and warm food, which on days such as this may turn out to be, are a definite plus. Nothing new is likely, but a few interesting species have been recorded, and that is what birding is all about.

As far as the weekend is concerned, it looks as though the wind direction may change, and instead of coming in from the west, easterlies are expected, if that should prove to be the case, the east coast may be the place to go. Passage birds will be driven in nearer the coast, so good views may be possible. Spurn Point may see me again.

Friday is due to be very damp by the look of things, but I will still have a trip up to Carsington. It is dry when I leave home but before I reach my destination the rain is falling, and looking at the sky, there is a lot up there.

I am a little late in starting out, so on my arrival, I decide to have an early lunch, a crisp bacon roll and a mug of latte should set me up for the day ahead. They are most pleasant and welcome, but set me up they do not. The heavens have opened and rain is lashing down. I dash to my car, and sit in this, waiting for the rain to stop. It does not. After half an hour I decide enough is enough, so make my way home. It is not often I have a complete washout, but today it is.

It looks as though this poor weather is likely to continue tomorrow, so I change my plans, and instead I will visit Eyebrook Reservoir and Rutland Water where there are hides. A few interesting birds have been reported lately, the pick amongst them being glossy ibis, American wigeon and grey phalarope, any of those would be most welcome.

I call in at Eyebrook Reservoir first, as there are no hides here, and driving down through Stoke Dry to the reservoir, I am delighted to see two red kites gliding over. Some greeting that! They were first introduced into Leicestershire some years ago, and they are now thriving, always a marvellous sight.

I park up by the side of the reservoir and start to scan the water. Although it is very dull and the light poor, the water is very calm, and the many birds are standing out well. Cormorant numbers are high, as are Canada and grey-lag geese. Teals and wigeons are well spread, with mallard numbers also high. A duck is flying fast and low over the reservoir, and even in today's poor light, it is showing much colour. As it comes ever closer, I realise it is a superb drake mandarin, they always brighten up a dull day.

Three birders walk up and as we greet each other, one says, 'Come for the phalarope I suppose?' I look at him, I thought the phalarope was at Rutland, but it looks as though the bird has transferred to Eyebrook. I quickly find out where they last saw the bird, it is on the opposite side of the reservoir, so I drive round.

I manage to park up in a good spot to look for the bird, and set myself up. I had been told to look for a little egret as the phalarope was feeding close to that bird.

The egret is soon located, white birds do stand out a bit.

There are many water birds in the area, coots especially so, and I concentrate on these, looking for a small bird spinning round in the water. After many minutes, my efforts are rewarded, a small bird spins out from behind a group of coots, and I have my quarry.

The bird is very accommodating, and I am able to enjoy watching it for several minutes. I do in fact, have my lunch whilst viewing the phalarope. I have mentioned previously how accommodating Arctic breeding species seem. I suppose human beings are not numerous in the areas in which they breed, the only thing they may see on two legs occasionally is a polar bear, and they move more often on their four legs. I doubt they could catch a phalarope in any case, or would wish to.

Time to move on to Rutland Water. As I arrive the rain commences, and as with yesterday, it does not stop. After many minutes I decide it is not worth the effort, so I cut my losses, and drive off home. In transit near to Market Harborough I see a further two individual red kites. I am surprised to see them in such conditions.

They started my day, and they have concluded it.

Well not quite. On my return journey home, I call in at the layby in Kings Bromley, here I see four little egrets.

Later in the evening, I am on the computer checking up on local bird reports, when I see a piece of surprising information, which also draws a wry smile to my face. I have today made a round trip of about one hundred and thirty miles to see a rare bird, when, if I had known it, I could have seen the same species at Chasewater, a round trip of about thirty miles. As compensation, Chasewater does not have red kites or mandarins.

Sunday dawns, damp, but I understand it may clear by mid-morning. The question now is, do I go across to Chasewater or visit Blithfield which seems to have a better range of species? Not being too confident of the weather forecasters I choose Blithfield, here I have hides.

By 10.30 a.m., it looks as though the forecasters have it right, blue sky is spreading and the sun is out. Blithfield is quiet, very few cars are parked up and no birders are in view, it looks as though I have the place to myself.

Initially not a lot is to be seen, so I decide to drive down Admaston Reach into Blithe Bay, and here things waken up. A great white egret is slowly walking along the shore, and whilst I stop to enjoy this bird, a small wader runs past. It is a turnstone, a very nimble little bird, which is living up to its name. The shore here is quite gravelly, and the bird is busily probing into this, not actually turning stones, but certainly turning gravel!

Moving on, as I round a bend, five little egrets are to be seen wading in shallow water and a flock of fifteen ringed plovers are feeding along the shore. I study these closely, but no little ringed plovers are among them. This is not really surprising, little ringed plovers are summer migrants, and by now the majority will have moved off south. Out in deeper water a largish wader is seen, a black-tailed godwit. Nothing special is to be seen among the ducks and gulls so I move round to Tad Bay.

Walking down through Stansley Wood I disturb a mixed flock of titmice. A mixture of blues, greats, coals, long-tails and a solitary marsh tit, and in the distance a great-spotted woodpecker can be heard drumming away. A pleasant enough greeting there. From the hide a wheatear is seen along the fence and out on the distant mud are three greenshanks. Over the water is a solitary black tern and two Arctic terns, the remnants of migrating species. Enjoy them whilst we can. Sitting out among the gulls are five great black-backed gulls, and, very obligingly fortunately, stands a yellow-legged gull. Easy to see from whence it gets its name.

Not a bad selection, nothing new, but several bits of quality, and before I forget, there are goodly numbers of swallows still hanging on.

Driving home through Kings Bromley, where do you think my car went? Today it was not little egrets which graced the layby, their big cousin has moved in. A great white egret was in the river, accompanied by three grey herons, a satisfactory conclusion to the day.

The final Monday in September has dawned in a distinctly autumnal manner with a slight frost. This quickly clears and a bright, clear day, lies ahead. By early afternoon I have completed all my chores so an hour or so out will not go amiss. A drive across to Blithfield where I can spend a few minutes viewing from the causeway will fit in nicely with the time I have available.

Little is to be seen from the Watery Lane car park, so I drive on across the causeway to Admaston Reach, things are a little livelier here. A flock of cormorants are feeding just off the causeway, very actively, causing quite a stir on the water. A few great crested grebes are on the fringe of all this activity, I think it is safe to say a shoal of small fish are being plundered.

Turning my attention to the northern side of the causeway, gulls are the principal birds seen, mostly black-heads but a few larger gulls are intermingling, mainly lesser black-backs.

Further down in Blithe Bay a great white egret is slowly walking the shore, and continuing down the bay, six little egrets can be seen. Whilst enjoying these a large bird of prey glides over, the osprey is abroad. It just circles slowly round, before flapping itself sway to its perch. Thanks to the leaf cover, and my angle of view, the osprey just vanishes into the trees, but never mind, I enjoyed its passing.

Time now to move on, after a very enjoyable half an hour or so. On my way home, passing through Kings Bromley can you guess where I end up? The layby! I pull in and see five little egrets, but no great white. After no little egrets seen yesterday, it is good to see them back, I missed them yesterday. They end a very pleasant time out, once again proving, you need not travel miles to see interesting and beautiful birds.

It is now Wednesday and my first opportunity to do a bit of birding for a couple of days. I have been into Lichfield to do some business, and I have an hour to spare, so on the way back home I will call in at the layby and pop across to Dunstall.

The layby has a flock of seventeen grey-lags on the river, the duck goosander is still in attendance, and the five little egrets are also on the meadow, once again consorting with the cattle. To add a little colour, two bullfinches are feeding on some ivy. To say a little colour does not do the bullfinch much justice, they are a most colourful and distinctive bird, always a delight to see.

As I drive down past the Dunstall Estate, pheasants are again very evident. I do not count them on this occasion, I am too busy avoiding running them over as they dash about on the road ahead. Flying seems to be the last thing a pheasant ever contemplates, no wonder they are shot. Running around on the ground is no way to escape the gun, I really do believe that given time, supposing they survive as a species that is, they will join the penguin and become flightless. The pheasants I 'chase' today had better learn about flight quickly, we are only days away from the start of the pheasant shooting season. It will be very interesting to see how many are still showing in a few weeks' time, unlikely to be anywhere near the numbers seen today.

Leaving the pheasants to get on with things, I drive down to the spot which overlooks Branston Quarry. As with everywhere currently, water levels are low, and bird numbers are also small. Two mute swans are to be seen, Canada geese can be heard but are not visible, and a few black-headed gulls are in the air. A little egret is hunched up on the shoreline and a small flock of house sparrows are fluttering about in the hedgerow, most noisily. That just about sums things up, time for home.

As I drive back though Dunstall things brighten up considerably. A merlin flashes out from a nearby field and for several seconds I am able to follow him, it being a male, as it races, low over the road ahead. I do not suppose I see him for more than ten seconds, it is all over so quickly, but what a climax to my short visit.

The weather forecast for the next few days looks quite reasonable, so I will have to start making plans for the weekend ahead, here the net will be most useful.

Prior to that I need to fill my car up with fuel. So a quick trip to Lichfield is required, and I will grab a few minutes' birding on my way back home. Living in a village as I do, petrol stations are no longer next door, so it is a question of filling up when you pass a station, or making a special journey, as I do today. Combining it with some time at Whitemoor Haye, will at least justify it all....

Sitting at my computer as I now am, I become conscious of a loud buzzing, looking at my windows I am surprised to see an hornet flying up and down them, sounding angrier by the second. I can only presume it had come in before I went out, and as that was over two hours ago, no wonder it sounds cross. We regularly have to rescue insects and spiders from inside the home and we have a plastic mug used for this purpose. Mug obtained. hornet caught, now released outside, we can now both get on with our business. Some insect, with an incredible pair of eyes, it gave the impression it was staring me out.

Back to the birds. Whitemoor Haye was quite busy. A good selection of birds on the lake, nothing extra special, although the pochards seemed to be slowly building up and the same thing applies to the lapwings, this is to be expected with September almost out. The first fieldfares of the season have already been reported from Cannock Chase. Does that mean winter is just around the corner?.

Driving down the rough lane I quickly came to a stop. The fly-tippers have been out and the lane is blocked with a load of builders' rubbish, with no way to drive round it. A call to Lichfield Council will have to be made on my return home.

I park myself and look across at the tawny owl tree, not today, just a couple of woodpigeons sitting out. The tree sparrow flock are actively feeding along the hedge and four yellowhammers are also seen, in today's bright sunlight, the three males look very canary-like, very aptly named these delightful birds. As I go to get back in my car, two red-legged partridges fly across the lane, their churring wings creating quite a noise. Game birds in flight are rarely silent.

Driving back slowly up the rough lane, I stop to watch a kestrel hovering over the lane. The barred tail is very clear, the bird being either a female or juvenile, I cannot see the bird's back to be absolutely sure. I watch the bird for several seconds before it glides off to repeat the exercise further across an adjoining meadow.

I stop once again at the lake. In the few minutes since I was last here, the Canada geese have moved in, well into three figures, and not to be outdone, a goodly number of cormorants have also joined in. A good illustration of just how quickly things can change, this is probably the reason birds have wings!

Time for home, and needless to say, my car turns, automatically, onto the Kings Bromley layby. I instantly stop. The layby is carless, but running about is a stoat, and for a few seconds I enjoy watching it dashing around. I have no idea what it is after, and I do not see it catch anything, just watching it is enough for me.

Now for what I really pull onto the layby for. Today I have seven little egrets, still amongst the cattle, a grey heron, a distant buzzard, and jackdaws are calling from the nearby church tower. Not a bad little haul that, I think you will agree.

Friday dawns a very pleasant day, and as Carsington Water again seems to have a few interesting species, I am back up to Derbyshire for a few hours.

I make my way directly to the Sheepwash Hide, from here a grey phalarope was reported yesterday. Although I have seen one recently, as you know, you can never have too much of a good thing! The hide is empty, so I sort out a good viewing spot and open up a viewing window, and settle myself down. Before I start birding, I become very conscious of a loud and angry sounding buzzing, and looking down the hide I see two hornets flying across a viewing window. As with the one I had back home a day or so ago, these insects cannot understand why they are unable to fly out, they are able to see but cannot get through, and they are getting more frustrated by the minute.

Time for the Brian George Hornet Rescue Service to come into operation. When I entered the hide, I had picked up the hide bird log book to see what had been reported, this I could now use to usher the hornets out. I open the viewing window, gently lower the book towards the hornets, and with a slow flick, out they both go.

Job done, I can now get on with my birding, leaving two, now very frustrated hornets, to get on with whatever they get on with!

I can only presume that the weather experienced this year has been very suitable for the hornets. They are not the commonest of insects to be seen, so to have been in their company twice, as I have recently, must be telling us something. Long may it continue, they are a most fascinating insect, and if you leave them alone, they rarely attack man, unlike their smaller cousin, the wasp.

Looking in the Hide Log I see pink-footed geese were reported early this morning, they would have been a good bird to have seen. Although the water level is still very low, few waders are to be seen, just three dunlins and one redshank, no lapwings which is a surprise. Teal numbers are high and a flock of wigeons are on the water, but apart from a little egret along the shore, nothing to get over excited about, and no grey phalarope.

I spend a further thirty minutes or so looking, during which time a few cormorants and great crested grebes swim into view, and as I am considering moving on, I hear geese calling. These are not Canada geese or grey-lags, I am listening to a shrill and lively 'kayak, kayak', an almost cackling sound—pink-foots! I quickly swing round to face the direction the calls are coming from and I am delighted to see a skein of seventeen birds gliding in to land on the reservoir. Unfortunately, they do not land in my line of vision, they sweep round a spit and vanish from sight. No complaints from me, I had experienced a wonderful thirty seconds or so, and collected a 'year tick'.

Time now for a celebratory crispy bacon cob and coffee, before I am off home to make my plans for tomorrow.

Spurn Point has been picking up a few interesting species, especially a few skuas and divers on passage, and as high tide tomorrow is around midday, it could bring a few of those birds in close to land, so Spurn it will be. An early start will again be required.

Although it is a bright morning, we had experienced a frost

overnight and I drive through several patches of thick mist but this, fortunately, quickly clears. On driving through Easington I must have been daydreaming, as I missed my turning for Kilnsea and ended up at Easington Beach. This is no problem I am pleased to say, having visited this spot, on previous occasions, I could just as easily sea watch from here as I could off Spurn itself. So I duly set myself up.

I am right about the tide, it is fully in, and apart from the odd angler, I have it all to myself. As I was sea watching, I had brought my 'scope and tripod with me, and these quickly proved their worth, I picked up a small flock of divers out on the sea, and focusing up I found they were red-throated divers, seven of them. A 'year tick' within minutes of arrival, now that cannot be bad. Further out a flock of scoters were visible, but hard as I worked these, they were all common scoters, nothing special hidden away amongst them. Goodly numbers of teals and wigeons were also on the sea, with just the odd gull passing through. I was very surprised with their numbers, they were few and far between.

A large, dark-looking bird, lumbered into view, and as it banked, I picked out the white patches on both the upper and lower wing surfaces—a great skua. A real bully boy this one, but today it was just passing through, there was nothing about for it to harass. They are the pirates of the northern oceans and will attack birds as large as gannets to make them disgorge their food, and birds the size of puffins are readily eaten whole. Not a bird to mess about with.

The tide retreats here very quickly, so I decided to move on down to Kilnsea to see what I can find in the Humber Estuary, but before I move off, I hear geese, almost a repeat from yesterday, except these are not pink-foots. A nasal sounding 'kr-rop, kr-rop' could be heard, only one goose sounds like this, the Brent goose. Over the sea a small skein of twenty or so birds are flying in, wings just clipping the surface of the sea. The distance they have probably flown, the English east coast must be a most welcoming sight. I know, seeing them is for me.

Now for a few minutes at Kilnsea. The Humber Estuary is really exposed, the tide had raced out exposing large areas of mud, on which were many waders and black-headed gulls. Food is plentiful in these conditions and watching the dunlins and knots is almost as though watching a feeding frenzy. Whilst enjoying all this activity, a sudden exodus of birds occurred from one area, and when looking more closely I could understand why. An Arctic skua had put in an appearance, and whilst it may not be as aggressive as its cousin, the great skua, the waders did not want its close attention. Whether the skua was in hunting mode or not I do not know, it quickly flies through and peace returns.

I had some time left so a walk down the canal could be of interest. This takes you down towards Spurn Point and has produced many interesting birds in the past.

Two warblers catch my attention in a small bush. I manage to obtain a decent view and they are two chiffchaffs, no doubt on their migration southwards. Further along the canal a small number of common snipe fly up as they heard my approach and quickly flew into the estuary. Continuing on my way, I picked up a black bird which was also eating hawthorn berries, and this was no blackbird, it was a superb male ring ouzel. I may have seen ring ouzel previously this year, but this bird was only about twenty feet away from me, and it was so interested in eating that it was not aware of my presence. I just stood still for a few minutes enjoying it all, binoculars were not needed that was for sure. Another bird on his way south, the next time I hope to see one of his kind will be in May.

Turning back a small flock of redshanks fly overhead, making their way into the estuary to feed, and two common sandpipers fly past me, as they progress down the canal. Not a lot else was seen so a few minutes in the churchyard will finish my day off.

I had chosen well. Two other birders were in the churchyard and they were enjoying two male pied flycatchers, needless to say I joined them, although when I told them about the ring ouzel they quickly departed. There were a lot of insects flying and the flycatchers were really filling themselves up, a good preparation for their departure south. I heard a short, soft call which I did not instantly recognise.

Fortunately, it repeated the call several times, a soft 'hueet' is the best way I can describe it. Eventually I tracked the bird down, and it was a willow warbler. I am so used to hearing them sing in the summer, I had completely forgotten what their call sounded like. Another bird making its way southwards. I wished all the migrants seen today good luck on their journeys and hope to see them all again next year,

That brought a most interesting day's birding to its conclusion, and increased my 'year list' by four very special species.

After all the excitement of yesterday, the question is 'how to follow that?'

Today also sees the completion of the month, and I have limited time available, so I will pop across to Albert Village Lake in Leicestershire for a quick look at the gulls.

Albert Village Lake does rather well for the more unusual gulls, it is right next door to a landfill site, which is regularly visited by the local winter gull population. I am hoping for something unusual, a white-winged gull, it is about time for the odd one to put in an appearance.

The journey across is uneventful and I am able to park up in a spot which overlooks the lake and is directly under the flypath of gulls coming over from the nearby landfill site. There are many gulls today, both on the lake and in flight, so I am going to have to concentrate hard. The weather at least is reasonable with little or no wind, so the act of birding is quite comfortable.

The two gulls in particular I am looking for are the glaucous gull and Iceland gull, both large gulls, and being white-winged gulls I am looking for gulls which have white primaries, not the black of our commoner species.

Of the larger gulls, lesser black-backed are certainly the commonest, with a few herring and great black-backed gulls. Needless to say, there are many black-headed gulls in attendance, but they are too small to interest me today.

I have some exciting moments, a few immature birds raise the temperature a bit, but all to no avail, so after a good hour spent, I call it a day. It will not be my last attempt, I am just probably a little early for these Arctic breeding species to have arrived so far inland. They will, I just have to hope to be available when they do. As I have said previously, you cannot win them all, today I did not, but I certainly did yesterday.

The month closes with my 'year list' standing at two hundred and nine, new species are not going to be easy to find, but we will try.

October has not commenced well. I have a problem with my foot. I cannot put it to the floor without pain, walking is very difficult. I have this occur occasionally, it is probably a touch of gout, and it normally takes three or four days to ease, my birding will now be very limited. Once it starts to ease off, I will at least be able to drive, it is my left foot and as my car is an automatic, the left foot is not used. Until then, my birding will be from my own garden, and it has not been very productive.

Fortunately, my feeders had all been filled up over the weekend, so provisions are available, the problem is, the birds are not. The odd house sparrow has put in appearance and the same thing applies to both blue and great tits. Starlings, which had been quite busy, are non-existent currently, and apart from the odd gull and rook flying over, little else has appeared on the scene. I can but hope things improve, and quickly.

As the week has progressed, my foot has improved, and today, the 4th October, I will be popping out for an hour or two. Nothing special has occurred in my garden over the past few days, a pair of greenfinches being the highlight. Today is however, a very special day, it is sixty years ago today that Dorothy and I were married, and had she still been here, I would not have been out birding on my own that is for sure, something a little more special than that would have occurred. Life however, is what it is, and I am just grateful for the life and time we spent together. One cannot ask, nor expect, more than that.

Back to the present. With the time I have available, a trip round Kings Bromley and Blithfield Reservoir should fit in well, and Kings Bromley will be my first stop. Before I even pull in on the layby, the little egrets can be seen, once again associating with the cattle. The cattle are no doubt disturbing many small insects and the like as they feed, and the little egrets are benefitting from this. Their behaviour is very similar to the way cattle egrets feed, hence my comments previously regarding any birders mistaking them for cattle egrets.

As I look further along the river, two grey herons are standing out on the bank and a great white egret is feeding in the river, and very actively so. Water is spraying off its bill on occasions, and it certainly appears to be finding something as its neck bulges as though food is passing down. A very contented bird one would believe.

Whilst all this is going on, a duck goosander swims slowly down the river, she too, diving frequently, hopefully as successfully as the egret.

Time to move on. I call in at the sailing club car park at Blithfield, and here I see two common sandpipers feeding along the shore and a southern cormorant is sitting out on the end of the jetty. A large flock of geese are in Mickledale Bay, the usual mix of Canada and grey-lags. As I am about to move off to Admason Reach three swallows fly past, they are a bit late, so I wished them luck.

In the reach, a small flock of teals are feeding in the shallows, the odd cormorant flies through and great crested grebe numbers are good. It is by now, a very bright afternoon, and two buzzards are enjoying the sunshine as they soar over the reservoir, and a kestrel puts in a brief appearance.

On the shore a party of pipits are feeding away very busily, not staying still for any length of time. Frustrating really, but after much effort I think they are all meadow pipits.

As I scan the water looking at passing gulls, I spot a gull sitting out on a buoy, quickly passing it off as a herring gull. For some reason I return to this bird, and on focusing up I see the bird has yellow legs. This is no herring gull, it is a superb full adult yellow-legged gull, and I nearly passed it by. It may not be a 'year tick', but it is the bird of the day in many respects, and I almost missed it. With gulls it always pays to at least look twice. A lesson there, no matter how good you may think you are. A useful ending to my trip out.

Friday has come in rather dull and as not a lot has been reported locally, I have decided to have trip up to the Staffordshire moors, see how the grouse are faring now the shooting season is almost two months in.

The journey up is uneventful and I arrive on Axe Edge Moor in deteriorating weather conditions, very gloomy in fact. I park up in my favoured spot on the moor and commence to scan round. A small flock of meadow pipits are near to hand and a pair or raven fly overhead, and that is about it.

A good half an hour passes. I hear the alarm call of red grouse in the distance, but they are not seen. Two walkers come into view, they stop and we talk.

They say they have seen no grouse as they crossed the moor, things are not looking good, I decide to give it another thirty minutes and then I will move on.

I am fortunate, it does not require thirty minutes. Within a few minutes two red grouse walk out of the heather and stand in full view, almost posing, and I am able to enjoy them for three or four minutes before they return to the heather and vanish from sight. They do not return, I hope this is a sign they have learned to keep to cover now the shooting season is open. I move on down to Tittesworth Water for a coffee and scone.

Swallow Moss will be my next destination, and this turns out to be a complete waste of time. The only bird seen being a magpie. As I have time, I decide to take the leisurely way back home and drive across country to Ashbourne, instead of the main route through Leek.

I am driving down a lane near to Warslow where I spot a flock of birds in a field. I stop to see what I have found. They are a flock of starlings, well into three figures and as I start to work my way through them, I become conscious of a tractor towing a wide trailer approaching me. There is no way it will be able to pass my parked car so I have to drive on a little way, where I fortunately find a wide verge where I can park and still study the starlings.

The tractor stops and the driver winds his window down, I wonder what he wants. He does not look very happy, and I am expecting some comment about my parking, when he asks, 'Am I bird watching?' On my reply of, yes, he asks would I like to see a barn owl? There is only one answer to that, the starlings are promptly forgotten, and he tells me to follow him. After a short distance he turns off down a track to a farm, and pulls in, and getting down from his tractor points further down the track to where a small barn is standing.

He tells me to drive down, I can park by the barn easily, and the barn owl is to be seen in the far-right corner of the barn where it roosts on a beam. The light in the barn is very poor as it has no windows just the door frame allowing light in, so the bird has to be really searched for. Also, the owl is rather nasty, and if approached too closely is likely to fly at you, the farmer in fact has had his cap knocked off twice recently. We have a joke about health and safety, and he waves me on my way.

I enter the barn cautiously and the corner favoured by the bird is very dark.

After a while I hear a shuffling and the owl appears further along the beam where there is more light, and is now visible. I can only presume the bird has become aware of my presence and has moved out to investigate, in view of the farmer's comments I stand quite still, hardly daring to breath. After about a minute the owl shuffles back out of sight, and I make my retreat.

What a superb way to end a very quiet day, a 'year tick' and a most unusual way to get one. As I drove back the farmer comes out of his house, so I am able to thank him. I had been a very lucky man.

Now what does tomorrow bring, apart from the rain that is forecast. North Wales looks as though it may be the driest area so I will visit the Point of Ayr, I have not been there for a few years, time to revisit. Come and join me.

I start out early, and it is a good job I do. The journey, which I anticipated at being a little over two hours, in fact has taken me over three and a half hours. A large accident has occurred where a HGV has shed its load all over the roadway, nothing can pass. The diversion is lengthy and slow, road works are also taking place in Flint. The net result being my late arrival at my destination.

The Point of Ayr lies at the entrance to the Dee Estuary, a few miles before you reach Rhyl. The tide retreats rapidly in such positions, and my late arrival means the tide is way out in the estuary, and apart from a few gulls and waders, all birds are distant specks.

One pool of water does at least have a small flock of pintails in attendance, the drakes looking particularly smart, and there are goodly numbers of black-tailed godwits to be seen. Dunlins and knots are well spread and the commonest ducks visible are shelducks.

I had hoped to see divers and grebes out on the water, but if there are any, they are far too distant to identify. The odd cormorant is flying across the water and a large flock of redshanks come flying in, they at least appreciate the exposed mud of the estuary.

On the shore are many lapwings, four to five hundred I would estimate and there is also a tidy flock of pipits on the shore. I work these hard looking for something a bit special, but they all look like meadow pipits. Two small waders fly in and land in a small pool. I am pleased they chose to do so, they were two sanderlings.

As my arrival was somewhat delayed, time has caught up with me, so I wend my way home, but not too far. As I drive out of the village of Talacre I spot three birders looking very intently into an adjoining field. I naturally stop, and I am very pleased I do so. They are studying a male Lapland bunting which is feeding in the field. A quiet day has now really woken up. I was very lucky to see the birders, otherwise I would have just driven past not knowing the bird was there. I frequently say birding is ninety per cent luck and ten per cent knowledge, today has proved that point. I now drive home a very happy man, with an unexpected 'year tick'.

Sunday is a far better morning, but as I have some work to complete a quick drive out for a couple of hours is all I can manage. Nothing of great interest has been reported locally so I will just have a drive to see what, if anything, I can find.

I head off towards JCB at Rocester, and as I am driving past Hawk Hills, a forested area north of Yoxall, I spot a large bird of prey sitting out on a bare branch in a tree. I pull in, it is a buzzard, and it looks as though it is thoroughly enjoying the warmth of the sun. I suppose a buzzard sitting out on a tree in Hawk Hills is very appropriate, the name must have originated from somewhere!

Whilst enjoying the bird I become very conscious of the beautiful colours of the trees. The area is mainly deciduous trees and the range of reds and golds to be seen is quite something. Autumn at its best. I am sure that if on holiday we would think how marvellous this all is, here I have not had to go on holiday, I have it all just minutes from home, as many of you too will have. We are very fortunate in the UK to have autumn colour such as this.

Not a lot more to report on the bird front until I end up at Croxall Lakes. Here the large flock of Canada geese are in attendance, as I work my way through them, I pick up a smaller bird. A lesser Canada goose, or cackling goose as it is now called. The last one of these I saw was up at Carsington, this could easily be my first Staffordshire record. An interesting enough bird to finish with.

I still have a little time available, so I will drive home via Dunstall as I am interested in seeing what the pheasant numbers now are as the shooting season has commenced.

I have to work hard to find any pheasants. In fields where I saw many just a few days ago, I cannot now find one. The first field which has many cattle in it, is totally devoid of pheasants, the second which contains sheep, likewise. It is not until I approach the hall itself that I see a pheasant, and 'a' pheasant it really is. A solitary male is strutting across a field among sheep.

Whether this dramatic fall in numbers is due to many being shot I do not know. Hopefully the birds will have learned quickly and moved into cover in the local wooded areas, where here they may avoid the gun.

This bird moving about completely in the open is asking for trouble. Although thinking about it, I have been told that shooting does not occur on Sundays, if that is so, this pheasant may be cleverer than first thought!

On checking my records later, I have recorded lesser Canada geese within the county previously, so today's bird is just a repeat, not that I am complaining.

It is now Wednesday, and I have my first opportunity of birding since Sunday. I only have a couple of hours available so a quick trip across to Blithfield Reservoir will have to suffice.

Little is to be seen from the two car parking areas, so I drive down into Admaston Reach. Decent numbers of teals and wigeons are on the water, with several cormorants and great crested grebes actively feeding. Further down Blithe Bay are large numbers of geese and gulls, along with many mallards.

Parking up I commence to study the geese. Several hundred are visible, a mixture of Canada and grey-lags, which is normal. I look hard for any other species tucked in amongst them, but nothing doing. Time to concentrate on the gulls. The bulk are black-headed and lesser black-backed, with the odd great black-backed and herring gull in the mix. A herring gull type takes off from a buoy, only allowing me a very brief view, but I suspect I have just missed out on a Caspian gull as it does not return.

I am very surprised at the lack of waders, just the odd lapwing is to be seen. They are all probably round in Tad Bay, but I do not have the time to visit there.

The day is absolutely superb for October. When I drove across, the temperature in my car read twenty-three degrees, and a soaring pair of buzzard are enjoying themselves. They just circle round in the warm air with hardly a movement of their wings, a wonderful example of flight, rising up in the air until they become mere specks. Great to be a large bird of prey in these conditions.

I slowly drive back and see two Egyptian geese fly in and land on the shore. I stop and look at them closely, they are not ringed so these are probably genuine wild birds and not escapees. Egyptian geese, as with Canada geese, escaped or were released from captivity many years ago and have successfully survived and bred in the wild, and are now very much part of the British scene. None has ever made the journey from Africa to the UK, they are not a migratory species, and they are not on their own regarding originally being introduced. Several birds and animals are not native, the little owl is another example, but occasionally, introduction goes very badly. The mink is probably the prime example, an animal that has been very destructive to some of our native species, and being introduced has very few natural enemies to keep it under control. Care needs to be taken when introducing/releasing species that are not here naturally, they should always be left where they were.

Getting off my soapbox I drive home, calling in at the layby in Kings Bromley needless to say. Today I have five little egrets. Now here is another bird which was not native to the UK, but unlike the Canada goose and Egyptian goose, it was not introduced, it arrived here completely under its own steam. I think we can safely say climate change is the reason. As things have slowly warmed up birds and animals have followed, this is how it has always been, where there is warmth and food readily available, they will move in. This is not migration, this is how animals have evolved and spread throughout the world. As long as conditions stay as they are, or even improve, they will remain and multiply, that is the way of nature. Darwin knew all about this many years ago, it is after all the survival of the fittest.

I have to smile to myself every time I see the little egrets at Kings Bromley. You will remember my telling you of the time a group of us drove all the way up to Anglesey, a round trip of three hundred miles in the hope of seeing a little egret, which fortunately we did. Now I have them almost coming in to see me, they are on my garden list. I have actually seen them from my garden.

That concludes a pleasant couple of hours, as I frequently say, it is not always the unusual, the common place can be equally interesting.

Friday is a very damp day, so any birding today will have to be done from the car. I will have a ride out and visit JCB at Rocester and call in at Blithfield Reservoir, on my return journey.

Considering the weather, I have great difficulty parking at Rocester, but eventually I manage. The usual collection birds are to be seen, not being fed today, and several shelduck are fighting, at least I could see they are fully fledged, and can fly. On the far side of the lake barnacle geese are feeding away. It is believed this flock commute between Carsington Water and Rocester on a regular basis. It is fact that I have never seen them at both locations on the same day, and I regularly call in at Rocester when returning from a visit to Carsington.

Now for Blithfield. The rain is still falling heavily. I position my car so I can open a window without the rain coming in. Most of the birds appear to be down the far ends of the reservoir, so I am not going to see a great deal today.

The usual teals and wigeons are to be seen in Admaston Reach and geese are grazing a nearby meadow, just Canada and grey-lags, with the odd cormorant and great crested grebe dotted about on the water.

A large gull catches my attention, although it is very distant. It appears to be a white-winged gull, no black being visible, but at this distance it is difficult to pick up a large amount of detail. It does not look quite large or heavy enough to be a glaucous gull, probably an Iceland gull, but I shall never know. Just another 'nearly bird'.

Time to return home, I have plans to make for tomorrow. I intend to visit Spurn Point once again, they have had some very interesting reports over recent days. Just to name a few. Richard's pipit, olive-backed pipit (see this one and it would be a 'lifer'), yellow-browed warblers—several, black redstart, rose-coloured starling and a few skuas and petrels have passed out at sea. One or two of those would not go amiss, so tomorrow will mean an early start. If you are up for it, come and join me.

I do make an early start, although the conditions are not very good. Steady rain is falling and it is a very dark morning, I just hope things improve as I journey east. Driving is not very good, especially on the M1 where spray is a problem.

Fortunately, conditions do improve and I arrive at Easington Beach in dry conditions, although it is very windy, almost gale force.

I set myself up for some sea watching, which will have to be from the car, making sure the wind will not be a problem. Very little is seen out at sea, the waves are all white capped due to the weather conditions. An odd gull battles through and a small flock of teals crash land onto the shore. If these birds have flown in from across the North Sea, they have had a tough crossing and will be very pleased to have reached dry land. I know they are ducks and can swim, but swimming in these conditions would not have been very comfortable for such a small duck.

Further out at sea a darkish looking bird catches my attention, as it flies very low over the water, almost skimming the waves as it rises above them to vanish into the troughs. Only shearwaters fly in this manner. I manage to get a good view in my 'scope, and I am pleased to see it is a Manx shearwater, I start my day off with a 'year tick'. After about another half an hour I am preparing to move on when two, heavy looking ducks come flying through, two duck eiders. I am pleased I had not moved on, they too are 'year ticks'. A superb start to my day out.

I drive on to Kilnsea, and here I have moved into a major 'twitch'. A large number of birders are to be seen, cars parked wherever the driver could. I am lucky, a car moves out just as I arrive, so I am able to park up comfortably.

Speaking to a group of birders I am informed a yellow-browed warbler, a Savi's warbler and a chiffchaff have recently been seen in the grounds of the local inn, and the olive-backed pipit is making fleeting appearances down the canal. A long-eared owl has also been reported from Sammy's Point. Time to get on with things.

I join about fifty birders in the inn grounds, manage to find a table to sit at, and add my concentration to things. It is not going to be easy, the wind is blowing the trees and bushes violently, so to get a good view of the three birds we are interested in will be difficult.

A good hour passes, with only a blackbird and a kestrel showing, when a shout goes up. A small bird has just landed in a nearby bush, and 'scopes and binoculars are focused there on. We are lucky, the bird pops onto the top of the bush, we have our Savi's warbler, only for about ten seconds, but we are all happy with that. A short time later the chiffchaff also puts in an appearance. This bird is more accommodating, it actually hops over the grass, it really wants to be seen. The yellow-browed it would seem, is not going to be so co-operative.

Whilst growing more impatient by the minute, a birder runs in. 'The yellow-browed in is the churchyard,' he shouts. A mass exodus takes place, luckily the church is almost next door, especially for me, I do not move that fast. This bird is really obliging, it is sitting out on a holly tree, in full view, you quickly realise where the name comes from, yellow-browed it most certainly is. We are able to enjoy the bird for a few minutes before it flies off. It is the best view I have had of the species, not that I have seen many.

Now for the top bird of the day as far as I am concerned—the olive-backed pipit. The chance of a 'lifer' looms. Having spoken to birders who have seen the pipit, it would appear to be nearer the top end of the canal, which is close to where I am now. So no driving is required.

I start my walk down the canal when I stop. A small bird has flicked up a bush, and I am delighted to see I have another yellow-browed warbler. You can never have too much of a good thing. I am able to enjoy this bird for a couple of minutes before it flies off, and the views I had were even better than the one seen minutes ago. It was obviously a different bird, the eyebrow was distinctly paler and the crown stripe was more visible, not as distinctive as that of a goldcrest, but visible nevertheless. Another cracking view. Now for the pipit.

I have noticed a group of twenty or so birders further down the canal, so I make my way towards them as quickly as I can. I have made the right decision, they had seen the pipit only minutes ago and they were also able to say it had been fairly active.

I wait about fifteen minutes before I get my first sighting of the bird, and I was very pleased I had done a lot of genning up on the bird the previous evening.

Had I not done so I could easily have mistaken the bird for a tree pipit, the differences being very marginal. The olive-backed pipit shows itself on several occasions, fortunately. The olive-green back was fairly distinctive, and the broad, buffish supercilium really stood out. Another important identification detail was the distinct dark and light spots on the rear of the ear coverts. No tree pipit has these head markings. My reading up on the bird has paid dividends, when hoping to see a new bird, it pays to go prepared. At times views can be very fleeting and minor detail is all you get. As 'lifers' go, this bird turns out to be very cooperative, and fully appreciated, especially by me.

Now for Sammy's Point. The car parking area is busier than when I was last here, although I cannot see any of the occupants, probably walkers. There are not many trees or large bushes at the Point, so searching for an owl is not too difficult, it just proves negative, no owl and little else. The tide by now is well out and all waders and gulls are very distant, apart from a goodly number of shelducks which are busily feeding in the pools remaining from the retreated tide. I have frequently found the Humber Estuary a marvellous spot to see shelducks, and they are a most attractive and easily identified bird, that is for sure. A change from pipit watching!

Three smallish and pale looking birds land in a nearby bush, not readily recognisable, concentration time is back. After a few moments they move into view. I am delighted to see they are three bramblings, a male with two females, three true winter migrants these. Unlike the Lapland bunting seen last week, which too are normally only seen in winter, they are so unusual I do not class them as migrants, they are vagrants. The brambling, however, is a true winter migrant, coming here from further north each winter, and then returning home to breed in the summer.

Take this as a warning and get your winter woollies ready!

I make my way back the short distance to my parked car, and as I prepare to drive off, a small party of pipits fly in and land on the car parking area. I rapidly raise my binoculars, but I am too late, a car drives in and chooses to park right where the pipits have settled. I have a feeling the two young lads in the car have parked up there quite deliberately, they clearly saw me looking in that direction, and their laughter as they get out of their car spoke volumes. All I can now do is put them down as meadow pipits, which is what they are most likely to have been.

That is that. A bit of a disappointing end to what has been a memorable day. Five 'year ticks', including among which is a 'lifer', it cannot get much better than that.

Sunday has come in very bleak, both weatherwise and healthwise. It is raining steadily and is forecast to last most of the day. On the health front I feel faint and have great difficulty in walking. I shall not be doing any birding today that is for sure. I have a feeling I am being affected by a new medication I am taking, so I will not take any more and try to get in touch with the doctor tomorrow.

The doctor confirms my thoughts regarding my medication. I now need another blood test to decide which medicine is appropriate, this I will have in three days' time. How I am currently feeling, birding is on the back burner for a few days, unless something arrives in my garden. How quiet things are garden-wise, that looks very unlikely.

Blood test completed, I now have to wait a few days for the results to become available.

It's now four days since I last did any birding, and added to this I am temporarily carless. My car was collected this morning for the repairs to commence and I cannot have a loan car until tomorrow at the earliest. Things do seem to be improving on the health front, so I am hopeful that give it a couple or more days I can start to get out a bit.

I did have a bit of excitement yesterday afternoon. A male great spotted woodpecker visited my peanuts, knocking them to pieces, much to the delight of a robin which gratefully picked up the fallen bits. It appreciated the woodpeckers' efforts no doubt, the robin did not have to do any work, he just enjoyed the fruits of another bird's labours.

I have been fortunate in one respect, not a lot has been reported locally, certainly nothing I had not previously seen, so I have not missed out on anything special. Among the birds reported, the one which really caught the eye has been great white egrets. Several reports have occurred, and yesterday seven different birds were seen. For a bird which is a relative newcomer to the UK, seven in one county is a good total. This is following the pattern first created by the little egret a few years ago, it will be very interesting to see if great whites increase at the same rate. Large white birds, the size of herons, would brighten up any waterside scene and probably have non-birders convinced they have seen storks. Now there is a thought.

There is a saying, 'Lightning does not strike twice'. Do not believe it. I picked up my loan car and within five hours I was involved in another accident. I will not go into details. Suffice to say, I am now temporarily carless, and likely to be so for the next two weeks or as my car is repaired.

The accident happened as I was returning home from a birdwatch at Blithfield Reservoir where I had had an enjoyable couple of hours. Winter waterfowl have started to return and I had seen several goosanders and goldeneyes, the latter especially are a delightful bird to see. Shelduck numbers were also good, a flock of seven of these were seen and among the geese flock were eleven barnacle geese. Teal and wigeon numbers were on the increase and the odd pochard was seen. The winter gull roost was starting to build up with large numbers of black-headed and lesser black-backed gulls among them. Among the cormorants were three of the southern variety, the most I have seen together here at Blithfield. All in all it had been a most pleasant couple of hours before disaster struck.

My birding will now be very restricted for at least a fortnight, but I will keep you informed of anything of interest I hear about, and I will start off with grey catbirds. No, I have not seen one, but they have hit the news, well one has!

Yesterday, 18th October, I saw a report on the BBC News that a grey catbird had been reported from Cornwall, and that hundreds of 'twitchers' were descending on the area. This is hardly surprising, as if my information is correct, it is only the second record of the bird being seen in the UK. The only other record was at South Stack, Anglesey, on the 4th October, 2001. Now, almost seventeen years to the day, we have our second, hence the 'twitchers' adrenalin rush.

The grey catbird is a North American species, breeding in central and eastern parts, which probably accounts for the bird being blown across the Atlantic, to end up on the southern-westerly tip of England. Depending upon how long this bird survives or remains in Cornwall, it could do much for the Cornish local economy, an ill wind for the catbird, benefits for locals—who knows? This bird is probably here due to the recent gales and tornadoes experienced in the States.

Unfortunately, the bird is unlikely to survive, due to our winter ahead and the lack of suitable food. Unlike my earlier comments on little egrets, this bird has not followed changing climatic conditions, it is probably the result of just extreme weather conditions. A case of being in the wrong place at the wrong time. Not that the 'twitchers' will be thinking about that, they have their nerves to calm down and a very special 'tick' to get.

Sunday is here, and that completes a week of no birding, apart from bits and pieces from my garden. The great spotted woodpecker has been a fairly regular visitor, but the robin appears to have found pastures new. An occasional woodpigeon now comes in to pick up the peanut scraps, but at least they are not wasted.

The odd interesting bird has been reported locally, and they have all come from Branston Gravel Pits. Here a long-tailed duck, grey plover and a black-necked grebe were seen, I would have liked the duck, the other two I have seen, fortunately.

Sarah was down Whitemoor Haye yesterday where she saw five fieldfares, her first for the season, she is one up on me there, although I saw them earlier in the year.

A bit of interesting news picked upon the net. You will remember recently, when I visited Spurn Point, I had hoped to see a rose-coloured starling, but failed.

Yesterday the news broke, one was seen in Ipswich, possibly the same bird, which seemed to be favouring one garden in particular. One house apparently, had over two hundred visitors coming in to see the bird, I just hope they took their boots off! A marvellous gesture by the owners to allow so many strangers into their house.

This reminds me of a similar situation near to home, many years ago, in 1991 in fact. A nutcracker, a member of the crow family, arrived in a garden in a small hamlet near to Stone, Staffordshire. Once the news was out, birders from all over the country descended on the scene. The owners of the property where the nutcracker was, now had large numbers of birders collecting outside their property in the hope of seeing the bird. Car parking was causing a problem, and the local police were involved.

The problem was resolved when a local farmer opened up his field for car parking, he made a nominal charge for this, and the owner of the property allowed birders in her garden, in small groups at a time, to see the bird. She made a charge for this and I believe that over the weekend she collected in excess of £2,000, for her favourite charity. Birders were happy, and so was a charity, even the police could relax and thinking about it, the farmer did not do badly out of it all.

When very rare birds do put in an appearance, thanks to the net, and many local bird hotlines, the news is now more easily obtained, and 'twitchers' are just waiting for the news. Distance to many means nothing, they just want the bird on their 'life list'. Whether you call this birdwatching or not is up to the individual, to many it is like train number collecting.

There is great excitement in seeing a rare or unusual bird for the first time, I am lucky in the fact it has happened to me twice this year. The stilt sandpiper and olive-backed pipit, but I would not have travelled the distances many birders had to see them both.

It also raises the question of climate change. 'Twitching' is probably a high carbon intensive way of birdwatching. Individually, a single car is not a great problem, but hundreds of cars chasing around after birds most weekends is a different matter. These vehicles, if in convoy, would cause major traffic problems as well as large carbon emissions, but I have never heard this point raised by birders. Are we helping to create a problem by chasing after the birds we love? That is a question we will all need to think about.

I have been to see my doctor this morning, and the news he gave me was not what I wished to hear. My problem was not the medication, he believes a minor stroke looks the more likely reason, and he is arranging a hospital appointment for me, at the earliest opportunity. I must confess I had thought that could have been the likely reason for how I felt, but you tend to lock those sorts of thoughts away. There is nothing I can do at present but wait to see what the outcome is.

One thing is for certain, birding is now most definitely on the back burner. It will be just a case of what I see in my own garden and if I pick up any interesting reports such as the recent grey catbird, which I believe to be worthy of discussion.

Today has been a day of mixed fortunes. Firstly a phone call from my motor insurance company. They are writing my car off, which was not expected., I cannot complain with their settlement figure, they were very fair, but it leaves me with the problem of finding a decent used automatic 4x4, petrol, and as I have found in the past, they are not easily come by.

Secondly, the hospital phoned. I have to go in tomorrow to see a specialist with regard to my suspected stroke. That appointment has been made very quickly, it was only yesterday morning I saw my doctor. No complaints with the NHS there.

Let us get back to birding. I actually managed a bit today. I was in my garden when I heard a loud mewing from above. Looking up I saw a small group of three buzzards, only twenty feet or so above my head. I have never been so close to buzzards previously, their markings stood out wonderfully clearly and it was obviously a pair with a fully-fledged juvenile. They just glided over, hardly a flap of their wide spread wings, and junior had quickly learned the tricks of the trade, it was not going to be outflown. It was even constantly moving its head from side to side as it studied the ground beneath, just as the adults were doing. I may have only seen them for less than thirty seconds, but it was a wonderful view, one I will long remember.

Then, watching the midday local news, I had to smile. A rhea has gone walkabout on a golf course near Evesham. It has apparently escaped from its home a few miles away, and taken up residence at the golf club. The bird's owner has been down several times, but the rhea keeps running off, it is enjoying its freedom too much. On the news today, to see this large, ostrich-like bird, walking about on the green, with golfers in the background playing golf, certainly looked a little unusual.

Thinking further. I wonder what the 'twitchers' will do about this bird. A bird which cannot fly and originates from South America, is unlikely to get onto the UK List! I am sure, however, there will be people who wish to see the bird, and why not, it is a bit of fun.

I am back from my hospital appointment and I am pleased to report the consultant did not believe I had experienced a stroke, he put it down to bad arthritis.

To make things absolutely certain, I am to have a scan, so I now await my appointment for this, and I understand they take time. The awkward side of this, is the fact he advised me not to do any driving until they were completely satisfied with my condition. This has stopped me looking for another vehicle, which, as I have said before, are difficult enough to find in any case.

It has also curtailed any serious birding. I am now confined to garden and local, and as I am not walking too well at present, local will mean local. Hopefully I will have something of interest to pass on, and as with the grey catbird and the rhea, if I should see any news of the unusual, I will let you know. The only good thing with all of this, is the fact it is near to the end of the year, and not the start.

The last two days have passed away quietly, but today saw a bit of excitement, and in my own garden. Unfortunately, it was only momentary. A small flock of fieldfares landed in my holly tree, but before I could have a good look at them and even count them, they were off. A car nearby sounded its horn, and that was that. There were probably ten birds or so in the flock, all I can do now is hope they return.

Hopefully they were accessing the quality of my holly berries, and will be back for them when the time is appropriate. I have at least now caught up with Sarah, my first fieldfare of the season.

I have been browsing the net, I think that is the right expression, I am not exactly a computer boff, to see what birds are about nationally, and I was very pleased with one piece of information found. There were several reports of waxwings being seen, unfortunately, all east coast. Norfolk had done very well with scattered reports along the northern shores of the county. None in great numbers, just in twos and threes, but it is a start.

It is a couple of years now since we had a 'fall' of waxwings, when they arrived in large numbers, and spread over many parts of the country. You will remember my experiences of seeing a superb flock at Frogatt, Derbyshire, in December 2016. It would be great to repeat that again, although knowing my luck, I will probably still be carless.

Of the birds regularly experienced in the UK, waxwings are the number one species for many a birder. They are an exotic looking bird, and they are more obliging than many a bird, frequently providing superb views. They seem to have no fear of man and can be approached closely. I have seen the odd one when in Norway, they are a near-Arctic breeding species, and they are just as obliging there. All we can do now is wait and see.

On checking the local bird line this morning, I realised I am missing out on the chance of seeing crossbills. In the popularity stakes, crossbills are probably only second to waxwings on most birders' lists, and several groups have been reported from Cannock Chase. They may as well be on the moon as far as my chances are concerned at present.

Cannock Chase is a good area for this bird, they feed on the seeds from cones and the Chase has large areas of conifers, planted by the Forestry Commission, and still maintained today. With the numbers of crossbills being reported currently, there was obviously a very good cone crop this early this year, so breeding numbers could increase. They are a very early breeding species, and dependent on the cone crop, can commence early February. Something to look forward to when I am again mobile.

During the morning there has been almost a passage of buzzards taking place. In the space of a couple of hours, I have seen seven fly over. I had my binoculars to hand, so I was able to study the birds well, and they were all the common buzzard, nothing extra exciting among them. Mind you, if I think back to fifty years ago, when I first came to live in Yoxall, if I saw one buzzard a year, it was worthy of note, so I should not knock seven in the matter of hours. I should be celebrating the fact.

The spread of this bird in relatively recent times is nothing short of phenomenal. With the introduction of myxomatosis to the rabbit population during the last century, buzzard numbers declined to such an extent, their future looked questionable. Once the danger of the disease was fully appreciated, and stopped being introduced, buzzards and other rabbit eaters, started their slow recovery. A clear illustration that if left alone, nature can take care of itself. Plus, the fact that without rabbits there would have been little chance for the reintroduction of the red kite, with its subsequent success.

When you add DDT and the like to the equation, you do wonder if we will ever learn not to meddle with nature. We are not the only animal to inhabit the planet, but we are the only one likely to destroy it. There ends my thoughts for the day!

The weather looks like it is trying to brighten up, so who knows, I may get a walk in this afternoon, see if I can find anything of interest locally.

The weather holds up, it is still bright although very chilly, so a short walk will not go amiss. I am fortunate where I live, although it is on a main road, I am almost opposite open fields which back onto the local river. The fields are council owned so access is available.

Today, as I slowly walk along, I become conscious of the call of a nuthatch, and after some time I finally locate the bird on an old silver birch tree. The bird is very actively feeding, working its way round the trunk of the tree, occasionally stopping to call. Probably celebrating some juicy find. A delightful sight and sound.

I have always considered the nuthatch to be the most colourful of our common woodland species. I jokingly refer to it as the kingfisher of the woods. On to Town Hill Bridge.

This bridge over the River Swarbourn, provides good views of the river, and downstream a pair of moorhens are busily feeding away in the shallows and a blackbird is scattering fallen leaves as it searches for food. I am about to cross the bridge to view upstream when a flash of yellow catches my attention. A male grey wagtail has arrived on the scene, and he is always welcome. They may be called grey wagtails, but their undersides are a brilliant yellow. Unfortunately, I only have the bird for less than a minute before it darts off downstream. I am not complaining, a minute in its company is better than no time at all. I now cross over the bridge.

Upstream the first birds I see are five mallards, two drakes and three ducks, they are just splashing about in the water as though they are playing games, and why not? The odd rook is standing about in the rookery, with the occasional caw ringing out, it will be a lot busier earlier in the new year when the rooks return to breed. This rookery has been here for many years. I have now lived in Yoxall for over fifty years, and it was here prior to my arrival. I must confess I am concerned about its long-term future, the trees are beginning to look decidedly frail. I often joke with people that to be a true village you must have a church, a pub, a post office, and most importantly of all, a rookery. Hang on rooks!

Whilst musing over the rooks, a movement on a nearby small ash tree catches my attention. A treecreeper is slowly working its way up the trunk, and the way it is probing its bill into the bark, it looks as though it is finding plenty of food. What it is eating I do not know, the tree unfortunately is on the opposite bank of the river, I presume it could be ants. Whatever it is, the treecreeper is happy.

That concludes a pleasant hour out, and it could not have been more local. I doubt if I was ever more than two hundred yards from home, it just shows what you may have available if you have the time to look. See what tomorrow may bring, I will probably have a short walk downstream. Join me if you have nothing better to do.

After a pleasant extra hour in bed, the clocks went back last night, it looks as though we may have a very good day ahead. Although overnight we had a frost, this has quickly gone and a bright and sunny day lies ahead. It is cold once again, but we can dress up against that.

I walk across to Bond End Bridge, disturbing a flock of about twenty house sparrows in a nearby hedge, they did not appreciate my passing. The river is very quiet, just a solitary moorhen swimming slowly downstream, so I pass over into the fields nearby. Here there is slightly more activity, two pied wagtails are associating with the cattle and a robin can be heard singing away. Robins are one of the few birds which sing all year, although they sing a different 'melody' in summer from winter. They are probably the most territory conscious of all our native birds, hence they are so vocal.

Progressing further up the field, a mistle thrush is seen hopping along, it soon flies off as it sees me, and a small flock of lapwings fly overhead, and that is about it.

After the quality of yesterday, today is a bit like 'after the lord mayor's show', but this is birding. Birds are not a commodity which can be ordered, they are there or they are not, all the birder can do is seek them out, if he is lucky. At least today, the sun is shining, that makes things a whole lot better!

Later in the afternoon, Sarah and Martin returned and they were full of the news they had seen a large number of little egrets on the main lake at Whitemoor Haye. They had been unable to count them accurately, but it turned out fifty-one had been reported. That is the largest number ever reported from a single location within the county, what a sight that would have been. If we have that sort of number in just one location, then how many have we spread all over Staffordshire?

This morning I really thought things were moving on the hospital front, I should have known better. I received a letter informing me that my MRI scan was to be on the 4th December, which I did not think was too bad. On reading the letter fully there was a questionnaire attached, and two of the questions concerned transplants and pacemakers, both of which I have. A phone call is made, and the result is I cannot have a scan, so I am back to square one, and I have now to contact my consultant to see where we go, and this I cannot do until tomorrow. This does surprise me, the hospital has all my medical records and details of my replacements and pacemaker are all on those, they obviously do not check prior to making appointments. A waste of time and money.

Whilst I was going about my household chores this morning, I heard a piece of very distressing news on the radio. The World Wildlife Fund had released the news that wildlife figures (all forms of wildlife), had reduced by an average sixty per cent in the last fifty years, and in some instances even higher losses were reported. Hedgehogs in the UK were down by seventy-two per cent, a phenomenal loss, no wonder I have seen none this year.

This loss is solely due to man. Wildlife does not eliminate itself, only we do it. The bulk of this loss is due to two main reasons, land usage and persecution.

The rainforests are being cleared at an alarming rate, and principally just to grow soya beans. One report I heard claimed an area the size of London is being cleared, every two days, this cannot go on. Large though the rainforests are, they cannot survive this rate of clearance. When you combine this with the number of animals being hunted for sale and also those being shot annually, this loss is easily understood.

The people doing all of this have no thoughts for the future, they will not be here, their interest is just for rewards today. But have you ever stopped to think where you sit in all of this? We are all part of it and jointly responsible. We want cheap food, we want to be able to go wherever we wish and hang pollution, we want more and more houses, which take over more and more land, and so we can go on.

Soon the only 'wild creatures' to be seen will be in zoos and collections. Children in the future will not have the pleasure of seeing a fox or badger, listening to a skylark or nightingale, these have almost gone now. Their connections with such things will only be by artificial means, TV, audio and books etc., the real wild world will no longer exist. You may think I am being melodramatic here, but with the world's population increasing at the rate it is, all of whom wanting their slice of the cake, tell me, please, how we will house and feed them? I am beginning to think that colonisation of another planet is definitely our number one priority, except will we quickly ruin that!

Anyway, let me climb down from my soapbox. Bird activity in my garden today has been very limited, but two grey squirrels did their best to entertain me.

They have been dashing round my garden like crazy, at times sitting up and facing each other as though boxing. I have never seen this type of behaviour previously, whether it was two males arguing over territory I do not know, they did not appear to actually strike each other, more as though displaying. They probably thought they are mad March hares. They at least brought a smile to my face, more than the WWF news had.

An interesting side to the squirrels' activity was the fact that two rooks were sitting on my fence appearing to be watching their antics. I studied then closely, the rooks that is, and I was conscious of the fact that they were turning their heads to follow the squirrels as they moved. I almost expected a round of applause, but that was taking imagination a bit too far, I think!

It is the end of the month, Halloween and all that. After three very cold nights, when we had frost, today has proved slightly milder, so a stroll locally is called for. I have not got a lot of time available, so a quick visit to Bond End Bridge will have to suffice, but it is at least a bit of exercise.

Since I was here a few days ago, the frost has caused a lot of leaves to fall, and the pathway is covered in multi-coloured leaves, looking very Autumnal and attractive. Had I been younger, much, and more agile, I would have enjoyed kicking up the leaves. Those were the days!

On glancing over the river bridge, I disturb a small flotilla of mallards, nine of them, which drift off downstream, passing a hunched up heron which is standing on the bank. The heron is not concerned about me, it just glares into the distance, had it not been the fact I can see its eyes, I would have thought the bird is asleep.

I cross the bridge to look upstream. Initially things are quiet until a pair of mallards crash land in the river. The noise of their arrival disturbs two dunnocks, which promptly fly off. A movement in a silver birch draws my attention.

I am delighted to see a party of seven long-tailed tits working their way through the tree, then a spot of yellow is seen, concentration time. Three siskins are among the party, two bright coloured males with one female, and these birds are every bit as agile as a titmouse. They regularly associate with titmice flocks, so it always pays to study the groups fully.

Whilst watching these birds a magpie commences to call from a cottage garden nearby, and it sounds very agitated, so I move back over the bridge to see what is going on. What is annoying the magpie I cannot tell, and as it sees me, it is off in any case.

In the garden is a large apple tree and spread on the ground beneath it are many fallen apples. Obviously, the owners are not apple lovers, but hopefully they are leaving the apples on the ground where they will soften up to be eaten by the birds. Migrant thrushes, fieldfares and redwings, will love these if they find them, and should they not, there are plenty of other things that will.

That brings October to a close, with my 'year list' standing at two hundred and sixteen, the chances of that increasing are now low. I am having trouble in making contact with my consultant, so as I am nowhere near knowing when I can drive again, my birding remains local. Rarities may not be available, but if you are prepared to look, there are still things to see and to learn.

At least November has commenced with my making contact with the hospital, and I now await information regarding another type of scan. Driving is still not on the agenda, so my birding continues to be limited. One thing I have been able to do is scan the net, and today I came across two very interesting and contrasting items concerning our oceans.

Firstly. Our ocean water temperatures have increased by one and a half degrees in the last twenty-five years, and although this may not sound a large amount, it is resulting in ice melting at both poles at an alarming rate. If this is not slowed down, and quickly, many islands will just vanish under the sea, and many large coastal cities will be permanently flooded. In the USA for instance, many of their coastal cities and towns which lie on the Pacific coast are particularly vulnerable, and they are not on their own. Mind you, their president does not believe in climate change, so what he is blaming for the calamity that has occurred in the States in recent times, I do not know.

With temperature increases of this size, it is not only flooding to be considered. A slight movement in temperature can destroy a coral reef for instance, and it does not stop there, it also destroys the creatures which rely on the reef for their very existence. This is also affecting British wildlife. Many fish and other sea creatures are slowly moving northwards as they escape the warmer waters, this also takes larger creatures with them. Many of our fish-eating birds, puffins being a good example, are having to move further north in pursuit of their favourite food. If this continues you will only be able to see puffins in Scotland and further north. For many creatures and plants, this will mean extinction, and I am not talking centuries away, this is just around the corner. Climate change is not a myth, it is racing along. When you combine this with the report issued by the WWF a few days ago, we should all be very concerned.

Now for some better news. Satellite photography has started to show us the current situation with whale populations. Since the control of whale hunting was introduced, their numbers have slowly started to increase but it has always been a problem to study them and find out their numbers. They travel such great distances you would never know how often you saw the same whale, so you could only at best assume their numbers. Now thanks to the improvements in satellite photography, they are able to study large areas of the oceans from space, to check upon the whales, and apparently, they will shortly be able to photograph everywhere, every twenty-four hours. If this is right, you could almost count every individual whale, now that would be something. Unfortunately, this development has not been made to help the whale, it has a military objective, but if the whale can find some benefit, it is better than nothing!

You will have noticed that no mention of the Rosliston Birders has been made recently, the reason being that due to my health problems I had decided it was time to 'retire', and the group is now being run by my old colleagues, Len and Roy, so they are in good hands. With my problems with walking any distance you can hardly lead people birding and I had to consider places to visit that suited me, which was not fair to them.

The first two days of November have produced nothing of special interest, although I have been out looking, not a lot seen or heard. It is almost as though the birds have gone away on holiday! Today, hopefully, things may be slightly better.

Sarah, on driving home yesterday, saw a small flock of wagtails in a field on the edge of the village. She could not stop due to traffic, but her first impression was pied wagtails. Flocks of pied wagails always interest me at this time of the year, you never know what may be tucked in among them. It is at least something positive to do today, plus a walk is good exercise.

It is not a bad morning, for November, decidedly pleasant. The field which has the wagtails in is being grazed by cattle, and their droppings are no doubt responsible for the insects on which the wagtails are feeding.

Several small parties of wagtails are flitting about, probably only a dozen or so in total, and they are very active. There are three extremely attractive males, very black and white. I am looking for paler, greyer looking birds, white wagtails, the continental species. Our pied wagtail is in fact a race, or sub-species of the white, which is classed as the nominate species, and is normally only found in the UK and occasionally on the west coast of Europe. The white, on the other hand, is spread all over mainland Europe, with a few arriving in the UK annually, especially on spring and autumn migration.

A flock of twenty or so goldfinches arrive on the scene, bringing in a real splash of colour, and they are a most argumentative flock of birds, harassing and chasing each other, even doing so with the wagtails. A movement on the ridge of the riverbank catches my attention, the heads of two red-legged partridges appear, they see me and quickly retreat.

Back to wagtail watching. After what seemed many minutes, three wagtails land close by, obviously unaware of me, and proceed to feed round a resting cow. I am very pleased they come in so close. One of the birds has a very grey back, only a slight amount of black on head and breast and paler looking wings—I have a white. It may not be a 'tick', but I do not see many each year, and a local one is a bit special.

The odd crow and magpie join in the proceedings and a grey heron can be heard from the river, but not seen. As I leave, two lesser black-backed gulls come in, but they only stay for a few seconds. A productive hour or so that has proved to be, home now for a spot of lunch and see how the soccer goes this afternoon.

The soccer did not go well, so I will not dwell on that. I did, however, pick up a bit of interesting news from the net. This news came from across the pond.

Birdwatchers in New York are going crazy over a drake mandarin duck which has appeared in Central Park, many travelling long distances to see the bird which is thought may be a true wild species. They have one or two captive birds in collections throughout the States, but this fellow is believed could be a true wild bird. It does, however, to my mind, beg the question what is a bird which originates in eastern

Asia doing on the east coast of America? To reach there it has flown all the way across North America, a long distance for a bird which I understand is not a migrant species. Anyway, it is up to our American friends to decide whether it is wild or not.

We are very fortunate in the UK. We are able to see mandarin ducks in many places, locally we have breeding populations. None of these have flown here, they are all descendants of introductions or escapees, but they are a most exotic addition to our bird list. I have even read reports which claim the UK has now got one of the largest populations of this bird, which has done much to help the bird avoid extinction. If that is the case it may not be long before we are sending birds back to their native home to help maintain their populations. This has happened previously.

The Hawaiian goose was almost extinct and if it had not been for a breeding programme carried out at Slimbridge, which enabled a reintroduction back home, the Hawaiian goose may well have been lost.

Collections and zoos are not all bad. Many a creature has been introduced back into the wild to help maintain wild populations, new blood is very necessary where populations are drastically reduced.

November 4th is upon us, and it looks as though we have a decent day ahead. It is a mild start and the evening is very promising for those wishing to celebrate Bonfire Night a day early. By afternoon, the sun is out brightly, so a walk is called for. I have not a lot of time available, so a walk up to the river will have to suffice.

At Town Hill Bridge a nuthatch is calling, which after several minutes searching I finally locate, and it is responded to by another nuthatch further down the river. Anyone would think it was spring, not the advent of winter. Things on the meadow are very quiet, a solitary moorhen is on the river and the odd jackdaw and rook can be heard. Nothing too exciting I am afraid, although a robin gives me a burst of song as I leave, always a welcome sound.

Walking back home I frighten a woodpigeon which is feeding on ivy berries. In the bird's panic I actually feel the draught as it flies, very low, above my head. I am very pleased it missed me, they are a bulky and heavy bird. It may not have been exciting along the river, it was nearly so, here!

Back home I decide to stock up my bird feeders, one or two are getting low, and whilst doing so I become conscious of a soft, almost melancholy whistling 'pyu- pu', being repeated. Only one bird sounds like this. Looking quickly skywards, I am delighted to see a small flock of golden plovers flying over. Seventeen of them, their white armpits (axillaries for the scientifically minded), showing well in the bright light of the day. Feeding the birds has really produced a bonus, it has been many a year since I last saw golden plovers over my garden. A perfect conclusion to the afternoon.

Last night, just as I was about to retire, I heard a tawny owl calling away. It was not the male hooting, it was a female calling and I can only presume something had disturbed her and she was giving vent to her feelings. Whatever the reason, I am just happy that we still have tawny owls locally, and trust she has a mate. Male tawny owls should soon be calling regularly as they sort out their territories and attract females which they do at this time of the year.

The month is slowly moving on, it is now the 8th and I have had little to report, apart from the owl. Today, however, things have brightened up somewhat. Locally, egrets are making the news, not that I am seeing any of them. Over a hundred little egrets have been reported, seventy-one at a single location. Where are they all coming from? Great white egrets are currently well up in double figures, and have been reported from eight different locations with seven being seen together on one occasion. Cattle egrets are also on the list, four at Belvide and one at Doxey Marsh.

Staffordshire birders are having a great time, not me unfortunately, I can only read about it!

Also, my garden has livened up a bit today. My gardener, Simon, has been in to give it a blitz and in doing so has exposed a good area of open soil, once he had departed the birds moved in. Greenfinches and goldfinches were the first to arrive, I presume fallen seed had been exposed, and these were quickly followed by a robin and blackbird. A woodpigeon stomped through, it was not going to miss out, and although not being an aggressive bird, its sheer bulk moved some of the smaller birds away. Two rooks flying overhead, obviously saw all this activity, and came down to investigate. Unlike the woodpigeon, their arrival did frighten all the birds away. They, however, did not hang around for long, and the smaller birds came back. Nothing special regarding species seen, but a good example of bird behaviour, and how they respond to us. How quickly they first arrived once Simon had left, it was just minutes. They had obviously been watching what he was doing, but how did they know the work he was doing was to their benefit. Bird brain, what a brain!

For a few days now it has been rather windy and wet, some very heavy showers in fact, but today, Saturday 10th, is a very pleasant morning, so I will have a walk up to Goose Green and Town Hill Bridge before the rain, which is forecast, arrives.

It really is a case of kicking up the leaves, with the recent winds many are now off the trees, it definitely is the 'fall' as our American friends call it, and some of the trees are even bare, looking quite sorrowful. Mind you, bare trees have one advantage, birds find it difficult to hide away, so we birders have a better chance of seeing them. Well, that is the theory!

Pleasant morning though it may be, the birds have other things on their minds, and few are seen. Swarbourn Meadow is totally birdless, well it was until a carrion crow flies over. The River Swarbourn is also deserted so I cross over onto Goose Green. There is at least a little more activity here.

A robin is singing delightfully, a female blackbird is sifting through a mass of fallen leaves, and rooks can be heard, several of them calling with a few in flight.

Jackdaws are not to be outdone, they too are active and noisy, anyone would have thought it was the start of the breeding season. It is amazing what a bit of sunshine can do!

A movement on the riverbank catches my attention, two pied wagtails are busily searching away, totally oblivious to me, such is their concentration on what they are doing. While this is going on I hear the mewing of a buzzard, but search as hard as I do, due to the trees I am unable to locate the bird. There is no mistaking this bird's call, and I would think it is probably soaring away on high, just enjoying itself, as I firmly believe large birds of prey do.

Walking back towards home I hear a loud schack, schack' ring out, fieldfares are about. A quick look across the Swarbourn Meadow and I see a large flock moving through the trees along the river, there must be over fifty birds visible, and they are all fieldfares, no redwings amongst them. The meadow may have been birdless on my way out, it certainly is not on my return home.

Lunch calls, and I can now have a quiet afternoon listening to the football, where hopefully, results will be better than last week. As with most things in life, you can but hope!

The weekend's football results were quite satisfactory, the five West Midlands clubs I am interested in, all won or drew, and plenty of goals were scored, I just wish my health had been as good.

Late Saturday evening I did something to my leg which has meant I can hardly walk, all I can do is hobble around, so even a short walk is out of the question.

This growing old lark is not funny! Consequently, my birding has all been in the garden, and not a lot is seen. Goldfinches have been plentiful, eating their fill of the sunflower hearts, I shall need to fill up their seed containers as soon as I am able. Apart from their activities, not a lot else has happened for me to see.

Locally it is again a case of egrets, little, great white and cattle egrets are still being seen regularly, and down Meadow Lane, here in Yoxall, a flock of over three hundred fieldfares were reported, not seen by me needless to say. So early in the year, that is a large sized flock, I thought the flock of over fifty I saw a few days ago was good, and if they were berry eating a few trees would be stripped bare.

I had a phone call this evening from my friend, Roy, he and some of the Rosliston Birders had been on Cannock Chase, and they had experienced a very good morning. Four birds in particular had made their day, a great grey shrike, crossbills, siskins and lesser redpolls, not a bad haul that. I have not seen a great grey shrike, crossbill or lesser redpoll this year, and to think they are so close to home, it is very frustrating. This, however, is birding!

Today is my normal weekly shop day, and as I am not driving at present, I am having to do it by taxi. One consolation of this is the fact that as a passenger I have a chance to look about me, leaving someone else to concentrate on the road ahead. The driver takes my usual route into Burton, this going via Dunstall, so I am able to have a look for the pheasants, to see how they have survived the shooting season so far.

As we drive down the lane where I saw many in September, I find the fields are totally devoid of pheasants, not a single bird. Whether this means they have been driven off by the guns, or have quickly learned to take to cover, I do not know. I suspect it is the first of my thoughts. Whatever your opinions are regarding shooting, we have to accept the fact that the birds were bred for the gun, and hopefully enough will have survived this to have learned from the experience. They may then breed next year and add to the wild population. The fact pheasants are common is due to this captive breeding, not all are shot, fortunately.

Driving further on, a flock of smaller birds catch my attention, the lane here is very narrow and the driver is going slowly. As we get closer I see they are a flock of mixed thrushes—redwings and fieldfares, about fifty or so of them. In the very bright sunlight of today the fieldfares look very grey, rather smart in fact, although only seen for seconds, they are a delightful sighting, and the redwings are my first for the season. Compensation for the lack of pheasants.

Today, it is Thursday, and I am able to walk comfortably at last, so a stroll up the village is called for. After two very dry and warm days, well warm for the time of the year, a walk on Goose Green and the Swarbourn Meadow should be very pleasant. Here I can walk alongside the River Swarbourn; where there is water there are usually birds. Well, that is the theory, let us see if it works.

Goose Green is at least very noisy, two magpies are complaining away, loudly, as is their wont. Two blackbirds are working their way through a patch of fallen leaves, scattering them in all directions, a robin is singing away from a nearby birch tree, and moorhens can be heard but not seen. The rooks and jackdaws are very vocal, as is becoming normal, and a dunnock gives a short cheep. Nothing dramatic, but all very pleasant, and as I am leaving, a grey heron glides in, landing further up the river.

Now for the Swarbourn Meadow. An old orchard lies adjacent to the meadow and from this a nuthatch can be heard, not seen on this occasion. Approaching the river I disturb a song thrush, always a delightful bird to see, their numbers have reduced dramatically in recent times. Years ago, they regularly bred in my garden, if I see one at home now it is worthy of note. Three duck mallards slowly drift past, quacking away as they do so, drakes do not quack. Although I am in full view, they appear oblivious of me, they obviously have more important things on their minds.

Here the river is tree lined, mainly birch and alder, and they are pretty well leafless, with small groups of birds flitting amongst them. I am glad I have brought my binoculars, and also the fact a bench is handy, so I can concentrate on these in relative comfort. A group of about twenty titmice are seen, blues, greats and coal tits, they are feeding away noisily and actively in a birch tree. Three tree sparrows are more interested in foraging away in a hawthorn bush, and hovering nearby is a kestrel, not that any of the small birds seem at all worried by it.

Walking on towards the end of the meadow, a flock of a dozen or so small birds land in an alder and promptly attack the cones. A few of the birds show flashes of yellow in their plumage, obviously siskins, but the remainder look rather drab.

Quickly focusing up I am delighted to see they are a mixture of female siskins and lesser redpolls, and I had insulted them by calling them 'drab'!

As I have said before, siskins are every bit as agile as titmice, and redpolls are no slouch either. They were swinging away on the cones, looking almost as though they were doing it for fun, busily picking out any seeds remaining and any small insect hiding away. In today's good light, the odd redpoll showed clearly why it is so called, the red forehead was quite distinct. After a few minutes they flew off further down river, and that was that.

When I came out for this walk, I little dreamed I would get myself a 'year tick', and where I had seen the redpolls was less than one hundred yards from home.

It cannot get much better than that. You just never know what you may find in your own 'patch', all you need to do is to go out and look for it. Going out today gave me my two hundred and seventeenth bird of the year, no complaints there, and not seeing them on the Chase no longer matters. It almost seems as though the birds came to see me—

now there's a thought!

Considering we are exactly half way through November, the weather at present is absolutely delightful. Not a cloud in the sky, the sun out all day and little or no wind, long may it continue. Walking back today I even see the odd small insect in the air, which was a bit unexpected. We now wait to see what tomorrow will bring. I have a blood test in the morning, but I may get a walk in during the afternoon.

After the brightness of the past few days, today is grey and gloomy, the best thing that can be said of it is the fact it is still mild for the time of the year. My blood test went fine and come early afternoon I have some time to spare, so a walk is called for. I decide to repeat my walk of yesterday in the hope I see the redpolls again.

One thing you learn when birdwatching is the fact of how quickly things can change. Hardly a bird to be seen or heard, today is solely a case of some exercise. Two blackbirds and a dunnock are all I see.

Back home I did at least have something of interest. My friend, Neil, of the Rosliston Birders, phoned me with an interesting story. A friend of his had seen a pair of magpies collecting bread from his garden, then taking it off to hide away in some nearby ivy and even placing some in guttering where they covered it with leaves. This is behaviour I had never seen or heard of previously with magpies, so some investigation is called for.

I have long been aware of the magpies' love of bright things. In my egg collecting days I often found bright things, silver paper and the like, in magpies' nests. The expression 'thieving magpies' is also well known. Although I do not know of any occasions when magpies have taken bright things from inside people's houses. I certainly never found any diamond rings in magpies' nests, mores the pity.

After much delving I have found reports of when food is abundant, magpies will carry it off and hide it away in various locations within their territory, even burying it in the ground. I knew jays did this, especially where acorns were concerned, but I was not aware that magpies did the same. The intelligence of members of the crow family, never fails to amaze me. You never stop learning in this game. I will view magpies with a little more respect in future.

Saturday is again a dull day, and there is little or no soccer being played today, to brighten the gloom. It is international break again. At least it is dry, so I can have a walk to see what I may find, I just hope the birds are not on a 'break'.

As I commence my walk conditions are improving, blue sky is starting to appear and the sun looks like it will put in an appearance—we can but hope. I have decided to go to see if the wagtails are still among the cattle.

I see little as I walk down, just a small flock of house sparrows in a garden hedge and three lesser black-backed gulls fly overhead. Further disappointment follows. Arriving at the gate I find there are no cattle in the field and after many minutes of searching, no pied wagtails either. They have no doubt moved on to wherever the cattle have. A bit of colour does however brighten up the scene, five goldfinches fly into an area where the cattle food had been stored, no doubt fallen grain is still available. The odd magpie is feeding in the field, and a carrion crow flies across, and that is about it. But stop, is it?

A bird's head is seen, it has a very distinct black moustache, it is a jay. Due to the vegetation in the meadow, had the bird not raised its head I would not have seen it. Jays are not rare birds, but they do tend to be rather secretive, heard more often than seen, and I have not seen many in the confines of my village. I have had the odd one on the garden very occasionally, but this is the closest to home for many a year.

They are certainly the most brightly coloured of the crow family. The bird hopped out into clearer view, slightly raising its crest as it did so, before flying off when the white rump combined with the blue and white on the wings were clearly visible.

Seeing this colour made me remember an old friend of mine who was a keen game fisherman and fly maker. He used to buy jays' wings from which he made a special fly for his fishing exploits. I always remember finding a dead jay in the road on one occasion, he was delighted to get the two wings. He made a very good supply of flies.

I still have time so I walk back to Bond End Bridge, the sun is by now out rather pleasantly, although it is still chilly. Birds are again at a premium. A single moorhen is on the river, two woodpigeons are in a local garden and a pheasant calls, only once. There is, however, other life in the river. Trout break the surface on several occasions, whether they are coming up for air or finding food on the surface I cannot tell, but one of them was a tidy sized fish, it would certainly have made a good-sized meal.

That concludes my walk, nothing overly exciting, but the jay helped to make it enjoyable nevertheless. I will now probably watch one of the rugby internationals which are being played this afternoon

The rugby was interesting, and England, who were playing Japan, won after a shaky start. Prior to darkness descending, two collared doves called in for a short while. I am pleased to have seen these as their numbers are greatly reduced at present, so they are welcome in my garden any time. A buzzard also glides over, so apart from the jay, two of the best birds of the day are seen from my own garden. Are they telling me something?

It is now Wednesday, and apart from my shopping expedition yesterday, I have not left the house since Saturday, but I will not dwell on that. Today, my gardener Simon is here, he is finishing off my back garden, much pruning and general work is required. After four hours of work he finally finishes, and things look much improved. I have several trees and large shrubs which had gone mad, these now look far tidier and more light can penetrate the garden. Bird life was at a premium as all of this was going on, but within minutes of his leaving, the first birds are back.

I have two large holly trees and titmice in particular, are very interested in these. No doubt many insects have been disturbed by the work done, and the birds are eager to seek these out. I also have a large buddleia which this year had flowered profusely, leaving many seed heads. Due to the cutting back, large numbers of seeds have no doubt fallen to the ground, several goldfinches and greenfinches are busily seeking them out. The odd woodpigeon joins in, and even a pair of blackbirds appear to see what is going on.

Unfortunately, the day has been damp and dull, light quickly fading, so this activity does not last long, but hopefully they all ate their fill. They have given me several minutes of enjoyment watching all this going on and they certainly added to the pleasure of the coffee I drank. As I mentioned previously, when Simon was last here, I am sure the birds can see just what is going on and come in to investigate if it is to their advantage. It is no different to birds following a plough, they have learned it will turn up food. Wild creatures are far cleverer than we give them credit for, they too can work things out, and do so regularly.

I forgot to mention. I woke up during the night to hear a tawny owl hooting. It was the male calling, so I now know we have both sexes locally. I hope they have met up, a breeding pair of tawny owls on my doorstep would be perfect.

Today is Thursday, 22nd November, and I mention the date as it may be the first day of real winter. I woke up to a very heavy frost which did not clear away until almost 11.00 a.m., the central heating was certainly required. It also heralded an increase in the number of birds visiting my garden, my feeders are very busy. I am pleased to see the numbers of house sparrows which had moved in. These birds had been rather thin on the ground recently, not today, well into double figures at times. A few starlings also appeared on the scene, these too had been in short supply of late.

Titmice and finches were also queuing up, at this rate I will shortly be having to go out and top up the feeders.

As I am writing this, a mass exodus takes place, madam sparrowhawk has arrived on the scene, she can clear a garden like magic. She hangs around for several minutes before moving on, and it is a good ten minutes before birds start returning.

A bit of excitement at least, well for me, I doubt if the small birds thought so!

The day has remained rather dull, but it is dry, so a walk after lunch may produce something of interest, we will see.

I am back from my walk, which was very quiet on the birding front. I visited Goose Green and Swarbourn Meadow, and apart from vocal jackdaws and rooks, a blackbird and a few woodpigeons, that was it. If it had not been for the activity in my own garden earlier in the day, you would have thought Yoxall was almost birdless. You get days like this, as I have said before, birds cannot be ordered, they are there or they are not, today was the latter. We now wait to see what tomorrow may bring.

When catching the news and weather on the TV, last night was the coldest night this year since February. I think I may be right about winter!

The weekend has arrived, and a dull and grey event it is too, but at least it is dry. Yesterday was a non-event as far as birding was concerned, but today things are different. I am invaded by starlings, not that I am complaining.

Nearby is a very old Scot's pine, I have mentioned it previously. There were originally two, and over the years it has been an attractive winter roosting tree for starlings, and today they are back.

Two flocks of over fifty birds in each, are whirling round in the sky, and occasionally one flock drops in on my garden, where they savagely attack my two fat ball containers. Pieces fly off, much to the pleasure of the woodpigeons waiting underneath, before the starlings depart. This is oft repeated, and no doubt both flocks are joining in. It will not be long before I am having to refill the containers, but that is what they are there for.

When watching the starlings' behaviour, it is surprising how much fighting and squabbling occurs. Considering the fact that birds in flocks are safer from predation, it is remarkable just how aggressive they can be against each other. They are also very noisy when in flocks, even small flocks of this size. No wonder they call a flock of starlings a murmuration, although I sometimes think they sound more like politicians at prime ministers questions time! Especially currently with all the arguments regarding Brexit, whether Brexit is good or bad, the referendum voted out, so for once I just hope they would forget party politics and do what the electorate wanted.

They are very active for about an hour, the starlings that is, not the politicians, before they fly off further afield. This time not going to their roost, probably seeking a change of diet. Thank you, starlings, you certainly brightened up my morning.

These two small flocks are probably local starlings flocking up for the winter. A large flock of about 4000 reported from Branston Gravel Pits, could well be continental birds which over-winter in the UK. Large numbers of continental starlings visit the UK each winter, probably doubling our native population. 'Brexit' will not stop these!

It brightens up slightly, the weather that is, so I will have a short walk up to Goose Green. Once again there is little to see, although the local robin is doing his best to cheer things up, very vocal today. I walk to the end of the green, hear the rooks and jackdaws, and as I am about to turn back a sharp 'sreeee, sreeee' rings out.

I swiftly swing round, but I am too late, the bird has vanished round a bend in the river and I have missed a kingfisher. I presume the bird had been perched on a nearby tree, and seeing me it took to flight. Although I did not see the bird, I at least heard it, so it is something to look or listen out for in the future. It is my first local kingfisher for some time, I am very pleased I decided to have this walk.

Yesterday evening I had a phone call from two friends from the Rosliston Birders, asking if I was free for a couple of hours birding in the morning? There was only one answer to that, so they are picking me up and we will spend some time at Croxall and Whitemoor Haye. A bit of serious birding at last.

At Croxall the Canada geese were well into the three hundreds, and the noise they were making was equal to their numbers, if ever birds wished to be seen and heard, this was it. Cormorant numbers were also high, a rough count of fifty-five was made. A few pochards and goldeneyes were also to be seen, with shelducks well into double figures. As we were about to drive off to the Haye, a flock of grey-lags flew in and joined in with the Canada geese. I would estimate we now had over five hundred geese on the water, and the noise was incredible. Nothing rare, but a memorable occasion.

The Tame Valley is well known for the winter flock of mute swans which collect here each year, and the commencement of their arrival was here to be seen. At least two hundred were feeding on a meadow, and it was interesting to see a good number of the birds were juveniles. We worked our way through the birds just in case an odd wild swan was to be seen, there was not, but it was probably a little early for their arrival.

Down the rough lane a flock of about fifty tree sparrows was seen, they were all roosting up at the top of an oak tree, and they were twittering away most musically, a delightful sound. Further down the lane the odd yellowhammer flew along the hedge and a lone male reed bunting stared us out for a few seconds.

In the newly quarried area, a flock of lapwings were to be seen, judging by their numbers, I would presume they were probably visitors from the continent. Tucked in amongst them were many starlings, the winter flock of those was also building up.

Back now to look over Whitemoor Lake.

One thing which was not to be seen were any geese, we know where they were. Several great crested grebes were on the water, along with more pochards and goldeneyes. Close in by the shore and out of the water were many teals and wigeons, the calls of the wigeons could be clearly heard, a little more melodious than that of the geese at Croxall!

On the far shore were more lapwings and among these were a few golden plovers and swimming just in front of them were three drake goosanders. Working our way further along the shore we picked out four little egrets, a couple of grey herons and a redshank. Not a bad little haul really. They brought the morning to its conclusion, a most enjoyable time, which in my current circumstances was most appreciated.

It is now Sunday, and once again it is very grey and dull. I doubt if I will do any birding today, soccer is taking over. The big match is on today, Aston Villa versus Birmingham City, the 'Second City Derby' as it is known. I have been a supporter of Birmingham City since I was twelve, and I used to follow them all over the country, from Torquay in the south to Newcastle in the north. I am an armchair supporter now, but they are still the first result I look for, and today's fixture, along with the return game at St Andrews, (Birmingham's ground), are the two matches which matter the most to the fans of both clubs. I have a feeling it will be Villa's day today, but we will see. I shall be tuning in to local radio at noon.

The soccer match was a most interesting and exciting game, six goals were scored so the paying spectators could not complain, unfortunately for me, the Villa scored four of them.

Come Monday, I manage a short walk, so Goose Green and Swarbourn Meadow, are my destinations. The Green is very quiet, just a nuthatch calling, but it is tucked away, so not seen. There is hardly a sound from the rooks and jackdaws, they are probably away in some local fields feeding, and nothing is on the river. No kingfisher today I am afraid! Time for the Meadow.

Here things start equally quietly, although I do flush a moorhen which flies off noisily, visible life at last. Progressing along the riverbank I stop, a very loud twittering is heard, and a large flock of titmice fly in and land on some alders. They are very active and feed away on the cones, there must be over forty birds in this flock. Concentrating my efforts I see blues, greats, coals and long-tailed tits and a single, more brownish-looking, titmouse. Before I can get a really good view of the bird, two magpies land in the alder, and the titmice are off. The bird is obviously either a marsh or willow tit, but which I will now never know, although a marsh is the more likely of the two. Further along the Meadow a grey heron glides in, just as it is about to land it sees me and that is the end of that. My afternoon stroll concludes, but very pleasant it has been.

I arrive home to receive a phone call from the hospital. I now have an appointment to see a neurologist, this is for the 9th December, not too long a wait. The surprising thing is the fact this is a Sunday. At last things seem to be on the move again. I just await confirmation.

Confirmation duly received, I can never remember having a hospital appointment on a Sunday previously, and it cannot come soon enough. During the night I had an unpleasant experience, a very dizzy spell and nearly falling over, so I have to take things easy for a while. It will be a case of birds in the garden once again, fortunately all my feeders are full.

Today, Thursday, is a damp and very windy day, but fortunately the temperature is not too bad. Deciduous trees are now almost completely bare, so birds are more easily seen. I have had goodly numbers of titmice on my feeders, principally blue and great tits, with a couple of coal tits making fleeting visits. It is interesting watching how they feed. The blues and great remain on the feeders eating their fill, the coal tits just dash in, grab a seed or nut, and promptly fly off with it. A nuthatch is very active, it regularly takes a sunflower heart or nut and flies onto my fence, where, placing it, promptly hammers it to pieces, a very energetic method of feeding. No wonder they are called nuthatches, mind you they do not hatch nuts, they hammer them to bits, we should probably change their name to 'nuthammerers'!

Greenfinch and goldfinch numbers are increasing almost daily, spending as much time on the feeders as on the ground, picking up fallen seed and nuts, here in company with the woodpigeons, their numbers too are on the increase. The house sparrows seem to have moved on, but the starlings are still winging their way around and attacking the fat balls. The rooks are also interested in the fat balls, and to see a rook dangling on a container is quite entertaining, the bird being far larger than the container it is swinging on. How the rooks ever learned to do this is a clear indication of the size of a bird's brain and their capability of learning, it also says much for the bird's perseverance! In the fullness of time, birds which do this will be the survivors, the ones which can adapt and learn to live alongside man. This, needless to say, does not only apply to birds.

As the day has progressed, it has become brighter and the sun appears. During early afternoon there is quite a movement of gulls, with several flocks flying over.

The majority being black-headed and lesser black-backed gulls, but the odd smattering of herring and great black-backed gulls can be seen. Taking into account the direction and height at which they are flying, I can only presume some ploughing is being done locally. The gull numbers are well up into the hundreds, quite spectacular really. It is also interesting to see the spread of ages among the birds, many juveniles are seen, especially amongst the black-heads, they have obviously had a good breeding season.

Nothing else to report, we now wait to see what tomorrow may bring. One thing we can be certain about, it will see November out, with most people's thoughts now being on Christmas!

I should not have said, 'Nothing else to report'. Just as I am about to close down for the day, a flash of colour arrives in my garden—two bullfinches call in. They are a pair, a male and female, and for about ten seconds or so they sit out on the top of my fence, looking most splendid in the remaining sunlight. Some bird, their appearance more than compensates my having stayed at home. You win some, you lose some, today I have won.

A final thought. As the day progressed, I began to feel far more comfortable, so, with a bit of luck, if this continues I may in fact get a walk in tomorrow. We will just have to wait and see!

The final day of November is here, and a very pleasant day it is too. Bright sunlight with just the chance of the odd shower, or so the forecasters claim. Unfortunately, things on the health front are not a lot better, so I will be unable to get out and enjoy it, so my only birding will be in the garden.

With the better weather the birds seem to have moved back into the countryside, only the odd bird in at a time. One thing I have noticed however, is that a few house sparrows have moved back, and they are visiting one feeder in particular, this contains sunflower hearts. I never see more than three birds on the container together, and surprisingly, they are always males. It may well be the fact I only have these three birds, as I never see more at one time. Only three or not, they are welcome back.

A grey squirrel has been doing its best to annoy me today. On five occasions at least, it has raided my fat ball containers, knocking them off their support, and then running off with a fat ball. Twice it vanished over the fence with a complete ball in its claws. I do not know how it managed to carry the fat ball.

Whether the squirrel is eating the balls or burying them, I do not know. All I do know is that it has cost me a few 'bob' today!

On one visit made, I did not see it come in, but on this occasion, I heard a magpie calling loudly. Looking out I saw a short tussle going on between the magpie and the squirrel, both wanting the same fat ball, and the magpie won. Twice it flew directly at the squirrel, making it retreat a yard or two, before chipping off a sizable chunk of the ball, with which it is able to fly off. In this battle a powerful and sharp bill were a better weapon than claws. You can see life in your own garden, given the time to look.

That sees November out, not the month I had anticipated, but life still went on. See what December has in store. Car or not, I am sure something of interest will pop up. All I am hoping for is good news come my hospital visit on the 9th, after which I may be able to start looking for a new car.

December has arrived, wet and miserable. We have that heavy

drizzle which soaks you to the skin eventually, so the fact I am not too mobile at the moment may not be a bad thing. Today is obviously going to be another day for studying birds in my own garden, and one thing is very noticeable, there is far more activity than yesterday. Whether this is due to the change in the weather, yesterday it was very good, today not so, is the probable reason. My supplies are easily obtainable, no searching required, so the birds are not out in the rain for long.

The first thing I notice is the number of house sparrows has increased, I counted eleven at one time, and these were a mixture of sexes. A decided increase on three yesterday. Goldfinches too are constant visitors, these at times also in double figures. I am beginning to think that goldfinches are rapidly becoming the number one garden bird, I certainly see more in my own garden that I do in the countryside. I may see flocks of fifty or so occasionally when out birding, but that is not a regular occurrence. In my garden they are almost a regular daily sighting, and as today, frequently seen in double figures. Long may it continue.

Titmice numbers are also good, blues and greats are constant visitors, but the top titmouse as far as I am concerned is the three long-tailed tits which visited the fat balls. Not only do they enjoy them, they also put on a superb acrobatic display as they hang onto the containers. I often refer to them as flying lollipops, probably not very complimentary, but with their long tails they are not unlike a lollipop! Lovely little birds.

With all this activity, ground feeders such as dunnocks and woodpigeons are enjoying themselves. Much seed is being scattered onto the ground and this is not going to be left. The two dunnocks are dashing around, as is their wont, life to them seems always a frenzy, whereas the pigeons are just standing about waiting for the seed to fall. They obviously know how to conserve their energy!

I had put some food scraps out for the larger birds and this is quickly consumed by jackdaws and magpies, with a blackbird picking up the smaller crumbs left behind by the larger birds. Nothing is going to waste that is for sure.

By lunchtime things have quietened down, just the odd bird popping in, a solitary buzzard glides over and a small flock of black-headed gulls also provide a fly-past. Nothing rare, but a very pleasant morning it had turned out to be, you are never alone with birds, even when at home.

I now have an afternoon of soccer to look forward to, my team, Birmingham City, are playing Preston and the match is on the radio, so I can listen to that. It is at least a bit of compensation for not being able to birdwatch.

The second day in December is a much better day, quite bright and relatively mild. The soccer went well yesterday, Birmingham City won 3 – 0, so that was certainly compensation for no birding. I am hopeful that come this afternoon I may get a short stroll in, we wait to see.

Yesterday afternoon my daughter, Sarah, went for a walk, and while going through the churchyard, she came upon a female sparrowhawk which had killed a woodpigeon. Sarah backed off to watch from a safe distance. Whilst doing so a lady walking from the opposite direction, saw what was going on, and promptly chased the sparrowhawk off. What she thought she had accomplished I just do not know. The sparrowhawk would now have to make another kill. All her action had done meant another bird, somewhere, was going to die, needlessly.

I am frequently amazed by people saying they do not like sparrowhawks and kestrels because they kill and eat other creatures. I remember once, when giving a lecture, this point was raised. The person who raised the question was not going to accept anything I said, his mind was made up. So I asked him the simple question, did he eat meat or fish? He did. There was little else left to say.

There is a slight difference in saying they kill and eat other creatures, they only kill to eat, unlike man who kills animals for fun so they may have a trophy hanging on their walls. The wild world is a hard world, but where survival is the name of the game, predation will go on, that is nature. No one is sorry for the worm the blackbird digs up from a lawn, they are only sorry when a sparrowhawk takes the blackbird! All three are equally important to the balance of nature, we certainly are not! So the next time you see a wild creature make a kill, either of an insect or an animal, marvel at the skill of the hunter. Be it a swallow or a golden eagle, you will have witnessed nature at its most spectacular.

The weather put paid to my opportunity of a walk, and things have not really improved. December so far has been garden watching, but it has also provided me with the opportunity of catching up on national and international wildlife news, and today, climate change is top of the agenda.

But before going into that, I received a surprise telephone call from an old bird watching friend of mine, who I have not seen or spoken to for about fifteen years. He moved down south when his company moved and since then our only contact has been the exchange of Christmas cards. He has been up here on business which he has completed a day earlier than anticipated, so he now has a day free. He phoned me in the hope I was available to accompany him on a day's local birding, as he wished to visit some of his old haunts. We had spent many a happy hour locally in the past, and he was no mean birder. I suggested we visited Croxall Lakes, Whitemoor Haye and finished off at Blithfield Reservoir. He obviously was not dressed for birding only having business cloths, but he did drive a 4x4 so we could drive round the shoreline at Blithfield. He was more than happy with my suggestion, and the thoughts of my having a full day's birding again was eagerly anticipated.

He was only staying at Uttoxeter, so he arrived bright and early. After a coffee and his enjoying the goldfinches on my feeders, he did not see these at home, we are on our way.

He was not familiar with the layby at Kings Bromley, so we call in here first, and it does not disappoint us. Five little egrets, three grey herons, a large mixed flock of Canada and grey-lag geese, a drake goosander, two little grebes and a circling buzzard overhead. My friend was suitably impressed.

On now to Croxall Lakes, and as this is my first serious days birding for some time, I will list the main birds as we see them, I may not get another day like this for some time yet, depending what happens on the 9th.

I think my friend is quite impressed with the fact I have a key which enables us to gain access. Birds at Croxall are rather widespread and take some finding, but we see great crested grebes, three of them, many cormorants, the odd teal and wigeon, a tidy little flock of tufted ducks along with the odd pochard. Gulls are plentiful, black-headed and lesser black-backed. Buzzards again put on a show, well two do, soaring high above us, and as we drive down the track, a sparrowhawk flies across.

We were not doing badly, and I am thoroughly enjoying myself, serious bird watching at last, and I am not doing the driving.

Whitemoor Haye now calls. We stop first to have a look over the lake. More Canada geese, mute swans, thirty or more of them, teals and wigeons are well into double figures and in various locations round the shore are seven little egrets. A small flock of seven dark looking geese catch our attention, they are on the far shore and not showing well. Eventually they move into a more open location, they are barnacle geese. My friend is delighted with these, they are a 'year tick' for him. Pochards, tufted ducks and mallards are well represented and a small group of seven goldeneyes, four of them glorious looking drakes, complete the scene. Well not quite, as we go back to the car a female kestrel pays us a visit, hovering very close by. As farewells go, that is not too bad. Now for the rough lane.

The quarrying down here has continued at quiet a rate since I was last along the lane, just a few weeks ago. The change is dramatic in a way, meadows where skylark sang are no longer here, a complete lunar landscape almost. The only consolation being that if left nature will quickly take over again. We live in hope.

Fortunately, much of the hedgerow has been left intact, enabling the tree sparrows and yellowhammers to continue their business. Tree sparrows are plentiful, one flock was well up in the twenties and there were three or four yellowhammers to be seen. We had very good views of these birds, they were landing on the lane collecting grit, so we just stood still watching them. We had their company for five or six minutes, enjoying every bit of it, until two magpies joined in. They quickly frighten the small birds off and then, realising we were there, they also fly off. Thank you, magpies.

Walking on further down the rough lane we see a small covey of six red- legged partridges and two male pheasants go dashing down the lane as they see our approach. Once again flight seems to be the last thing they think about, luckily for them, they find a gap in the hedge and dash through that. Peace returns.

Reaching the corner of the lane we stop and turn back. A movement in the hedge catches our attention, and we find ourselves looking at three goldfinches, always a bird to enjoy. We reach our car without further adventure and proceed to Blithfield Reservoir.

Time is now rapidly running away with us so a quick decision is made. We will visit the Watery Lane car park for a view down the reservoir, and then cross the causeway to have a drive down Admaston Reach. At this time of the year the hours of good daylight are not long, and today has, unfortunately, been rather dull in any case, just about remaining dry.

There are many birds to be seen, the bulk I must admit are gulls, and we drop on two yellow-legged gulls amongst them, another 'year tick' for my friend. Several pochards and tufted ducks are on the water, with many cormorants and great crested grebes accompanying them. Teals and wigeons are plentiful round the reservoir edges and a small flock of meadow pipits are busily feeding away on the shore. Small flocks of goldeneyes are scattered across the reservoir and a carrion crow does us a favour.

It lands on the shore and promptly flushes two redshanks that we had not seen. Unlike the magpies at Whitemoor Haye, we did thank this bird!

Driving across the causeway two oystercatchers fly over, calling loudly as they do so, they are rarely silent. Admaston Reach also has goodly numbers of teals and wigeons with a large flock of mallards out on the water. Driving slowly down the Reach, a line of little egrets are walking the shore, seven of them, almost in a military manner.

In Dairy House Reach large numbers of gulls are again in attendance, among them are several great black-backed gulls, the largest number I have seen together for some time. Thanks to the water levels still being low, we did not have to drive so far to see these birds. More little egrets are to be seen and whilst enjoying these a great white egret saunters round the corner of the bay.

My friend is absolutely delighted with this bird, it is a 'lifer' for him. We may have a few spread round Staffordshire, but they are few and far between in his neck of the woods. We stop to enjoy this bird, you do not rush off from a 'lifer', even if it is not yours. After several minutes the bird turns back and takes to flight.

We concentrate our efforts back on the water. Mute swan nunbers are really building up, a large flock is regular here during winter, and frequently the odd wild swans, whoopers and Bewick's are to be found amongst them. Not today I am afraid.

Shelduck numbers are high. I stop to count these, thirty-one, that is probably the highest number I have ever seen at Blithfield.

As we are about to leave, a large mixed flock of geese come in, very noisily needless to say. The bulk are Canada and grey-lags, but a paler looking bird is picked up. Closer scrutiny shows this to be a bar-headed goose, not a bad bird to finish up on.

My friend drove off home a very happy man, three 'year ticks' and one of them a 'lifer', that is a good day out for anyone. Me, I was just so pleased to have at long last, well it seems long last, got in a day's birding. Nothing new for me, just a good number of cracking birds.

Now back to the international conference taking place in Poland, where Sir David Attenborough made a speech to the delegates. In this he told them that climate change was humanity's greatest threat and could mean the collapse of civilisation and the extinction of much of the natural world is on the horizon. The question is, is anyone listening?

Poland, the country in which the meeting is being held, is claimed to use more coal per head of the population than any other. The USA has withdrawn from the Paris Agreement which aimed to control the rate of the rise of the world's temperature, and emerging countries, such as India and China are using fuels, coal especially, at an alarming rate. As has been said by many people, it is the time for action, words are not enough.

In my lifetime I have witnessed many changes. Things which were once common place, are now almost rare. Birds, which I know the best, have reduced in numbers at an alarming rate. This past summer I saw less swallows, house martins and sand martins than for many a year, swifts were almost rarities. Even the commoner warblers such as blackcap, willow warbler and chiffchaff, which you would expect to hear from any piece of woodland, were very thin on the ground.

I do, seriously, believe we are too late, the good times are now behind us. The days when cuckoos called, skylarks sang above many a field, and blackbirds chased each other round in the garden, are now almost gone, along with much else. I wish you luck, Sir David, but I am afraid few who are in the position of being able to do anything about it, are even listening. The most powerful man in the world, President Trump of the USA, does not believe in climate change in any case, so what chance have we?

December, so far, apart from my day out with my old friend, has not been a good month for birding. It is now the 6th, and I have done little. Even my garden has been quiet over the past two or three days, and yesterday it rained almost non-stop all day, although in the midst of all the rain I did have an amusing incident, which brightened up the day appreciably.

I have a small garden pond and alongside the edge of this I have a life-sized plastic grey heron, it has been there for some years, my late wife Dorothy bought it for me. Today I noticed a great tit trying to land on the bill of the bird, which due to it being smooth plastic and sloping downwards, did not give the bird any real grip, with the result the great tit kept on slipping off. The bird was nothing if not persistent, although unsuccessful. This went on for several attempts on the bird's part, before it gave up and flew off. What it was all about I have no idea, whether any small insects were on the heron I do not know, I certainly saw nothing when I went out to look. Whether the bird was just enjoying itself or not I will never know, there has been no repeat.

It has also been a period of frustration, both white-fronted geese and a Slavonian grebe have been reported, and the long-tailed duck is still at Branston Gavel Pits. All three would have been 'year ticks' for me had I not been carless.

The one consolation now, is the fact that my hospital appointment is only days away, so who knows. I may have some good news. We can but hope!

Today I have to go into Lichfield where I have some business to complete, and on the return journey I manage a couple of minutes' birding. My taxi driver drives slowly past the Kings Bromley layby, and I am delighted to see we have three little egrets in attendance with a drake goosander on the river. A mixed flock of Canada and grey-lag geese are on the meadow, a grey heron is stalking fish upstream, and a robin is heard from the churchyard nearby. Some serious birds again, my first since my day out with my friend. To complete the picture, as we drove over the River Trent, two more goosanders flew down the river, this time both ducks. This drake I saw a short time ago may have the start of a harem!

Friday dawns very damp, but by lunchtime it has brightened up considerably. My proofreader, Evelyn, has called to take me out for a spot of lunch, which is much appreciated, and thoroughly enjoyed. Not driving currently, this is a most pleasant break.

On my return home a bit of excitement awaits me. A carrion crow has knocked one of the fat ball containers onto the ground, and several of the fat balls have rolled out. The crow is now able to hack them to pieces, and it is doing so with relish.

Bits are flying everywhere, much to the pleasure of two starlings which are collecting them up. The starlings appear to have no fear of the crow which is only feet away, not that it seems the slightest bit interested in the starlings, it has other things on its mind. Fat balls which usually last days are consumed in just minutes. A crow's bill is a very good tool, time now to replace the fat balls.

I had filled up the sunflower heart containers early on, and while I was away these have obviously been fully appreciated. They are both now just about half full, or should that be half empty? These too will have to be replenished before the day is out. The way things are going with my birds today, I will shortly need a bank loan!

There is little doubt I will be refilling the sunflower heart containers. A flock of eleven goldfinches are now in the garden, five on one container, six on the other, with the hearts reducing at an alarming rate. To add to this, three woodpigeons are eating the fallen hearts, at least nothing is going to waste.

Sunday has finally arrived, and I am back from my hospital appointment. I had a thorough examination and many tests, I was there for half an hour, but unfortunately, I now have to wait for the results of the tests. He did, however, warn me that the chances of my driving again are not good. There is a problem with my right foot where when relaxed, my foot turns to right angles and consequently would rest on my accelerator which means I could press this pedal when I thought my foot was on the brake pedal. If that should prove to be the case, driving would most certainly not be possible. That means I am still unable to drive, so the chances of obtaining a new vehicle this year has gone and possibly gone for good. My birding for the remainder of the year is going to be local, very much so, and how it is looking, this also applies for the future. The most important thing is that I keep myself mobile, so that I can continue to walk..

The day itself is very pleasant for the time of the year, so a short walk after lunch will be taken. I will visit Goose Green again and call in on Swarbourn Meadow on my return journey.

Goose Green is again quiet, although the rooks and jackdaws are expressing their opinions a little more, and a moorhen is busily hunting away on the river. I can hear titmice calling, but cannot find them, and a kestrel flies through. She, it being a female, brings at least a bit of quality in.

On to Swarbourn Meadow. Here a carrion crow is letting rip, what has upset it I do not know, but it is certainly informing the world it is not happy! Two magpies further down the river are also letting vent to their feelings, and then I see what has upset them. A buzzard is sitting out on the top of a tree and our noisy birds do not appreciate the bird's close proximity. Why they should worry I do not know, a buzzard is not going to attack them, although they may try to drive the buzzard off.

They do not, it is just a noisy stalemate.

Approaching the end of the Meadow, I disturb a small flock of linnets, about ten of them, but they do not hang around, they are quickly off into the distance. One thing which is noticeable from when I was recently along the river, there are no fish rising to the surface. The colder weather now being experienced, has obviously affected insects and the like, which are remaining deeper in the water, and the trout are doing likewise.

That ends an enjoyable stroll, back home now for a pleasant mug of hot coffee, and see what the birds are up to in my own garden. Not a lot, I just manage to refill my food containers as the rain starts to fall. I had been indeed fortunate.

Monday is a very busy day and birding is not on the agenda, but fate at times can come to your aid. Early afternoon, I am doing some work in my study, when a movement outside, on my sunflower heart containers, catches my attention. I am delighted to see six siskins on the containers, three of each sex. For the next few minutes, they attack the hearts with gusto, with much going onto the ground beneath. The woodpigeons are going to enjoy themselves when they find these fallen hearts.

Unfortunately, I did not have their company for long, they were obviously just passing through, but I am not complaining. Siskins are not regular visitors to my garden, so just having them for a few minutes is a bonus. Their bold colours certainly brightened up a gloomy afternoon, especially as light rain is now beginning to fall.

During the past few days, I have been very inactive. Early in the week I had a fall which has kept me fully housebound, having injured my back, so any birds seen have all been from or in my own garden. Fortunately, they have been very active, so I have at least had things to see.

The most interesting were a party of eleven long-tailed tits which spent nearly an hour attacking my fat balls. Even when larger birds came in, they only flew off to a nearby tree, and once the coast was clear they were back again. Unfortunately, from my point of view, they were obviously on passage as they have not been back.

The last couple of days have been very cold, the frost today is still on the ground in patches as darkness returned, which is why the birds have been so active. I managed to struggle out late this afternoon to fill up many of my containers, and I have hardly returned in before birds are back feeding. They are most certainly stocking up in preparation for another cold night ahead. At this time of the year they need all the help we can give them.

Feeding the birds is now big business, and it is doing much to help many birds survive, and as the human population increases and more houses are required, feeding the birds takes on a totally new aspect. We are destroying their natural territories so fast that the only way many will survive is by moving in and living close to us. Our own gardens will then become their territories, and feeding them will help their survival.

Some of my friends have learned about my car problems, so the opportunity of another day's birding has arisen. They are visiting Doxey Marsh over at Stafford, and have a spare seat in the car, needless to say, I gladly fill it.

Driving across Cannock Chase we see buzzards, ravens and a jay, a good enough start to our day out, and we arrive at Doxey to find only one car on the car park. We are going to have the place to ourselves by the look of things. Doxey, being completely open to the public, has many public footpaths, and can get rather busy at times with dog walkers and cyclists, which can interfere with the birding. Not necessarily intentionally, just the movement and noise generated can be sufficient to drive birds off. Today we may be lucky.

Doxey Marsh covers a large area and I am unable to walk those sorts of distances, but I can make the first couple of lakes, or Flashes as they call them here, and then take myself back to the car to await their return. I have no intention of limiting their day out. This understood, we are off.

Several good birds have been reported from Doxey recently, not 'ticks' but certainly birds I would like to enjoy once again. We park up and walk the short distance to the first of the Flashes, the name of which eludes me. A large number of waterfowl are to be seen. Many Canada and grey-lag geese, the largest number of shovelers I have seen for a long time, pochards and tufted ducks are not to be outshone, neither are gadwalls and mallards are their usual plentiful selves. The pick of the waterfowl, are a pair of pintails, the drake of which is looking quite colourful, he is rapidly coming out of his moult. When you include other water birds to these, this Flash has a very high number of birds in attendance. As we are about to move on, two little egrets fly in, not a bad goodbye that.

Moving on towards Boundary Flash, I wave my friends on, so they can cover a much larger area than I can currently, and I will see them back at the car.

Approaching the Flash a family party of five bullfinches are feeding in the hedge, it looks like they are eating ivy berries or some small insects which may be on the berries. They are oblivious to me, so

I am able to enjoy them for two or three minutes before they move on. In the small trees above where the finches were seen, long-tailed tits are foraging away, always a pleasant sight, and from the undergrowth beneath a robin is singing. All in all, very pleasant.

Boundary Flash is well vegetated, it has thick areas of reed with areas of open water. A viewing platform is available, and if I am able, I can walk to the end of the Flash where a rise provides views over the area, and towards the River Sow which runs through the reserve. The reserve actually has two rivers running through it, the River Sow and the Darling, which have made it a superb wetland site, flooding occurring frequently.

My friends have moved on from here so I have things to myself. Initially it is just coots, moorhens, mallards and Canada geese, until three grey herons fly in, and their arrival does me a great favour. They land on the edge of a reed bed, and in doing so, flush out four snipes, which I had not seen. These birds provide me with a fly-past, they glide directly overhead to land in the reeds behind me. Some greeting that.

A decent selection of gulls are on the Flash, with a few great black-backed and common gulls amongst them. A small flotilla of pochards join in and I count seven little grebes scattered round the Flash, that is not to be sniffed at, especially as they outnumber the great crested grebes, I can only see three of those. From out of a reed bed two more little egrets strut, in the shallow water their yellow feet can be clearly seen, that always makes identification positive.

Moving on round the Flash towards the way to the rise I mentioned, I stop, a low but harsh 'chup' rings out. Just in front of me a male reed bunting has popped out of the reeds and is sitting on the top of a small bush, simply glaring at me.

We are no more than ten feet apart, and for about thirty seconds he just sits there staring straight at me, it has been a long time since I was this close to a reed bunting. They may not be rare, but this bird has made my day, an absolute cracker this one.

He moves on and so can I. Approaching the rise I stop to admire a kestrel, a male, which is sitting out on the top of a stump, that is until he spots me, and is off..

From the rise a good panoramic view of the marshes can be made.

A flock of woodpigeons, a good hundred or more, are feeding amongst the cattle and further grey herons are along the Sow. Whilst enjoying these a large white heron walks into view, or more accurately, a great white egret appears and when you see the two together you can appreciate the size of the bird, to all intents and purposes, it is a white heron. Close to the cattle a large flock of wigeon are also grazing, and their delightful whistling call can be heard. Few ducks quack, irrespective of what Walt Disney may think!

I am about to move off, when a couple of birders approach me. 'Have I seen the cattle egrets?' they ask. You know the answer to that, no. Apparently, just over the other side of the rise, there are two in a field with a few cattle. I only need to walk a short distance to see them. I thank them and I am on my way.

I am pleased to say they were right about the distance. In a field beyond a hedge, were the two cattle egrets, sharing the field with a few cows. I know I have seen these birds previously, but you can never have too much of a good thing. When combined with the little and great white egrets seen, to have all three at one location is a bit special to say the least, and don't let us forget the grey heron. We have seen four family members today.

Time to make my way back, my friends will not be long now and they can walk far faster than me. I pause at Boundary Flash for a few minutes, and if ever I was in the right place at the right time, this is it. Approaching the viewing platform, a call is heard from the reed bed which I just do not recognise instantly. It is quite musical, although a bit penetrating, a three-note whistle 'tit-looe'. I know I have heard it before, but I just cannot recall it. The bird is well hidden within the reeds and I am beginning to give up on ever identifying it, when the bird chooses to cooperate, out it walks—a green sandpiper. For no more than ten seconds the bird stands clear of the reeds before with a quick turn, it is back into cover. If ever I was meant to see a bird, that was it. And I now know what they sound like. I must admit the bird's behaviour did surprise me a little. I have never thought they were birds which seek cover like this, most of my sightings have always been in the open.

You never stop learning in this game. A great finish to my trip to

Doxey, no 'year ticks' but some wonderful birds, and that is what it is all about.

My friends incidentally had done equally well, they beat me in one sense, they had seen three green sandpipers on Tillington Flash, so we are all happy. As we were about to drive off a great spotted woodpecker flew into the car park and landed on a tree. We were able to watch this bird for two or three minutes before it flew off, and that bird did finish off my visit to Doxey.

We drive home via Blithfield Reservoir to spend a few minutes seeing the gulls coming in for their nightly roost. Large numbers of black-headed and lesser black-backed gulls are easily picked out. Great black-backed gulls are also in decent numbers, well scattered among the other gulls, with the odd common gull flying through. One of my colleagues draws my attention to a pale looking gull which has landed, very conveniently for us, on the causeway wall. He has picked up an Iceland gull. The white primaries were showing clearly at this close distance, no mistaking this bird for a herring gull. Although I have seen one previously, none of my friends had seen one this year, so they were delighted with their 'year tick'. A great conclusion to a most interesting day out.

Listening to the latest forecast regarding climate change, what the scientists say is frightening. At the rate ice is thawing at the poles, sea levels will rise many feet, and this is in a relatively short period of time.

At the current conference in Poland, all I seem to be hearing is platitudes, no single country seems to be grasping the seriousness of the situation. Kuwait, China, Russia and the USA do not believe it in any case, and with three of those being among the major industrial countries in the world, who are probably polluting the world the most, we have no chance.

At my age, why should I be worried, I shall not be here to see it happen, and I believe that is what the world's leaders are thinking. If it will not affect them, why worry?

The climate change conference is finally over, and they have agreed to aim to limit the increase in carbon levels, note I say aim, but I could see little of how this was going to be accomplished. Many, many fine words once again, but most of the conservation and scientific bodies did not see a lot to be happy about, and I trust them far more than any politician.

The cold weather has continued which has meant much activity in the garden. Nothing extra special has paid me a visit, but the goldfinches and greenfinches have been constant visitors to my feeders, plenty of colour there. The titmice numbers have increased and the starlings and house sparrows are not far behind. Several rooks have been in attacking the fat balls, with many of the ground feeders waiting patiently underneath, nothing has been wasted that is for sure. It has been a time of regularly topping up the feeders, but it looks as though things may change by tomorrow, temperatures look like rising. We will see.

On Sunday, Sarah had a bit of luck. She and Martin were down Whitemoor Haye where they were studying the large goose flock, and she picked out two pink-footed geese amongst them. These were her first of the year, so she came home highly delighted, and why not? Fortunately, I have seen pink-foots this year myself, so she could not gloat!

Another trip out looms. Two of my friends are visiting Attenborough Nature Reserve, would I like to accompany them? There is only one answer to that. They can only make it a morning visit which suits me fine. Attenborough, as I am sure I have mentioned previously, is a very large reserve, and I normally only manage to make the Kingfisher Hide, so a morning is ideal.

It is a rather chilly morning, so before we venture forth a quick visit to the café is called for. A mug of hot coffee, and we are on our way.

Reports of red kite had been made from the opposite side of the River Trent, so my two friends who had not seen kites this year, made that their initial destination and would call in at the Kingfisher Hide for me on their return. That suited me fine,

I could settle down in the hide and really work the water in front. I had brought my 'scope with me specifically to do this, and walking is not exactly my better point at present.

The usual activity was going on near the visitor centre, young children thoroughly enjoying themselves feeding the ducks, geese and swans. Who knows, this could also be the start of a lifelong long love affair with birds for one or two of them, just like it had for me. One of the parents, seeing me carrying my equipment, asked me about two of the birds they were feeding, they could not have chosen two more attractive birds to feed, they were two drake red-crested pochards. I explained what they were and told them a bit about the birds. I think someone would be on the net later that day.

I was pleasantly surprised by the number of Egyptian geese to be seen, well up into double figures, and further out on the lake were tufted ducks and pochards. As I started to walk down the track to the hide, a Cettis warbler breaks forth, and there is no mistaking this little fellow, some voice, and as with the robin, it calls throughout the year, not just in the breeding season. Very cooperative, I love birds which announce their presence.!

I first started visiting Attenborough well over twenty years ago, and the reason was the Cetti's warbler. They had slowly moved up country and commenced to breed at Attenborough, which was the nearest breeding location to home at that time. Their numbers have slowly built up and several pairs are regularly seen here. Unlike many of the warblers seen in the UK, they are a resident not a summer migrant, and for at least two years now, a pair have bred near the car parking area. When visiting during the breeding season you can regularly hear at least one calling, you hardly need to move from your car. It does not seem all those years ago that I used to drive down to Dorset just in the hope of seeing the bird. I now have them at Whitemoor Haye, less than ten miles from home. Their spread has been amazing.

A little way down the track I stop on the bridge, just as a gravel barge passes beneath, disturbing the birds somewhat, and here I see three further red-crested pochards, a drake with two ducks and a great crested grebe pops up, sees me, and quickly dives again.

Further down the track is a viewing screen which overlooks Tween Pond. On a spit just in front of the screen are four common snipes and two oystercatchers, and on an island further out, are several cormorants, a couple of grey herons and a little egret. Black-headed gulls are plentiful and gadwall numbers are good. On now to the Kingfisher

Hide.

This I have all to myself, my friends by now being well on their way to kite seeking. This hide overlooks Clifton Pond, usually the most productive of the lakes, and today is no exception. The usual large concentration of gulls are to be seen. Black-headed and lesser black-backed being the most numerous, but several herring gulls are on show, plus a small number of common and great black-backed. One of the latter is close in and it looks huge, they are indeed a large bird when seen this close. I would not like to tangle with one, that is for certain.

Waterfowl are plentiful, with forty or so gadwalls being a very good number to see. Shovelers and shelducks are well accounted for, tufted ducks, pochards and mallards are in very good numbers and the odd goldeneye can be seen. Cormorant are well over fifty. Little and great crested grebes are dotted about, accompanied by the inevitable coots and moorhens, along with the odd grey heron. A decent mixture.

Time now to concentrate on the islands to see if we can find any waders.

After much searching, I finally come across a group of small waders, what have we here? I am thankful I brought my 'scope, they are quite a distance away. They turn out to be five dunlins and two green sandpipers and further on I spot several lapwings roosted up. Looking through these I pick out five golden plovers, they give me four different waders. Clifton Pond has done very well.

At this stage in the proceedings, two birders arrive in the hide, rather breathlessly. 'Had I seen the great white egret?' they ask. My answer to that was obviously no. Apparently the bird had been seen just minutes ago, flying over the nearby Tween Pond and heading in this direction. I certainly had not seen the bird and it is unlikely I could have missed such a large white bird flying in.

The bird is not to be seen round the shores of Clifton Pond nor on the water, so I suggested we concentrate our efforts on the reed beds, it could easily have vanished in those without my spotting it. I can understand their interest in the bird, they have never seen one previously, I have done very well with them this year, not that it is time to gloat.

Whilst searching I found out the birders were two recently retired friends, who had only taken up birding recently. On learning this, I raised the question had they ever seen dunlin, green sandpiper or golden plover—the answer was no, we could at least put that right.

I swung my 'scope round to where I had last seen the birds, and they were still there. I called them over, they did not have 'scopes, and showed them the three birds. They were delighted to see them. I was also able to explain that all the three birds were in winter plumage, hence the fact they did not look quite like the illustrations in their guides. They made a note of my field guide so I have a feeling their local book shop is due two sales. Can I ask for commission?

Back to great white egret seeking. My two friends appeared whilst doing so. They had seen the red kite, only fleetingly, it was some distance away, but they were happy. I pointed out the waders to them and got back to egret hunting. We now had five pairs of eyes seeking it out.

Many minutes passed until a slight movement in the reed bed caught my eye, I quickly brought this to the attention of all, concentration time is nigh. After what seemed almost an eternity, out walked our friend, it is indeed a great white egret, and the powerful, yellow looking bill, showed it to be an adult. I did not realise it, but for one of my friends it is a 'year tick', a 'lifer' to the two newcomers to the game. The had now seen four birds for the first time, it is all new when you first start, and good luck to them.

Two small birds caught our attention in the reed bed. A pair of reed buntings were actively searching for food, so we were able to enjoy them for a few minutes.

The male at the very least gave us a colourful send off. Mind you they were not the last birds we saw. Two common snipe flew in, to promptly vanish into the reeds, much to the pleasure of the two newcomers to birding.

Time has now caught up with us, so off home we trudge, after a most pleasant, few hours. My friends said they hoped to get out again before the end of the year, if they do, they will give me a buzz. I eagerly await.

I have yet to hear from the hospital, so with Christmas now being just a few days away, I think it is safe to say my serious birding for the year looks over, unless I hear from my friends.

I shall keep my eyes open on my garden, and if things improve, I may yet manage a walk locally, time will tell. The annoying thing is the fact that we still have a few very interesting birds locally, which had I been mobile, I could easily have seen. Frustration is the name of the game!

Christmas is now just five days away, and at last things have improved with my back. It is a very pleasant day, bright and sunny, so a stroll out after lunch will not go amiss.

I am pleased to say the birds have come out to greet me. My first port of call is Goose Green, and here a large mixed party of titmice are busily feeding. Whether the improvement in temperature has encouraged the emergence of small insects I do not know, but the birds are all happy enough. I patiently make my way through the flock, it totals thirty-seven birds, a mixture of blue, great, long-tailed, coal, plus a pair of marsh tits, most of our local titmice, only the willow tit is missing. As well as actively feeding, they are also very vocal, and I spend an enjoyable, few minutes watching them before they move on. Walking on further down Goose Green I spot a largish bird of prey approaching. At first, I think it may be a goshawk, but as it gets nearer, I realise it is a female sparrowhawk. I have mentioned previously that female birds of prey are usually larger than the males, and at distance a female sparrowhawk can be easily confused with a male goshawk, not today, unfortunately. A grey wagtail is foraging away along the river bank and two moorhens are squabbling over something or other. A decent bit of action. Now for the Swarbourn Meadow.

A pair of blackbirds are busily feeding on the meadow, and the way they are behaving they do look like a true pair. Very sociable. A grey heron takes off from the river as I approach, and surprisingly, a jay flies through, not a bird I see that often locally. Apart from those, things are rather quiet, just a chaffinch calling, and then I stop. As what I can best describe as a gravelly twitter is heard, and I do not readily recognise it. Slowly making my way in the general direction of the sound it suddenly hits me, it is the flight call of the siskin. I quicken my pace to see a small flock of about a dozen birds land in a silver birch. They are evenly spread sex wise, half of each, and they noisily attack the cones which hang on the tree. Unfortunately, they are only visible for a minute or two, before they are once again up and away. A short time it may have been, but for me it was a delightful couple of minutes.

The weather has now decided to change and drizzle is starting to fall, but luckily, I am only a short distance from home. I may have only been out for an hour or so, and I doubt if I have walked above a quarter of a mile in total, but it was certainly a most pleasant time. Nothing rare, but plenty of activity from the birds, which is what matters.

Whilst I have been out, the birds in my garden have been busy, one fat ball container lies empty on the ground and my sunflower containers need refilling. My birds certainly keep me active enough, that is for sure!

Another friend has heard about my problems with my car, and he has suggested a morning at Blithfield Reservoir, that suggestion is not going to be turned down.

He collects me on a bright and dry morning, perfect conditions for birding. We drive straight to Stansley Wood and proceed directly down to the hide overlooking Tad Bay. Water levels have improved since I was last here, now visible in front of the hide. Teal numbers are high and they are mainly in the shallows round the edges of the reservoir. Wigeon on the other hand are out on the grassy areas, grazing away. A large mixed flock of Canada geese and grey-lags are also on the shores and tucked in amongst them are nine barnacle geese, they were unexpected.

On the water are many cormorants and great crested grebes, along with coots, these I would estimate are well into three figures. Duck numbers are also good. Tufted ducks and mallards are well accounted for, and the number of shelducks is also impressive. Goldeneyes and goosanders are up in double figures, although the gadwall and pochard numbers looked low. They could quite easily be round in Blithe Bay. What was also noticeable was the very low numbers of lapwings. Usually, they are in three figures, not today, just twenty or thirty of them were to be seen. Blithfield is a large water however, and we were only viewing a small area of it.

Away from the water, two buzzards flew across, quite lazily, and raven could be heard but not seen. A small bird of prey was spotted over the woods, the way it was flying we presumed it to be a sparrowhawk, and a wren let rip from undergrowth near to the hide. We could not see it, but something had obviously upset the bird, although no other bird was heard.

At this point a couple came in and explained they had only recently joined the West Midland Bird Club and this was their first visit to Blithfield. They were new to birding and were very pleased for us to point out the birds to be seen, many of which were obviously new to them.

Whilst doing this, a woodpigeon commenced to call from near the hide, and one of the birders asked the question of how did we know it was a woodpigeon and not a collared dove? They were seeing both in their garden and were interested in how to tell which was which by their calls. This fortunately was easy to explain,

The woodpigeon has a five-note call, with the emphasis on the first 'coo', with the collared dove having a three-note call, the emphasis on the middle 'coo'. The woodpigeon cooperated well, calling several times so they quickly picked up on what was said. The collared dove they would have to wait for, none were calling at Blithfield.

Whilst having our final look round, two grey herons flew in, quickly followed by five little egrets, as send offs go, that was nay bad! The little egrets really did excite our new friends and they now learned to look out for their yellow feet when next seen.

Driving home we stopped in Newtonhurst Lane to have a closer look at the barnacle geese, and as we were doing so, we were delighted to see a great white egret walk down Tad Brook. This was a bit special, especially for my friend, he had not seen one previously this year. That brought a most pleasant morning to its conclusion.

Today is turkey collection day, and in transit to my butcher in Armitage, I have a pleasant, few seconds. My taxi driver is forced to stop, a covey of nine red-legged partridge decide to cross the road at that moment, and they were in no hurry. Had my driver not been considerate, we could easily have been eating partridge at Christmas instead of turkey! On my return journey, a little egret is visible at the Kings Bromley layby and a kestrel is hovering near to the church. Three bits of quality seen, the turkey run had been worthwhile in more ways than one. Being a passenger instead of a driver does at least enable you to see things, so that is some consolation for not being able to drive at present.

Sunday, 23rd December has dawned wet and miserable, the only consolation being the temperature, mild for time of the year, and no snow is forecast. One thing the rain has done is bring a lot of birds into my garden, with much activity on my feeders.

The majority of birds to be seen are blue and great tits, in double figures at times, feeding on both the sunflower hearts and fat balls. Two greenfinches, a male and female, are also regular visitors to the sunflower hearts, much to the delight of three woodpigeons. These birds are actively picking up the fallen hearts, so nothing is going to waste. An amusing incident happens, a seed falls on the back of one of the woodpigeons, and before it can turn to take the seed, one of its companions picks it off its back. A slight battle ensues between the two, but this does not last long, they quickly return to eating the fallen hearts. It was like two small children squabbling over a sweet in the playground. It certainly brought a smile to my face. I am frequently surprised by the antics of the birds', at times they are almost human.

A flock of Canada geese fly over, very low and noisily. I can hear their honking clearly from within my home. How low they are flying I can only presume they are coming into land on a nearby farmer's field, and there must have been well over fifty of them judging by the noise. Canada geese rarely do things quietly, they are, after all, originally from the American continent. I will say no more!

Christmas Eve has dawned bright and crisp, frost being very evident, and the cold weather has brought in the birds. The fat balls are being devoured by a flock of starlings, I count seventeen in the garden, almost queuing up to get onto the fat balls. Whilst on the subject of starlings, according to local reports, over five thousand of them can be seen at Branston Gravel Pits, quite a murmuration (the collective name for a flock of starlings). These may well be continental birds as large numbers migrate across each winter.

Greenfinches have also moved in, several of those have been attacking the sunflower hearts. Looking at the containers, it will not be long before I am having to refill them. The usual goldfinches and titmice are to be seen and the ground feeders are very active. At times like this garden birding is most enjoyable.

The bright weather has continued, and as my back is now almost normal, a short walk is called for, so after an early lunch I am on my way. Walking down my drive I hear a racous 'krownt', only one bird sounds like this, and looking up a grey heron is flying overhead. I do not know what has upset the bird, but it is certainly letting rip. A good start to my walk.

I am only going as far a Goose Green, and I arrive to find it almost birdless, they are obviously all in my own garden! Three rooks fly over and a chaffinch is calling, and that is that. Back to Swarbourn Meadow, will that be any better?

Marginally. A small party of titmice are on the alders, just blues and greats, and a pair of magpies are stalking the meadow, not that they appear to be finding a lot. Things then brighten up. High above, a buzzard flies through, 'mewing' loudly, always a welcome sight and sound, and as I turn for home, a mallard splashes down in the river. Only a few birds seen, but the grey heron and the buzzard were definitely worthy of mention, it is always a bonus to see and hear birds.

Christmas now awaits, tomorrow it will most definitely only be birds in the garden, apart that is, from the one on my plate!

Christmas Day has come in dull with a slight mist, but at least it is not raining and the conditions for anyone travelling are not too bad, not that I am.

Bird activity in my garden was very much on the agenda early on, although it has quietened down recently, they have no doubt eaten their fill. One thing which is very noticeable is the number of house sparrows seen, well into double figures, and two of them in particular raise my interest levels.

Outside my kitchen window I have a nest box, which has housed the odd pair of great tits in the past, and today a pair of house sparrows are paying a great deal of attention to the box. They are going in and out of the box frequently, with the male sitting on the top of the box twittering away occasionally, whilst the female is inside.

You would think the breeding season had arrived, not midwinter. This performance carries on for several minutes before they too depart.

I will have to see if this is repeated, they were obviously a pair, but could just have been searching for insects in the box. Time will tell whether they were seeking out a home. Should they want it, it is vacant and available to rent, at not a very excessive rate!

With the milder weather over the Christmas period, things quietened down in the garden, the birds were obviously finding food further afield. The most exciting bird which called in to see me, or to be more accurate, flew through, it did not stay, was a superb male sparrowhawk, I doubt if I saw it for more than three seconds, but that was sufficient time to appreciate the bird's agility. Having seen a female a few days ago, we may well have a pair locally, that could be good news.

On checking the local birdline, I see we had waxwings quite near to home, five were reported from Hednesford, only twenty minutes or so away, had I been able to drive. As I cannot, they may as well have been on the moon. Unfortunately, they were reported on one day only, so there was little point in Sarah and me chasing them.

My house sparrows are still showing interest in my bird box. I feel sure that if they had only been seeking small insects, they would have by now cleared the box out. I shall just have to be patient and wait to see what happens over the next few weeks.

Friday, 28th December, and I am at last able to get in a local walk, not far, just Goose Green, but that will at least be a change from my garden.

The rooks at the nearby small rookery are very noisy, five nests still remain from the last breeding season, and two of the rooks are standing on two of the nests, looking as though they have already staked their claim. A blackbird is calling and a distant robin can be heard, almost spring-like, except my calendar tells me it is still December.

Goose Green is also alive with bird sounds. The rooks and jackdaws from the local main rookery are very noisy and active today, and two mallard ducks are quacking away, quite agitatedly. I cannot see them, but I know they are females because only the female quacks.

Walking further down the river I hear a call, momentarily I do not recognise it, but it soon hits me—I am listening to a bullfinch. Search hard, I cannot locate the bird, it is tucked away in thick vegetation on the opposite side of the river. As I move on a moorhen almost frightens me to death, it literally flies off from under my feet. A further blackbird and robin are also singing away, very pleasantly I add, and as I stand to enjoy their refrains, a sudden movement in a nearby bush catches my attention.

A small bird is actively seeking out food in the thick lower branches of the bush, I cannot see it clearly, but judging by its size I presume it to be a wren. After a minute or two I decide to move on and then stop. The bird has popped out and I find I am looking at a chiffchaff. Not unusual, some do over-winter, but looking at this bird, something about it is not right. Concentration time is nigh!

Then I realise, it has black legs and a very dark bill. Our common chiffchaff has paler legs and bill; I have a different race here, and I am pretty sure it is the Siberian race, to use its scientific name 'tristis'. This is one for the field guide when I get back home.

A quick look over Town Hill Bridge produces nothing, and the Swarbourn Meadow is almost as quiet, just a chaffinch calling and a pair of magpies feeding on the meadow. What they are finding is not clear.

Birding is now over, I have not brought my notebook with me, so I want to check things up whilst still fresh in my memory. I am pleased I do, it is the Siberian race, as well as the detail mentioned previously, it also lacked any yellow tinges and the cheeks were quite dark. I am more than satisfied, and it is another 'tick' for the year. It has been many a year since I last saw a Siberian race bird, and as it is likely to be my last 'year tick' of 2018, I am delighted to have seen it.

We have several birds which have different races, the chiffchaff has three which can be seen in the UK. Our regular species, which is a summer migrant, is classed as the British and western European race, scientifically known as collybita, then we have the Scandinavian race—abietinus, and finally the Siberian race—tristis.

The more you become involved with bird study, being able to classify races becomes a challenge, it concentrates the mind somewhat. Plus, it is always interesting to know where your bird may have originated from.

Whilst talking about 2018, have you ever thought how much dates influence your lives? From the day you were born, which you celebrate annually, the legal age to drive, to drink, coming of age, and various other things, age dominates our lives.

Wildlife does not know how lucky it is, it just has two aims in life. Firstly, survival and, the second is the continuation of the species, and it does not need a calendar for that. It knows when it is old enough to breed, it does not have to be told, it just gets on with life. We, for all our so-called intelligence, have to be told most of this and even have laws passed which control what we do, and we believe we are above the animals. As I have mentioned previously, unlike us who kill indiscriminately, animals only kill to defend or eat, and in many cases they do not have to kill to defend, a show of strength usually suffices. We have much to learn from our 'lesser' animals.

Those, old enough, will probably remember the hit song by Doris Day *Que sera, sera*, (Whatever will be, will be), that probably sums up life much more than any regulation or resolution. Just let the wild side get on with it, without our interference it can manage well.

Back to 2018. We now only have three days left. What I may see on the bird front is purely up to chance, but one thing I do know for certain, I shall not be making any RESOLUTIONS!

Chance has indeed taken a hand. A phone call from my friends, and tomorrow they are off to Cromford and Carsington Water. My friends wish to try to get hawfinches on their 'year lists', and also the great northern diver has been showing well at Carsington. Did I fancy a few hours out? I do not think I need to answer that question!

Roads are quiet after Christmas and we arrive at Cromford and park up. A quick coffee is called for, the day may be reasonable weatherwise, but there is a decided chill in the air, it is after all the end of the year.

There is a lot of activity in a nearby tree, this draws our attention, were we going to hit the jackpot right away? No, it was a mixed flock of titmice along with a few chaffinches. A quick look over the canal, just mallards and moorhens, so we make our way to the church and the bridge over the river, where we can also look up to Willersley Castle, a favoured haunt for hawfinches in the past, will we be lucky today? I fortunately, have seen both our target birds so I am under no pressure.

We enter into the church ground first, here we have many yew trees and I have seen the hawfinches occasionally hiding away in these, not today. As compensation, we do see a few goldcrests, of both sexes, so that is a good enough start. A song thrush is hopping about among the gravestones, and as I have said before, they are no longer as common as they once were. A robin gave us a brief burst of song, and that was that. Now for the river bridge.

The Derwent is flowing quite rapidly. It is carrying a lot of water and is a deep colour, one can but presume a lot of water has run off into the river. Once again, no hawfinches are seen, but as we bring our heads up above the level of the bridge parapet, we hear a noise below, a drake goosander takes off and flies upstream. His departure flushes a male grey wagtail which had been on the riverbank and we had not picked it up. Always a special bird to see, however fleetingly, as this one is today.

Crossing the bridge, we look downstream, not a lot occurring. We scan the trees along the riverbank, hawfinches occasionally are seen here, but our luck, or lack of it, continues—no hawfinches. As we are about to turn to walk towards Willersley Castle, a dark bird comes hurtling down the river, to vanish under the river bridge—a dipper. Several pairs breed along the River Derwent and they are fairly regular sightings here at Cromford, but never guaranteed, so we are delighted to see this one, even though it is only for a few seconds. We now move on towards the entrance to Willersley Castle.

It is only a castle by name, it is a café and religious teaching centre, and the grounds have many mature trees, which are frequently visited by hawfinches. Would they be so today? We are rapidly reaching our last chance. Many of the trees are distant so it is a 'scoping job, but we came prepared. We searched the high ridge beyond the castle, a few jackdaws and woodpigeons were about it. Moving down the slope we have a bit of excitement, we really thought we had located one, unfortunately, beautiful though the bird is, it is a male bullfinch. Any other day and we would have spent time enjoying this fellow, but today we are after his larger cousin.

Out last throw is to study the tall trees of the nearby cottages, and our luck finally turns. At the top of a tall tree are three heavy looking small birds. We have our birds—hawfinches. They are just sitting out, they could almost be sleeping, and they are not a 'scope job, these are enjoyed through our binoculars, unfortunately, not for long. A convoy of motorcycles come through, and the noise from their exhausts frightens the birds off. Ah well, that is that. We are not grumbling, we have chalked up a few very choice birds. How would Carsington fare? After a coffee we will find out.

We call in at the Sheepwash car park initially, and whilst talking about car parks, as I am a blue badge holder, all our parking today is for free. That is probably the main reason why I have been invited out!

We make our way down to the Sheepwash Hide, but things here are relatively quiet, goodly numbers of teals and wigeons, a few mallards and tufted ducks, and that is about it. The Spit has cormorants and grey herons, plus a solitary shelduck. My friends decide to pop down to the Paul Stanley Hide to see if there is anything tucked away further up the water. I remain where we are, they will call for me on their return journey.

As so happens in this birding game, shortly after my friends leave, it brightens up a little. Two ringed plovers fly in, escorted by an oystercatcher, a decided improvement. To really liven things up, a gaggle of very noisy grey-lag geese fly in, these crash land right in amongst the teals and wigeons, scattering them far and wide. I have a smile on my face, I doubt if the ducks had.

My friends return, they too have seen ringed plovers, plus several common snipe and little grebe, so they were happy and not too upset about missing the oystercatcher.

We drive round to the main car park, have a quick coffee and make our way to Stones Island. Whilst walking down, we hear a soft barking sound coming from the direction of the surfing club. Only one goose sounds like this, we have barnacle geese. A quick look, confirms that twenty-six geese are on a meadow near the shore.

Our roaming flock are at Carsington today, as you will remember I have previously mentioned the flock appears to commute between Carsington and the JCB lakes at Rocester. Today is obviously the turn of Carsington, and we are happy with that. I always think that barnacle geese are a most delightful bird to see.

Proceeding down Stones we spot two dunlins, busily foraging away in a small pool of water. They look as though they are thoroughly enjoying themselves. Whilst watching these two, a pair of oystercatchers fly in, so my friends have pulled that one back

It is now time to put our 'scopes to work, we have a large expanse of water to cover if we are to find the diver. We split the area into three, each working their own. It is many minutes before we strike lucky. One of my friends has found the bird right over near the dam, the distance it is away he did a thoroughly good job.

The view is not the best, but a diver is a large and heavy looking bird, and the neck and winter colouring, make it easily distinguishable from a cormorant. We were happy enough, we had found our quarry. We enjoyed the bird for several minutes before it faded from view, that bringing our day out to its conclusion, and successful it had been.

This morning, the final day of the year, my garden has been taken over by woodpigeons. At one time I had nine in the garden, all pecking away at my lawn.

What they were after I have no idea, although they did give the appearance of swallowing something. After they departed, I went out to look, nothing visible, so it remains a mystery. I cannot believe it was ants at this time of the year, but I could be wrong. It is likely to remain one of life's little mysteries!

As you by now know, Sarah and Martin used to join forces and have a bird race with me on January 1st, when we each hoped to chalk up our first fifty birds of the year. Thanks to my current situation, that will not happen come 2019. Usually, we would spend the last day or two checking up on what was to be seen locally, so we could plan our day and hopefully start the year off well, but not this coming new year.

This afternoon I hope to visit Goose Green again, to see if the Siberian chiffchaff has remained *in situ*, if it does so that could at least be a quality bird to start the new year on. We wait and see.

Although the day commenced grey and drab, it has now brightened up considerably and for the end of late December it is quite mild. I arrive on Goose Green to find it very quiet, definitely an 'after the Lord Mayor's Show' type of feeling.

Two carrion crows are on the green seeking out food, not very successfully.

Rooks and jackdaws can be heard but not seen, with a solitary robin giving out a short burst, and that is it. No chiffchaff today, it was probably just passing through and little else to brighten up the scene.

Swarbourn Meadow is a lot livelier. A party of linnets are working the silver birches and a little further along a mixed flock of titmice are doing likewise, except they are feeding on alders. I notice something very grey further downstream, so I approach with caution. As I get closer, I realise it is the head of a grey heron which was showing up above the bank, the heron being in the river. Not wishing to disturb the heron I cut back across the meadow where I see a blackbird and two magpies. Those bring my years birding to an end, well almost…

Home for a coffee and top up all my feeders in preparation for Jan 1st, now just hours away. I have a feeling the new year is going to start rather quietly, but before that, wait, what do I hear?

A mewing is heard above, and a buzzard comes over, slowly flapping its wings as it drifts across. A good finale to my year's birding, no complaints from me.

Whilst I had been out there has obviously been much activity in my garden. One of my fat ball containers has been knocked to the ground and emptied, probably by squirrels, and two of the seed holders need topping up. Be interesting to see if the birds thank me come the new year!

The year has not yet finished. A rook comes in and lands on the fat balls' pole, nothing unusual in that, but what followed was unexpected. The rook moved onto the arm which was supporting one of the fat ball containers, and then leant down to take hold of the container with its beak, and slowly pulled this up. Once it had done this, it positioned the container along the arm for support and proceeded to hack the fat ball to pieces. After a time, the container worked free and hung down once more, the rook then repeated the process of raising it again. I watched the rook repeat this manoeuvre several times over a twenty-minute period, during which time three fat balls were demolished, not all eaten by the rook I hasten to add, other birds were eagerly eating the scraps which had fallen to the ground. I now know why my fat balls vanish so quickly! The question this raises is how did the rook learn to carry out this operation and is it the only one which has done so? Unfortunately, one rook looks very much like another, so unless I see more than one rook queuing up to tackle my fat balls in this manner, I shall never learn the answer to that question. An interesting conclusion to a year's birding. You never stop learning.

I have reached the stage where this narrative concludes, not in the manner of which I anticipated, but one can do little regarding fate and illness. My final year saw two hundred and eighteen birds on my year list, two of which were 'lifers', which is not bad, even though it could have been more. When I look at the birds reported locally, I could have increased my year's total by at least ten, but it was not to be. I still had many pleasant hours thanks to birds I did see, and I am sure there is more to come in the future.

As you know, I first became involved with birds when I was five, feeding my first ducks, fell in love with them when I was six and saw my first ever kingfisher, and now in my eighty-fifth year I am still seeking to learn more. That will never stop, hopefully.

I have made many friends along the way, many of whom are part of this story, having both helped me and shared with me many of these adventures. They are far too numerous to mention, but they know who they are...

There are three, however, who helped to make it all possible. My late wife, Dorothy, whose love, friendship and support was the major factor, my daughter, Sarah, who has shared many of these happy hours, and Evelyn Syer, a friend and fellow birder, whose work as my proofreader has enabled this narrative to be completed.

Without them, it would never have been possible—I thank them.

I hope you, having read this, will gain as much from watching and studying birds as I have. You can be alone even when with people, with birds you are never alone, let them become your friends, they will not let you down. Birds may have frustrated me at times, but I have never had an argument with one!

Birders, as a group of people, are happy to share their experiences with you and assist when they can. You obviously will always get the odd exception, but they are not worth worrying about, and you will have seen the times when they have helped me see birds. Do not be shy, get out there and join them

Before closing, it may be of interest to see the range of species I have seen over these eighty years, the totals as they currently stand:

UK life list., seen in the UK.—392
Total seen in the UK, not all on UK list—426
(This includes hybrids and escapees)
Local—area covered by the West Midland Bird Club—315
Garden or seen from garden—110
Total abroad—308
Birds on UK list, but only seen abroad—38
Seen Abroad, not on British List—55
Total of species seen—519

Those to newcomers may look large figures, but to 'twitchers' they are very average. They will see well over three hundred different species in a year, my best ever, you will remember, was in 2012 when I saw two hundred and fifty-five, and that year I travelled many miles to see them. Whether I will see any new species in the future is now down to whether I will be allowed to drive again, and that is looking doubtful. I had always hoped to reach the four hundred mark on my seen in the UK life list. As things stand at present that is unlikely to ever materialise. That, however, is not what is important, I still have birds to see and much to learn, even from the birds in my own garden.

To bring my efforts back into perspective. There are birders with the obsession of seeing the highest number of species in a single year, and they travel the world to do this. I will not mention cost, they obviously are not poor. I think the record now stands at 6,833, this accomplished by a Dutchman, Arian Dwarshuis. Someone, someday, will break the 7,000. I know one thing for certain, it will not be me!

Looking back on these eighty years, I have been a lucky man. I have visited many countries, met many people, seen great beauty. Not only birds, I have marvelled at the skill and poise of dolphins, the size and beauty of whales, swam with seahorses, stood, open mouthed, watching the skill of chamois as they leapt from crag to crag and smiled at the antics of Alpine marmots. All of this is down to a magic moment when a kingfisher landed on my father's fishing rod. What is it they say about from tiny acorns mighty oak trees grow? I owe that kingfisher a debt that can never be paid. There is a wonderful world around us, just take a bit of time and go out to explore and enjoy. The way the world is going, we may not have it for much longer.

The last ten years have also taught me something else, time, if you let it, really does heal. It does not do it on its own, you have to take charge, sorrow is one thing, feeling sorry for yourself is something totally different. The big thing I have found is to have an interest, what that interest may be is not important, having the interest is what matters most. If your interest can be shared with other people, so much the better. I have referred to life as being similar to a limited overs cricket match, you only have one innings, so get out there and make that 'score'.

A final thought. If enough of us become interested in, enjoy and care for the wildlife that surrounds us, we may yet save the planet. "We can destroy or cherish, the choice is ours." Nine simple words, quoted by Sir David Attenborough in the BBC TV programme, *The Blue Planet*, but words so succinct. Now that is something to ponder.

Goodbye and happy birding.

Brian C George.

APPENDIX I
SEQUENTIAL LISTING OF THE BIRDS SEEN IN 2018, BY DATE AND LOCATION, IN MY EIGHTIETH YEAR OF BIRDING

1st January
Home.
- 1. Rook
- 2. Blackbird
- 3. Magpie
- 4. Long-tailed Tit
- 5. Dunnock
- 6. Starling
- 7. Woodpigeon
- 8. Carrion Crow
- 9. Blue Tit
- 10. Great Tit
- 11. Coal Tit
- 12. Chaffinch
- 13. Robin
- 14. Greenfinch
- 15. Bullfinch

Kings Bromley
- 16. Mallard
- 17. Black-headed Gull
- 18. Mute Swan
- 19. Buzzard
- 20. Jackdaw

Croxall
- 21. Great Crested Grebe

Catton.
    22. Pheasant (Complete Albino)

Whitemoor Haye
    23. Coot
    24. Tufted Duck
    25. Canada Goose
    26. Great White Egret
    27. Raven,
    28. Lesser Black-backed gull
    29. Golden Plover
    30. Lapwing
    31. Wigeon

Blithfield Reservoir
    32. Goldeneye
    33. Cormorant
    34. Teal

Dunstall.
    35. Grey-lag Goose

2nd January
Home.
    36. Goldfinch
    37. House Sparrow

Barton Marina
    38. Moorhen
    39. Pochard

3rd January
Barton Marina
    40. Little Grebe

Croxall
    41. Mistle Thrush

Whitemoor Haye
    42. Yellowhammer
    43. Tree Sparrow
    44. Song Thrush

Kings Bromley
    45. Little Egret

Blithfield Reservoir
    46. Great Black-backed Gull

6th January
Blacktoft Sands
    47. Wren
    48. Grey Heron
    49. Cetti's Warbler
    50. Shelduck
    51. Marsh Harrier
    52. Bewicks's Swan

7th January
Chasewater.
    53. Great Northern Diver
    54. Goosander
    55. Herring Gull

8th January
Blithfield Reservoir
    56. Nuthatch
    57. Shoveler
    58. Oystercatcher
    59. Little Owl

9th January
Woodhouses
    60. Collared Dove

10th January
Alrewas.
    61. Kestrel

Barton Marina.
    62. Gadwall

12th January
JCB Lake – Rocester
    63. Barnacle Goose
    64. Common Gull
    65. Ruddy Shelduck

13th January
Darley Dale
    66. Hawfinch
    67. Great Spotted Woodpecker

14th January
    Dunstall
    68. Linnet
    69. Merlin

15th January
Whitemoor Haye
    70. Whooper Swan

Catton Park
    71. Stock Dove
    72. Redwing

19th January
Tittesworth Water
>73. Mediterranean Gull
>74. Reed Bunting

20th January
North Cave Nature Reserve
>75. Green Woodpecker
>76. Brambling
>77. Redshank

Doncaster Services—M18
>78. Pied Wagtail

21st January
Catton Park.
>79. Fieldfare

26th January
JCB Lakes —Rocester
>80. Red-crested Pochard

27th January
Checkley
>81. Peregrine Falcon

28th January
Cannock Chase—Whitehouse
>82. Sparrowhawk

1st February
JCB Lakes—Rocester
>83. Egyptian Goose

2nd February
Axe Edge Moor
    84. Red Grouse
    Swallow Moss
    85. Hen Harrier

3rd February
Drakelow
    86. Jay

8th February
Newton Solney
    87. Cattle Egret

10th February
Attenborough Nature Reserve
    88. Water Rail

11th February
JCB Lakes—Rocester
    89. Cape Shelduck
    90. Mandarin

17th February
Draycott-in-the-Clay
    91. Red-legged Partridge

18th February
Albert Village Lake.
    92. Black-throated Diver
    93. Iceland Gull

19th February
Whitemoor Haye
    93. Meadow Pipit

21st February
Blithfield Reservoir
    94. Cormorant – Sinensis

24th February
Blacktoft Sands – RSPB
    96. Goldcrest
    97. Bearded Tit
    98. Curlew

25th February
Yoxall – Home
    99. Siskin

Whitemoor Haye
    100. Skylark

2nd March
Blithfield Reservoir
    101. Yellow-legged Gull

4th March
Alrewas – National Memorial Arboretum
    102. Rough-legged Buzzard

11th March
Whitemoor Haye
    103. Chiffchaff

17th March
JCB Lakes – Rocester
    104. Red Kite

Tittesworth Water.
    105. Marsh Tit

24th March
Blacktoft Sands – RSPB
    106. Grey Partridge
    107. Avocet
    108. Bittern

25th March
Blithfield Reservoir
    109. Little Stint

31st March
Eyebrook Reservoir
    110. Common Snipe
    111. Smew

1st April
Tittesworth Water
    112. Scaup

3rd April
Whitemoor Haye
    113. Corn Bunting
    114 Sand Martin

6th April
Blithfield Reservoir
    115. Osprey

7th April
Whitemoor Haye
    116. Swallow

Croxall – Broadfields Farm Meadow
    117. White Stork

Blithfield Reservoir – Stansley Wood
　　118. Blackcap

Hoar Cross
　　119. Treecreeper

8th April
Croxall Lakes Nature Reserve
　　120. Willow Warbler

Whitemoor Haye
　　121. House Martin

9th April
Carsington Water
　　122. Willow Tit

Blithfield Reservoir
　　123. White Wagtail

12th April
Whitemoor Haye
　　124. Common Crane

13th April
Blithfield Reservoir
　　125. Yellow Wagtail
　　126. Little Ringed Plover

14th April
Dunstall
　　126 Lesser Spotted Woodpecker

15th April
Tucklesholme
　　127. Caspian Gull

16th April
Bearda Hill Woods
    128. Pied Flycatcher

Nr Blackshaw Moor
    129. Goshawk

Dane Bower – Chimney Layby
    130. Ring Ouzel

18th April
Blithield Reservoir
    131. Arctic Tern
    132. Little Gull,
    33. Common Sandpiper

19th April
Blithfield Resevoir
    134. Common Tern

Cannock Chase – Coppice Hill
    135. Cuckoo

Blithfield Reservoir
    136. Ringed Plover

20th April
Whitemoor Haye
    137. Lesser Whitethroat

Alrewas – Arboretum
    138, Common Whitethroat

Blithfield Reservoir
- 139. Little Tern
- 140 Wood Warbler

21st April
Attenborough Nature Reserve
- 141. Sedge Warbler

22nd April
Blithfield Reservoir
- 142. Black Tern

27th April
Blithfield Reservoir
- 143. Swift

29th April
Cannock Chase – Seven Springs
- 144. Garden Warbler

4th May
Croxall Lakes Nature Reserve
- 145. Reed Warbler

Cannock Chase – Seven Springs
- 146. Redstart.

JCB Lakes – Rocester
- 147. Bar-headed Goose

5th May
Blacktoft Sands
- 148. Grasshopper Warbler
- 149. Montagu's Harrier

Swinefleet.
    150. Dotterel

12th May
Paxton Pits Nature Reserve
    151. Turtle Dove
    152. Nightingale

13th May
Cannock Chase
    153. Hobby

18th May
Stauton Harold Reservoir
    154. Grey Wagtail

Kings Bromley Layby
    155. Kingfisher

19th May.
Bempton Cliffs RSPB
    156. Gannet
    157. Kittiwake
    158. Puffin
    159. Razorbill
    160. Shag
    161. Fulmar
    162. Guillemot
    163. Rock Dove
    164. Sandwich Tern
    165. Rock Pipit
    166. Feral Pigeon

25th May.
Attenborough Nature Reserve
    167. Greenshank

26th May
Cromford
> 168. Dipper

Tittesworth Water
> 169. Spotted Flycatcher

Bearda Hill Woods
> 170. Tree Pipit

1st June
Blithfield Reservoir.
> 171. Black-tailed Godwit

9th June.
Catton Hall.
> 172. Honey Buzzard

16th June
Blacktoft Sands RSPB
> 173. Spotted Redshank
> 174. Garganey
> 175. Black-necked grebe

21st June
Blithfield Reservoir
> 176. Green Sandpiper

22nd June
Canock Chase – Upper Longdon
> 177. Woodlark

23rd June
Swallow Moss
> 178. Whinchat

1st July.
Cannock Chase—Cadet Camp
    179. Stonechat

4th July
Blithfield Reservoir
    180. Spoonbill

5th July
Blithfield reservoir
    181. Wood Sandpiper

7th July
Blacktoft Sands RSPB
    182. Ruff

14th July
Derbyshire Bridge
    183. Wheatear

1st August
Alrewas Gravel Pits
    184. Curlew Sandpiper

3rd August
Carsington Water
    185. Lesser Canada Goose (Cackling Goose)
    186. Whimbrel

Blithfield Reservoir
    187. Turnstone

4th August
Old Moor RSPB
    188. Temminck's Stint

8th August
Blithfield Reservoir
    189. Common Scoter

10th August
Blithfield Reservoir
    190. Sanderling

11th August
Far Ings
    191. Snow Goose
    192. Knot

17th August
Hoar Cross
    193. Tawny Owl

18th August
Reedness.
    194. Bar-tailed Godwit

25th August
Axe Edge Moor
    195. Twite

1s September
Frampton Marsh.
    196. Stilt Sandpiper (Lifer)
    197. Long-billed Dowitcher

7th September
Blithfield Resersoir
    198. Pintail

8th September
Chowder Ness.
    199. Red-necked Phalarope

13th September
Blithfield Reservoir
    200. Water Pipit

15th September
Spurn Point
    201. Scarlet Rosefinch

Kilnsea Wetlands Nature Reserve
    202. Grey Plover

Sammy's Point
    203. Short-eared Owl

22nd September
Eyebrook Reservoir
    204. Grey Phalarope

28th September
Carsington Water
    205. Pink-footed Goose

29th September
Easington Beach
    206. Red-throated Diver
    207. Great Skua
    208. Brent Goose

Kilnsea.
    209. Atctic Skua.

5th October
Warslow.
    210. Barn Owl

6th October
Point of Ayr
    211. Lapland Bunting

13th October
Easington Beach
    212. Manx Shearwater
    213. Eider

Kilnsea
    214. Savi's Warbler
    215. Yellow-browed Warbler

Spurn Point – Canal
    216. Olive-backed Pipit (Lifer)

15th November
Yoxall – Swarbourn Meadow
    217. Lesser Redpoll

28th December
Yoxall – Goose Green
    218. Siberian Chiffchaff

APPENDIX II
NAME CHANGES

NAME USED IN OLDER GUIDES	INTERNATIONAL NAME OR NAME NOW IN REGULAR USE AND IN NEW FIELD GUIDES
Bewick's swan	Tundra swan
Lesser Canada goose	Cackling goose
Shelduck	Common shelduck
Shoveler	Northern shoveler
Wigeon	Eurasian wigeon
Pintail	Northern pintail
Teal	Eurasian teal
Pochard	Common pochard
Scaup	Greater scaup
Eider	Common eider
Scoter	Common scoter
Goldeneye	Common goldeneye
Red grouse	Willow ptarmigan
Ptarmigan	Rock ptarmigan
Capercaillie	Western capercaillie
Pheasant	Common pheasant
Divers	Loons
Slavonian grebe	Horned grebe
Storm petrel	European storm-petrel
Leach's petrel	Leach's storm-petrel
Cormorant	Great cormorant
Shag	European shag
Fulmar	Northern fulmar
Gannet	Northern gannet
Great white egret	Great egret

Bittern	Eurasian bittern
Spoonbill	Eurasian spoonbill
Honey-buzzard	European honey-buzzard
Buzzard	Common buzzard
Marsh harrier	Western marsh harrier
Goshawk	Northern goshawk
Sparrowhawk	Eurasian sparrowhawk
Kestrel	Common kestrel
Hobby	Eurasian hobby
Peregrine	Peregrine falcon
Moorhen	Common moorhen
Coot	Eurasian coot
Purple gallinule	Purple swamp-hen
Corncrake	Corn crake
Crane	Common crane
Oystercatcher	Eurasian oystercatcher
Avocet	Pied avocet
Stone-curlew	Eurasian stone-curlew
Dotterel	Eurasian dotterel
Ringed plover	Common ringed plover
Golden plover	European golden plover
Lapwing	Northern lapwing
Knot	Red knot
Woodcock	Eurasian woodcock
Snipe	Common snipe
Turnstone	Ruddy turnstone
Whimbrel	Eurasian whimbrel
Curlew	Eurasian curlew
Redshank	Common redshank
Greenshank	Common greenshank
Grey phalarope	Red phalarope
Skuas	Jaegers
Herring gull	European herring gull
Common gull	Mew gull
Kittiwake	Black-legged kittiwake
Guillemot	Common guillemot

Puffin	Atlantic puffin
Rock dove/feral pigeon	Common pigeon
Woodpigeon	Common woodpigeon
Collared dove	Eurasian collared dove
Turtle dove	European turtle dove
Ring-necked parakeet	Rose-ringed parakeet
Cuckoo	Common cuckoo
Nightjar	Common nightjar
Swift	Common swift
Hoopoe	Eurasian hoopoe
Kingfisher	Common kingfisher
Bee-eater	European bee-eater
Wryneck	Eurasian wryneck
Green woodpecker	European green woodpecker
Skylark	Eurasian skylark
Shore lark	Horned lark
Swallow	Barn swallow
House martin	Common house martin
Rock pipit	Eurasian rock pipit
Dipper	White-throated dipper
Wren	Winter wren
Robin	European robin
Nightingale	Common nightingale
Redstart	Common redstart
Stonechat	Eurasian stonechat
Wheatear	Northern wheatear
Blackbird	Common blackbird
Waxwing	Bohemian waxwing
Grasshopper warbler	Common grasshopper warbler
Reed warbler	Eurasian reed warbler
Pallas's warbler	Pallas's leaf warbler
Chiffchaff	Common chiffchaff
Fan-tailed warbler	Zitting cisticola
Pied flycatcher	European pied flycatcher
Bearded tit	Bearded reedling
Nuthatch	Eurasian nuthatch

Treecreepr	Eurasian treecreeper
Golden oriole	Eurasian golden oriole
Jay	Eurasian jay
Magpie	Black-billed magpie
Chough	Red-billed chough
Jackdaw	Western jackdaw
Raven	Northern raven
Starling	Common starling
Tree sparrow	Eurasian tree sparrow
Chaffinch	Common chaffinch
Serin	European serin
Goldfinch	European goldfinch
Greenfinch	European greenfinch
Siskin	Eurasian siskin
Linnet	Common linnet
Scarlet rosefinch	Rosefinch or Common rosefinch
Crossbill	Common crossbill
Bullfinch	Eurasian bullfinch
Lapland bunting	Lapland longspur
Reed bunting	Common reed bunting

Many bird clubs are also using these names in their bird reports, so I am sure it will not be too long before they become common practice. I only wish that many of the species prefixed 'common', were so! It may be a good idea to take a copy of this list for future reference, although it only covers the species more regularly seen in the UK, with the odd exception.

APPENDIX III
ADVICE FOR NEWCOMERS

I am frequently asked by newcomers to birding, how can they learn? Before I can attempt to answer this question, I need to know how much they wish to learn.

There are many different types of birders, from the ones who just love birds to those who specialise in just one or two species. Let us commence at the very beginning. The main reason people start to birdwatch is because they wish to identify the birds they see, how best can they do this?

Binoculars and a field guide are absolutely necessary, but do not rush to buy, especially your first pair of binoculars. Look at what other birdwatchers are using and when you do go to buy, try as many pairs as you can. Also, do not be afraid of buying a second-hand pair, there are many birders who change their binoculars more often than they do their cars. Also, make sure they are waterproof—bird watching is not only done in dry conditions! I have two pairs of binoculars myself, one being an 8x42 which I use when in woodland conditions, out walking and at home, my other pair are a 10x42, ideal where distance is involved. I suggest you do not consider a telescope until you have really judged just how serious a birder you wish to become.

Always remember, you buy in haste, you repent at leisure!

Now field guides. There are a range of these available, and they vary in quality considerably. The first question you need to consider is once again, how serious a birder do you wish to become, and are you likely to travel abroad to see birds? Also, remember size is important, if you wish to take your field guide with you, it must fit your pocket.

If your interest is just local and always in the UK, then you need a simple guide, and the one which I believe fits this purpose is the *RSPB Handbook of British Birds*. This publication covers the 270 commonest birds found in the UK with a further twenty-six rarer species sometimes seen in the UK. It not only covers identification, it also looks at many other aspects, it is more than just a field guide. It is also well illustrated. Should you go abroad on holiday, especially to Europe and round the Mediterranean, you will require a guide which covers the birds of Britain, Europe and North Africa, and these obviously start to increase in size. One I have found as a suitable in between, and still fits the pocket, is the *Hamlyn Guide to Birds of Britain and Europe*, by Bretel Bruun. This guide covers 530 birds and has 465 distribution maps.

Two further publications, which I personally believe to be the best of their classs, but are not pocket size, are *Birds of Europe with North Africa and the Middle East*, by Lars Jonsson, my particular favourite field guide, and Collins *BIRD GUIDE*. The latter was voted the bird book of the year when first published, and many claim it to be as essential to birdwatching as a pair of binoculars. I have one piece of advice concerning the Collins book, buy the large format edition, the book has over 3,500 illustrations and I believe you need the larger size to pick out all the detail.

Now you have your optics and field guides sorted, how do you learn more, and also where do you go to see all these birds?

From reading this book you will have learned that I was a tutor at both the University of Birmingham and Keele University, where I taught bird study courses.

Many similar courses are being taught today at many centres throughout the country, the only problem with some of these courses is that they have now become more academic. The majority of birders love birds, want to see birds and be able to recognise them, they would never class themselves as ornithologists. This is where bird clubs come into their own.

Most counties or large cities have their own birdwatching clubs, run by experienced and enthusiastic birders. Here you can join people with a range of experiences, attend illustrated indoor meetings and go out on regular field meetings. Many of these clubs even have their own nature reserves and it is the best way to learn just what your local area has on offer. Many operate their own bird lines so you can phone or text to obtain the latest information. Membership fees are usually very reasonable. You can easily obtain details of your local group via the

Internet.

Moving up a degree or so, we have the county wildlife trusts, most counties have their own and they do wonderful work locally to protect wildlife. Here you can do voluntary work, I am a volunteer warden, or just enjoy the facilities and visiting the many nature reserves under their ownership. Many of the county trusts allow fellow members free admittance to their reserves. Several of these trusts run educational programmes where you can learn more.

Then at the top of the so to speak, you have the national organisations, of which the RSPB is probably the most well-known, and membership of these organisations allows you access to some of the finest nature reserves in the UK. We must not forget the National Trust, they too own many acres of the best British countryside, some home to our rarest birds.

One final point. You will at times need to take down details of birds you see which you cannot recognise, so a note book and pen are also pieces of required equipment. I have moved on from those to having a pocket recorder, you can speak much faster than you can write, so the quicker you can get any information down, the better. Birds do have a nasty habit of flying away!

So it is all out there, with many people willing to assist you. Go out with these people, most are only too willing to pass on their knowledge and experiences, just open your mind to what you may learn, and then, as with me, you have many years of both pleasure and learning ahead. And who knows, one of you may be the new David Attenborough. Remember one thing, we all start life with a blank page, it is what we write on it that matters.

The Author

I was born in an old area of Birmingham, Saltley, where many of the houses did not have gardens, as they were back-to-back with a communal yard. Here birds were at a premium. I was very fortunate, on Sunday afternoons, after lunch, and weather permitting, my parents would take me to the local park to feed the ducks. At an early age I knew what mallards, coots, moorhens and swans looked like.

In 1939, just prior to war breaking out, we moved to Great Barr, a suburb of Birmingham where green fields were then abundant, and because of the war, remained so for many years. My father, who was in a reserved occupation, and did not have to join the forces, was a keen fisherman, and I was able to join him on many an occasion. On one of these trips out, a magical moment occurred, well magical as far as I was concerned. My father had his rod in a rest and a kingfisher landed on his rod.

For just a few seconds, I gazed at the most beautiful thing I had ever seen, and that was that. Birds and I began an eighty-year love affair which still continues today.

Since then, I have studied birds in Egypt and most countries in Europe as far north as Spitsbergen, and continue to do so today, although I do not travel so far now being a blue badge holder and not too mobile.

I was a freelance journalist for several years, writing nature features for a local newspaper, the *Birmingham Evening Mail*, and also several national magazines.

I also jointly presented a natural history radio programme for the then BBC Radio Birmingham and for thirty years I was a part-time tutor for both the University of Birmingham and Keele University, teaching wildlife subjects. This I continued to do on a private basis until recently.

My late wife, Dorothy, was also a keen naturalist, and we jointly organised bird study tours to Europe, where we studied birds not regularly seen back home, and also in the UK.

My aim has always been to try to involve as many people as possible in the love of the countryside, as I firmly believe the world will not be saved by politicians.

The only chance it has is for the people to care.

I hope that by reading this book, others will feel the same, so that young children in the future, too, can feed the ducks.

One final thought. A truly wonderful world lies outside your doors, and it does not cost you anything to go out and see it. You will find many new wonders, and probably make many new friends, you may even bump into me—now there is a thought. All you require is the inclination to do so, and as happened to me, you will not turn back.